"I know of no one else drawing breath who has Teresa Morgan's remarkable combination of classical learning and theological profundity. In this book she puts it to powerful, arresting use, showing us how the restoration of trust leads at last to the reconciliation of all things."

—MATTHEW V. NOVENSON
Princeton Theological Seminary

"Teresa Morgan has long been recognized for her groundbreaking interdisciplinary work on *pistis* in the ancient Greco-Roman world. *Trust in Atonement* now establishes her as a prophet who speaks directly to our fractured times. Dealing directly with the many and varied critiques of atonement, Morgan—quite remarkably—develops a new model that is at once faithful to scripture and pertinent to this moment."

—GABRIELLE THOMAS
Emory University

"In this stunning book, Teresa Morgan refuses to be constrained by the narrowness of academic analysis alone. Through a penetrating examination of the connection between trust and atonement, this study illuminates how the relationship between humans and God is put right and considers the implications for interpersonal relationships. It offers rich insights into what it means to forgive and to trust, and how one then enacts restorative justice. This is a book that must be read—and more than that, acted upon—in order to build a fairer and more compassionate society that is renewed in the image and love of God."

—PAUL FOSTER
University of Edinburgh

"The fruitfulness of Morgan's decisive turning of *pistis* in the direction of trust is clearly seen now as she eloquently develops a new, theologically and pastorally constructive turn in understanding of Christ's role in bringing reconciliation. Morgan very effectively combines the fruits of her classical and biblical research with insights from trauma studies and many other areas important for life today."

—PETER OAKES
University of Manchester

"Teresa Morgan has developed a fascinating new model of the atonement based on the New Testament concept of *pistis*, or trust. She unpacks Christ's work as a mediator by renewing our attention to this central biblical concept in dialogue with contemporary psychology and social science, with a vision wide enough to include not just the ways Christ reconciles us to God but also the ways he reconciles the natural world and transforms our relationship to it. This is theology that is at once biblical-historical, contemporary–social scientific, and philosophical-systematic."

—ROSS MCCULLOUGH
George Fox University

"'Reconciled diversity' is a buzzword in missiology. What is often overlooked, however, is the issue of trust (*pistis*). In this well-written book, Teresa Morgan makes a compelling case for the importance of trust in understanding what God has done in Jesus Christ, and how his faithfulness invites us to the mission of healing relationships."

—STEFAN PAAS
Vrije Universiteit Amsterdam

"In this work of constructive theology, Teresa Morgan develops an impressive model of at-one-ment as the rebuilding of trust that was started in the incarnation. This 'therapeutic trust' was as appealing in the early Roman Empire as it still is in modern conflict resolution. In a bold, Simone Weil–like argument Morgan shows how suffering and wrongdoing are often intertwined and that a therapy of trust is crucial for victims and perpetrators alike."

—GEORGE VAN KOOTEN
University of Cambridge

"In this engaging, rich, and generative study, Teresa Morgan develops a new constructive theological account of the atonement as the restoration of trust between God and humanity through Jesus Christ. Morgan shows how a trust-based approach to atonement can enrich our thinking about the most acute and challenging aspects of our lives: violence, war, trauma, abuse, and environmental degradation. Readers will discover much food for thought to reconfigure their understanding of the central icon of the Christian faith: the crucified Christ."

—DAVID G. HORRELL
University of Exeter

"The fields of New Testament and classical Roman studies are once again indebted to Teresa Morgan, who offers here not only an innovative model for the atonement centered on trust, but a comprehensive and humane theology of the New Testament that will be useful for scholars and those in ministry alike."

—TIMOTHY MILINOVICH
Dominican University

"In a bold hermeneutical study, Morgan moves from historical to theological studies, mediating central ideas from early Christianity successfully into modern life."

—CILLIERS BREYTENBACH
Humboldt University Berlin

"Teresa Morgan's fascinating model of the atonement is the natural next step in her work on the multidimensional theme of trust. Her proposal is at once focused and far-reaching, provocative and pastoral. Morgan's attention to the trust and trustworthiness of Jesus, on the one hand, and to our contemporary context and concerns, on the other, makes this book a significant contribution to both the academy and the church."

—MICHAEL J. GORMAN
St. Mary's Seminary and University

TRUST IN ATONEMENT

GOD, CREATION, AND
RECONCILIATION

TERESA MORGAN

WILLIAM B. EERDMANS PUBLISHING COMPANY
GRAND RAPIDS, MICHIGAN

Wm. B. Eerdmans Publishing Co.
4035 Park East Court SE, Grand Rapids, Michigan 49546
www.eerdmans.com

© 2024 Teresa Morgan
All rights reserved
Published 2024

Book design by Lydia Hall

Printed in the United States of America

30 29 28 27 26 25 24   1 2 3 4 5 6 7

ISBN 978-0-8028-8337-7

Library of Congress Cataloging-in-Publication Data

A catalog record for this book is available from the Library of Congress.

IN LOVING MEMORY:

Florence Gertrude Randle (1862–1904)

Florence May Randle (1889–1956)

Florence May Kendall (1912–1990)

Jean Mary Brown (1934–2018)

Contents

	Preface	ix
	List of Abbreviations	xi
	Introduction	1
1.	**Wrongdoing and Suffering, Trust and Mistrust**	35
2.	**Trust after Trauma, Conflict, and Offending**	85
3.	**The Trust and Trustworthiness of Jesus Christ**	117
4.	**Trust in Creation**	159
5.	**As We Forgive**	196
	Conclusion	221
	Works Cited	227
	Index of Subjects	255
	Index of Scripture	259

Preface

This book was begun while I was on research leave under the auspices of a Leverhulme Trust Major Research Fellowship and a Templeton Foundation grant for the project "The Philosophy, Theology, and Psychology of Christian Trust in God." It is related to all three of the books that have been or will be published as a result of those grants, and I am grateful to both organizations for their generous support.

Cilliers Breytenbach and Susan Grove Eastman read the whole manuscript in draft, and Daniel McKaughan, Robert Morgan, and Clare Rothschild read individual chapters. I benefited greatly from their comments and criticisms, and I feel very fortunate to have such wise and gracious colleagues. Lectures and seminar papers introducing the material were given at the Society for New Testament Studies Conference (2024), the Society of Biblical Literature Annual Meeting (2023), the Australian Catholic University, Candler School of Theology, Emory University, the Logos Institute of St. Andrews University, as the Prideaux Lectures of the University and Diocese of Exeter (2022), and to the Community of St. Anselm at Lambeth Palace, and I am grateful for the lively engagement of colleagues and students on all those occasions. Warm thanks are due to Trevor Thompson and the editorial and production teams at Eerdmans for their encouragement of the project and meticulous work throughout the publication process.

This study grew out of *The New Testament and the Theology of Trust: "This Rich Trust"* (Oxford: Oxford University Press, 2022). Having written a chapter in that book on the role of the trust between God, Jesus Christ, and humanity in Jesus's death, I came to think that this was a topic that deserved some more thought. I did not expect "some more thought" to take me into the realms of conflict resolution, the restoration of trust after trauma and offending, altruism, spite, mediation, and reconciliation in the animal and plant kingdoms, and forgiveness

PREFACE

and reconciliation between human beings. The argument in chapter 3 of this book, however, is an expansion of chapter 4 of *The Theology of Trust*. In this book, I have also modified my earlier argument, often in small ways, looking for better interpretations of texts, and sometimes in substantial ways as I have sought to develop the theological model further. In the introduction to this study, I offer summaries of my earlier work on New Testament *pistis* and introductions to the study of trust in history, the social sciences, philosophy, and psychology (pp. 7–23) including updated versions of material that appears in the introduction to *The Theology of Trust*. In chapter 1, my reading of Genesis 1, anti-ableist readings of healing miracles in the gospels, and the sections on wrongdoing, suffering, and *apistia* in the gospels and Romans (pp. 38–41, 57–59, 63–76) are also reworked (in the last case, extensively) from *The Theology of Trust*. In chapter 5, the section on entrustedness (pp. 207–10) draws on one section of chapter 7 of *The Theology of Trust*. The overall shape of this study, however, along with most of its material, is considerably different from the sketch from which it grew, and offers, I hope, a fuller and more persuasive account of the role of *pistis* in its aspects of trust, trustworthiness, faithfulness, and entrustedness in the at-one-ment of humanity with God through Jesus Christ.

Abbreviations

AB	Anchor Bible
Anim. Behav.	*Animal Behavior*
CBQ	*Catholic Bible Quarterly*
EC	*Early Christianity*
ExpTim	*Expository Times*
Faith Philos.	*Faith and Philosophy*
FemT	*Feminist Theology*
Front. Psychol.	*Frontiers in Psychology*
Int	*Interpretation*
Int. J. Philos. Relig.	*International Journal of the Philosophy of Religion*
Int. J. Psychol. Relig.	*International Journal for the Psychology of Religion*
J. Comp. Psychol.	*Journal of Comparative Psychology*
J. Disabil. Relig.	*Journal of Disability and Religion*
JSNT	*Journal for the Study of the New Testament*
J. Trust Res.	*Journal of Trust Research*
Ment. Health Relig. Cult.	*Mental Health, Religion & Culture*
PNAS	*Proceedings of the National Academy of Sciences*
Proc. R. Soc. Lond. B	*Proceedings of the Royal Society B: Biological Sciences.*
SJT	*Scottish Journal of Theology*
TDNT	*Theological Dictionary of the New Testament.* Edited by Gerhard Kittel and Gerhard Friedrich. Translated by Geoffrey W. Bromiley. 10 vols. Grand Rapids: Eerdmans, 1964–1976
TS	*Theological Studies*
WBC	Word Biblical Commentary

Introduction

Atonement stands at the heart of the good news that Christians embrace and proclaim.[1] In English, atonement (or "at-one-ment," as it is sometimes spelled to highlight its derivation) describes the state of being "at one" with another person, in harmony with them, or reconciled with them after conflict.[2] The first followers of Jesus shared the life-changing experience that, through Jesus Christ, they had been reconciled with God, and it had been made possible for humanity to live in its right relationship with God as it had not done since the beginning of human existence. Celebrating that experience, sharing the joy and hopefulness of

1. The word "atonement" is first used of the relationship between God and humanity by William Tyndale in his 1526 translation of the Bible: "For God was in Christ and made agreement between the world and himself and imputed not their sins to them: and has committed to us the preaching of the atonement" (2 Cor 5:19, spelling modernized). Tyndale probably did not coin the word, which is used by several other writers in the early sixteenth century of relationships between human beings as well as between humanity and God.

2. In this sense "at-one-ment" is a synonym for reconciliation (in German, for instance, "reconciliation" and "atonement" are both rendered by *Versöhnung*). Those who write about reconciliation in a Christian context in English use it in two ways, which we can call "reconciliation wide" and "reconciliation narrow," after the distinction between "ethics wide" and "ethics narrow" coined by May Edel and Abraham Edel, *Anthropology and Ethics* (Springfield: Thomas, 1959), 8. John Hick speaks, similarly, of atonement "broad" and "narrow" in *The Metaphor of God Incarnate* (2nd ed.; Louisville: Westminster John Knox, 1993), 12. "Reconciliation wide" is a synonym for "at-one-ment" and covers all the ways in which God restores human beings to their right relationship with God through the life, death, and work of Jesus Christ. "Reconciliation narrow" refers to one group of models of how God does this, which focus on Jesus as mediator between God and humanity. These are often developed out of passages in which the Greek terms *katallagē* and *katallassein*, "reconciliation" and "reconcile" (which are also common elsewhere in Greek in contexts of diplomacy and political or legal mediation) appear (e.g., Rom 5:10–11; 11:15; 2 Cor 5:18–20).

INTRODUCTION

it with others, and offering others the chance to share it became their life's work. They were convinced that returning to God brought new life, hope, and freedom from the tyranny of the wrongdoing and suffering that blight our lives and make us damage each other and ourselves. Putting this restoration at the center of their worldview framed, and continues to frame, Christians' understanding of God, their humanity, and all their relationships.

In everyday life, there are many ways in which people who have been estranged or in conflict can be reconciled with the help of a third party. The third party may actively mediate between them. Perhaps she quietly pays off a debt one owes to the other, enabling them to get back on terms. She might intervene with a fourth party who has been making trouble between them. Or she might be so radiantly kind, friendly, and good to both parties that they become ashamed of their behavior and make up.

Early Christians were convinced that Jesus Christ was the means of their at-one-ment with God. (Although the term "atonement" is a modern coinage, I will use it throughout this study in the broad sense in which it is often used today, to refer to the return of humanity to its right relationship with God, however the means of return is understood.) The way Jesus lived, taught, and acted, however, together with the way he was betrayed, executed, and then experienced by his followers as risen and exalted, did not fit straightforwardly within any one existing tradition about how God (or gods) might act to save human beings from the consequences of their own wrongdoings or from oppression by others.[3] Jesus's followers therefore drew on multiple stories and images of how God had acted in the past, or might act in the future, which were current in Jewish tradition and the gentile world around them. Jesus could be seen as having offered himself as a sacrifice, in the hope that God would respond. His death could be understood as making or marking a covenant or new covenant between God and humanity (sacrifices could be made, in Jewish and gentile tradition, for all these reasons).[4] He could be seen as having offered himself as a ransom to a metaphysical power of evil to free humanity from its clutches. Or perhaps he had acted like a scapegoat, taking on himself the punishment due to humanity for its disobedience to God. Some identified him as God's general in an ongoing war with evil, in which the decisive battle had been won in his crucifixion and resurrection but which

3. Pp. 46–49.

4. On the death of Jesus as a "supplicatory offering," see Adela Yarbro Collins, "The Metaphorical Use of *Hilastērion* in Romans 3:25," in *Sōtēria: Salvation in Early Christianity and Antiquity. Festschrift in Honour of Cilliers Breytenbach on the Occasion of His 65th Birthday* (ed. David S. du Toit, Christine Gerber, and Christiane Zimmermann; Leiden: Brill, 2019), 278.

Introduction

would not be over until the end time. Others saw him as something like God's ambassador, interpreting God to humanity and bringing the two together. God could be recognized as loving the world so deeply that God sent God's Son into it, so that those who were able to recognize him could respond with love and trust and enter eternal life. Or perhaps Jesus was, and is, an example of someone who loves God so fully, is so faithful to God, and obeys God so perfectly that he changes humanity's understanding of what a relationship with God can be and inspires others to follow his example. Most early writers drew on more than one of these ideas, exploring what each might contribute to understanding what they and their communities believed God had done through Christ.

Out of these images and narratives, a wealth of theories or models of atonement has developed. Different groups and individuals at different times have preferred one to another, but no one model has been accepted as orthodox at the expense of the rest. They have continued to coexist and grow in number, exploring different aspects of the mystery of divine revelation and action in the world. Diverse and nuanced, they are often grouped into broad types such as ransom, satisfaction, penal substitution, or moral influence.[5] Every type has been both defended and criticized. If, for instance, Jesus has to fight and defeat the powers of evil, and if there is any real jeopardy in that battle, does that not suggest that the powers of evil are as powerful, or almost as powerful, as Godself? If Jesus had to sacrifice himself or take punishment due to other people to enable God to be reconciled with humanity, does that not make God disturbingly transactional, even punitive, in God's dealings with humanity? And what kind of God colludes in his Son's agonizing death? If Jesus's death compensates for all human sins, does that leave human beings with enough moral responsibility for themselves? And what of the sins that have been committed since the crucifixion? On the other hand, if human beings are capable of responding to Jesus Christ as Son of God, taking responsibility for their wrongdoing, and repenting and asking for

---

5. On the range of models of atonement and their strengths and weaknesses see especially Paul S. Fiddes, *Past Event and Present Salvation* (London: Darton, Longman & Todd, 1989); John McIntyre, *The Shape of Soteriology* (Edinburgh: T&T Clark, 1992); Fleming Rutledge, *The Crucifixion: Understanding the Death of Christ* (Grand Rapids: Eerdmans, 2017); Eleonore Stump, *Atonement* (Oxford: Oxford University Press, 2018), 3–112; William Lane Craig, *Atonement and the Death of Christ: An Exegetical, Historical, and Philosophical Exploration* (Waco: Baylor University Press, 2020); Oliver D. Crisp, *Approaches to the Atonement: The Reconciling Work of Christ* (Downers Grove: InterVarsity, 2020). Taking a nontraditional approach and identifying "final Adam," "Son of God," "Spirit," "Wisdom," and "Logos" as models of Christ's mediating or saving action, see Patrick Cousins, "Roger Haight's Theology of the Cross," *Heythrop Journal* 58 (2017): 78–90.

INTRODUCTION

forgiveness, why did Jesus need to die? Why would Jesus have needed to die for his example to inspire people to follow him and seek to become more like him?[6]

The idea that God can save human beings either from the consequences of their own wrongdoings or from suffering at the hands of others goes back deep into Israelite and Jewish tradition, and I will return to it in chapter 1.[7] Most classical models of atonement concentrate on the idea that God saves human beings from a state of sin, the sins they enact in that state, and the consequences for the sinner. The major modern contribution to thinking about atonement, however, has come from theologians for whom the burning concern of human life and Christian life, and therefore Christian theology, is the liberation of the poor, the marginalized, and the oppressed of the world, including the materially poor, slaves and the descendants of slaves, women, people of color, the politically unenfranchised, and all those deprived by others in any way of the opportunity to thrive.[8] Developing alongside the struggle for political and economic freedom and justice among the poor in Latin America in the mid-twentieth century, liberation theology was quickly taken up by other oppressed and marginalized groups around the world.[9] Liberation theologians have criticized classical models of atonement

6. It is sometimes suggested that one or another of these models is outdated because the imagery it draws on (for instance, that of cosmic war or feudal honor codes) no longer plays a large part in our worldview. See, e.g., Crisp, *Atonement*, 70 (on honor codes); Christian A. Eberhart, "Atonement," in *Atonement: Jewish and Christian Origins* (ed. Max Botner, Justin Harrison Duff, and Simon Dürr; Grand Rapids: Eerdmans, 2020), 19 (on Roman law). From this point of view, trust is a strong concept with which to approach atonement, since it is agreed to play a central role in relationships and societies in every time and place.

7. Gentiles usually envisage gods as saving them from suffering; see p. 46.

8. Studies of suffering together with wrongdoing and altruism in the animal kingdom have not yet become part of thinking about atonement, but chapter 4 will argue that they have a role in it, and there, too, suffering is one focus.

9. Among seminal studies in liberation theology see especially James H. Cone, *A Black Theology of Liberation* (Philadelphia: Lippincott, 1970); Gustavo Gutiérrez, *A Theology of Liberation* (Maryknoll: Orbis, 1973); Katie Cannon, *Black Womanist Ethics* (Atlanta: Scholars Press, 1988); Joanne Carlson Brown and Rebecca Parker, "For So God Loved the World?" in *Christianity, Patriarchy, and Abuse: A Feminist Critique* (ed. Joanne Carlson Brown and Carole R. Bohn; New York: Pilgrim: 1989), 1–30. Criticizing various aspects of classical models, including their apparent acceptance of violence and their consequentialism, and in particular the idea that suffering can be redemptive, see notably Rosemary Radford Reuther, "Christology: Can a Male Savior Save Women?" in *Sexism and God-Talk: Towards a Feminist Theology* (Boston: Beacon, 1983), 116–38; Simon S. Maimela, "The Atonement in the Context of Liberation Theology," *International Review of Mission* 75 (1986): 261–69; J. Denny Weaver, *The Nonviolent Atonement* (Grand Rapids: Eerdmans, 2001), especially 96–121; Jennifer Buck, "Feminist Philosophical Theology of Atonement," *FemT* 28 (2020): 239–50; Jamall A. Calloway, "The Purpose of Evil Was to Survive It: Black and Womanist Rejecting the Cross for Salvation," *FemT* 30 (2021): 67–84. Chigor Chike, "Black Chris-

Introduction

on some of the same grounds as earlier writers but also on grounds of their own. Traditional models can be seen as too individualistic: too concerned with the salvation of individuals rather than the reshaping of societies. They are criticized for not doing enough justice to God's care for and identification with the poor and oppressed, and for not explaining how God's actions through Christ liberate and empower people to fight against social injustice happening now. "What is the relationship between salvation and the process of human liberation throughout history?" asks Gustavo Gutiérrez, answering that the work of Christ is "human liberation . . . liberation from sin and all its consequences: despoliation, injustice, hatred."[10] Classical models can appear to glorify suffering in a way which people who have suffered brutal and systematic oppression over years and generations find grotesque and unacceptable. The same models have often (in practice if not in principle) reinforced the power of the powerful over the powerless by encouraging the already powerless to follow Christ by embracing humility, suffering, and self-abnegation.[11] A credible model of atonement, for liberation theologians, must not glorify oppression or suffering in any form. It must show that although suffering is sometimes necessary in the fight for justice and freedom, God does not validate it for its own sake and is always on the side of those who suffer. As James H. Cone puts it, the gospel is "a story about God's presence in Jesus' solidarity with the oppressed, which led to his death on the cross. What is redemptive is the faith that God snatches victory out of defeat, life out of death, and hope out of despair."[12] A good model must show that God's actions in Christ change the

---

tology for the Twenty-First Century," *Black Theology* 8 (2010): 357–78 outlines sometimes distinct developments in recent Black Christology and soteriology in South Africa, the United Kingdom and the United States. James Cone and Douglas John Hall are among those who emphasize that liberating the oppressed also liberates their oppressors; see Timothy Hegedus, "Douglas John Hall's Contextual Theology of the Cross," *Consensus* 15 (1989): 23. We will also consider the suffering that our own wrongdoings cause us. Joyce Murray, "Liberation for Communion in the Soteriology of Gustavo Gutiérrez," *TS* 59 (1998): 54 notes that Gutiérrez distinguishes liberation "from" oppression and "for" love and communion, both of which are necessary for salvation. Liberation theologies also tend to emphasize the salvific aspects of Jesus's earthly life and teaching as well as his death. Not addressing the whole of Jesus's life and ministry but making the same argument is Teresa Morgan, *The New Testament and the Theology of Trust: "This Rich Trust"* (Oxford: Oxford University Press, 2022), 196–281.

10. Gutiérrez, *Theology of Liberation*, 83, 90.

11. Arnfridur Gutmundsdottir, *Meeting God on the Cross: Feminist Christologies and the Theology of the Cross* (Oxford: Oxford University Press, 2010), 4, 57–114. The theology of the cross was revitalized after the Second World War by the need to respond to the suffering and hopelessness of those who had survived (3).

12. James H. Cone, *The Cross and the Lynching Tree* (Maryknoll: Orbis, 2011), 150. Diane Leclerc and Brent Peterson, *The Back Side of the Cross: An Atonement Theology for the Abused and*

INTRODUCTION

world in practical ways, making people more equal, more just, more empowered, and more compassionate. For a feminist theologian such as Elizabeth Johnson, a good model must show how Christ's death involves "the self-emptying of male [or any other] dominating power in favor of the new humanity of compassionate service and mutual empowerment."[13]

Liberation approaches to atonement have received their own share of criticism. Like "moral influence" models, they tend not to explain why Jesus had to die (some explicitly reject the idea that he did have to die). They do not always seek to show *how* Jesus Christ's triumph over death makes possible the practical, physical, this-worldly work of liberation. As we have already noted, there is no one accepted model of atonement that says everything we might want to say about God's work for humanity through Christ. One of the key contributions of liberation theology, however, to which this study is indebted is an overdue reminder that, in pre-Christian traditions and surely also for Christians, God wills and works to save the suffering as well as the sinful.

There are many wide-ranging and nuanced surveys and discussions of existing models of atonement, and the aim of this study is not to add another. But the differences of emphasis between the many models, ancient and modern, raise the question what a model of atonement deserving of discussion should aim to include. Everyone, I think, would agree that it should draw on the scriptural traditions that give rise to the concept, while recognizing that no one model can do justice to the whole range of biblical language and imagery of Jesus's saving work. Granted that existing models agree up to a point on what atonement achieves, a new model could usefully pay some attention to where they disagree. Did Christ have to die and, if so, why? How important is humanity's response for the effectiveness of God's salvation? Are not only Jesus's death but also his earthly life and actions, resurrection, and exalted life salvific? Everyone would surely agree that any model should be as coherent, compassionate, and relevant as possible. To anyone for whom the Christian witness to what God has made possible for humanity through Christ offers a possibility for meaningful existence, exploring the nature of our right relationship with God, what must change in ourselves and our lives for us to be at one with God, and how that change is possible is so fundamental

---

Abandoned (Eugene: Cascade, 2022), offers an interpretation of the cross and resurrection for the abused that is also an exceptionally rich pastoral resource.

13. Elizabeth Johnson, *She Who Is: The Mystery of God in Feminist Theological Discourse* (New York: Crossroad, 1992), 190–91. Dorothy A. Lee, "Sin, Self-Rejection and Gender: A Feminist Reading of John's Gospel," *Colloquium* 27 (1995): 51–63, in the context of a feminist argument, makes the point that subaltern groups do not only suffer but also sin. But, they sin in different ways from hegemonic groups and need to change in different ways too.

Introduction

that any model of atonement that does not speak to our sense of ourselves in our world as well as our fears and hopes will not speak to us at all.

This book offers a new model of atonement through the restoration of trust between God and humanity that seeks to be biblical and relevant, coherent and compassionate. Even if we accept that no single model can do justice to the diversity of early images and traditions about the meaning of Jesus's life and death, or to the complexity of what Christians' relationship with God and Christ means to us today, we may still wonder whether we need yet another. The language of trust, however, is so ubiquitous in the earliest Christian writings, including writing about the death of Christ, and so fundamental to the earliest Christian teachings that the absence of an existing model of atonement to which trust is central is a surprising lacuna that invites exploration.

Trust in the Earliest Christian Writings: The Interpretation of Christian *Pistis*

This study arises indirectly from the findings of the 2015 study *Roman Faith and Christian Faith*, which is a historical investigation into the meaning and operation of *pistis*, *fides*, and related concepts in the world of the early Roman Principate and the earliest churches.[14] Greek and Latin were the dominant languages of this world (Aramaic, which Jesus and his first followers spoke, was also widespread in the East), and *pistis* and *fides* each had a wide range of meanings that were almost, though not quite, coextensive.[15] Both can mean "trust," "trustworthiness," "faithfulness," "loyalty," "good faith," "honesty," "credibility," "confidence," "assurance," "pledge," "guarantee," financial "credit," legal "proof," "credence," "belief," a "position of trust/trusteeship," a "trust" in the sense of something with which one is entrusted, "protection," or "security."[16] The most common meanings of both terms in literature and documents are relational "trust," "trustworthiness," and "faithfulness." *Pistis* and *fides* are interesting to students of Christianity because they are also the terms that, in Christian contexts, are usually translated "faith"

14. Teresa Morgan, *Roman Faith and Christian Faith* (Oxford: Oxford University Press, 2015).
15. Morgan, *Roman Faith*, 7, 20–21.
16. The nearest Aramaic equivalent, *hêmānûtā'* (related to Hebrew *ĕmûnāh*) has a narrower range of meaning, but trust is also central to it. *Pistis* (like *fides*) is an "action nominal," a type of noun common in Greek and Latin that is derived from a verb and expresses both active and passive meanings of that verb. *Pistis* is therefore the trust I put in you and the trustworthiness I attribute to you, or my faithfulness to you and yours to me. *Pistis* is also a social virtue; I cannot trust if there is no one to trust, so my trustworthiness is linked with your trust.

7

INTRODUCTION

or "belief."[17] For modern Christians, however, faith and belief (German *Glaube*; Spanish *fe*; French *foi*) are rather different from trust, trustworthiness, or faithfulness, and they may be rather different from each other as well. This raises the question whether the earliest surviving Christian writings, which are in Greek, use *pistis* language in its most common, first- and second-century meanings or in a distinctively Christian sense.

Roman Faith analyzes all the New Testament passages in which *pistis* language appears. It finds that they almost always follow contemporary usage, using the noun *pistis*, the verb *pisteuein*, the adjective *pistos*, and their relatives mainly to refer to relationships of trust, trustworthiness, and faithfulness, but occasionally using *pistis* or *pisteuein* to refer to belief and believing. A few passages use *pistis* language in more unusual ways that prefigure the distinctive concept Christian "faith" would eventually become. The body of teaching, for example, entrusted by the apostles to later generations, can be called "the faith."[18] Occasionally, *pistis* seems to refer not just to the relationship of trust between God and Christ and Christ's followers but to the bond that trust creates, and perhaps even to the community created by the bond.[19] In these ways, first-century Christians were already beginning to stretch and adapt *pistis* language for their own theological and organizational purposes. Most often, however, *pistis* to early Christians meant relational trust, trustworthiness, faithfulness, or entrustedness.[20]

17. "Belief" refers here to the cognitive attitude that takes something to be the case or regards it as true, but it is worth noting that early Christian belief is a complex attitude based on the coherence of multiple claims. E.g., belief in the resurrection is based on a combination of direct experience, report, the interpretation of passages of scripture, and the coherence of all these things with the hopes of Jesus's followers during his earthly life and after the resurrection experiences. See Morgan, *Theology of Trust*, 99–109. Greek in general usually uses "thinking" language (e.g., *nomizein, phronein, dokein*) together with *peithesthai* rather than *pistis* language to refer to belief. English can speak of "believing in" a person in a sense that seems to encompass both trust or confidence and belief, but with most philosophers currently writing about trust I distinguish between trust and belief, so I will avoid this potentially ambiguous phrase. English translations of the Bible tend to translate *pistis* language with "belief" or "faith" and their relatives, but the New American Bible makes more use of "trust."

18. Morgan, *Theology of Trust*, 322–23.

19. Morgan, *Theology of Trust*, 265–66, 278, 322.

20. On the role of "loyalty" as part of early Christian *pistis*, see Morgan, *Theology of Trust*, 4 n. 19, 51, 159 n. 76, 160–61. The fact that relational trust and its relatives dominate early Christian *pistis* does not, of course, mean that early Christians did not hold beliefs; they certainly did. But *pistis*, for Christians, is above all a life-changing commitment to God and Christ that demands more than belief. In the world of the early principate, both Jews and gentiles could believe that many things were true about heavenly beings (such as angels or the gods of polytheism) without worshipping them; belief was distinguishable from veneration or worship. It is debated

Introduction

The centrality of *pistis* to early Christian thinking and practice is clear throughout the earliest writings, including the writings of the New Testament with which this study is concerned. *Pistis* language is present in every New Testament text apart from 2 John. It appears fourteen times in the five chapters of 1 Thessalonians, probably the earliest surviving Christian writing, and is central to some of the most influential passages of Paul's letters. Jesus uses *pistis* language in every layer of tradition in the Synoptic Gospels, and it appears a hundred times in the Gospel of John, usually in the mouth of Jesus.[21] *Pistis* language is used of God and human beings, individuals and groups, of God's action through Christ, of conversion, and of life in communities of the faithful. By the time Paul wrote, Christians were already referring to themselves as *hoi pistoi* or *hoi pisteuontes*, "the faithful." These terms remained their preferred self-designation for centuries ("the faithful" is still often used today).[22] Occurrences of *pistis* language far outnumber those of other concepts central for early Christians such as love, righteousness, salvation, and hope, and no other corpus of texts, Jewish or gentile, uses it so heavily. *Pistis* language forms the single most dominant cluster of terms and concepts in New Testament writings and in early understandings of Christians' relationship with God, and this in itself is a reason to ask ourselves what role it plays in the at-one-ment of humanity with God.

Over time, as we have begun to see, Christian *pistis* and its equivalents in other languages used in early churches became increasingly complex, encompassing not only trust, trustworthiness, faithfulness, and belief, but also confidence, hope, the "leap of faith," the "eyes of faith," worship, a body of teaching, good works, fideism in the modern sense of a conviction held independently of (or even in spite of) reason, and "the faith," meaning Christianity as a whole. In this process, trust became less interesting to most theologians than belief, knowledge of God, or the

---

at what point Christian veneration for Jesus Christ amounted to worship, but there is no doubt that Christ-confessors were called from the start to make a life-changing commitment to Jesus Christ and take a decisive step beyond believing things about him. The term they use for that step is *pistis/pisteuein* not just in the sense of propositional "belief" but also in its relational "trust" sense. Through time, belief became increasingly central to Christian confession, but that is beyond the scope of this study.

21. This points to the possibility that the historical Jesus called people to trust probably in God, though possibly also in himself. The Synoptic Gospels often leave open whether Jesus is telling the disciples to trust in God or in him, but John's Jesus urges them to do both. See Morgan, *Roman Faith*, 350–51, 354–59, 400–401, 424.

22. The participle *hoi pisteuontes* could mean "the faithful" or "the believers." The adjective *hoi pistoi* could mean "the faithful" or "the trustworthy." Since they are used interchangeably from before our earliest evidence, and since commitment to God and Christ involves relational trust as well as believing, both are best translated as "the faithful." The two variants may have arisen in different communities as equally good translations of an Aramaic original.

INTRODUCTION

content of doctrine. As a result, almost no theologies of trust have been written, though trust in God and God's faithfulness remain popular subjects for pastoral writing.[23] If trust and its close relatives form the dominant meanings of *pistis* language at the roots of Christian tradition, however, trust is evidently a concept worth considering not only historically but theologically. If trust plays a leading role in the earliest Christian accounts of the relationship between God, Christ, and humanity, how should we understand it theologically, in all the contexts in which it appears?[24] How might that understanding affect our understanding of Christian faith or Christian life more broadly?

These questions led to the writing of *The New Testament and The Theology of Trust*, which investigates how the New Testament uses *pistis* language to describe and explain the importance of trust between God, Jesus Christ, and humanity in the Christ event, Jesus's earthly life and teaching, his death, and his exalted life. [25] *The Theology of Trust* explores not only the trust that human beings are invited to put in God and Christ but also the trust that God and Christ put in one another and the trust that both put in humanity. It proposes that trust between God, Christ, and humanity is both what philosophers call "three-place" (i.e., trust for something, in this case salvation) and "two-place" (i.e., a relationship that is valuable in itself).[26] It seeks to show how God is understood as faithful to God's people through time and also as capable of doing a "new thing" (in the words of Isaiah) and surprising humanity. The book considers the riskiness of trust for everyone involved and argues that God practices "therapeutic trust" in humanity, by which God offers the possibility of salvation, knowing that human beings will probably respond imperfectly at first, while also allowing the possibility that their trust will strengthen over time.

The Theology of Trust argues that people put their trust in Christ in every aspect of his earthly life and work, death, resurrection, and exalted life, and that trust

23. The most important exception is the work of Pierangelo Sequeri; see pp. 17–18.

24. Morgan, *Roman Faith*, 117–20, 128–37, 178–88, 196–200, 238–39 offers a number of reasons why *pistis* may have become so important to Christians so soon in addition to the possibility that Jesus called people to trust: it is prominent in the exodus narrative; it is widely treated in the early principate as a paradigmatic virtue of times of crisis and an opportunity and building block of new societies; and both the Jewish scriptures and gentile writings can speak of God (or gods) as trustworthy.

25. The idea of trust is not always expressed in *pistis* language: *paratithenai* and *parathēkē*, terms for entrusting someone and for something which is entrusted, also appear, and the language of confidence, hope, and obedience is also closely related to trust. Morgan, *Theology of Trust*, 8, 295–98 discusses these alongside *pistis* language, but for present purposes we can focus on *pistis*.

26. Philosophers can also speak of "one-place" trust, a generically positive attitude toward trust that can precede specific instances of trust.

10

Introduction

contributes to salvation everywhere that it occurs.[27] It also argues that human beings' response to Christ is always partial and imperfect. Nobody fully understands Jesus Christ in every aspect of his nature or work any more than anyone fully understands God, and even those who put their trust in him often fail through fear, doubt, or temptation, but even imperfect trust is enough for salvation. The book looks at the widespread but neglected New Testament concept of "entrustedness," by which God and Christ entrust apostles, other individuals, and whole communities with gifts such as leadership, preaching, and healing, and responsibilities for stewarding God's creation until the end time. Finally, it explores the almost undiscussed phenomenon of "propositional trust," "trusting that" something is true, suggesting that this is at least as important for Christians as believing or knowing that something is true.

One chapter of *The Theology of Trust* begins to outline the role played by trust in the death and resurrection of Jesus, particularly in the undisputed letters of Paul. That chapter is the germ of this book, which takes it further in several directions. The argument of *The Theology of Trust* that every aspect of Christ's existence is salvific raises the question why a whole book should be devoted to trust in relation to Christ's death and resurrection. The cross, however, is so central to Christian thought and devotion, and so challenging to faith and reason alike, that if trust is to be seen as playing a significant part in humanity's at-one-ment with God, the role of the cross deserves more investigation than that earlier book could give it.

WHY TRUST?

As I noted above, all models of atonement, more or less directly, are developed out of ideas and images scattered throughout the Hebrew Bible and New Testament, including ideas of sacrifice, ransom, substitution, mediation, reconciliation, propitiation, love, imitation, and cosmic war. The "trust" model developed here is no exception. Indeed, since *pistis* and its relatives are ubiquitous in New Testament writings, including in passages about the cross, there is a strong reason prima facie for considering the role of *pistis* in at-one-ment. Trust has a further claim on our

---

27. In New Testament studies this approach goes back to Ernst Fuchs and Gerhard Eberling in addition to liberation and systematic theologians who have recently argued for it, including Edward Schillebeeckx, Jakub Trojan, and Kathryn Tanner. See, e.g., Aloysius Rego, *Suffering and Salvation: The Salvific Meaning of Suffering in the Later Theology of Edward Schillebeeckx* (Leuven: Peeters, 2006), 289–96, 304–5; Kathryn Tanner, *Christ the Key* (Cambridge: Cambridge University Press, 2010); cf. Jakub S. Trojan, *From Christ's Death to Jesus' Life: A Critical Reinterpretation of Prevailing Theories of the Cross* (Bern: Lang, 2012), 378.

INTRODUCTION

attention. In the past half-century, research into trust has burgeoned, especially in philosophy, psychology, and the social sciences.[28] Scholars have become fascinated by the power of trust to create and sustain relationships and communities, small and large, simple and highly complex. Some have suggested that this trend is fueled by a growing fear that societies, organizations, and individuals around the world are becoming less trusting and less trustworthy, and that this poses a significant threat to their flourishing and even survival. Some are particularly interested in how trust can be rebuilt in individuals and societies after conflict, trauma, or crime. The philosopher Thomas O. Buford speaks for many when he says that trust is so important that it can be called our "second nature": "when trust is present we have a basis of community, of hope, and of goals. When it is absent or significantly diminished, fear of others enters accompanied by isolation, instability, and confusion over norms that govern our lives."[29] Trust is increasingly recognized as fundamental for everything from the psychological integrity of individuals to the negotiation of interstate relations, and that suggests another reason to consider the role of trust in at-one-ment between God and humanity.

Several slightly different definitions of trust are in circulation across disciplines, but this definition of relational trust aims to cover all its most widely accepted elements:

> Trust is the action of putting something (which might include an object, an outcome, or oneself), or the attitude of willingness to put something, in someone else's hands (i.e. in their power, responsibility, and/or care), on the basis (which might be e.g. a belief, hope, wager, or assumption) that the other will respond positively (for instance, because she is willing and/or able to do so, and/or because she is encouraged to do so by one's trust).[30]

---

28. For overviews of research on trust see Onora O'Neill, *A Question of Trust: The BBC Reith Lectures 2002* (Cambridge: Cambridge University Press, 2002); Katherine Hawley, *Trust: A Very Short Introduction* (Oxford: Oxford University Press, 2012); Dale E. Zand, "Reflections on Trust and Trust Research: Then and Now," *J. Trust Res.* 6 (2016): 63–73; Nicole Gillespie, "Trust Dynamics and Repair: An Interview with Roy Lewicki," *J. Trust Res.* 7 (2017): 204–19; Morgan, *Roman Faith*, 15–23 (on the historiography and sociology of trust) and Morgan, *Theology of Trust*, 8–22 (on philosophy and psychology).

29. Thomas O. Buford, *Trust, Our Second Nature: Crisis, Reconciliation, and the Personal* (Washington, DC: Lexington, 2009), 8, 1. Most trust theorists assume we have an innate disposition to trust; see, e.g., Eric Schniter, Roman M. Sheremeta, and Daniel Sznycer, "Building and Rebuilding Trust with Promises and Apologies," *Journal of Economic Behavior and Organization* 94 (2013): 242–56.

30. Morgan, *Theology of Trust*, 22. This definition encompasses both two- and three-place trust, though not one-place trust, which is not a feature of New Testament writings, where trust

Introduction

Since I have also mentioned propositional trust, it is worth offering a definition of that too: "trusting that" means entrusting something or someone, or being willing to entrust something or someone, to a proposition about which one accepts that one is not certain.[31]

It is generally agreed that one can hold an attitude of trust at a given moment without acting on it and also act with trust while holding an attitude, say, of fear or doubt, but that ideally attitude and action go together. The fact that attitude and action do not always go together is significant for this study, because sometimes New Testament writings suggest that a person acts with trust without feeling it, or without feeling it unequivocally: perhaps because they are taking a deliberate risk or because they feel fear or doubt.

Recent work in the philosophy of trust was initiated by a groundbreaking essay by the moral philosopher Annette Baier.[32] Baier observed that modern Western philosophy had taken little interest in trust and had not recognized that it has both positive and negative aspects. She offered a definition and exploration of "morally proper" trust.[33] Baier proposed that trust often involves reliance but that it is distinct from reliance because one can be let down by someone or something on which one relies, but one can be betrayed only by someone one trusts.[34] When I trust a person, I depend on her goodwill toward me, which means that I am vulnerable to her, so "trust . . . is accepted vulnerability to another's possible but not expected ill will (or lack of good will) toward one."[35]

Baier argues that we trust people, despite the fact that it makes us vulnerable, because, as human beings, we are not self-sufficient practically or emotionally.[36] This fundamental observation about human existence, she suggests, has been too little recognized by Western moral philosophers, who have tended to see trust as a

---

is always in relation to God, Christ, or someone such as an apostle entrusted with a role by God and Christ. In a case of three-place trust, when we trust someone to respond positively, we cannot necessarily be sure that they will succeed in doing what we trust them for.

31. On how this differs from belief see Morgan, *Theology of Trust*, 325–26.

32. Annette C. Baier, "Trust and Antitrust," *Ethics* 96 (1986): 231–60.

33. Baier, "Trust and Antitrust," 231–32.

34. Baier, "Trust and Antitrust," 234–35.

35. Baier, "Trust and Antitrust," 235. Arguing that trust is not the same as reliance see also Hawley, *Trust*, 3–6; Morgan, *Theology of Trust*, 24–25. There are too many cases in which one can rely without trust and vice versa for this to be satisfactory. E.g., I can rely on my enemy to want to defeat me without trusting her; I can trust my partner to bring home a pint of milk and also pick one up myself on the way home, so I am not relying on him.

36. Baier, "Trust and Antitrust," 236. See also Adam Seligman, "Trust, Experience, and Embodied Knowledge: Lessons from John Dewey on the Dangers of Abstraction," *J. Trust Res.* 11 (2021): 5–21.

INTRODUCTION

type of contract that autonomous individuals make voluntarily on the basis that it is in their interest.[37] This kind of contract making, Baier holds, may be available, even normal, for "adult males whose dealings with others are mainly business or restrained social dealings with similarly placed males," but it is not normal for human beings in general.[38] Elsewhere in human life—among family members, lovers, friends, the vulnerable and those who care for them, and all those of unequal power or status—trust looks very different.[39] Very young children, for example, can be seen as trusting parents over whom they have very little or no control. This kind of trust is not rationally assessed, nor is it earned by the trustee, but it is given prima facie, and it is not contractual in any obvious way because it does not negotiate for a specific return.[40] One implication of Baier's argument, which is significant for our study, is that the trust people give each other in relationships is not necessarily (though it can be) wholehearted or unreserved from the start. It can begin as something tentative, provisional, and subject to confirmation by further experience. This is what is sometimes called "thin" trust, which, if all goes well, becomes "thicker"—firmer and more wide-ranging—over time.

Baier's approach to trust was one of the inspirations for the development of a new field of ethics: the ethics of care. Care ethicists argue that human beings are always interdependent and are created and thrive in relationships.[41] Like Baier, they resist the assumption that ethical agents are independent, autonomous, and act mainly in the public sphere.[42] Care, which is both an attitude and a practice (though not necessarily both simultaneously), is seen as the fundamental human good, and some care ethicists argue explicitly that care requires trust.[43] In recent years, care ethics has increasingly interested theologians, for whom it is axiomatic

37. Baier, "Trust and Antitrust," 244–53. She identifies this form of thinking especially with Kant.

38. Baier, "Trust and Antitrust," 248.

39. Baier, "Trust and Antitrust," 249–50. Baier draws here on the work of Carol Gilligan, *In a Different Voice: Psychological Theory and Women's Development* (Cambridge: Harvard University Press, 1982).

40. See Jacopo Domenicucci and Richard Holton, "Trust as a Two-Place Relation," in *The Philosophy of Trust* (ed. Paul Faulkner and Thomas W. Simpson; Oxford: Oxford University Press, 2017), 149–60. They also describe some of the ways in which trust can be unwelcome or difficult or put relationships under tension.

41. Virginia Held, *The Ethics of Care: Personal, Political, and Global* (Oxford: Oxford University Press, 2006), 46.

42. S. Ruddick, "An Appreciation of Love's Labour," *Hypatia* 17 (2002): 214–24; Michael Slote, *The Ethics of Care and Empathy* (London: Routledge, 2007), 1.

43. Daryl Koehn, *Rethinking Feminist Ethics: Care, Trust, and Empathy* (London: Routledge, 1998), especially chapter 3; Held, *Ethics of Care*, 30, 37; Eva Feder Kittay, *Love's Labors: Essays on Women, Equality, and Dependency* (2nd ed.; Oxford: Abingdon, 2020), 34–35.

14

Introduction

that human beings exist in a relationship with God that is often characterized as one of care.[44]

I mentioned earlier the concept of "therapeutic trust," a concept that is gaining interest among moral philosophers.[45] We trust someone therapeutically when we act toward them with trust, even though we do not know whether they will respond by being trustworthy, or even when we suspect they will not prove trustworthy. In a classic example developed by the philosopher Karen Jones, imagine that I go away for the weekend, trusting my teenaged children not to hold a party and make a mess of the house.[46] I may suspect that they will do just that, but I hope that by trusting them I will demonstrate that trust is an important aspect of adult life and something they should take seriously. Even if they do not prove trustworthy this time, I hope that next time they may respond a bit better until, eventually, they become trustworthy adults. One of the strengths of the concept of therapeutic trust is that it emphasizes that trust can take a step into a situation in which trust does not yet exist and make possible and initiate a relationship, or an aspect of a relationship, that develops through time. *The Theology of Trust* argued that therapeutic trust is characteristic of God, who entrusts Jesus Christ—that radically atypical and unexpected type of messiah—to the world and trusts human beings to be able to respond to Christ, knowing that some people will fail, at least at first, and that probably everyone will fail up to a point, but knowing that humanity is capable of responding eventually.[47] The concept of therapeutic trust will also be important in this study, where I will argue that God acts with grace by placing therapeutic trust in humanity, an act that changes humanity's understanding of what is possible for it and thereby what is possible for it in relationship with God.

A small but growing number of philosophers of religion and theologians has also begun to investigate the possibility of trust between humanity and God. In 1956, the philosopher and theologian Knud Eijer Løgstrup began his monograph *The Ethical Demand* by discussing the love command in the gospels. Løgstrup argues that the love command expresses the recognition by Jesus (or the gospel

44. E.g., Barry R. Sang, "A Nexus of Care: Process Theology and Care Ethics," *Process Studies* 36 (2007): 229–44; F. de Lange, "The Heidelberg Catechism: Elements for a Theology of Care," *Acta Theologica Supplementum* 20 (2014): 156–73; Helenka Mannering, "A Rapprochement between Feminist Ethics of Care and Contemporary Theology," *Religions* 11 (2020): 185–97.

45. E.g., H. J. N. Horsburgh, "The Ethics of Trust," *Philosophical Quarterly* 10 (1960): 343–54; Karen Frost-Arnold, "The Cognitive Attitude of Rational Trust," *Synthese* 191 (2014): 1957–74.

46. Karen Jones, "But I Was Counting on You!" in Faulkner and Simpson, *Philosophy of Trust*, 90–107; Michael Pace, "Trusting in Order to Inspire Trustworthiness," *Synthese* 198 (2020): 11901.

47. Morgan, *Theology of Trust*, 68–72.

INTRODUCTION

writers) that human beings are interdependent by nature. Jesus commands his followers to accept this and learn to depend on one another for everything that is most important in their lives. To depend on one another, however, Løgstrup argues, human beings must learn to trust. Trust is fundamental: "It is a characteristic of human life that we normally encounter one another with natural trust."[48]

Løgstrup describes trusting as "to lay oneself open."[49] When we trust, we "dare to come forward in the hope of being accepted ... Through the trust which a person either shows or asks of another person he or she surrenders something of his or her life to that person."[50] If another person surrenders him- or herself to us in this way, we have the power to care for them or to do them harm, but, for Løgstrup, this is no choice at all: "out of this basic dependence and direct power arises the demand that we take care of that in the other person's life which is dependent upon us and which we have in our power."[51] Caring for another person, however, does not mean that we objectify or disempower them. "Responsibility for the other person never consists in our assuming the responsibility which is his or hers."[52] Løgstrup sees this pattern of self-surrender and care without disempowerment at the heart of human beings' relationship not only with one another but with God.

Joseph J. Godfrey's 2012 monograph *Trust of People, Words and God: A Route for Philosophy of Religion* draws on Baier's work to argue that salvation does not depend only on belief (as Christians sometimes argue) but also on the attitude and action of trust.[53] He identifies four main types of trust, which share the quality that they make us "receptive to enhancement," changing and enlarging us in positive ways.[54] Among much else, he argues that trust can coexist with doubt and skepticism;[55] that we can envisage trust in God as similar to trust between human beings;[56] and that trust can be a basis for knowledge "insofar as knowledge can be supported by taking well the reliable word of another person."[57] Godfrey's book

48. Knud Eijer Løgstrup, *The Ethical Demand* (Notre Dame: University of Notre Dame Press, 1997), 8.

49. Løgstrup, *Ethical Demand*, 9.

50. Løgstrup, *Ethical Demand*, 10, 17.

51. Løgstrup, *Ethical Demand*, 28.

52. Løgstrup, *Ethical Demand*, 28.

53. Joseph J. Godfrey, *Trust of People, Words and God: A Route for Philosophy of Religion* (Notre Dame: University of Notre Dame Press, 2012), ix, 87, 89.

54. Godfrey, *Trust of People*, 89.

55. Godfrey, *Trust of People*, 168.

56. Godfrey, *Trust of People*, 396–99.

57. Godfrey, *Trust of People*, 198 and chapter 6.

Introduction

is a study in the philosophy of religion, not in Christian theology, but he suggests, surely rightly, that it offers much for theologians to think about.[58]

In recent years, some philosophers of religion have become interested in trust through their interest in Christian faith or belief. Among others, William Alston, Robert Audi, Richard Swinburne, and Nicholas Wolterstorff have recognized the role of trust in faith in the course of investigating the nature and foundations of belief in God, and Audi has discussed it at length.[59] Daniel McKaughan has gone further, arguing that Christian faith is primarily relational rather than primarily cognitive and showing that his model of faith fits well with the way in which New Testament writings describe *pistis* toward God and Christ.[60] He also argues that people of faith can be said to have faith, and be faithful or trusting toward God, even at times when they are suffering from doubt or lack of belief.[61]

One of the very few theologians with a significant interest in trust and, in particular, the trustworthiness of God is Pierangelo Sequeri.[62] In his magisterial study *Il Dio affidabile* Sequeri argues that God is not an object of knowledge. The reality of God can be discerned only in an encounter of trust with the God who is *affidabile*, that is, reliable, trustworthy, and dependable.[63] Sequeri grounds this argument in an anthropology that insists on the centrality of trust to all kinds of

---

58. Godfrey, *Trust of People*, chapter 11 and following.

59. E.g., Nicholas Wolterstorff, "The Assurance of Faith," *Faith Philos.* 7 (1990): 398; William P. Alston, "Belief, Acceptance, and Religious Faith," in *Faith, Freedom, and Rationality* (ed. J. Jordan and Daniel Howard-Snyder; Lanham: Rowman & Littlefield, 1996), 3–27; J. L. Schellenberg, *Prolegomena to a Philosophy of Religion* (Ithaca: Cornell University Press, 2005), 106–26; Richard Swinburne, *Faith and Reason* (2nd ed.; Oxford: Oxford University Press, 2005), 147–58; Robert Audi, "Belief, Faith, and Acceptance," *Int. J. Philos. Relig.* 63 (2008): 87–102; Robert Audi, *Rationality and Religious Commitment* (Oxford: Oxford University Press, 2011). Benjamin McCraw, "Faith and Trust," *Int. J. Philos. Relig.* 77 (2015): 141 suggests that it is now a platitude that faith in God involves trust, which is surprising given how little it is still explored.

60. E.g., Daniel McKaughan, "On the Value of Faith and Faithfulness," *Int. J. Philos. Relig.* 81 (2017): 7–29; Daniel McKaughan, "Cognitive Opacity and the Analysis of Faith: Acts of Faith Interiorized through a Glass Only Darkly," *Religious Studies* 54 (2018): 576–85.

61. Daniel McKaughan, "Action-Centered Faith, Doubt, and Rationality," *Journal of Philosophical Research* 41 (2016): 71–90; Daniel McKaughan, "Faith through the Dark of Night: What Perseverance amidst Doubt Can Teach Us about the Nature and Value of Religious Faith," *Faith Philos.* 35 (2018): 195–218.

62. Daniella Ricotta, *Il Logos, in verità è amore: Introduzione filosofica alla teologia di Pierangelo Sequeri* (Milan: Ancora, 2007), 51–70.

63. Pierangelo Sequeri, *L'idea della fede: Trattato di teologia fondamentale* (Milan: Glossa, 2002), 64.

INTRODUCTION

human knowledge.[64] Human beings have an innate tendency to trust, and trust fulfills one of our basic needs, enabling us to see one other and be seen, to recognize one another and be recognized.[65] In a relationship of trust and faithfulness, we know one another and are known for who we are—a personal orientation that is also ethical. For Sequeri, the reality of another that we experience in encounter with that other, whether human or divine, we also experience as true and good.[66] Sequeri's work has not been translated into English and is notoriously difficult to read in Italian, so it has been little discussed by Anglophone scholars, but it shares some of their interests. Trust, for Sequeri, is essential if we hope to come to know and love God.

All these studies have made advances in our understanding of trust, including the way we think about trust between human beings and God. They share the view that trust and its relatives are as central to the relationship between God and humanity as they are to relationships between human beings. They point to divine-human trust as life-giving and life-enhancing, risky but necessary, not necessarily incompatible with fear or doubt but equally formative for our sense of ourselves and of God, and foundational to our knowledge of God. None of these studies more than touches on the idea of trust in the Bible, but one of the aims of *The Theology of Trust* was to show that the idea that trust is central to the divine-human relationship is deeply rooted in scripture and Jewish and Christian tradition. This study seeks to develop that line of thought further, particularly in relation to atonement.

The study of trust, including trust in God, also has a substantial history in social psychology, the psychology of religion, and psychotherapy. David H. Rosmarin and his research group have developed an account of what it means to trust in God that involves both believing and feeling that God is taking care of one.[67]

---

64. Pierangelo Sequeri, *Il Dio affidabile: Saggio di teologia fondamentale* (Brescia: Queriniana, 1996), 354–55; Sequeri, *L'idea della fede*, 194.

65. Sequeri, *Il Dio affidabile*, 135; Michael Paul Gallagher, "Truth and Trust: Pierangelo Sequeri's Theology of Faith," *Irish Theological Quarterly* 73 (2008): 11–13.

66. Sequeri, *Il Dio affidabile*, 378–88.

67. David H. Rosmarin, Kenneth L. Pargament, and Annette Mahoney, "The Role of Religiousness in Anxiety, Depression, and Happiness in a Jewish Community Sample: A Preliminary Investigation," *Ment. Health Relig. Cult.* 12 (2009): 97–113; David H. Rosmarin, S. Pirutinsky, and Kenneth I. Pargament, "A Brief Measure of Core Religious Beliefs for Use in Psychiatric Settings," *International Journal of Psychiatry in Medicine* 41 (2011): 253–61; Steven Pirutinsky and David Rosmarin, "My God, Why Have You Abandoned Me? Sexual Abuse and Attitudes towards God among Orthodox Jews," *Ment. Health Relig. Cult.* 23 (2020): 579–90. They describe six "core domains" that identify subjects as trusting in God: (1) God has constant regard for all worldly affairs; (2) God has absolute knowledge of what is in people's best interests; (3) no power is greater than

Introduction

Neal Krause and his research group have argued that, in the Christian groups they studied, those who express strong trust in God also tend to have confidence that God is just.[68] Their findings echo the conviction of New Testament writers that trust in God and Christ goes hand in hand with the experience of God's justice and care. Psychologist and psychotherapist Doris Brothers has explored the effects of trauma on trust in her influential study *Falling Backwards: An Exploration of Trust and Self-Experience*. Brothers argues that trust is essential to human beings because a positive experience of the self is impossible in its absence.[69] Without trust we cannot function: it is "the glue of self-experience."[70] What is more, trust in others and trust in ourselves are equally important. Brothers identifies four dimensions of trust that ideally operate in us to roughly equal degrees:

1. Trust-in-others, which sees others as trustworthy providers of experiences that for us are part of ourselves (self-object experiences). For example, I might trust others to affirm my sense of myself as a musician.

2. Trust-in-self, which sees oneself as capable of eliciting self-object experiences

---

God; (4) God must be involved for anything to occur; (5) God is merciful and generous; (6) God is righteous in judgment.

68. N. Krause, "Trust in God and Psychological Distress: Exploring Variations by Religious Affiliation," *Ment. Health Relig. Cult.* 18 (2015): 235–45; N. Krause and R. D. Hayward, "Assessing Whether Trust Offsets the Effects of Financial Strain on Health and Well-Being," *Int. J. Psychol. Relig.* 25 (2015): 307–22. Almost all early experimental studies on trust in God assumed that trust is equivalent to holding a set of beliefs, while in philosophy the differences between trust and belief are increasingly emphasized; see Morgan, *Theology of Trust*, 12–17. Challenging the psychological model on the basis of work in philosophy is Joshua N. Hook et al., "Trust in God: An Evaluative Review of the Research Literature and Research Proposal," *Ment. Health Relig. Cult.* 24 (2021): 745–63. Psychological models also assume (and in this matter are closer to most New Testament writings) that children are born with the capacity and impulse to trust.

69. Doris Brothers, *Falling Backwards: An Exploration of Trust and Self-Experience* (New York: Norton, 1995) with a critical review of thinking about trust in psychotherapy on 5–30. On the developmental foundations of trust see also Jon G. Allen, *Trusting in Psychotherapy* (Washington, DC: American Psychiatric Publishing, 2021), chapter 2. The link between trauma and the erosion of trust, and its effects on the ability of trauma victims to make successful relationships and engage effectively with the world around them, is much discussed in social psychology and psychiatry; see, e.g., Andreas Ebert et al., "Modulation of Interpersonal Trust in Borderline Personality Disorder by Intranasal Oxytocin and Childhood Trauma," *Social Neuroscience* 8 (2013): 305–13; Gianni Guasto, "Trauma and the Loss of Basic Trust," *International Forum of Psychoanalysis* 23 (2014): 44–49.

70. Brothers, *Falling Backwards*, 31. Ana-María Rizzuto, "Religious Development beyond the Modern Paradigm Discussion: The Psychoanalytic Point of View," *Int. J. Psychol. Relig.* 11 (2001): 201–14 makes a similar argument and also argues that religious faith requires the same social conditions as interpersonal trust to develop well (203–4).

INTRODUCTION

from others. For example, I might trust myself to present myself to the world in such a way that it sees me as a musician.

3. Self-as-trustworthy, which sees oneself as able to provide trustworthy self-object experiences for others. For example, I might trust myself to provide my colleagues with the confirmation they need that they are intellectuals.

4. Others-as-self-trusting, which sees others as trusting of their ability to provide trustworthy self-object experiences. For example, I might trust my colleagues to be able to show me that they are intellectuals.

Those who have suffered trauma often lose one or more of these dimensions of trust. Trauma damages our trust not only in others but also in ourselves and our relationship with the world around us.[71] Without it we tend to lose empathy with others and may be attacked by feelings of anger or shame.[72] Brothers's model emphasizes how significant it is for people not only to be able to trust but also to be trusted—to feel that they are seen as trustworthy.[73]

Brothers shows how the world in which we trust and feel trusted is the world that we experience as real, and in which we experience ourselves as real. Those who do not trust themselves to show themselves to the world and be seen by others, or who do not trust others to show themselves to them and be seen, can come to feel that they are not quite real in the everyday world, or that others are not quite real in their world. They may then look for security in dreams or fantasies that seem safer than the surrounding world—and there they may become trapped.[74] If we ask, "Whom do we trust?" or "By whom do we feel trusted?" we are also asking "Who is real for us?," "In what relationships do we experience ourselves as most real?," "In what world are we material?," and "In what world do we matter?"[75]

These are not only universal human questions but profoundly theological ones. Brothers's exploration of how failing to learn to or losing trust can cause us

71. Brothers, *Falling Backwards*, 55–57.

72. Brothers, *Falling Backwards*, 57–60. Brothers notes that the betrayal of trust does not typically destroy self-trust in adults but does in infants and children.

73. Brothers, *Falling Backwards*, 209–30.

74. Brothers, *Falling Backwards*, 64–68, 70–73, 114–18.

75. Cf. Pieter D. Craffert, "I 'Witnessed the Raising of the Dead': Resurrection Accounts in a Neuroanthropological Perspective," *Neotestamentica* 45 (2018): 1–28, who argues that human experiences of physical or metaphysical phenomena can be so divergent that they can be described as living in different worlds. Wilfried Härle and Reiner Preul, eds., *Glaube* (Marburg: Elwert, 1992), 1–2 note the need for more discussion about the relationship between divine-human *pistis/fides* and the fulfillment of human personhood from a theological perspective.

20

Introduction

to feel trapped in a destructive reality—one where we are unable to access a life in which we would be able to grow, thrive, and make good relationships—has uncanny resonances with some New Testament images of what it means to live in a state of sin and suffering, a state which New Testament writers sometimes explicitly call *apistia*, a lack of trust in God. Brothers's emphasis on the importance of creating or restoring trust for those who do not have it if they are to live fully as human beings, in themselves and in relationships and communities, powerfully echoes New Testament writings' insistence on the power of trust to bring humanity into more abundant and eternal life.

When people cannot develop trust, or lose trust, they often also lose hope. The relationship between trust and hope is not widely discussed in psychology, but it is explored in an article by Matthew Ratcliffe, Mark Ruddell, and Benedict Smith.[76] Citing the 1999 United Nations Istanbul Protocol, which states that victims of torture often have "a sense of foreshortened future without expectation of a career, marriage, children, or normal lifespan," Ratcliffe, Ruddell, and Smith investigate how torture and other kinds of trauma "can lead to a loss of 'trust' or 'confidence' in the world. This undermines the intelligibility of one's projects, cares, and commitments, in a way that amounts to a change in the structure of temporal experience."[77] Those who lose trust can cease to be able to look forward, to have confidence in the future, or to hope. The organic connection between trust and hope is another that will recur in our exploration of the role of trust in at-one-ment between God, Christ, and human beings.

Recent work in philosophy and psychology tends to focus on individuals and to assume that people in different places and times trust in much the same ways. Historians and sociologists are more interested in groups and whole societies and the distinctive patterns that trust can form in different places and times. Medieval historian Ian Forrest, for example, in his study *The Trustworthy Men: How Faith and Inequality Made the Medieval Church*, shows how relationships of trust between English bishops and small groups of leading "trustworthy men" in parishes shaped the administration of medieval England.[78] Robert Putnam,

76. Matthew Ratcliffe, Mark Ruddell, and Benedict Smith, "What Is a 'Sense of Foreshortened Future'? A Phenomenological Study of Trauma, Trust, and Time," *Front. Psychol.* 5 (2014): art. 1026.

77. Ratcliffe, Ruddell, and Smith, "Foreshortened Future," 1. See United Nations, *Istanbul Protocol: Manual on the Effective Investigation and Documentation of Torture and Other Cruel, Inhuman, or Degrading Treatment or Punishment* (Geneva: Office of the United Nations High Commissioner for Human Rights, 1999), 47.

78. Ian Forrest, *The Trustworthy Men: How Faith and Inequality Made the Medieval Church* (Princeton: Princeton University Press, 2018).

INTRODUCTION

in *Bowling Alone: The Collapse and Revival of American Community*, argues that declining participation in group activities from the mid-twentieth century onward degraded trust within American society and put society and its institutions at risk.[79] A growing body of work in conflict studies focuses on the role of trust in different parts of the world in helping societies to recover after the destruction and trauma of war, and sometimes on the different ways in which trust operates, or fails to operate, in those complex and fragile situations. I will discuss some of these studies in chapter 2, together with the role that churches are taking in some countries to try to restore social trust. The importance of trust is a common theme of historical and sociological studies across place and time, but trust does not always operate in the same way in different societies. One of the aims of any study of trust in Christianity, including this one, is therefore to explore the ways in which Christian trust is distinctive.

Roman Faith and Christian Faith argues that sources of the early Roman Principate, written around the time that Christianity emerged, largely agree that trust between family members is strong and reliable. Trust between friends or trading partners, in contrast, is desirable but not easy, while political institutions tend to be untrustworthy, and emperors are often seen as less trustworthy than anyone. This profile of (mis)trust, it suggests, is not surprising in the aftermath of a turbulent period of Roman conquest and exploitation of neighboring states, which overlapped with a devastating civil war in Rome, both of which dramatically degraded trust in politics and political institutions. It may also help to explain why the Christian call to trust in a wholly trustworthy God was appealing to some people.

The Theology of Trust argues that trust takes an equally distinctive but different shape in New Testament writings. In broad terms, God takes a risk on humanity, entrusting Jesus Christ to the world, trusting him to be able to form trust relationships with those who encounter him, and trusting humanity to respond. This is risky especially because God is acting indirectly through Christ and because Jesus is not a traditional messiah. In his earthly life, death, and resurrected and exalted life, however, Jesus mediates between God and humanity, trusting and trustworthy to both, to bring humanity back to trust in God and to keep it in that relationship until the end time.

This brief summary of some of the most influential developments in trust research in recent years across different disciplines begins, I hope, to show why trust is an interesting concept in Christian theology, not least in connection with atone-

---

79. Robert Putnam, *Bowling Alone: The Collapse and Revival of American Community* (New York: Simon & Schuster, 2000).

Introduction

ment. Trust is found everywhere in early Christian writings, describing the relationship between God and humanity that is restored through Jesus Christ. Outside biblical studies, trust is widely agreed to be so basic to human life that neither individuals nor groups can survive, let alone flourish, without it. It is so important that we take significant risks to establish and maintain it, making ourselves vulnerable and surrendering ourselves to others. People cannot always trust all at once or once for all, but trust can begin as one step toward another—something relatively "thin" and limited that, ideally, grows through time. As it grows, it can sometimes be an attitude, sometimes an action, sometimes both. It can coexist with fear and doubt and can also wobble and fail without failing ultimately. It acts as a basis for relational knowing. It is good for many purposes and intrinsically good as part of a relationship. Without trust, both love and hope become much harder to practice. Where we trust is where we see and are seen; where we feel real and material; where we matter. Trust can be not only a desirable acquisition and condition but the starting point of new or renewed life in relationship.

Theology and History

The model of atonement developed here begins with historical readings of New Testament writings and particularly the undisputed letters of Paul. Since the relationship between historical criticism and theology in New Testament studies is a matter of much debate, it is worth saying a little about how this study treats the relationship between the two.

As a historian by training I do not share the view, which goes back to Johann Philipp Gabler and was influentially restated in the late twentieth century by Krister Stendahl, that we need to establish the historical status of New Testament writings before thinking theologically with them; that, as Stendahl put it, the "descriptive task" precedes the "theological task."[80] For one thing, it is a truism of modern historiography and theology alike that the study of the material world can neither prove nor disprove any argument in metaphysics.[81] For another, Gabler's and Stendahl's claims rely implicitly on the hope that historical study

80. Krister Stendahl, "Biblical Theology, Contemporary," *The Interpreter's Dictionary of the Bible* (ed. G. A. Buttrick; 4 vols.; Nashville: Abingdon, 1962), 1:418–19. James Barr, *The Concept of Biblical Theology: An Old Testament Perspective* (London: SCM, 1999), 202–4, argues that the meaning the Bible had remains its only meaning, though he accepts that even historical "description" uses modern categories of thought, so no reading is free of interpretation (204–5).

81. The idea that God acts in history, of course, challenges simple understandings of this boundary but is beyond our scope here.

INTRODUCTION

can establish facts or truths that correspond reliably to the reality of the past, but historians are much more wary of making that claim. Our evidence for the past—especially from two millennia ago—is fragmentary, partial in both senses of the word, and endlessly debatable. The study of ancient history cannot lay an unproblematic foundation for anything else. Theology, moreover, can equally well be done through the lens of philosophy, literary criticism, aesthetics, and other disciplines.

That said, like almost all Christians, I take early witness in general, and that which has become scriptural in particular, to be foundational to faith. At a minimum, it transmits and interprets the witness of some of those who were closest to the Christ event and whose lives were transformed by it, together with the communities they formed, and communities of the faithful through time have found it reliable and fruitful for shaping and guiding their relationship with God, their earthly life, and their hope. Many Christians go much further, affirming the scriptures as theologically infallible, inerrant, or even literally true at every point. Christian tradition, however, has never claimed that there is no mystery about God or divine action for the world, nor that New Testament texts were dictated by God to their writers, so almost all those who affirm biblical infallibility or inerrancy also accept that testimony to God's actions mediated through human writers needs to be interpreted.[82] In this context, historical-critical interpretation is an important tool by which we try to understand better what the earliest surviving witnesses to the Christ event and the good news experienced, understood, and wanted to communicate about what they and their communities understood as God's action through Christ for the world.

Another contribution historical-critical study of the Bible can make to faith is to identify ideas, themes, or ways of thinking in the texts that evolving Christian tradition has forgotten, overlooked, or developed to the point that they have changed significantly. I have argued that one such theme is the importance of the relational aspects of *pistis* (i.e., trust, faithfulness, trustworthiness, entrustedness) for early Christians. Another theme, as chapter 1 will argue, is that salvation can, and should, be equally for wrongdoers and for those who suffer. By excavating themes such as these from the texts, historical study of biblical writings can offer faith and theology new food for thought and new starting points for development, and this is the aim of the historical passages in the following chapters. In *The*

---

82. There are, for instance, traditions that God dictated the Torah to Moses, and that the Qur'an was orally revealed by God to Muhammad via the angel Gabriel, but there is no comparable tradition about New Testament writings, though the author of Revelation (1:19) describes himself as having been commanded to write what he sees.

Introduction

Theology of Trust I suggested that book should be seen as a work of theological reflection arising from historical investigation on the theme of *pistis* in the New Testament, or what Heikki Räisänen described as "theologizing about the sources" as a way of reflecting on their significance in the present.[83] This study, in developing its model of at-one-ment, goes further toward constructive theology and can perhaps be called a type of "New Testament theology."

In developing their model of at-one-ment, the following chapters will often draw, in conventional historical-critical fashion, on interpretations of the text that I argue their creators intended. Sometimes they will offer a reading that, I suggest, the earliest readers of a text could plausibly have heard in it, whether or not it was at the forefront of the writer's mind. For example, the discussion of Jesus's attacks on Pharisees in chapter 1 will note that early readers could also have understood something of the Pharisees' point of view.[84] Sometimes what follows will draw implications out of a text that I will argue constitute a historical-critically responsible reading, though I doubt they describe what the author primarily or consciously intended to say. For instance, the discussion of wrongdoing in Romans 1 will argue that when Paul describes many of the sins of gentiles as attitudes and behaviors imposed on them by God as a result of their failure to acknowledge God, many of these attitudes and behaviors are forms of suffering as much as sin, and it will infer from this that Paul recognizes, implicitly though not explicitly, that gentiles suffer as well as sin.[85] Sometimes a reading will be drawn out of the text that I will argue is coherent with the thinking of the text, even though I doubt that anyone in the first century would have seen it, and we can see it only from our different cultural perspective. I will argue, for example, that Jesus's aim when healing can be seen not as to valorize the normative body over the nonnormative but to bring people to consciousness of their need for salvation.[86]

Though *pistis* language is ubiquitous in New Testament writings, some texts are more fruitful than others for thinking about at-one-ment through trust, so the gospels and Paul's undisputed letters will appear more often than other writings. The argument, however, does not try to weave the texts it draws on into a single narrative. Though many writings shed light on the topic, to find them illuminating we do not need to find them all completely coherent (and to claim that they are

---

83. Heikki Räisänen, *Beyond New Testament Theology: A Story and a Programme* (2nd ed.; London: SCM, 2000), 203, though Räisänen is more optimistic than I am that this exercise can take historical criticism as its foundation. See similarly Gerhard Ebeling, *Word and Faith* (London: SCM, 1963), 94, 96.

84. Pp. 65–66.

85. P. 73.

86. Pp. 58–59.

INTRODUCTION

would be historically irresponsible). Nor does what follows have anything to say about one of the most controversial topics in New Testament studies: the historical Jesus. Since thinking about the significance of the cross and resurrection, by its nature, postdates both, the center of gravity of thinking about atonement is always a postresurrection perspective.[87]

At each point I will try to be clear what kind of reading is in play. It is, I believe, imperative that we write theology that is deeply and responsibly rooted in scripture, which both acknowledges and respects the intentions of its writers and first listeners as they responded to the revelation of God through Christ to them, and recognizes our own needs as we respond to God's revelation through Christ in our time and place.

The model of at-one-ment sketched in this study is developed primarily out of Paul and particularly Romans not because Paul or Romans has special status among New Testament writings but because Paul is the author who most often links *pistis* language explicitly with the death of Christ. Even so, what he says is often brief and allusive, and we must draw implications out of it. Our own experience, however, and the individual and communal reception and testing of theological ideas, are part of the argument for those ideas along with their scriptural roots and intellectual coherence. To be taken seriously, they need to resonate and to shed some light on our situation, and to meet our needs as people of faith who are seeking God and greater understanding of God and our life in God's and Christ's hands.

OUTLINE OF CHAPTERS

Theology, as noted above, draws widely on other disciplines and experiences in framing its key concepts and arguments, from formal logic to literary criticism to everyday life. Images and models of atonement are eclectic, borrowing from religious ritual, government, law, warfare, diplomacy, commerce, social codes, ethics, human rights discourse, environmentalism, and the spectrum of human relationships to describe and interrogate how we understand at-one-ment between

---

87. Many scholars would now accept that Jesus may have foreseen his arrest, and even his death, soon before the event if not earlier in his mission, but how he understood it remains speculative and, in New Testament writings, is always framed by the experience of the crucifixion and resurrection. Some of the key questions about the concept and practice of "New Testament theology" are set out in Christopher Rowland and Christopher Tuckett, eds., *The Nature of New Testament Theology: Essays in Honour of Robert Morgan* (Oxford: Blackwell, 2006), xi–xii.

Introduction

God and humanity.[88] This study takes inspiration from several fields in which trust is much discussed: studies of conflict resolution, the psychology of trauma, and programs for the rehabilitation of ex-offenders as well as studies of altruism and spite in the animal kingdom.

We saw at the beginning of this chapter that atonement can be treated as a synonym for reconciliation, but that it is helpful to distinguish between "reconciliation wide," which includes all models of atonement, and "reconciliation narrow," which understands Jesus specifically as mediating between God and humanity as, for instance, an ambassador might mediate between two peoples. Models of "reconciliation narrow" often begin from Paul's use of *katallagē* and *katallassein*, "reconciliation" and "reconcile" (Rom 5:10–11; 11:15; 2 Cor 5:18–20) but usually argue that the concept of reconciliation can be detected in other New Testament writings where those terms do not appear.[89] This study begins from the observations

---

88. Surveyed by Natalie Kertes Weaver, *The Theology of Suffering and Death: An Introduction for Caregivers* (London: Taylor & Francis, 2012), 46–74.

89. Some of these studies have argued that the theme of reconciliation (i.e., "reconciliation narrow") is more widespread than we usually assume, especially in Paul's Letters, notably Ralph P. Martin, *Reconciliation: A Study of Paul's Theology* (Atlanta: Knox, 1981). On reconciliation in Paul see especially Cilliers Breytenbach, "Salvation of the Reconciled," in *Grace, Reconciliation, Concord: The Death of Christ in Graeco-Roman Metaphors* (Leiden: Brill, 2010), 171–86; Juan Manuel Granados Rojas, *La teologia de la reconciliacion en las cartas de san Pablo* (Estella: Verbo Divino, 2016). Granados Rojas emphasizes that, for Paul and his followers, reconciliation is above all transformation (129), and justification is ancillary to it. Breytenbach shows how in Jewish tradition God often changes God's attitude in order to be reconciled with humanity, but for Paul it is always humanity that is changed while God remains the same. On reconciliation in New Testament writings and in theology see also Peter Stuhlmacher, "The Gospel of Reconciliation in Christ: Basic Features and Issues of a Biblical Theology of the New Testament," *Horizons in Biblical Theology* 1 (1979): 161–90; Margaret E. Thrall, "Salvation Proclaimed: 2 Corinthians 5.18–21: Reconciliation with God," *ExpTim* 93 (1982): 227–32; Peter Stuhlmacher, *Reconciliation, Law, and Righteousness: Essays in Biblical Theology* (Philadelphia: Fortress, 1986), 1–15; Arland J. Hultgren, *Christ and His Benefits: Christology and Redemption in the New Testament* (Philadelphia: Fortress, 1987); C. F. D. Moule, *Forgiveness and Reconciliation and Other New Testament Themes* (London: SPCK, 1998), 3–17, 41–46; Colin E. Gunton, ed., *The Theology of Reconciliation* (London: T&T Clark, 2003), especially essays by Christoph Schwöbel, "Reconciliation: From Biblical Observations to Dogmatic Reconstruction," 13–38 and Douglas A. Campbell, "Reconciliation in Paul: The Gospel of Negation and Transcendence in Galatians 3:28," 39–65; Corneliu Constantineanu, "Pauline Scholarship on Reconciliation: A Review of the Related Literature," in *The Social Significance of Reconciliation in Paul's Theology: Narrative Readings in Romans* (London: Bloomsbury, 2010), 25–42; Gerald Downing, "Reconciliation: Politics and Theology," *Modern Believing* 58 (2017): 3–15. Against the idea that there is a "doctrine of reconciliation" at all in the New Testament, see Ernst Käsemann, "Some Thoughts on the Theme 'The Doctrine of Reconciliation' in the New Testament," in *The Future of Our Religious Past: Essays in Honour of*

INTRODUCTION

in *Roman Faith and Christian Faith* and *The Theology of Trust* that in multiple New Testament passages God is faithful to humanity and by implication trusts Jesus with the work of atonement. Jesus is both faithful to God and trusts humanity to respond to him, and humanity is called to trust in a trustworthy God and in Jesus Christ in order to be restored to its right relationship with God. *Roman Faith* also shows that *pistis* and *fides* language is constantly invoked in the wider Greek and Roman world in writings about reconciliation between individuals and groups, whether on the level of state diplomacy or mediation in the private sphere.[90] The trustworthiness of mediators, and the trust that those seeking a new or restored relationship need to be able to put in each other, are key aspects of the practice of at-one-ment at all levels of ancient societies, both human and divine, so we can expect early Christians to have heard the language of trust associated with the work of God through Christ as language of reconciliation or atonement. "Reconciliation," however, is a more generic term than "trust," which is one means by which reconciliation can be achieved. To explore atonement by the creation or restoration of trust, therefore, is to explore it through a concept that is not only far more common in New Testament writings than "reconciliation" language as such but also has more specific content.

The following chapters explore what it might mean, to early Christians and to Christians now, to think of Jesus Christ as restoring humanity's relationship with God through trust in his death and resurrection. They do not go on to consider explicitly the implications of a trust model of atonement for Christians' understanding of God and God's relationship with humanity more widely (as *The Theology of Trust* began to do), but the idea that God seeks to reconcile humanity to Godself through trust does have some implications for our view of God.[91] It suggests that what God seeks with humanity is a relationship that brings wholeness of life and identity to human beings, individually and corporately, and the ability to embrace life and relationships to the full. It proposes that God is willing to act in a new way to achieve this by sending into the world a radically unexpected kind of messiah. By sending this messiah into the world, God takes the risk of trusting humanity therapeutically, inviting it to respond with trust, even though God knows that human beings—selectively deaf and resistant, fearful

---

Rudolf Bultmann (ed. James A. Robinson; London: SCM, 1971), 49–64, with the critique of Martin, *Reconciliation*, 71–79. No study to date that focuses on reconciliation, however, has discussed the role of *pistis* in reconciliation. In contrast, the focus of this study is on the role of *pistis*, specifically in at-one-ment, rather than on what is usually identified as reconciliation language.

90. Morgan, *Roman Faith*, 85–108.

91. One cannot, of course, talk of God in terms of any human attribute or activity without anthropomorphizing, if not mythologizing, and in the modern world this way of talking is always open to question, but that discussion is beyond the scope of this study.

28

Introduction

and doubtful, skeptical and prone to fail as we are—will quite likely not be able to trust absolutely all at once. God takes this risk not only because of the life-giving and relationship-strengthening power of trust, but because being trusted is empowering and God seeks with humanity a relationship that not only brings life but empowers humanity and entrusts it with work to do in partnership with God for the world. For the sake of this relationship, God is willing to limit God's power and control in the world and give great freedom to the world. None of this amounts to a new understanding of God, but it highlights certain aspects of God's relationship with humanity through the lens of trust.

I mentioned above that classical models of atonement focus on the restoration of sinners while liberation theology focuses, strongly though not exclusively, on the liberation of the suffering and oppressed, and I suggested that a model of atonement should, ideally, be able to show how Jesus Christ saves people from both wrongdoing and suffering. Chapter 1 argues that several different types of wrongdoing appear in the Hebrew Bible (and, indeed, in the gentile world), in-cluding willful, collective, and inherited sin, different kinds of foolishness, and even bad moral luck, together with several theories of how wrongdoing comes about. All these involve people trusting in the wrong people or places, or not at all, and all bring suffering to wrongdoers and others. Sometimes suffering itself leads to wrongdoing, so wrongdoing and suffering are closely entwined, and both can alienate people from God. The Hebrew Bible also offers several visions of different kinds of saviors who save God's people in different ways both from suffering and from the wrongdoing that is often its cause.

Christ-confessors inherit all this complexity, so New Testament writings also offer different explanations of the causes of wrongdoing, show wrongdoing and suffering as closely entwined, and use a wealth of images to show Jesus Christ as liberating people from both suffering and wrongdoing. This chapter also acknowl-edges that natural suffering can alienate people from God but suggests that this, as a different kind of suffering, needs to be addressed separately and falls outside the scope of this study. One of the ways in which wrongdoing and the suffering it brings are described in New Testament writings is as *apistia*, the absence of trust, or trust in the right places, so, looking ahead to chapter 3, this chapter begins to consider the relationship between wrongdoing, suffering, and *apistia* in Paul's Letter to the Romans.

Chapter 2 turns to three other fields of study. It explores the role of trust in the restoration of societies after conflict, in which many people have done wrong, many have suffered, and many have both done wrong and suffered; in work with survivors of trauma, who need to learn or relearn to trust both themselves and others in order to make new relationships and a new life; and in the rehabilitation of ex-offenders, who have often both suffered and done wrong and need to be

29

INTRODUCTION

restored to mainstream society after paying a penalty. Case studies in these fields show how, in very different areas of life, wrongdoing and suffering are deeply entangled, and how the creation or re-creation of appropriate trust is widely recognized as central to processes of healing and restoration. In all these situations, mediators are commonly involved in the process of seeking to develop or restore trust, and in all of them some of the most trusted and effective mediators are those who have themselves done wrong and/or have suffered in the same ways as those with whom they work. Having been where others are now, they are seen as trustworthy and can both work with those who seek at-one-ment and walk with them on their journey.

One insight shared by work in all these fields is that the attitude and action of trust, which ideally go together, can also be separated, so that, for instance, people can take a step of trust before they feel trusting of others. Another is that trust can be incremental; one can start with minimal, "thin" trust, which can grow stronger and extend its reach as other parties are found to be trustworthy. A third insight, related to both of the first two, is that it is possible for parties to failed relationships to take a first step of trust before the truth (or truths) of their situation have been recognized, before anyone has repented of wrongdoing, and before any act of forgiveness. This is important for chapter 3, which argues that God reaches out to humanity, by grace, with therapeutic trust before humanity has repented or sought forgiveness, creating a space into which humanity can step and begin the process of self-recognition and change.

Chapter 3 begins with Paul's sketches of the significance of the death of Christ in Romans 3, Galatians 2, and Philippians 3 and seeks to show how the trust between God and Jesus Christ, together with the therapeutic trust that God and Christ offer to humanity, makes possible the restoration of trust between humanity and God. This idea resonates with references to the idea of Christ as mediator elsewhere in Paul and other writers, while the idea that human beings are called or recalled to salvation through trust in God and Christ runs throughout the New Testament. God's outreach of trust shows humanity, trapped and demoralized in its wrongdoing and suffering, that to God it is still precious and still worthy of trust. By trusting humanity to respond to Christ with trust, God also entrusts it with a share of the power that is needed to bring it back to its right relationship with God and changes what is possible for humanity in response.

God and Jesus Christ trust one another as God and wholly faithful human being, as Father and Son by the gift of the holy spirit, and as preexistent Father and Son.[92] Both trust humanity to respond to Jesus in both his incarnate and exalted

92. Here and elsewhere, I do not capitalize the (holy) spirit in order to distinguish the spirit

Introduction

life. Even through death Jesus's relationship both with God and with humanity proves indestructible, even if we envisage him as doubting himself in Gethsemane or on the cross.[93] His actions break the human cycle of failed trust, wrongdoing, and suffering. On the cross the Father's and the Son's shared commitment to humanity is revealed to its fullest. There is nothing humanity can do that puts it beyond saving, no suffering out of which God cannot bring new life, and no situation in which God and Christ will not offer and invite restorative trust. Under the cross humanity, with everything it is capable of and everything it is worth to God, is most fully revealed to itself.

Jesus creates from the cross a space in which God reaches out with trust to humanity, and humanity is invited to take a step of trust with Christ into relationship with God. The crucifixion achieves this on its own, but the resurrection acts as an extra grace for the disciples, shattered by Jesus's arrest and death, and for the present, in which we still so often feel as if evil and wrongdoing rule our world. At this point, this chapter parts company with chapter 4 of *The Theology of Trust*, which saw the resurrection as a necessary part of the process of at-one-ment.

Mediators do not normally have to die to bring at-one-ment to others, but this chapter argues that Jesus had to die because he could not be other than he was, wholly trusting and trustworthy toward God and humanity. More than that, he dies as a grace because human beings do have to die, spiritually, to a life dominated by wrongdoing and suffering.[94] We have to "get out" of the life we are in and live in a new life with new relationships and new hope. To enable us to go through this death, Christ shows the way; we travel with him in spirit, and the exalted Christ travels with us.

I construct a fictional scenario to explore how the invitation to trust in God and Christ might offer new life to a person who is suffering abuse and a person who is both a victim and a perpetrator of abuse. Using the image of God as gardener who "composts" wrongdoing and suffering to create new life, I argue that God's action in Christ acts as a sign that this is not a world in which evil that is done must stay done, creating suffering and more evil as its effects reverberate through time, place, and relationships. Rather, this is a world in which human wrongdoing and suffering are disrupted by new life and hope, and in which entering a relationship of trust with God and Christ can change those who trust for good. In this

---

of God, as understood by New Testament writers, from the Holy Spirit later understood as a person of the Trinity.

93. P. 69.

94. On grace itself see especially John Barclay, *Paul and the Gift* (Grand Rapids: Eerdmans, 2015); on the relationship between grace and trust, see below, pp. 122–23, 128.

INTRODUCTION

model, God is always ready to act for humanity and receive humanity back to its right relationship with God, but God does not force people to trust. People must respond to God's grace, to the revelation of God's and Christ's trustworthiness, and to the promise of new life by taking a step of trust into the space in which reconciliation is possible.

This chapter follows much of the research described in chapter 2 in seeing appropriate trust as an essential first step in reconciliation, after which people can begin to face their past or present, articulate it, repent, seek forgiveness, and contemplate offering forgiveness, as they need. Like work in these disciplines, it recognizes that facing the past and present, repentance, and seeking and offering forgiveness are all highly demanding forms of mental, emotional, and social work that can take years and may not be completed within a lifetime, a theme we return to in chapter 5. Sometimes, coming to trust may create or restore a relationship absolutely and forever. Sometimes it may be just the first step that makes further steps possible. This model follows New Testament writings, however, in recognizing that people often struggle to trust and waver and fail in trust, but if they continue to want and work to trust, failures of trust do not end God's relationship with them. However carefully the gardener cultivates her flower beds, weeds will continue to spring up until the last day, and God continues to work with both flowers and weeds until the end time.

Most of this study focuses on atonement between God and human beings, but chapter 4 turns to the rest of creation. It asks whether we can envisage not only human beings but also other created beings as estranged from God by suffering or wrongdoing and the loss of trust, and as reconcilable with God, directly or indirectly, through Jesus Christ. It argues that there is biblical warrant for seeing nonhuman creation as both suffering and doing wrong and investigates recent work in animal and plant sciences that argues that animals and plants can both suffer and, in some cases, act with deliberate "spite."[95] It explores how Jesus is portrayed as mediating between God and nonhuman creation not only as a person who acts and dies for humanity, but also as part of creation that lives and dies for creation as a whole and calls the whole of creation to respond. Returning to the life sciences, I look at how animals and arguably even plants can recognize and act as mediators, restoring harmony in groups after conflict and harm within and even across species. I consider ways in which we might envisage animals or plants coming to at-one-ment with God through Christ and propose that human beings, in imitation of Christ, might have a role to play in such a process. Finally, this chapter reflects on whether, at a time of crisis in humanity's relationship

95. Pp. 171–72.

Introduction

with the natural world, we can see practices of trust and trustworthiness in the animal and plant worlds as revelations calling human beings back to our right relationship with God.

The fifth chapter turns to at-one-ment in human beings' relationship with one another, which is often understood in terms of bilateral, face-to-face repentance and forgiveness. It argues, first, that Christian at-one-ment between human beings is never bilateral but is always trilateral because it is mediated by Jesus Christ. Second, it argues that we should see repentance and forgiveness between human beings, like that between human beings and God, as made possible within a framework of the (re-)creation of trust. Finally, this chapter argues that Christians can see themselves as entrusted by God and Christ with work to do for the creation of trust and at-one-ment in this world. It looks at some New Testament passages that speak of followers of Christ as "entrusted" with work for God in the world, arguing that human beings are entrusted, among other things, with following and imitating Christ by acting as mediators in human relationships. Entrusted individuals and communities can re-create the space paradigmatically created by the cross, into which people may take a step of trust to meet Christ, and in which they may begin to work toward recognition of their suffering and wrongdoing, forgiveness, and reconciliation. At times—for many different reasons—it may not be possible for individuals or groups who have done wrong and suffered to confront one another directly, and then entrusted individuals and communities can offer a place where they can work separately to come to terms with what has happened and begin a journey into new life. We should recognize, however, that to create spaces like these, Christian individuals and communities must be trustworthy, and recent catastrophic failures of trustworthiness among church leaders entrusted with the care of others have made this work much harder.

We have seen that *pistis* language encompasses trust, trustworthiness, faithfulness, and entrustedness as well as a range of other concepts that are less relevant to this study. For convenience, the following chapters will sometimes talk about "trust" as a shorthand for all these concepts, but where it is important to clarify which concept is in play, they will distinguish between them.

CHAPTER 1

Wrongdoing and Suffering, Trust and Mistrust

Human life is beset by the mistakes we make, the damage, intended and unintended, we do to one another, and the suffering we cause to ourselves and others by our failings. Like inhabitants of a wet climate who develop many words for rain, we have large and varied vocabularies for these behaviors: wrongdoing, transgression, offense, iniquity, misdeed, sin, error, lapse, suffering, trouble, adversity, trial, passion, affliction, sorrow, pain. We distinguish between willful and accidental harm, direct and indirect damage, and the harm we do out of laziness, foolishness, carelessness, malevolence, and bad moral luck.[1] We differentiate between individual and corporate responsibility for damage done and between direct responsibility and responsibility by association. We recognize the difference between suffering we bring on ourselves, suffering that comes through our connections with others, and suffering that falls on us because we are in the wrong place at the wrong time.[2] We also recognize that these categories can overlap and have blurred and contestable boundaries. Is a small child who repeatedly does what he has been told not to do being willfully naughty, or is he challenging contestable parental boundaries in the only way he knows? If I cannot afford to buy food that is sustainably produced, am I to blame for the damage my eating habits do to the environment?

1. A person has "bad moral luck" when they are in a position in which they cannot make a morally good decision; see, e.g., Thomas Nagel, *Mortal Questions* (New York: Cambridge University Press, 1979); Bernard Williams, *Moral Luck* (Cambridge: Cambridge University Press, 1981).

2. The idea of collective wrongdoing and guilt may be more readily accepted in Jewish and Christian traditions because their sacred texts were probably composed and largely interpreted by members of dominant social groups who had the most political and cultural agency. They also recognize, however, that subaltern groups have relatively little agency and bear relatively little responsibility for collective states, and such groups are liable to suffer more than they do wrong.

35

CHAPTER 1

What is more, wrongdoing and suffering are everywhere entwined not only because my wrongdoing may cause you to suffer and vice versa, but also because my wrongdoing may arise from my experience of suffering and vice versa. Many of us have had the experience of saying or doing something hurtful to someone who did not expect it of us and feeling bad afterward; we betrayed their trust and, if we have a tender conscience, we suffer for it. Probably everyone has had the experience of saying or doing something harmful in reaction to something that we perceive has been said or done to us; we lash out because we feel hurt or betrayed.

Suffering and wrongdoing of all kinds test our trust and often damage or break it. Psychologists, together with philosophers of trust and care ethicists, hypothesize that infants have a disposition to trust, and that trust tends to fail first in human relationships when people experience betrayal.[3] Some people may break trust before their trust is betrayed, but either way, once trust is damaged, even young children can quickly become both untrusting and untrustworthy. They may withdraw from relationships or start to behave antisocially, and this further undermines their trust in others and that of others in them. Some of those who have been treated unfairly or unkindly stop looking for fairness or kindness, and those who live in an atmosphere of conflict can become hardened to it and expect nothing else. Those who have lost trust often struggle to trust even people who have not hurt them and whom they have not hurt. They may decide they can trust only themselves, but they can also struggle to trust themselves, because of their experience that trust has proved misguided in the past. They can struggle to trust that it is worth even trying to trust people or things around them. Even when those who have, for whatever reason, lost trust long to repair it, restoring trust can be difficult or impossible without help.

Not every failure of trust, of course, destroys our capacity to trust ourselves or others. Nobody is perfect, and most of us have let other people down, and have been let down ourselves, without experiencing acute suffering or the failure of relationships. The times when trust does fail, moreover, can teach us necessary lessons. We need to be not only trusting toward those around us but also alert, discerning, and sometimes skeptical. Our relationships are sounder when we do not rush to trust people who may not be able or willing to respond or encourage people to trust us for things we cannot provide. It is important not only to make relationships of trust but also to learn to trust appropriately and discriminatingly. Even so, most people would agree that our lives are better—more peaceful, less stressful, more fulfilled, and more optimistic—where our trust relationships are strong, and we should be wary even of minor failures that chip away at our capacity to trust and be trusted.

3. Above, pp. 18, 20 n. 72.

36

Wrongdoing and Suffering, Trust and Mistrust

Trust, the ways in which trust fails, and the interaction of wrongdoing with suffering are as complex in stories of the relationship between humanity and God as they are in stories about human beings. In Christianity and the traditions that shape it, human beings can fall out of trust with God intentionally or unintentionally, through willful disobedience, foolishness, or disastrous mischance. They can suffer for their own failures of trust or because their ancestors or other members of their community have failed. They can also challenge God or break trust with God over what they experience as undeserved suffering at the hands of other people, which God has not prevented, ended, or punished, or even at God's own hands.

In Christian tradition, in which the relationship between God and humanity is characterized centrally as *pistis*, damage to trust between God and humanity strikes at the heart of the relationship. This chapter aims to show how, for New Testament writers and the traditions on which they draw, wrongdoing and suffering are deeply entwined in human experience, and both can be seen as damaging trust between human beings and God. We will encounter several kinds of wrongdoing as well as more than one kind of suffering: the willful, the associative, the foolish, the reactive, and the frankly ambiguous. In chapter 3, however, I will argue that the Christ event makes possible humanity's release from the power of all kinds of suffering and wrongdoing. We should expect that a God who seeks a relationship of trust, love, peace, and more with humanity would act to enable humanity's release from both suffering and wrongdoing, if either might form an obstacle to the relationship, and this, I will argue, is what we find.

BAD FROM THE START?

In Jewish and Christian thinking about the divine-human relationship, human sin or wrongdoing is anything that puts human beings out of their right relationship with God.[4] In the Hebrew Bible, this is most often deliberately bad behav-

---

4. The most common Hebrew terms usually translated "sin" are *ḥṭ'*, *pšʿ*, *ʿwn* [ʿ*wy/w*]. In the LXX and New Testament the most common term is *hamartia*. We also find in Greek *paraptōma*, *parabasis* (referring to an individual mistake or transgression), *parakoē* (disobedience), *adikia* (injustice), *asebeia* (impiety), *anomia* (lawlessness), and occasionally the generic *kakia* (badness). They are surveyed by G. Quell, J. Bertram, and G. Stählin, "ἁμαρτάνειν," *TDNT* 1:274–78 (Hebrew Bible), 1:286–89 (LXX), 1:293–96 (New Testament), and by Robin C. Cover and E. P. Sanders, "Sin," in *Anchor Yale Bible Dictionary* (ed. David Noel Freeman; 6 vols.; New Haven: Yale University Press, 1992), 6:31–47. *Hamartia* can mean any kind of "error," but it usually refers (in Greek in general and in the LXX and New Testament) to something for which a person

37

CHAPTER 1

ior, individual or collective, by human beings. Alternatively, as Carol Newsom has demonstrated, human beings can be seen as simply bad by nature.[5] A third strand of biblical thinking shows people as internally divided and often suffering from the fact that their passions work against their moral convictions to drive to

---

held responsible, though responsibility does not always imply individual willful wrongdoing. It can have cultic, legal, or ethical dimensions, with the emphasis in the New Testament on the ethical. *Paraptōma* more often means a "stumble" or "blunder." *Asebeia* and the *para-* terms are particularly favored by Paul and his followers, whereas *anomia* is favored by John. Stählin and Sanders both take it as uncontroversial that wrongdoing in the New Testament is willful sin, but this chapter argues that the picture is more complex.

Paul's understanding of God's righteousness and the "righteousing" of human beings is a matter of long-standing debate, to which we cannot contribute at any length here. In the Greek of Paul's day, however, in broad terms *dikē, dikaiosynē, dikaioun*, and their relatives have three ranges of meaning and four spheres of operation: they can refer to what is required, what is morally right, or what is customary according to the gods or God, according to the laws of a state, according to human society, or according to individual conscience. (Further meanings are less relevant to this context.) A human being who is *dikaios* may be in right standing with the divine, obedient to human laws, in tune with the conventions of their society, or in line with an accepted standard of morality, and their *dikaiosynē* may consist in an attitude, actions, or, ideally, both. Much debate in ancient philosophy, ancient forensic oratory, and the modern study of the Bible and theology turns on the relationship between divine command, human law, and custom, and on the relationship between what is morally right and what the divine, the law, or society requires. For Paul (as for faithful, law-observant Jews in general) much of this complexity is sidestepped, because he takes for granted that the only arbiter of what is required, morally right, or customary is God, and that, in societies of the faithful, human laws and both individual and social behavior should all be in accordance with what God requires. Paul is less clear about whether *dikaiosynē* inheres primarily in attitude, action, or both, but it seems likely (as Rom 7:15–20 suggests) that for Paul, as for most people in his world, attitude and action ideally go together. Much of the modern debate about *dikaiosynē* and related concepts in Paul focuses on whether he understands it judicially or morally, but if Paul, with Jews in most contexts, takes for granted that the judicial and the moral converge in the nature and operation of God's *dikaiosynē*, there is surely for him (whether or not there is, or should be, for later Christians) no meaningful distinction between judicial and moral *dikaiosynē*. This study, therefore, takes God's *dikaiosynē*, as understood by Paul, as bringing those who trust back into their right relationship with God. Here, I speak of right in the sense that it fits with what God requires of humanity—which is, by definition, what is morally right, and with what God would like to be God's customary relationship with humanity—and in the sense that it puts human attitude, action, and relationships with both God and other human beings on the right footing. This is not far from Käsemann's view in *New Testament Questions of Today* (London: SCM, 1969), especially 169–80; see also Morgan, *Theology of Trust*, 63–64.

5. Carol A. Newsom, "Models of the Moral Self: Hebrew Bible and Second Temple Judaism," *Journal of Biblical Literature* 131 (2012): 5–25. This, as she notes, raises questions about both human beings' responsibility for their actions and God's responsibility, but these are beyond the scope of this chapter.

Wrongdoing and Suffering, Trust and Mistrust

them toward wrongdoing.[6] Prophetic and wisdom writings in particular speak of the wrongdoing that arises from "foolishness," which has a spectrum of meaning from intellectual to moral deficiency, including delusion and unintended mistakes caused by fate.[7] We can go further and see, in some passages, distinctions between wrongdoing as active or reactive, intentional or unfortunate, or an action or a state. We can also see wrongdoing everywhere entwined with suffering, with both challenging trust.

Most Jewish and Christian interpretations of the disobedience of Adam and Eve in the garden understand it as a willful sin and their expulsion as punishment (Gen 3:16–24).[8] There are, though, subtleties in the story and its context in the creation narrative that have always invited further reflection. In both creation narratives (Gen 1:1–2:3; 2:4–25), humanity is in a relationship with God from its beginnings.[9] This relationship can be seen not only as one of authority and obedience but also as one of trust. When, for instance, God places the human in charge of Eden and commands him not to eat the fruit of a particular tree, God does not police the garden. God seems to trust the human, and later the man and woman, to do as God tells them, perhaps as part of their stewardship (2:16–17; cf. 2:15). When the serpent approaches the woman (3:1), she repeats what she has been told about eating the fruit, quoting what God said (3:3; cf. 2:17). Her repetition of God's words underlines them but also suggests that the woman trusts God. She

---

6. Newsom's account of internal conflict offers a background for texts like Rom 6–8, which makes it less likely that Paul must have drawn on Platonism, as argued by Emma Wasserman, "Paul among the Philosophers: The Case of Sin in Romans 6–8," *JSNT* 30 (2008): 387–415.

7. The words for "fool" and "foolishness" used in the LXX and New Testament are *mōros* and *mōria*, respectively. In the LXX, these words translate a range of Hebrew terms. E.g., in Isa 32:5–6 the fool is one who has willfully broken off his relationship with God. Cf. Ps 93(94):8; Jer 5:21. But in 2 Sam 24:10 David describes himself as having been foolish in the sense of deluded rather than sinful, though he accepts his guilt. Similarly, in Job 16:7 becoming a fool is a punishment for thinking of oneself as wise. In Sir 4:27 a fool lacks understanding, but if he has power he may also be dangerous, and in Sir 25:2 foolishness is a moral blunder. But often Ben Sira describes fools as those who are not wise and should be excluded from the company of the wise, with no suggestion that they have done wrong (e.g., 18:18; 19:11, 12; 20:13, 16, 20).

8. Though Irenaeus, *Against Heresies* 3.23.1–33.1; 5.29.1 recasts God's response to Adam and Eve as formative and educational, and Philo may also have known of this interpretation in Jewish circles. See Teresa Morgan, "To Err Is Human, To Correct Divine: A Recessive Gene in Ancient Mediterranean and Near Eastern Religiosity?" in *The New Testament and the Church: Essays in Honour of John Muddiman* (ed. John Barton and Peter Groves; London: Bloomsbury, 2015), 68–72.

9. Humanity is created in God's image, blessed, and given a relationship with the rest of creation on the basis of its relationship with God at 1:26–29, and it is created and placed in Eden to curate it at 2:7–15.

39

CHAPTER 1

accepts God's words as they were spoken and is doing what she has been told without questioning it.

The serpent does not try to persuade the woman that she is a free agent, that God cannot tell her what to do, or that she should test the boundaries of the relationship. He undermines her trust, making her wonder whether God was telling the truth when God said that eating the fruit of the tree would lead to death and whether she was right to have trusted God.[10] He then encourages her to trust him instead, when he tells her that eating the fruit will give her knowledge of good and evil (3:5).

In this light, the actions of the woman and man look less like willful disobedience than a naive or foolish response to the undermining of their trust.[11] They are immediately followed by another failure of trust. When God asks the man whether he has eaten the fruit, the man blames the woman for his actions (3:12). The man and woman are in a relationship of care, which can also be seen as a relationship of trust. The woman was made because "it is not good that the man should be alone," and she is described as the man's helper (2:18, 20). When the woman involves the man in her disobedience, she fails in her care for him. When the man takes the fruit, he apparently trusts the woman, but when he blames her for the fact that he has willingly eaten it, he implies that he was her victim and breaks trust with her. What follows is not only disobedience to God and punishment but further trust, failures of trust, and renewals of trust between God and humanity that characterize the whole of human history.[12]

A generation later, the pattern of loss of trust leading to wrongdoing can be seen again. The children of Adam and Eve grow up, through no fault of their own, in a world of suffering, and we may wonder if their trust in God is a little less than completely secure as a result. In Gen 4:3–5 Cain and Abel both make offerings to God, but Cain's is rejected. Cain is angry, as he can see no reason for the rejection (4:5). God's response is to imply that Cain, unlike Abel, is being tested because he cannot be trusted to "do well" and not to give in to the sin that is "lurking at the

10. Noted by John Skinner, *A Critical and Exegetical Commentary on Genesis* (2nd ed.; Edinburgh: T&T Clark, 1930), 75–76; cf. William Curtis Holtzen, *The God Who Trusts: A Relational Theology of Divine Faith, Hope, and Love* (Downers Grove: IVP Academic, 2019), 155–56.

11. Phyllis Trible, "Eve and Adam: Genesis 2–3 Reread," in *Womanspirit Rising* (ed. Carol P. Christ and Judith Plaskow; 2nd ed.; San Francisco: Harper & Row, 1992), 79, suggests that the serpent approaches the woman first because she is more intelligent or has more initiative or greater sensibilities than the man, who follows her lead silently and passively. In this scenario, the woman's trust is undermined by doubt and the man's trust by fear of God (cf. 3:10).

12. God's speech act at 3:16–19 implies that the relationship between Adam and Eve will no longer be based on trust but instead on mutual need and experienced with pain.

40

door" (4:7).[13] When Cain kills his brother, on one level he commits a willful sin. On another, we can imagine him, hurt and resentful at apparently not being trusted when he has not done anything wrong, thinking that if God is not going to trust him, he may as well deserve it.

In these stories, human actions that, from one perspective, are willful wrongdoings and betrayals of trust are, from another, reactions to the perception that God has not trusted those involved. This perception brings suffering in the form of doubt, and suffering leads the sufferers to do as much damage to the relationship as willful wrongdoing might have done. The tragedy of both stories, from this perspective, is that if Eve and Cain had trusted more rather than less, or trusted God rather than the snake, both suffering and wrongdoing might have been avoided.[14]

Later in Genesis we begin to find the suggestion that humanity has, by nature, an inclination to do wrong which has to be combated (e.g., Gen 4:7; 8:21).[15] God's expulsion of Adam and Eve from the garden does, however, bring suffering on generations of their descendants, who share their hard life without having shared their disobedience. That God punishes children for the wrongdoings of their fathers becomes a running theme of biblical and other writings both as an explanation for present suffering and as an incentive to obedience (e.g., Exod 20:5–6; 34:6–7; Num 14:18; Deut 5:9–10).[16]

The story of the great flood is the first in which God apparently decides to punish humanity as a whole for its universal willful sinfulness. "The Lord saw that the wickedness of humankind was great in the earth and that every inclination of the thoughts of their hearts was only evil continually . . . and it grieved him to his heart" (Gen 6:5–6).[17] It is worth noting that even this strong formula does not necessarily imply that human wickedness extended beyond a particular generation.

---

13. Gordon J. Wenham, *Genesis 1–15* (WBC 1; Waco: World Books, 1987), 104, notes that several of the many explanations that have been proposed for God's rejection of Cain's offering do not see Cain as blameworthy.

14. Ancient Jewish commentaries, unlike Christian commentaries, do not suggest that Adam's sin has been inherited by his descendants. Though Genesis allows us to see the behavior of Eve, Adam, and Cain as understandable, they are still presented as culpable.

15. Carol A. Newsom, "When the Problem Is Not What You Have Done but Who You Are," in Botner, Duff, and Dürr, *Atonement*, 71–88 argues for a strand of thinking in the Hebrew Bible, perhaps arising from the destruction of Judah in 586 BCE, according to which people fundamentally lack moral agency, such that they must be transformed from without.

16. Alternatively, e.g., Deut 24:16; Jer. 31:29, God is sometimes understood as deliberately eschewing such punishment when it could have been exacted, while elsewhere, e.g., Lev 26:39; Isa 65:6b–7, later generations are described as suffering for both their own and inherited wrongdoings.

17. Translations are from the NRSV unless otherwise noted.

CHAPTER 1

What is more, no sooner has God resolved to wipe out humanity (6:7) than we hear that "Noah found favor in the sight of the Lord . . . Noah was a righteous man, blameless in his generation; Noah walked with God" (6:8–9). The flood generation is not, in fact, "only evil." (Noah's wife and children were presumably not all bad either, since they were also allowed to survive to repopulate the world.) Nor do we hear that the birds and animals and "creeping things" that are destroyed by the flood are evil (though it is not impossible that verses 11–12 refer to the violence and corruption of both nonhuman and human "flesh"). The flood generation is near universally or collectively rather than universally wicked.

In later books, wrongdoing occasionally arises from attitudes or behaviors that in other circumstances would be recognized as normal and appropriate.[18] The most notorious case is that of Jephthah (Judg 11:29–39). Leading the Gileadites in a war against the Ammonites, itself the result of repeated failures of trust between the two peoples, Jephthah vows under the influence of the spirit of God (11:29) that if God gives him victory, he will offer the first thing that emerges from his house to meet him on his return as a sacrifice to God (11:30–31). After he defeats the Ammonites, the first thing to greet him on his return is his daughter (11:34). He is horrified and tears his clothing in grief (11:35). Like Adam, and even more shockingly, Jephthah also tries to shift the blame for the situation, telling his daughter, "You have struck me down and brought calamity upon me" (11:35), as if she has in some way broken trust with him. He does apparently sacrifice his daughter (11:39), but it seems clear that he and his community both know it is a monstrous thing to do.[19] The writer concludes, "there arose an Israelite custom that for four days every year the daughters of Israel would go out to lament the daughter of Jephthah the Gileadite" (11:39–40). Jephthah does wrong out of a laudable desire to serve his people with the help of God. His vow proves terribly misjudged out of thoughtlessness, overconfidence, perhaps too much trust in his own judgment, or even bad moral luck, but not out of any ill intention.

In the flood story, the wrongdoing of a generation leads all but one family to die. In Isaiah 53 the pattern is reversed.[20] The "man of suffering" (53:3) bears the wrongdoings of his people and is "wounded" and "crushed" because of their sins

18. This type of wrongdoing may arise when people pursue opportunities without thinking through their consequences, sometimes with terrible results.

19. Though it has been suggested that the reference to the daughter's virginity points to her remaining a virgin rather than being sacrificed.

20. According to the pattern of the scapegoat, the goat was driven out of the community after the community's wrongdoings were laid symbolically on it. The suffering servant is taken to suffer willingly, but so, probably, was the scapegoat. Sacrificial animals in general in the ancient world were required to appear willing to be sacrificed and, if they did not, were sometimes reprieved.

42

and guilt (53:5–6, 8, 10–11). The people are said to have done wrong collectively—probably, since the context is the aftermath of the Babylonian conquest and exile, over more than one generation—but the man of suffering himself has done no violence (53:9). He allows himself to be "numbered with the transgressors" without being one of them (53:12), and he is compared to a lamb led to ritual slaughter, which must itself be unblemished (53:7). Cilliers Breytenbach has shown how, in the Septuagint version of this passage, the Mediterranean motif of the person who dies voluntarily on behalf of another individual or a group is blended with the common language of sacrifice.[21] The suffering servant also invokes the scapegoat (e.g., Lev 16:21–22) and even figures who represent the whole of their people in war or cult.[22] We do not have to condone the idea that one person *should* suffer to make possible divine forgiveness, nor that suffering is justified by its consequences, to recognize the psychological power and cultural significance of this pattern. In addition, Isaiah 53 exemplifies the complexity of much prophetic thinking about wrongdoing and suffering. The people whose wrongdoings the man bears are also said to suffer (53:4): they are in need of healing (53:5) as well as forgiveness of their wrongdoings. Their suffering is apparently partly self-inflicted (e.g., 53:6) but has also been inflicted on them by others (e.g., Isa 52:1–2), and they need to be restored to their right relationship with God on both counts. At the same time, the condition of the people under their wrongdoing and suffering means that they do not recognize the suffering servant as their liberator (cf. Isa 53:5). He does his work in collaboration with God (52:13; 53:4) unacknowledged—he is even regarded as punished by God for being particularly despicable (53:3–4)—and makes possible the at-one-ment of Israel with God before his people are in a position to ask for it. For Christians, this theme that God and his servant act to restore God's people to their right relationship with God even before they are able to respond prefigures the therapeutic trust of God and Christ in the Christ event.

THE VARIETIES OF MESSIAHS

In New Testament scholarship, wrongdoing or sin is usually understood as either an individual act of willful rebellion against God or a state in which humanity

---

21. Cilliers Breytenbach, "The Septuagint Version of Isaiah 53 and the Early Christian Formula 'He Was Delivered for Our Trespasses'," in *Grace, Reconciliation, Concord*, 83–84, 93.

22. E.g., the young David in 1 Sam 17:32 or the Israelite high priest. See, e.g., Crispin Fletcher-Louis, "The High Priest in Ben Sira 50," in Botner, Duff, and Dürr, *Atonement*, 89–111, arguing that the high priest in Ben Sira becomes the location of the at-one-ment of God and humanity.

CHAPTER 1

collectively persists until the Christ event makes possible its release and return to its right relationship with God. Much of the rest of this chapter will argue that there are further complexities in New Testament writings' representation of wrongdoing, suffering, and their interaction. First, however, it is worth touching briefly on the wealth of recent scholarship about messiahs and messianic ages to remind ourselves of the traditions inherited by Christians about saviors and salvation, which also attest that human beings can both do wrong and suffer, that suffering and wrongdoing are often intertwined, and that those who put their trust in God can hope to be released from the power of both.

In the Hebrew Bible and other Second Temple writings, God is often spoken of as saving Israel and triumphing over her enemies. In addition, the idea of a leader figure who is tasked by God with saving a chosen group goes back at least to Moses, who rescues the Israelites who are enslaved, through no fault of their own, in Egypt. This idea becomes more prominent around the time of the Babylonian exile, though it is never equally important in all texts or strands of tradition. Such leaders—acclaimed, imagined, or foretold—take many forms. They may be anointed kings of Israel,[23] angels, priests, or persons who have, in some form, both an earthly and a heavenly life.[24]

Writings that look forward to or remember the return from the Babylonian exile tend to link Israel's present suffering with the wrongdoing of earlier generations

23. Note also, probably, in this regard the Persian king Cyrus, assuming that he is treated as a messianic figure at some point in the evolution of Deutero-Isaiah. See Lisbeth Fried, "Cyrus the Messiah? The Historical Background to Isaiah 45:1," *Harvard Theological Review* 95 (2002): 373–93; John F. A. Sawyer, *Isaiah through the Centuries* (Hoboken: Wiley-Blackwell, 2018), 262–70.

24. On the varieties of messiahs, see, e.g., Jacob Neusner, W. S. Green, and Ernest Frerichs, eds., *Judaisms and Their Messiahs at the Turn of the Christian Era* (Cambridge: Cambridge University Press, 1987); William Horbury, *Jewish Messianism and the Cult of Christ* (London: SCM, 1998), 5–108; John J. Collins, "Pre-Christian Jewish Messianism: An Overview," in *The Messiah in Early Judaism and Christianity* (ed. Magnus Zetterholm; Minneapolis: Fortress, 2007), 1–20; Andrew Chester, *Messiah and Exaltation: Jewish Messianic and Visionary Traditions and New Testament Christology* (Tübingen: Mohr Siebeck, 2007); Adela Yarbro Collins and John J. Collins, *King and Messiah as Son of God: Divine, Human, and Angelic Messianic Figures in Biblical and Related Literature* (Grand Rapids: Eerdmans, 2008); Markus N. A. Bockmuehl and James Carleton Paget, eds., *Redemption and Resistance: The Messianic Hopes of Jews and Christians in Antiquity* (London: T&T Clark, 2009); Matthew V. Novenson, *Christ among the Messiahs: Christ Language in Paul and Messiah Language in Ancient Judaism* (Oxford: Oxford University Press, 2012); Novenson, *The Grammar of Messianism: An Ancient Jewish Political Idiom and Its Uses* (New York: Oxford University Press, 2017); J. Thomas Hewitt. *Messiah and Scripture: Paul's "in Christ" Idiom in Its Ancient Jewish Context* (Tübingen: Mohr Siebeck, 2020). On God in the Hebrew Bible as both judging and saving the suffering, see also Lucien Richard, *What Are They Saying about the Theology of Suffering?* (New York: Paulist, 1992), 16–17.

44

Wrongdoing and Suffering, Trust and Mistrust

and possibly also the writer's own generation, suggesting that God's people need to be saved from both. We have already seen an example from Deutero-Isaiah. Sometimes the prophet's portrait of wrongdoing and suffering is quite complex. The prophecies of Deutero-Zechariah, for example, dating probably to the Persian period, distinguish between the enemies of Israel (e.g., Zech 9:1–8; 10:11), her sinful leaders (e.g., 10:2–3), and the rest of God's people, who look forward to liberation by the triumphant king who will defeat their enemies (9:9), bring them home from exile, and restore them to wealth and plenty (9:16–17; 10:8–12). There is a hint (10:6) that this restoration follows a time of divine rejection, perhaps primarily of Israel's leaders, but the remembrance of past punishment is less prominent than the celebration of the people's future release.

In other contexts, salvation involves release from suffering with no intimation that restoration is also needed after wrongdoing. The singer of Psalm 35, for example, prays, "Contend, O Lord, with those who contend with me; fight against those who fight against me!" (35:1 [NIV]). The theme of the whole psalm is that the singer is a good and pious person who has provoked no one, and those who are attacking and causing him suffering are evil and unjust. First Maccabees begins its account of the Maccabean wars of liberation from the Seleucid monarchy with a stark description of the evils inflicted on Israel and her suffering. The writer observes that some Israelites, under pressure, conformed to the customs of their rulers (1 Macc 1:43; 2:15) but does not suggest that Israel's oppression was in any way the result of her wrongdoing. In his song of exhortation, delivered just before he dies, Mattathias, the uprising's first leader, tells his sons to remember a series of heroes of Israel's past from Abraham to Daniel who were rewarded for their faithfulness to God, signaling that Israel's salvation is the reward of faithfulness and not a release from the consequences of sin. In addition to saving God's people from wrongdoing or suffering in the present or hoped-for near future, God or God's savior can also be envisaged as eschatological judge (e.g., Ps 37:10–13; Ezek 20:33–38; 39:2; Dan 12:1–2).

From this complex tradition, Christians inherit broadly four models of what a savior may do. He may save his people from suffering caused by others, from their own wrongdoings, from the painful consequences of their wrongdoing, or some mixture of all three.

The concept of a triumphant savior figure, whether human or divine, is widely shared across other Near Eastern and Mediterranean societies.[25] When Near East-

---

25. On Near Eastern messiahs, see, e.g., Thomas L. Thompson, "The Messiah Epithet in the Hebrew Bible," *Scandinavian Journal of the Old Testament* 15 (2001): 57–82. On Greek and Roman savior figures and cult to savior figures in this period, see Johan C. Thom, "God the Savior in

CHAPTER 1

ern or Mediterranean gods or human beings are acclaimed or prayed to as past, present, or hoped-for saviors, they are most often envisaged as saving a people from suffering. Usually this suffering is caused by other people, but sometimes it is caused by natural disasters, which themselves can be seen as either punishments for human wrongdoings against the gods or simply hazards of a volatile environment. In a recent study of salvation in the Greek world, Theodora Jim has shown how representing Greek gods as saviors and establishing cults to savior gods began to become more common in the fifth century BCE and increased significantly from the fourth century onward.[26] From the late fifth century and throughout the Hellenistic period, it also became increasingly common to honor and offer cult to human political and military leaders identified as saviors.[27] Individuals could pray to saviors for protection from a wide range of dangers, including being captured in war, being attacked while traveling abroad, and being subject to unjust lawsuits. Savior gods were often invoked when a slave was being manumitted. Communities and states could also pray to savior gods for protection from their enemies, divine support in war, and liberation from tyranny, drought, earthquakes, or plague.[28] Peoples of the Mediterranean and Near East could therefore envisage divine or human saviors as liberating them from either unmerited suffering at the hands of other people or the natural world or suffering that they had brought upon themselves by their own transgressions or those of their community. This tradition would also have been familiar to early Christians and probably foremost in the minds of some gentiles.

Savior figures, Jewish and gentile, could save in a number of different ways. New Testament writings employ a wide range of terms to depict how Jesus Christ saves.[29] He can be said to "give his life a ransom [*lytron*]" (Mark 10:45 // Matt 20:28), to "release" (*exairein*) human beings from the power of "the present evil age" (Gal 1:4), or to "redeem" (*exagorazein*) human beings (Gal 3:13; 4:5; cf. Rom 3:24; 1 Cor 1:30, using *apolytrōsis*). Jesus can be a sacrifice for human wrongdoings (Heb 9:26), "our paschal lamb" who has been sacrificed (1 Cor 5:7), or the "lamb

---

Greco-Roman Popular Philosophy," in du Toit, Gerber, and Zimmerman, *Sōtēria*, 86–100; T. S. F. Jim, *Saviour Gods and Sōtēria in Ancient Greece* (Oxford: Oxford University Press, 2021).

26. Jim, *Saviour Gods*, 119–39. This is strikingly close in time to the period in which messianism became more significant in (some) strands of Judaism. At 249–56 Jim discusses savior gods in Roman religion.

27. Jim, *Saviour Gods*, 166–213.

28. Jim, *Saviour Gods*, 46–79 (individuals), 80–117 (communities). Extreme natural phenomena could be seen as punishments for wrongdoing, but usually they seem to be regarded as the inevitable evils of a volatile environment.

29. On terminology, see, e.g., McIntyre, *Soteriology*, 26–52; J. G. van der Watt, ed., *Salvation in the New Testament: Perspectives on Soteriology* (Leiden: Brill, 2005); Breytenbach, *Grace, Reconciliation, Concord*; du Toit, Gerber, and Zimmerman, *Sōtēria*.

of God who takes away the sin of the world" (John 1:29). A new covenant can be sealed by the blood of Jesus (Luke 22:20; 1 Cor 11:25; cf. Matt 26:28 // Mark 14:24). Jesus can become a "curse" (*katara*) for others (Gal 3:13) or a "supplicatory offering" (*hilastērion*) for the forgiveness of wrongdoings (Rom 3:25).[30] He can be seen as reversing the death (1 Cor 15:21–22) or wrongdoing (Rom 5:12) that came into the world through Adam, a wrongdoing of which all Adam's descendants have suffered the consequences.[31]

These terms direct attention variously to Jesus as saving people from wrongdoing of different kinds, suffering, or both, and they are sometimes suggestively ambiguous. The concept of ransom (*lytron*; Mark 10:45 // Matt 20:28), for example, can refer to one person securing the release of another from some kind of imprisonment or constraint that they have brought upon themselves, whether foolishly or through force of circumstances (for instance, if they have gotten into debt), or in cases where they are more or less innocent victims (for instance, if they have been captured in war). When Jesus uses *lytron* in saying that "the Son of Man came not to be served but to serve, and to give his life a ransom for many," the word could mean either of the meanings above or both; the story in which it appears and its immediate context do not define which sense Jesus has in mind.[32]

---

30. On this interpretation of *hilastērion*, see Yarbro Collins, "Metaphorical Use of *Hilastērion.*"

31. He can also enable God to justify or make righteous those who trust in him (e.g., Rom 3:30; 8:33) though he does not justify himself. On the (debatable) incidence of forensic metaphors, particularly in Romans, and their meaning see Andre B. du Toit, "Forensic Metaphors in Romans and Their Soteriological Significance," *Verbum et Ecclesia* 24 (2003): 53–79, which also emphasizes the limitations of this language, which focuses on human guilt.

32. We usually assume that, in context, ransom is from willful sin, but see also p. 2. Whether the ransom logion originates with Jesus is much disputed; see, e.g., Rainer Riesner, "Back to the Historical Jesus through Paul and His School (The Ransom Logion–Mark 10.45; Matthew 20.38)," *Journal for the Study of the Historical Jesus* 1 (2003): 171–99 (in favor); Michael Wolter, *Jesus von Nazaret* (Göttingen: Vandenhoeck & Ruprecht, 2019), 302–3 (against). On *lytron* as not best interpreted as cultic sacrificial terminology, despite the echo of Isa 53, and hence reading Mark 10:45 as not referring to atonement sacrifice here, including a discussion of recent scholarship, see David S. du Toit, "Heil und Unheil: Die Soteriologie des Markusevangelium," in du Toit, Gerber, and Zimmerman, *Sōtēria*, 202–5. Luke uses the related *lytrōsis* in Zechariah's song at 1:68 to bless God, who has saved his people from their enemies and "the hand of all who hate us" (1:71, cf. 1:73, though he mentions the forgiveness of wrongdoings later at 1:77), and at 2:38 where the prophet Anna tells those who are awaiting the redemption of Jerusalem (again, probably, from its suffering) that she has seen God's salvation (cf. 2:30). Luke 24:21 uses the related verb in a similarly open way, while Acts 7:35 uses *lytrōtēs* of Moses, who delivers Israel from her oppressors. Romans 3:25, however, and likely 1 Cor 1:30 (in light of 1 Cor 13:3, followed by Titus 2:14 and 1 Pet 1:18) use it with a cultic implication (Christ delivers people from wrongdoing), while Heb 9:12, unsurprisingly, uses *lytrōsis* with clear reference to atoning sacrifice for sin.

CHAPTER 1

The idea of Jesus as sacrifice also bears multiple possible meanings. Sacrifices, Jewish and gentile, were offered in the process of admitting to a fault and asking a god to forgive it, not to exact punishment for it, or to send no further punishment for it. They could be offered after some kind of estrangement between the god and the worshiper to restore good relations without an admission of guilt.[33] Sacrifices were also offered as thanksgivings for victories, for blessings or gifts received, or in recognition of an ongoing good relationship between a deity and his or her people. They could recognize or seal an agreement or covenant between people in the sight of a god or between people and a god. Hebrews 9:26, for example, describes Jesus as a sacrifice for humanity's (collective) wrongdoing, but the paschal lamb that Paul invokes at 1 Cor 5:7 is a remembrance and celebration of the sacrifice that averted suffering from the Israelites when God sent the last and greatest plague on Egypt.[34] There is no direct evidence, but it is possible that this was the earliest meaning of this image, one that was available to Paul's first listeners (though Paul implies in 1 Cor 5:8 that what the lamb has released the Corinthians from is a state of "malice and wickedness," which is apparently their own). Catrin Williams has argued that the author of John 1:29 deliberately weaves together allusions to the Passover and Isaiah's servant poems to create the vision of a Passover lamb who, uniquely, takes away the world's sins (whether universal or not, or willful or not, is left unstated, and other passages of the gospel arguably allow both interpretations). Other commentators have heard here an allusion to the apocalyptic lamb who fights evil in Jewish apocalyptic writings and the book of Revelation (e.g. Testament of Joseph 19.8; Rev 7:17; 17:14; cf. 1 Enoch 90.38). Any of these allusions could have been detected by John's first audiences.[35] Meanwhile, when Jesus is remembered in the Synoptic Gospels as saying on the last night of his life that a covenant is sealed in his blood (Matt 26:28 // Mark 14:24; cf. Luke 22:20, which adds "new"), this covenant can be understood as being like the covenant with Abraham or Moses, which marks a new beginning in the divine-human relationship based on a new initiative by God and a new response from humanity, or as

33. Justine Potts, *Confession in the Greek and Roman World: A History of Religious Transformation* (Oxford: Oxford University Press, forthcoming).

34. Sacrifices of a lamb are referred to in almost a hundred passages of the Hebrew Bible and are made for various purposes including as a "communion offering" (e.g., as a thanksgiving or affirmation of the covenant, Lev 3:6–7) and as a purification offering after an individual has done wrong (Lev 4:32–35).

35. Catrin Williams, "'Seeing,' Salvation, and the Use of Scripture in the Gospel of John," in Botner, Duff, and Dürr, *Atonement*, 131–54. The Eastern church fathers saw a reference to Isa 53:7 here, while Western fathers preferred to see reference to the paschal lamb. The options are set out by Raymond E. Brown, *The Gospel according to John I–XII*, AB 29 (New York: Doubleday, 1966), 58–63.

48

like the new covenant, for instance, of Jer 31:31, which follows Israel's sin and repentance.[36] Since Jesus calling people to repent of their (individual or collective) sins is a strong theme in Mark and Matthew, we tend to assume that the covenant at Matt 26:28 and Mark 14:24 is of the first type, though neither gospel uses explicit covenant language elsewhere. Luke, however, may take a slightly different view. He mentions the covenant obliquely at 1:55 and explicitly at 1:72–73 when he makes Mary and Zechariah respectively celebrate the coming of Jesus as a remembrance of the covenant with Abraham.[37] Zechariah glosses what Jesus will bring both as salvation "from our enemies and from the hand of all who hate us [with no indication here that we have provoked their hatred]" (1:71) and as "salvation . . . by the forgiveness of . . . sins" (1:77). Mary's song focuses entirely on the helping of the faithful poor and oppressed by the bringing down of the powerful (1:50–53), in which God acts "according to the promise he made to . . . Abraham and his descendants forever" (1:55). For Luke, therefore, the covenant may be primarily the covenant with Abraham the righteous that releases people from suffering and inaugurates a new people of God, to which he can, but does not always, append the idea of a covenant for the forgiveness of sins.[38] Connecting the Abrahamic covenant with the theme of raising the lowly and bringing down the powerful fits with Luke's well-recognized concern for the poor and marginal, whom we would expect to need salvation from suffering as much as, if not more than, from sin.

The language of messiahship testifies to messiahs as saving people from wrongdoing (willful or not), suffering, or both, and to the possibility of salvation

36. Mark and Matthew draw on Exod 24:8 here, whereas Luke draws on Jer 31:31; W. D. Davies and Dale C. Allison, *A Critical and Exegetical Commentary on the Gospel according to Saint Matthew* (3 vols.; London: Bloomsbury, 1988–1997), 3:472–75 regard the words in the Synoptic Gospels and Paul as all recalling the Sinai covenant from Exod 24:8. Brian J. Capper, "The New Covenant in Southern Palestine at the Arrest of Jesus," in *The Dead Sea Scrolls as Background to Postbiblical Judaism and Early Christianity* (ed. James R. Davila; Leiden: Brill, 2003), 90–116, especially 99–101, describes the "new covenant" among rural Essenes as "a mutually supportive friendly society" (100).

37. Zechariah's song also celebrates the birth of his son John (1:76–78), but much of it looks forward to the coming of Jesus as savior (1:68–75). In 1:77 John will bring people knowledge of the salvation from sins that Jesus will bring.

38. Discussed by Torsten Jantsch, *Jesus, der Retter: Die Soteriologie des lukanischen Doppelwerks* (Tübingen: Mohr Siebeck, 2017), 144–49. Acts also refers to the covenant twice. First, Acts 3:25 refers to the covenant that God made with Abraham, to which Peter appends the idea that God sent Jesus to bless the Jerusalemites "by turning each of you from your wicked ways" (3:26). Second, in Acts 7:8 the covenant refers simply to the covenant with Abraham. This suggests that the covenant is again primarily the covenant with Abraham, which marks a new relationship between God and humanity, but does not respond to human sin, to which Luke can append the idea that a new covenant also releases from sin.

CHAPTER 1

from one's own wrongdoings and their consequences or those of others. Some New Testament authors adapt this language more strongly than others to their dominant understanding of how Jesus Christ saves people and what he saves them from. In at least some writings, however, we can see traces of multiple understandings. We can also hear, in the variety of images for Jesus as Messiah, a challenge to Jewish and gentile, and ancient and modern listeners alike. Where do you stand before God? What do you need: salvation from your own wrongdoing, your state of sin, your suffering, or the suffering imposed on you by others? What are you asking for? What does God ask of you? Few people in any generation stand before God in unshaken trust and trustworthiness, but when God offers you trust anew, how will you respond?

It is not only in individual terms and images of atonement, however, that we can hear different ways in which Christ is envisaged as saving and different ideas about what humanity is saved from. We can also find them in passages of narrative and argument. In these passages, we also encounter *pistis* language in connection with various understandings of salvation.

WRONGDOING AND SUFFERING IN THE GOSPELS

All four canonical gospels introduce their story of Jesus's earthly ministry as one of sinful humanity called to repentance or rebirth. All four represent John the Baptist as preparing the way for Jesus, and the Synoptic Gospels remember him as preaching repentance from sins (Matt 3:2 // Mark 1:4 // Luke 3:3).[39] In the Gospel of John, meanwhile, we see John the Baptist refer to Jesus as the one who takes away the sins of the world (1:29). According to Mark and Matthew, Jesus begins his ministry where John the Baptist left off, calling people to repent because the kingdom is at hand (Matt 4:17 // Mark 1:15). Not surprisingly, the implication is normally taken to be that everyone has done wrong and needs to be forgiven, though the evangelists, focused on the importance of repentance, have little to say explicitly about whether wrongdoing is universal, collective, or inherited, or whether or not it is willful.

Before the appearance of John the Baptist, however, Matthew, Luke, and John prepare listeners in slightly different ways. Matthew sticks with the theme of wrongdoing: the angel tells Joseph that his wife's son will be called Jesus, "for he will save his people from their sins" (Matt 1:21). (From what kind of sins we do not

39. In these texts, the quotations from Mal 3:1 and Isa 40:3 point to coming judgment, release from sin, and release from suffering.

50

Wrongdoing and Suffering, Trust and Mistrust

know.[40]) Luke's birth narrative, as we have seen, refers to both the wrongdoing and suffering of God's people. The Lukan Zechariah is told that his wife will bear a child who will prepare Israel for the Lord by turning their hearts, probably from wrongdoing (Luke 1:17), though the people might also need to be turned from their mistrust of God following suffering. Gabriel's prophecy to Mary (1:32–33) affirms that Jesus will reign over the house of Jacob forever, hinting at the liberation of Israel from either suffering, wrongdoing, or both. Mary's hymn of praise focuses on God's promise to Abraham and his helping of "his servant" Israel by putting down the powerful (who could be foreign oppressors or the wealthy of Israel) and exalting the oppressed (1:51–55). Zechariah's song of praise mentions both the relief of Israel's suffering and the forgiveness of her wrongdoings, which could be individual, collective, or inherited (cf. 1:71, 74, 77–79). The Prologue of John meanwhile is ambiguous. Jesus is the light who comes into the world to give power to those who respond to him to become children of God (John 1:9, 12), but nothing is said in this passage about their present state of sin or suffering.[41]

The double theme of salvation from wrongdoing (individual or collective) and from suffering (caused by oneself or others) that begins to emerge in these passages can be detected elsewhere in the Synoptic Gospels and is underlined in passages in which Jesus either criticizes those who are hostile to him or shows compassion for those who are vulnerable or distressed.

The Matthean and Lukan John the Baptist tells those who come to him for baptism (Pharisees and Sadducees in Matthew; "crowds" in Luke) to "bear fruits worthy of repentance" (Matt 3:8 // Luke 3:8). Jesus, directly or indirectly, says repeatedly that he has come to call wrongdoers to repentance or to call people to repent (e.g., Matt 9:13 // Mark 2:17 // Luke 5:32; Matt 6:12 // Luke 11:4; cf. Matt 7:5 // Luke 6:42; Matt 7:21–23 // Luke 13:25–27; Matt 21:32). The parables of the end time in Matthew and Luke highlight the grim fate of those (e.g., the unforgiving slave, the laborers in the vineyard, the tremulous custodian of one talent) who, for whatever reason, have not done as their master commanded when he returns to judge their faithfulness (Matt 18:34; 25:30 // Luke 19:27; Matt 21:41 // Luke 20:16). At the Last Supper, Matthew's Jesus says that his blood is poured out "for the forgiveness of sins" (26:28). At Matt 18:6 (// Mark 9:42 // Luke 17:2), Jesus also calls down woe on anyone who makes one of the "little ones" who trust in him do wrong. A "little one" could be a child or any innocent or vulnerable person, and the saying implies that when one person corrupts another, both are morally damaged. The early

40. In Matthew the magi come to pay homage to a newborn king of the Jews (Matt 2:2), leaving open what this king might be destined to achieve.

41. See below, pp. 55–56.

51

CHAPTER 1

sermons in Acts, which may remember something of the earliest postresurrection preaching, refer to Jesus's death for the repentance and forgiveness of Israel or call to their listeners to repent (e.g., Acts 2:38; 3:19; 5:31; 10:42).[42]

When people come to Jesus, they sometimes do so in consciousness of their own wrongdoing. The woman who anoints Jesus's feet in Luke's Gospel (7:36–50) is identified as a sinner. As she works, she weeps and kisses Jesus's feet (7:38), suggesting that she repents of her wrongdoings. Jesus tells her that her trust has saved her and her sins are forgiven (7:50, 48). Sometimes, however, people who are castigated for wrongdoing seem to have meant well or to be saying or doing something humanly understandable. In all four gospels, someone (according to John, Simon Peter) draws a sword and attacks those who are arresting Jesus (Matt 26:51–54; Mark 14:47; Luke 22:50–51; John 18:10–11). In all but Mark's version, Jesus rebukes them, but it is hard not to think that this response to a moment of terror and disaster is, at least, understandable. After the transfiguration in the Synoptic Gospels, Jesus descends from the mountain to find that some of the disciples have tried and failed to heal a boy with a demon (Matt 17:14–20 // Mark 9:14–29 // Luke 9:37–43). Jesus criticizes the disciples for their lack of faith and prayer (Matt 17:17, 20 // Mark 9:19, 29 // Luke 9:41), but a charitable reader (ancient or modern) might think this was, at worst, a failure motivated by aspiration. When Peter protests against Jesus's first passion prediction in Matthew and Mark, Jesus rebukes him, "Get behind me, Satan!" (Matt 16:23 // Mark 8:33). Peter may be mistaken in protesting, but loyal protests by a friend against a heroic figure going into danger are commonplace in ancient literature, and early listeners would surely have heard, as we do, loyalty and good intentions in Peter's words.[43] It is possible, in these and similar stories, to say and do wrong with the best of intentions.

Jesus's rebuke to Peter implies that those who do wrong or are in a state of sin are in league with or under the authority of Satan. Those who put their trust in Jesus seek or embrace the kingdom of God by putting themselves, instead, under his authority. For the Synoptic writers, however, to be under a power hostile to

42. So, e.g., Graham Stanton, *Jesus of Nazareth in New Testament Preaching* (Cambridge: Cambridge University Press, 1974), 67–85, though this is debated by, e.g., C. K. Barrett, *A Critical and Exegetical Commentary on the Acts of the Apostles* (London: T&T Clark, 1994), 22–23, who argues that what looks like "primitive" theology is not necessarily early.

43. Cf., e.g., Andromache begging Hector not to go back into the fight (Homer, *Iliad* 6.405–465) and Ismene protesting Antigone's plan to bury her brother Polynices and receiving as violent a rejection as Peter (Sophocles, *Antigone* 28–81). This also underlines that those who put their trust in Jesus do not become sinless. Trust is a long-term relationship with ups and downs, and those who trust may also relapse into wrongdoing at times; see Morgan, *Theology of Trust*, 258–68.

52

Wrongdoing and Suffering, Trust and Mistrust

God does not necessarily mean that one is a wrongdoer. Whenever Jesus releases someone from an evil or unclean spirit, he releases that person from the power of evil, but in none of those stories or references is the person suffering said to be a wrongdoer.[44] When Jesus says in Matt 9:36 and Mark 6:34 that he has compassion on the crowds who gather around him because "they were harassed and helpless, like sheep without a shepherd," he suggests that the crowds are vulnerable and suffering (he could be referring to either political or metaphysical oppression) rather than sinful. Matthew 10:6, invoking in addition the tradition that a political leader will one day gather in all the tribes of Israel before finally defeating her enemies, allows a similar reading when Jesus sends out the disciples to preach to the "lost sheep of the house of Israel," telling them (without sin or repentance language) that the kingdom of heaven is at hand. When Matthew's and Luke's Jesus tells his followers to "ask; and it will be given to you" (Matt 7:7–11 // Luke 11:9–13), he may be referring to their everyday needs and the relief of the suffering of hunger or illness, but he can also be heard as referring to the suffering that evil inflicts on human beings.

There are well-recognized hints in all four gospels that Jesus was seen by some around him as potentially the kind of political leader especially associated with saving Israel from suffering at the hands of her enemies.[45] At Matt 14:1–2 (// Mark 6:14–16 // Luke 9:7–9) Herod Agrippa apparently fears that Jesus may be John the Baptist raised from the dead. This is an unexpected claim and does not play any obvious role in the narrative, so it may remember a story that circulated at the time. If so, and if Josephus is right that Herod had John executed because he thought he might be a political threat (*Antiquities* 18.118), there may be a trace here of a suspicion circulating during Jesus's Galilean ministry that he was fomenting political trouble or even had active political ambitions.[46] John's Gospel attributes

---

44. Mark 1:23–28 // Luke 4:33–37; Matt 8:16–17 // Mark 1:32–34 // Luke 4:40–41; Matt 4:24 // Mark 3:11 // Luke 6:18; Matt 8:28–34 // Mark 5:1–10 // Luke 8:26–39; Matt 9:32–34 // Luke 11:14–15; Matt 12:22–24 // Mark 11:14–15; Matt 17:14–21 // Mark 9:14–19 // Luke 9:37–43a.

45. Recently discussed from varying perspectives by Robert D. Rowe, *God's Kingdom and God's Son* (Leiden: Brill, 2002); Brendan Byrne, "Jesus as Messiah in the Gospel of Luke: Discerning a Pattern of Correction," *CBQ* 65 (2003): 80–95; Wayne Baxter, *Missing Matthew's Political Messiah: A Closer Look at His Birth and Infancy Narratives* (Philadelphia: Pennsylvania University Press, 2017); Max Botner, *Jesus Christ as the Son of David in the Gospel of Mark* (Cambridge: Cambridge University Press, 2019); Serge Ruzer, *Early Jewish Messianism in the New Testament* (Leiden: Brill, 2020), 43–68; Isaac W. Oliver, *Luke's Jewish Eschatology: The National Restoration of Israel in Luke-Acts* (Oxford: Oxford University Press, 2021).

46. Alternatively it is suggested by Adela Yarbro Collins, *Mark: A Commentary* (Minneapolis: Fortress, 2007), 303–4 that John or Jesus is imagined here as the kind of exceptional individual who can return from the dead (such as Protesilaos or, according to some, Nero), but this is

CHAPTER 1

to Jesus during his ministry in Galilee a fear that the people want to carry him off to make him king (6:15) and, implausible as this sounds in these terms, it may also attest that some people had political ambitions for Jesus at a relatively early stage of his ministry. Suspicions about this could have formed one basis for the later plot against Jesus in Jerusalem. All four gospels report that when Jesus was handed to Pilate, he was accused of having called himself the "King of the Jews." In all four, Pilate asks him whether he is the king of the Jews, and at John 18:34 Jesus indicates that he suspects that people have claimed this of him, though he does not answer Pilate directly.[47] The gospels conspire to award as little of the blame for the crucifixion as possible to the Roman authorities, but they all also agree that Jesus was crucified under a placard alleging that he was identified as, or identified himself as, the king of the Jews (Matt 27:37 // Mark 15:26 // Luke 23:38 // John 19:19), suggesting that Pilate was concerned that Jesus might lead or form the focus of an uprising to liberate Israel from oppression, or at least that he was prepared to take seriously worries among the Jewish leadership to that effect.

Elsewhere, a saying of Jesus about swords hints that if he did not harbor political ambitions for himself, his language could encourage the thought in others. In Matt 10:34–36 and Luke 12:51–53 Jesus says that he has come to bring not peace but a sword, while at Matt 26:52 and John 18:11, as we have seen, he has to stop one of his followers from fighting his arrest, telling them that those who live by the sword die by it. There is no strong indication that Jesus ever saw himself as a political, much less a military leader, but if others could see him that way, and if some of his words and actions could be seen as encouraging that possibility, such a hope would likely have been associated with the idea that Jesus would save Israel from her suffering under Roman rule.

To these hints that Jesus was remembered by some in his lifetime as having been sent to release Israel from oppression, we can add the stories and sayings that speak to his concern for the liberation of the poor and oppressed, and that have been brought increasingly into discussions of atonement by liberation theologians.[48] We have already mentioned the songs of Mary and Zechariah. At the beginning of

---

a very rare type in the ancient world and not associated with a change of identity such as is suggested here. Moreover, there is no strong reason to think that John was regarded by anyone as this kind of hero. Nor do the Greek heroes mentioned above return with greater power, like Elijah, to herald a greater event.

47. Cilliers Breytenbach, "'Wie geschrieben ist' und das Leiden des Christus: Die theologische Leistung des Markus," in *The Gospel according to Mark as Episodic Narrative* (Leiden: Brill, 2020), 365–66. At John 18:36, Jesus assures Pilate, "my kingdom is not from this world," strengthening the implication that he knows people have claimed that he does have political ambitions.

48. Above, pp. 4–6. See, e.g., Cone, *Black Theology*; Jon Sobrino, *Jesus the Liberator: A Historical-*

Wrongdoing and Suffering, Trust and Mistrust

his ministry, according to Luke, Jesus affirms in the Nazareth synagogue that the prophecy of Isa 61:1–2 has been fulfilled. Later he assures John the Baptist that, in his ministry, "the poor have good news brought to them" (Matt 11:5 // Luke 7:22). Despite the differences between Matthew's and Luke's beatitudes, both attest to Jesus's concern for the vulnerable. Matthew's Jesus prophesies that the meek will inherit the earth and that those who hunger and thirst for righteousness or justice will be satisfied, while all those who are persecuted will receive their reward in heaven (Matt 5:5–6, 11). Luke's Jesus proclaims that the poor, the hungry, those who weep, and those who are hated are all blessed, while those who are rich, those who laugh (at their own good fortune or others' suffering?), and those whose reputation in this world is high will be punished under God's kingdom (Luke 6:20–26). Luke also offers a memorable parable of intersectional suffering (18:1–8). A widowed woman goes to court and seeks justice against an adversary who, the story implies, is persecuting her unjustly. The judge, an unjust man himself, does not want to give her justice, but she is so persistent that eventually he does. Jesus commends her persistence in the face of inequality and discrimination as a form of the trust and faithfulness that the Son of Man will be pleased to find on earth when he comes. In these sayings and stories, we are not usually told whether suffering is caused by people's own wrongdoing or that of others (though we usually assume the latter), but the focus is clearly on Jesus's ministry as relieving suffering.

In places, as we have seen, John's treatment of suffering and wrongdoing parallels that of the Synoptic Gospels, but in some respects it is significantly different. In a handful of verses (e.g., John 3:19; 8:43–44; 10:3–4, 14, 26), associated by some commentators with a "final redactor" of the gospel, Jesus seems to speak as though human beings are already divided into those who prefer light to darkness (3:19) and "know" their "shepherd" (10:4, 14) and those who prefer darkness and "belong to your father, the devil" (8:44) and will "die in your sins" (8:24). Whether those who prefer light do so because they are not sinful; or because they are less sinful than those who prefer darkness, or differently; or because, despite what looks like the predestinarian thinking of these passages, they are only different from those who prefer darkness in making a choice to "receive" Jesus, is never clear. Elsewhere (e.g., John 1:29; 3:14, 17; 5:14, 24) the gospel seems to assume that everyone is a wrongdoer—whether by individual or collective responsibility or association is not usually specified—but those who choose to trust or believe in Jesus are saved and will not be condemned (e.g., 8:24).[49]

Theological Reading of Jesus of Nazareth (Maryknoll: Orbis, 1993); Rosemary Radford Ruether, *Women and Redemption: A Theological History* (2nd ed.; Minneapolis: Fortress, 2012), 167–269.

49. Just occasionally, whether an individual has done wrong willfully or not is specified:

CHAPTER 1

Even John, however, who is radically negative about those he casts as hostile to Jesus—particularly most "Jews" and the Jewish authorities—does not wholly obscure that those his Jesus calls children of the devil are, by their own lights, law-abiding and well-intentioned people of faith. They "search the scriptures" because, as observant Jews, they believe that eternal life is to be found through them (5:39–40). Though Jesus does not sympathize with them, we may sympathize with their reluctance to accept that the scriptures tell them to put their trust in an unknown and adversarial Galilean preacher. Jesus acknowledges that they keep the law, even if they do not interpret it as he would prefer (e.g., 7:19, 22–24). When Jesus says and does what to them are outrageous things, they do not leap to the conclusion that he is willfully evil but think he must be possessed by a demon (8:20; 10:20). Even when they plot to kill him in chapter 11, they do so out of fear that he will cause so much trouble that the Romans will crack down on the whole nation and abolish the temple cult (11:48). In coming to their decision, they cite (ironically, from Christians' point of view, but traditionally and reasonably from their own) that "it is better for you to have one man die for the people than to have the whole nation destroyed" (11:50). As we have begun to see, and will see further in the Synoptic Gospels and in Paul's criticisms of his fellow Jews, individuals and groups that New Testament writers condemn as wrongdoers can also be seen as well-intentioned, faithful people who have sometimes suffered themselves and are doing their best for those in their care in difficult situations.

The trend of John 3:10–21, as we have seen, is to suggest that everyone is sinful but that those who put their trust in Jesus will not be condemned, whether or not they have been predestined to "come to the light" (3:20). John 3:14 suggests a little more: "Just as Moses lifted up the serpent in the wilderness, so must the Son of Man be lifted up." The brass serpent on a pole that Moses erected in the desert (Num 21:8–9) was put up as a sign of God's power to cure people from snakebite. Here, as in healing stories, those who put their trust in Jesus and come to eternal life are by that token released from suffering.[50] Poisonous snakes threaten a form

---

the man blind from birth has not (John 9:2), but the man by the pool at Bethsaida and the woman taken in adultery have (5:14; 8:11). Interestingly, neither the man nor the woman is said to *pisteuein* in Jesus before the man is healed and the woman is released from condemnation, though the man does later (9:38). Nor does the man by the pool at Bethsaida *pisteuein* (5:6–8), though he obeys Jesus's command to walk. Perhaps their roles in Jesus's self-revelation are more important within the stories than their own attitudes, though these passages also reinforce the sayings of 5:21–22 and 6:65 that Jesus himself or God choose to whom life is given.

50. Brown, *John I–XII*, 133 notes that the midrash of the serpent story in Wis 16:6–7 emphasizes its salvific function; cf. John 12:31–32, which is without saving language but contrasts the people whom Jesus draws to himself with the destruction of the "prince of this world."

56

Wrongdoing and Suffering, Trust and Mistrust

of natural suffering for human beings, but in 17:15 Jesus, returning to this theme, suggests that the suffering of his followers comes from the devil through human beings. There he prays to God, "I am not asking you to take them out of the world, but I ask you to protect them from the evil one."

It is tempting to assume that in the gospels the *locus classicus* of the idea that Jesus saves people from suffering is his healing miracles. The suffering at issue here is usually, nowadays, taken to be natural suffering rather than suffering as a consequence of wrongdoing (in line with John 9:3 and despite Matt 9:2 // Mark 2:5 // Luke 5:20). Natural suffering is not our focus in this study, so if these stories are about natural suffering, they fall outside our remit.[51] In recent years, however, a new way of reading them has developed that puts them within our scope.

The idea that Jesus releases people from natural suffering has a long history going back to antiquity. It invokes the Isaianic tradition that the messiah will heal the sick and a widespread assumption, both ancient and modern, that illness and disability are, if not the consequences of sin, then misfortunes from which anyone would want to be cured. Christians have always turned to Jesus Christ in need, and Christ is universally recognized as having compassion on the suffering. In recent years, however, the assumption that everyone needs to be released from illness or disability has been criticized by some commentators as ableist. It is argued that this type of reading disempowers and discriminates against those who live with disabilities or chronic illnesses, identifying their lives with inadequacy, abnormality, failure, and sin. It encourages the physically normative to marginalize and degrade others by offering them sympathy but not acceptance or respect.[52]

---

51. Natural suffering can also cause people to lose trust in God. In a striking recent case, see Arndt Büssing, Klaus Baumann, and Janusz Surykiewicz, "Loss of Faith and Decrease in Trust in a Higher Source During Covid-19 in Germany," *Journal of Religion and Health* 61 (2022): 741–66. In my view, natural suffering needs to be discussed separately, as it is arguably not a departure from the good order of the world in relation to God, as we find with wrongdoing and its consequences, but weaves together natural suffering and suffering caused by human wrongdoing. See Gerald W. Peterman and Andrew J. Schmutzer, *Between Pain and Grace: A Biblical Theology of Suffering* (Chicago: Moody, 2016). The authors emphasize God's use of human agents to enact his plan of salvation, culminating in Jesus Christ, who shares human suffering, alleviates it, and offers a model for his followers. They also, like this chapter, underline the way in which sin reverberates through generations, damaging those who did not commit it.

52. See, e.g., Nancy L. Eiesland, *The Disabled God: Toward a Liberatory Theology of Disability* (Nashville: Abingdon, 1994); Julia Watts Belser and Melanie S. Morrison, "What No Longer Serves Us: Resisting Anti-Ableism and Anti-Judaism in New Testament Healing Narratives," *Journal of Feminist Studies in Religion* 27 (2011): 153–70; Thomas E. Reynolds, "Theology and Disability: Changing the Conversation," *Disability and Health* 16 (2012): 33–48; Julia Watts Belser, "Violence, Disability, and the Politics of Healing," *J. Disabil. Relig.* 19 (2015): 177–97. Nicole Tillotson, Monica

CHAPTER 1

Those who live with chronic illnesses or disabilities often decisively reject the assumption that nonnormative bodies or minds need to be pitied or cured.

A less discriminatory approach to Jesus's "healing" miracles invites us to reconsider what those who seek change need to be released from, and whether they all receive the same response from Jesus.[53] In several healing stories, Jesus seems to give someone what they ask for, but also something they did not seem to be asking for. For example, he tells the woman with the hemorrhage, "Your trust has healed you" (Matt 9:20–22 // Mark 5:25–34 // Luke 8:43–48), using the verb *sōzein*, which in the gospels and elsewhere in Greek regularly means "to save." His response hovers semantically between healing and salvation. Has the woman not only been healed from her illness but also saved? Perhaps she has done, or inherited, some wrong we do not hear about, or perhaps she is saved from the suffering she has endured from a society that, in the belief that it is doing God's will, wrongly shuns her because she is ritually unclean.

Jairus seeks healing for his daughter and Martha for her brother Lazarus (Mark 5:23; John 11:21). Both, instead, are given a resurrection. These resurrections do not abolish the natural phenomena of suffering and death, which both resurrectees will experience again, unless the end time comes first. Jesus, however, explicitly tells Martha that what she should be trusting him for is not her brother's healing but eternal life, and Lazarus's resurrection is a sign of that for which people rightly trust in Jesus. Looking for healing, Jairus and Martha are given something much greater: an assurance of God's power and eternal life for everyone that transcends sin, physical illness and disability, and mortality itself.

In these and similar stories we can see people coming to Jesus seeking relief from what they (and those around them) apparently think of as their natural suffering, but being given something different and greater: sometimes release from the power of wrongdoing over their lives, and sometimes release from the suffering caused by their misunderstanding of their situation or the misunderstanding of those around them.[54] What they are given is also a teaching for wider society. Characters in the gospels who seek healing for someone else—such as the

---

Short, Janice Ollerton, Cassandra Hearn, and Bonita Sawatzky, "Faith Matters: From a Disability Lens," *J. Disabil. Relig.* 21 (2017): 319–37 explores how people living with disabilities describe them in light of their faith.

53. Amos Yong, "Many Tongues, Many Formational Practices: Christian Spirituality/Formation across Global Christian Contexts," *Spiritus* 31 (2009): 179 n. 30 notes an exception: John Hull has suggested that Luke 18:35–43 is told as much to illustrate the *pistis* and "conversion" of the blind man as it is to illustrate his desire for healing.

54. Cf. stories in which Jesus expels demons from people who, speaking for the demon, resist (e.g., Mark 5:7 // Luke 8:28; Mark 1:24 // Luke 4:34).

paralytic's trusting friends, Jairus the synagogue leader, the anonymous centurion, the Roman official, and the Canaanite woman—all represent the social networks around individuals who are identified as in need, and their acts of trust can be seen as expressing social assumptions that, with the best intentions, do wrong by wanting to "normalize" people whose bodies, minds, or behaviors are different from their own. When Jesus gives a person who is healed not quite what they, or those around them, asked for, he challenges everyone's assumptions, suggesting that what they should be asking for is not the homogenization of the natural variety of human life and experience, but a saving, life-giving relationship of trust that transcends the limitations of human existence. In the process, Jesus reminds listeners that the most important aspect of any teaching or action of his may not be whether it releases someone from suffering or wrongdoing, or what kind of suffering or wrongdoing, but the (re)new(ed) relationship with God that it makes possible.

WRONGDOING AND SUFFERING IN THE NEW TESTAMENT EPISTLES

Even this brief overview of wrongdoing, and the relationship between wrongdoing and suffering, in the gospels points to more complexity in the picture than we sometimes recognize. Some of the same complexity is detectable in the New Testament epistles. The epistles often indicate that Jesus, as Messiah, saves people from willful wrongdoing, but they are also threaded with language and imagery that hints at other kinds of wrongdoing and suggests that Jesus also saves people from suffering.

We will look in more detail below at Paul's language in Romans, which links both wrongdoing and suffering with *pistis* language.[55] In 1 Corinthians, Paul repeatedly exhorts the Corinthians to stop sinning or to punish sinners, with a strong implication that these sins are their own. In 1 Cor 4:18 Paul states that some have become arrogant. In 5:1–2 he claims some are arrogant (with perhaps an implication that they are trusting their own judgment too readily) and immoral and that they should "drive out the wicked" (5:13). In 6:7–8 Paul writes that they should stop wronging and defrauding one another and later says they should not become idolaters and immoral (10:6).[56] All this reflects the reproving tone of the letter as a whole and the situation that prompted it, and the proclamation that

---

55. Pp. 71–76.

56. Cf. 2 Cor 12:20–21; 13:2 where Corinthians behaving badly also seem to be personally responsible for their wrongdoings.

CHAPTER 1

"Christ died for our sins" (15:3) is the culmination of this aspect of the letter as well as part of Paul's argument about future resurrection.[57] To the Galatians, however, Paul writes in rather different terms. Having responded well to Paul's preaching (Gal 1:6), they are now deserting it, but Paul does not call their desertion wrongdoing. They are being disturbed and thrown into disorder by people who deserve to be cursed for their wrongdoing (1:7–9). They are stupid (*anoētos*), bewitched (3:1), and need to be corrected (3:7). Once enslaved to "beings that by nature are not gods" (4:8), they must not relapse but hold fast to God, Christ, and the gospel as preached by Paul. Paul clearly thinks the Galatians are accessible to reproach and can mend their ways, but he represents them as more foolish and vulnerable than sinful, more wronged than wrongdoing. (Perhaps they have trusted too readily in the "other gospel" of 1:6.) The Thessalonians receive a different kind of letter again. When Paul speaks of the Thessalonians as turning from idols to serve God (1 Thess 1:9), we could look forward to Rom 1:18–21 and suggest that the Thessalonians were sinners for not having acknowledged the God of Israel earlier, but there is no hint of that in this letter. Nor does Paul suggest that the Thessalonians were suffering before they heard the gospel. He presents them rather as having taken the opportunity to acknowledge and serve the "living and true God" (1 Thess 1:9) and to be saved from the "wrath that is coming" (1:10).[58] At 1 Thess 1:6, 2:14, and 3:3 he indicates that persecution and affliction followed their conversion,

57. Elsewhere referring to Christ's death, Paul says he "died for us." Breytenbach shows how Paul's thinking moves from the inherited phrase "for our sins" to thinking of Christ as dying "for us" (i.e., for the benefit of and, in 2 Cor 5:14 and Rom 5:6, in the place of) or for all of "us" (Jewish and gentile) as an expression of love, for our salvation, and in a prolepsis of the final judgment that makes possible new life in Christ even before the end time. See Cilliers Breytenbach, "The 'For Us' Phrases in Pauline Soteriology: Considering Their Background and Use," in *Grace, Reconciliation, Concord*, 59–81; Breytenbach, "'Christus starb für uns': Zur Tradition und paulinischen Rezeption der sogennanten 'Sterbeformeln,'" *Grace, Reconciliation, Concord*, 95–126. In 1 Cor 1:27–28 Paul reminds the Corinthians that they were chosen by God, despite their weakness, lowliness, and foolishness. At 2:14, he states that only the spiritual receive the gifts of God's spirit, but at 3:1–3 the Corinthians are still "fleshly" and not spiritual "infants in Christ" who are not ready for solid food. This state, Paul says, will persist as long as they are jealous and quarrel with each other. This may suggest some tension between Paul's acceptance of the Corinthians' infant state and his holding them to account for their wrongdoings, but the solution may be that the kinds of bad behavior Paul castigates are everyday wrongdoings that everyone should know not to commit.

58. Cf. Pieter G. R. de Villiers, "Safe in the Family of God: Soteriological Perspectives in 1 Thessalonians," in van der Watt, *Salvation*, 317–20. We assume that future "wrath" will fall on those who have not acknowledged God and Christ, but Paul does not specify here whether this will include those who have not heard the gospel. This may have been a strategic approach in preaching, particularly to gentiles, who may not have seen themselves as suffering at the time when they were evangelized or as being sinful for not having worshiped the God of Israel before they heard the gospel.

Wrongdoing and Suffering, Trust and Mistrust

and that he sent Timothy back to Thessalonica to check whether they had been "shaken by these persecutions" (3:3) and tempted away from Paul's teaching (3:5). He rejoices that they "continue to stand firm in the Lord" (3:8), and encourages them to continue to do good and abstain from evil (5:15, 22). Evil is a force that needs to be resisted, but Paul implies that the Thessalonians are well prepared to do so.[59] In these letters, Paul writes in different terms according to the situation he is addressing and can represent his communities as vulnerable and misled as well as responsible for their own wrongdoing.[60]

Four accounts of Paul's own call, by Paul himself and (probably) one of his followers, add further complexity to this picture. In Gal 1:14 he explains, "I advanced in Judaism beyond many among my people of the same age, for I was far more zealous for the traditions of my ancestors" (NRSVue). In Phil 3:4–9 he says that his zeal in persecuting the church was based on his commitment to his own Pharisaic tradition (3:5–6), though he has now come to think that righteousness comes solely from God through the *pistis* relationship between God, Christ, and the faithful (3:9). In both passages Paul presents himself as more misguided in honest zeal than sinful in the years in which he persecuted Christ-confessors, even though he (tacitly) recognizes that he was in the wrong. First Timothy 1:12–13 goes further, saying on Paul's behalf, "I am grateful to Christ Jesus our Lord, who has strengthened me, because he considered me faithful and appointed me to his service, even though I was formerly a blasphemer, a persecutor, and a man of violence. But I received mercy because I had acted ignorantly in unbelief." Though the writer makes clear that Paul's violent persecution of Christ-confessors was wrong, it is presented not as willfully sinful but as understandable given his background and perhaps temperament.[61] The Letter to Titus, whose tone in general is sharper than that of 1 Timothy, also has a harsher description of Paul (and others) before his call or their conversion, describing them as "foolish, disobedient, led astray, slaves to various passions and pleasures, passing our days in malice and envy, despicable, hating one another" (3:3). Even so, this passage represents Christ-confessors before their confession less as willfully sinful than as misled, enslaved, and perhaps wrongdoers by association.

---

59. Reemphasized probably by a follower of Paul at 2 Thess 2:2–12; 3:3.

60. At 1 Thess 5:10 Paul refers to the fact that "Christ died for us" so that the faithful may live together with him, whether dead or alive when he comes, but even here he does not refer to Christ as having died for the Thessalonians' sins. We might assume that this was his original preaching to them, but even if so, it is striking that their putative sinfulness does not feature in this letter. At the least, Paul seems to be focusing on the opportunity they have taken rather than their release from sin or suffering.

61. Acts also represents Paul as violent in his persecution of Christ-confessors (8:1, 3), and Christ's words at Acts 9:4 imply reproach, if not condemnation, and not excuse.

CHAPTER 1

Other writers who draw on Paul take his language in slightly different directions. Hebrews, for example, understands the sacrifice of Christ consistently as expiating human wrongdoing (Heb 2:17; 7:26; 9:13–14, 15, 28; 13:11–12; cf. 10:26). The author seems to see wrongdoing, in line with one strand of Jewish tradition, as willful disobedience against God (2:2; 3:8–12; 4:7–13), though at 5:2 he distinguishes the "ignorant and wayward" from others.[62] The author also refers to the devil at 2:14–15 as holding humanity in slavery by its suffering of the power of death. The Pastoral Letters focus on life in a church rather than on community members' condition before they became Christians, though we have already seen what 1 Timothy has to say about Paul's life before his call. First Timothy 1:15 refers to Jesus as coming into the world to save sinners, but 2 Tim 1:9 refers, a little more ambiguously, to Jesus as saving community members and calling them to a holy life "not according to our works." The immediate point here is that it is God's grace, not human works, that makes possible human beings' calling, but the writer does not specify the nature of the barrier to human beings' living a holy life previously. Both letters occasionally suggest that people are responsible for their own wrongdoing and offenders need to be punished, notably Alexander and Hymenaeus, who have blasphemed and been handed over to Satan in punishment (1 Tim 1:20) and who are used as an example of culpable profane talk that makes other people godless (2 Tim 2:16). First Timothy 1:3–7, however, describes untrustworthy teachers of the law as people who want to be teachers but do not understand what they are saying, suggesting that they may be more misguided than willful wrongdoers. Bishops and, in the last times, everyone must try to avoid falling into the devil's trap (1 Tim 3:7; cf. 6:9) or falling victim to deceitful spirits (1 Tim 4:1–2) and being corrupted (1 Tim 6:5; cf. 2 Tim 2:14), while 2 Timothy encourages community members to be kind to one another, so that those who have been trapped by the devil's snare may be granted repentance by God and return to their senses (2:24–26). In these passages, wrongdoing, at least in the community of the faithful, seems to be more a matter of individuals' being misguided, victimized, and trapped by hostile powers than a matter of willful wrongdoing, and the emphasis is on the importance of avoiding traps and helping others out of them rather than on liability. Just as some of Paul's emphasis on the Corinthians' responsibility for their sins may be due to the situation that 1 Corinthians addresses, so 1 and 2 Timothy may have arisen in communities in which the writer felt that it would be more productive to encourage and strengthen people's resolve

---

62. Harold W. Attridge, *The Epistle to the Hebrews* (Philadelphia: Fortress, 1989), 143–44 notes the connection with sacrificial regulations in the Hebrew Bible (e.g., Lev 4:2) that prescribe sin offerings only for "unwitting offenses" and not willful sins.

than attack them for their imperfections.[63] This, though, in itself points to the range of Christian ideas about wrongdoing and suffering, their causes, how they should be addressed, and human responsibility that writers could draw upon as they thought appropriate.[64]

How Trust Fails: Wrongdoing, Suffering, and *Apistia* in the Gospels

Throughout New Testament writings, the right, saving, cleansing, life-giving, or "righteousing" response to God and to Christ is *pistis*.[65] The negative forms of the *pistis* lexicon (*apistein, ou pisteuein, apistos, apistia*) are less common but also appear.[66] They feature in many of the same contexts as the positive forms,

63. The tone of Titus in this respect is again sharper, emphasizing that bishops and their families must be "blameless," implying that they are responsible for their actions (1:5–9), and referring to "rebellious people" and "deceivers" who must be silenced (1:10–11). Even in these cases, since these people are community members, we may suggest what the writer does not—that they may be well intentioned even if, in the writer's eyes, they were wrongheaded.

64. 1 Peter offers listeners a mixture of images that tend in slightly different directions. In 2:24 and 3:18, the author writes that Christ bore human sins on the cross, whereas 1:14, 18, 22 and 2:9–10 suggest rather that before the Christ event the writer's audience were ignorant and their existence was pointless and limited: they were "no people" because they were not God's people, while now they are "a chosen people, a royal priesthood, a holy nation, God's own people" (2:9). This tells us that pre-Christian existence is of little, if any value, but not whether it is a life of sin or suffering. The thinking of 1 John, meanwhile, often parallels that of the final version of John's Gospel. For instance, 1 John 3:4–10 suggests that those who do wrong belong to the devil and have neither seen nor known Christ, and the coming of Christ has revealed who belongs to God and who does not. 1 John 1:7 and 2:2, however, refer to Christ as cleansing human beings from their wrongdoings or expiating them.

65. "To righteous" is the neologism used by some commentators to avoid the historically specific (Lutheran) overtones of "to justify" and what some hear as the judicial overtones of "to make right." I take it that Paul thinks that people who put their trust in God and Christ are both put into their right relationship with God and are internally reoriented toward righteousness (see above, p. 38 n. 4, though I would leave open the possibility that the process of orientation, like that of trust, can take time). As a result, I use both "to righteous" and "to make right," and occasionally "to justify."

66. John connects *ou pisteuein* twice explicitly with wrongdoing. In both cases the wrongdoing is failure to trust in Jesus (John 8:45–46; 16:9). Elsewhere we can infer that *ou pisteuein* is linked to condemnation (e.g., 4:48; 5:38, 47; 6:64; 10:25–26; 12:39; at 3:18 those who *ou pisteuein* have already been condemned). But in some passages it is disciples or those apparently open to trust who *ou pisteuein* (3:12; 14:10; cf. 20:25), so their failure is part of their ongoing relationship with Jesus.

CHAPTER 1

especially in relation to forgiveness, eternal life, power, or the end time, and, like the positive forms, may relate to God, Christ, or both. We might expect that not putting one's trust in God or Christ would be a sin for which the one who does not trust would be personally responsible. In practice, failure to trust, like trust itself, can be more complicated: a matter of misunderstanding or misguidedness or a response to suffering rather than willful wrongdoing. It can also bring suffering with it and cause others to suffer or even to do wrong.

For John, some people cannot believe or trust in Jesus because they do not "belong to my sheep" (10:26; cf. 3:18; 4:48; 8:45–46; 12:39; 16:9), but the Synoptic Gospels assume that everyone is capable of trust. One of the clearest identifications of the failure to trust (and also to be trustworthy) with willful wrongdoing occurs in the Matthean Jesus's attack on the scribes and Pharisees (Matt 23:1–36). "You tithe mint, dill, and cumin, and have neglected the weightier matters of the law: justice and mercy and *pistis*" (Matt 23:23; cf. Luke 11:42). The scribes and Pharisees believe that they are serving God rightly, but Matthew accuses them of failings that prevent them from seeing that they need to come to a (re)new(ed) relationship with God. They misunderstand what is most important about the law. They are more interested in their own status than in doing God's will (Matt 23:6–12). They fail to practice what they preach (23:3, 13–15, 23–30). Their interpretation of the law overburdens those they teach (23:3–4). As a result, they betray innocent people who rely on them, blocking the entrance to the kingdom from them (23:13), making them as bad as themselves (23:15–16; cf. Matt 10:1–36; Luke 10:12–15), and leading them into hell (Matt 18:6–9; cf. Matt 15:1–20 // Mark 7:1–23; Luke 11:37–44).[67] They have failed to trust in God and instead have persecuted, and continue to persecute, the prophets, wise men, and scribes sent by God (Matt 23:30–36; cf. Matt 11:18–19; 21:23–27; 23:37).[68]

Matthew marks out three ways in which people fail in trust. First, they may fail to trust in God and those who speak in God's name. Second, they may trust their own judgment of how to serve God too readily. And third, they may fail to be trustworthy toward God or those innocents who trust them (and who seem here to be led primarily into wrongdoing rather than suffering).[69] Most commentators take these passages as evidence of conflict between Matthew's community and some other Jews, and probably also as remembering conflict between the histor-

67. Luke 6:43–44 links this image with the bearing of rotten fruit.

68. To justify their refusal to listen they make perverse claims about Jesus and try to mislead others with them (e.g., Matt 12:24–30 // Mark 3:22–27 // Luke 11:15, 17–23).

69. Similar themes appear, e.g., at Matt 4:1–7; Luke 4:1–4, 9–12 (Jesus resists the temptations to serve himself or exercise inappropriate power over others but remains obedient to God); Matt 9:13 (the Pharisees serve God inappropriately).

64

Wrongdoing and Suffering, Trust and Mistrust

ical Jesus and the religious authorities. They are also a warning to Matthew's own community: at your peril do you fail in trust in God and in Jesus, or in trustworthiness toward your fellow human beings.[70]

Our reading of Genesis 2–3, however, suggests another perspective on this passage. Israel, in both Jesus's day and Matthew's, was suffering under Roman rule (though there had been political changes in the interim). Freedom to practice the law could have been limited or abolished by the Roman administration at any time. Any activity, from prophecy to armed uprising, that could have been interpreted by Rome as seditious had the capacity to provoke a brutal response. In this situation, no prudent or caring religious leader would have been likely to endorse anyone in danger of attracting negative attention from the Roman authorities. If the religious authorities in the gospel are hostile to prophets, wise men, scribes, the righteous, or "the one who comes in the name of the Lord" (Matt 23:34–35, 39), their response can be heard as rooted in Israel's suffering and their care for their people. If they do focus on keeping the rituals of the law rather than what Matthew identifies as justice, mercy, and trust (23:23), it may be because they seek to preserve the identity of their people through shared ritual at a time when thinking on a larger and more idealistic scale about what Israel owes to God seems out of reach. Even Matthew's claim that the scribes and Pharisees inappropriately seek their own honor (23:2–7) may emerge from a context in which they believe that their people need to see that their own leadership is still in place and they are not wholly at the mercy of the Roman administration. No doubt Matthew himself is not inviting his listeners to sympathize with the scribes and Pharisees in the agonizingly difficult and dangerous circumstances of Jesus's time or his own, but we cannot rule out that his listeners recognized the difficulty of the Jewish authorities' situation, and how difficult it would have been for them to risk trusting in such an unexpected kind of messiah. Many of Matthew's listeners probably had similar experiences of Roman rule. Whether they did or not, it is open to us to see in the apparent *apistia* of Matthew's religious authorities not a simple case

---

70. The scribes and Pharisees have likely inherited their practice, so to the extent that it is (in Matthew's view) misdirected, their sin can be seen as inherited rather than as their own initiative. This is true even if Matthew's larger point is that the authorities should have recognized Jesus as the Messiah, because here he is not only criticizing them for that but also for their understanding and keeping of the law. Acts continues the challenge, particularly to "Jews," to repent and *pisteuein*, but postresurrection repentance is focused on past failures to recognize Jesus's identity and mission (e.g., Acts 2:22–40; 3:11–26; 7:51–53; 9:4). Outside Jerusalem, the call to trust is sometimes offered as an opportunity rather than a call to repentance (e.g., 8:37–38; 13:16–39) but 17:30 suggests (perhaps based on knowledge of Paul's Letter to the Romans) that gentiles, too, need to repent as they recognize the "unknown God" as the God of Israel.

65

CHAPTER 1

of willful wrongdoing but a response—imperfect but perhaps the best they could offer in the circumstances—to Israel's suffering.

At Matt 6:24–34 and Luke 12:21–34, Jesus tells his followers not to worry about their life and calls them *oligopistoi*, people of little trust, if they do (Matt 6:30 // Luke 12:28). As in Jesus's attack on the scribes and Pharisees in Matthew, this looks initially like criticism of a willful failure of trust. Many of Jesus's audience, however, will have lived in a precarious economy in which the one bad harvest, one poor year for fish, one serious illness in a family, one epidemic or plague of vermin, could make the difference between survival and destitution or death.[71] If people worried about their life, it was often because life was precarious and suffering endemic, and both Jesus and the evangelists would have known this as well as their audiences. When the evangelists put exhortations to trust in Jesus's mouth, therefore, they surely do so not taking the failure of appropriate trust to be necessarily a form of willful wrongdoing but recognizing that it must sometimes be an almost inevitable and understandable consequence of suffering, which Jesus addresses not simply by castigating his followers but by offering them reassurance and a different vision for their life.

Jesus's warnings about the sin of *apistia* in Matthew are not directed only at the Jewish authorities. No one in Matthew (or any other gospel) fails in trust more often or more variously than Jesus's own disciples. In Matt 18:6, as we have seen, Jesus warns them against untrustworthiness both toward God and toward those who trust in Jesus: "If any of you put a stumbling-block before one of these little ones who trust in me, it would be better for you if a great millstone were fastened around your neck and you were drowned in the depth of the sea."[72] In Luke 18:9–14, Jesus tells the disciples a parable unique to this gospel "to some who trusted in themselves that they were righteous and regarded others with contempt" (18:9). A Pharisee, who trusts his own judgment of how to serve God, is found to be less righteous than a wrongdoer who beats his breast and prays for mercy, and followers of Jesus must make sure that they are not like the Pharisee.[73] Not only are the disciples at risk of *apistia*, however, they are also vulnerable like "little ones" themselves. In all three Synoptic Gospels in his prophecies of the end

71. Though Kimberley Bowes, ed., *The Roman Peasant Project 2009–2014: Excavating the Roman Poor* (Philadelphia: University of Pennsylvania Press, 2020) warns against assuming that all peasants are uniformly and extremely vulnerable to human and natural disasters.

72. Matt 18:6 // Mark 9:42, though there *eis eme* is probably an interpolation.

73. Matt 18:6 is part of a discourse addressed to the disciples and there is no sign that others are present. Luke 18:9–14 is one of a series of stories and sayings addressed to the disciples from 17:22, and there is no indication of a change of addressee at 18:9.

Wrongdoing and Suffering, Trust and Mistrust

time, Jesus warns the disciples (or some of them) that when that time comes, they and others will risk being led astray by false messiahs (Matt 24:4–5 // Mark 13:4–6 // Luke 21:8–9).

In practice, the disciples' failures of trust tend to be failures of fear or doubt, weakness, or lack of self-confidence rather than arrogance or injustice. They betray *apistia* or *oligopistia* when they panic during a storm at sea (Matt 8:26 // Mark 4:40 // Luke 8:25), fail to walk on water (Matt 14:30–31), cannot heal as Jesus does (Matt 17:20; cf. Matt 17:17 // Mark 9:19 // Luke 9:41), or cannot believe that he has risen (Luke 24:11; cf. Luke 24:41; John 20:25). No ordinary human being, however well-intentioned or committed to Jesus, trusts perfectly.

At the same time, there is no sign in these narratives that if those who have put their trust in Jesus are trying to trust and be faithful, their periodic failures cause the failure of the relationship as a whole.[74] When the disciples fail to cure a boy with a demon, for example (Matt 17:14–18 // Mark 9:16–27 // Luke 9:38–42), Jesus says, "You faithless [*apistos*] and perverse generation, how much longer must I be with you?" (Matt 17:17 // Luke 9:41; cf. Mark 9:19). But then he heals the boy, and the disciples go on following him, so his question sounds like an expression of exasperation rather than condemnation. In Mark's version of the same story, the boy's father, who both *expresses pistis* and asks for help with his *apistia*, receives help just as others do who are praised for their *pistis* (Mark 9:24). The text offers no comment on the man's unusual words, but Mark may intend his audience to infer that *pistis* that asks for help, even though it knows it is imperfect, is given it. In Luke's account of the resurrection, the disciples do not believe the women who first report that Jesus has been raised from the dead (Luke 24:11), and when they see him themselves, they are *apistos* with joy (24:41), but they are not criticized for their *apistia*.[75] In John's Gospel, Jesus does occasionally criticize followers who have trusted in him or (in the case of Nicodemus at John 3:12) have perhaps shown the capacity for trust but not become followers. "Do you not believe [or "trust"] that I am in the Father and the Father is in me?" Jesus asks Philip (14:10) when Philip asks to be shown the Father.[76] But after the resurrection, Thomas's insistence "Unless I see the mark of the nails in his hands . . . I will not believe" (20:25) is met by the command, "Become not untrusting, but trusting" (20:27)

---

74. Except, we assume, in the case of Judas; see below, pp. 69–70.

75. This is the only time anyone is said to be, paradoxically, *apistos* with joy. Perhaps Luke is conveying that they could hardly believe their eyes; cf. the long ending of Mark 16:11, 14, 16.

76. Elements of both belief and trust may be involved here, since *pisteuein* is part of the disciples' commitment to Jesus as well as their knowledge of him (cf. John 14:9).

CHAPTER 1

together with the affirmation, "Blessed are those who have not seen and yet have come to believe [or "trust"]" (20:29).[77] Thomas's failure to trust is not ideal, but it is also not a deal-breaker.

In all these stories, people who ought to trust in Jesus, have trusted in him, or want to do so all trust imperfectly or fail altogether at some critical moment. Often within the story, their failure is understandable. They live in times when it is natural and reasonable for the poor to worry about their life and for community leaders to worry about their political overlords. Ordinary people cannot walk on water or expel demons. The news that Jesus has been raised from the dead is beyond extraordinary; anyone might fail to believe it, especially (men of the first century might think) when it is reported by women. Failure to trust in God can stem from arrogance or hostility to God or too much trust in oneself, but it can also stem from lack of self-confidence, vulnerability to corruption, or suffering. Nowhere, however, is there any sign that Jesus rejects those who want to trust but fail.[78] If they want to trust, or have trusted, and want to remain in their relationship with Jesus, they can and do. In this, Jesus's followers are a microcosm of Israel with its checkered post-Abrahamic history of trust and failure to trust in God for diverse reasons. They are also a preview of those who put their trust in Jesus after the resurrection and Pentecost, who, as early (and later) Christian writings abundantly attest, will struggle as much as the disciples to keep the *pistis* they confess.

Within the gospels, Matthew 18 offers a hint that, even after Pentecost, imperfect trust and failures of trust may not be deal-breakers. Matthew is the evangelist who stresses most often that those who reject Jesus are destined for the "outer darkness" (e.g., 22:13) or "furnace of fire" (13:42, 50), but even he hints that, until the Son of Man returns, those who have trusted and then failed may be restored to the community. When Jesus describes how community members should solve their problems (Matt 18:15–20), he concludes that when all avenues of reconciliation have failed, the transgressing member should be excommunicated and treated "as a gentile and a tax collector" (18:17).[79] Gentiles and tax collectors are paradigmatic outsiders, but they are also among those with whom Matthew's Jesus associates

77. On this translation of 20:27, see Morgan, *Theology of Trust*, 106–7. At 20:29 both belief and trust are involved, since Thomas has just come both to believe that Jesus has indeed risen and to affirm him as Lord and God (20:28).

78. *Apistia* therefore refers either to absolute nontrust or inadequate trust within a relationship with Jesus, and this complexity is what Matthew seeks to clarify by sometimes referring to the disciples' *oligopistia*.

79. On parallels to 18:17 in synagogue regulations and parallels to the passage as a whole in 1QS V, 24–VI, 1; CD IX, 28, as well as early Christian parallels, see Ulrich Luz, *A Commentary on Matthew* (3 vols.; Minneapolis: Fortress, 2001–2007), 2:453.

Wrongdoing and Suffering, Trust and Mistrust

(8:5–7; 9:11–13; 15:21–28), to whom he preaches (9:10), whose *pistis* he praises (8:10; 15:28), and who become his disciples (9:9). If gentiles and tax collectors can put their trust in Jesus and become followers in Matthew's Gospel, then 18:17 suggests that the door remains open even for those who have been expelled to return to the community.[80]

Among human beings in the gospels, Jesus is the paradigm of trust in God. Even he, however, can be shown as wavering in trust in response to suffering. In Gethsemane, Jesus prays for release from his imminent suffering: "but not what I want, but what you want" (Matt 26:39 // Mark 14:36 // Luke 22:42).[81] There is no *pistis* language in this scene, but elsewhere obedience to God's will is a mark of trust and faithfulness, so the fact that it is necessary for Jesus to affirm his obedience here suggests that his trust has come under attack.[82] At this point in the gospels, Jesus's prayer in Gethsemane is, for many, shocking, and some commentators see it as reflecting a memory of the trauma of that night. Whether or not this is the case, it is significant that it appears in all three Synoptic Gospels. Jesus's affirmation of his obedience indicates that even if his trust in God has wavered, it has not failed, but perhaps it also hints that he does not have complete trust in himself to will what God wills. If so, he responds by reaffirming his obedience. "Not what I want" suggests that just as it is God's will that he is serving, it is by God's will, not his own, that he will remain faithful. At this moment we can see Jesus, as the human paradigm of trust and faithfulness, also offering an exemplary response for times when trust comes under attack or fails. At his moment of greatest temptation and greatest risk, he replaces any trust in himself or his power with trust and obedience to God.

All four gospels, however, also accept that people can fail in trust in a way that breaks their relationship with Jesus once for all. We can assume that Judas, as a disciple, at one time was in a relationship of trust with Jesus (or thought he was, or was believed to be). When Jesus, in the Synoptic Gospels, foretells his betrayal, he says of him, "Woe to that one by whom the Son of Man is betrayed. It would have been better for that one not to have been born" (Matt 26:24 // Mark 14:21; cf. Luke 22:22). Even the sin of Judas, however, is treated with unexpected complexity, in different ways, by different writers. John 12:4–6 shows him protesting at the anointing of Jesus with expensive oil that could have been sold to feed the poor.

---

80. This is compatible with Matt 16:19; 18:18 if we assume that the disciples have the authority not only to expel wrongdoers but to readmit the penitent into the community.

81. Cf. John 12:27, indicating that John knew of this tradition and shows Jesus not asking for relief.

82. Possibly by the devil, since this scene distantly echoes the temptations in the desert.

69

CHAPTER 1

John glosses his protest as hypocritical—Judas held the communal purse and stole from it (12:6)—but he does not make Jesus rebuke Judas directly: Jesus only tells Judas to let the woman do what she wants (12:7). The fact that John feels the need to gloss what Judas says suggests that it may have occurred to him, as it occurs to many modern readers, that, on the face of it, Judas's words were not unreasonable. Matthew, Luke, and John (Matt 26:23–25; 27:9–10; Luke 22:21–22; John 13:18; 17:12) all make Jesus affirm that Judas's betrayal is necessary and foretold by the scriptures, a saying that led some later commentators to the view that Judas could not be held wholly or individually responsible and might not even have been exercising free will (cf. especially John 13:2, 27). Matthew, meanwhile, claims that when Jesus was condemned, Judas repented, telling the chief priests and elders, "I have sinned by betraying innocent blood" (27:4). He raises the question whether Judas never expected Jesus to be convicted, and his betrayal was as much blind or misguided as willfully sinful.

Some of the most powerful depictions of people failing decisively in trust appear in prophecies and parables of the end time. Jesus foretells that there will come a time when the *pistis* of his followers is judged once for all, and on that day they must show the divine judge that they have, on balance, been *pistos*. At the end of the parable of the talents, for example, the slaves who have multiplied their talents are commended as trustworthy (Matt 25:21 // Luke 19:17; Matt 25:23). The slave who has not, and who is clearly though implicitly untrustworthy, is castigated as wicked and worthless (Matt 25:26, 30; Luke 19:22) and, in Matthew's Gospel, flung into the eschatological outer darkness where there are weeping and gnashing of teeth (Matt 25:30).[83] Like the betrayal of Judas, however, this story is not as straightforward as it might seem, and it is significant that many modern readers feel that the slave with the one talent has been treated unfairly. Perhaps he did not know what to do for the best or did know but was afraid to do it: he says that his master has a reputation as a hard man. Perhaps he did not trust himself to succeed. Perhaps he did not think that the master had entrusted him with enough to invest to make any significant or reliable return. (One talent is far from a negligible sum, but five talents would be much better.) Being entrusted with anything is demanding, and we can imagine that the failure of the slave might be due to inexperience, timidity, or bad experiences of his master in the past. Though Matthew and Luke tell this parable to urge the faithful to remain

---

83. See further pp. 209–10. Luke's Jesus warns that the "master . . . will come on a day when [his slave] will not expect him and at an hour that he does not know" (12:46). He will punish the servant whom he finds has not been faithful and prudent (12:42), and will "put him with the *apistoi*" (12:46).

70

faithful until the master's return, to modern and, quite possibly, first-century ears, it is also a reminder that even the most catastrophic failures of trust may have a backstory.[84] A failure of trust often emerges from a complex environment in which trust is subject to temptation, suffering, and self-doubt and may already have been undermined even by the person who is apparently offering trust.

All the gospels emphasize the importance of trust, not least because they are, in part, teaching texts that aim to fortify community members and keep them faithful. They all also look forward to a day when the faithful are encouraged to believe that everyone will finally be held to account. But later developments in eschatology, from the doctrine of purgatory to Origen's hope that, ultimately, all human beings will be reunited with God, testify to what the gospels already recognize: trust is complicated, demanding, and insecure, often for understandable reasons, and until the end time it is likely to remain so.[85]

WRONGDOING, SUFFERING, AND *APISTIA*
IN THE LETTER TO THE ROMANS

Paul has more to say about wrongdoing than most New Testament writers, and more to say on the subject in Romans than in any other letter. Romans is also the letter in which he speaks of *apistia* and *apistein* in connection with both wrongdoing and suffering, and one (together with Galatians and Philippians) in which he speaks of right standing between God and humanity as restored through *pistis*. Chapter 3 develops a model of how at-one-ment between God and humanity is offered through the *pistis* of Christ, drawing especially on Paul's Letter to the Romans. As a preliminary, it is worth saying something here about Romans' representation of wrongdoing, suffering, and the failure of trust.

In Rom 1:17 Paul proclaims, on prophetic authority, that "the one who is righteous will live by *pistis*" (cf. Hab 2:4). The possibility for life-giving *pistis* is mediated by the gospel, "the power of God for salvation to everyone who *pisteuein*" (Rom 1:16). The gospel reveals the righteousness of God "from *pistis* to *pistis*." I have

---

84. Some patristic commentators suggest that the servant who was given one talent was less able than the rest, though they do not absolve him of having done the wrong thing with it. Origen, *Commentary on Matthew* 67 goes further, describing this servant as typical of many of the faithful, who do fear God but waste their energies, so that, without being blameworthy, they end up with little to show for their activity. Such people, he says, interestingly, often see God as harsh and implacable. Without wanting to seem to contradict Matthew, he evidently has some sympathy for them.

85. E.g., Origen, *On First Principles* 2.11.5, 7; 2.11.6–7.

CHAPTER 1

argued elsewhere that this refers in part to the trust and trustworthiness of God, which is answered by human trust and faithfulness.[86]

Next Paul says that the wrath of God is being revealed against the impiety (*asebeia*) and unrighteousness (*adikia*) of those who "by their wickedness suppress the truth" (Rom 1:18). These are gentiles, who should always have glorified and been grateful to God (1:21) because God has always made "what can be known about God"—including perhaps *pistis* (cf. 1.16)—known to everyone in the created world (1:19–20). The gentiles, however, became empty in reasoning (1:21); in their supposed wisdom they became fools (1:22) and exchanged worship of God for worship of created beings (i.e., idols; 1:23). The gentiles' failure to acknowledge God has led to every form of vice from gossip to murder (1:24–31).[87] Paul claims that they know that those who practice such things deserve death, but they not only continue to practice them but endorse them in others (1:32), causing yet more wrongdoing.

Paul's tenses in this passage deserve some attention. What can be known about God's justice is (or should be) plain to gentiles in the present (1:19), and they know God's decree, though they do not follow it (1:32). The causes, however, are in the past, when gentiles did not honor God, their hearts were darkened, and they became fools (1:21–22).[88] Paul evidently thinks that contemporary gentiles are wrongdoers, but they may be wrongdoers by inheritance, who do not actively do wrong themselves or who are stuck in their wrongdoing despite themselves (not unlike the well-intentioned but conflicted character in Rom 7:15–20, who, Paul says, does not act himself, but is acted on by sin).[89]

---

86. Morgan, *Roman Faith*, 286–87.

87. These wrongdoings are enacted mainly on the human level, but verse 30 includes "God-haters" (*theostygēs*) followed by the "hybristic" and "arrogant" (*hybristēs, hyperēphanos*) who are also associated, in the New Testament and in gentile discourse with arrogance and self-will toward the divine. In classical Greek, *theostygēs* means "hated by the gods," but commentators agree that it must be active here, as the Vulgate takes it to be.

88. Susan Grove Eastman, "The 'Empire of Illusion': Sin, Evil, and Good News in Romans," in *Oneself in Another: Participation and Personhood in Pauline Theology* (Eugene: Wipf & Stock, 2023), 162–63 points out the importance of the connection between "distorted perception, falsehood, and violence" in this passage, but that it does not make clear where final responsibility for evil rests. She suggests that attributing evil to human beings is socially and theologically unsatisfactory, because it tends to justify further violence in the name of eradicating evil, and therefore Paul's other model, that sin is something human beings suffer under and from which they have to be liberated, makes an essential contribution to both our as well as his understanding of how evil may be overcome.

89. In light of our reading of Genesis 3 and 4, we might consider the possibility that the gentiles turned from God because they felt rejected by God, though Paul does not say so.

Wrongdoing and Suffering, Trust and Mistrust

Another striking aspect of this passage is that most of the vices Paul lists at 1:26–27 and 1:29–31 are things to which gentiles are "given over" by God. Whether we understand these activities as punishments actively inflicted by God, or whether, more neutrally, God "surrenders" gentiles to them (another possible meaning of *paradidonai*), these are consequences of gentiles' original wrongdoing, not new or willful sins. Wrongdoing, for gentiles as, later, for Jews, can be something not intended or even accidental but imposed upon one as a penalty. Yet another notable aspect of this passage is that most of the vices listed are also forms of suffering. Communities marked by greed, malice, murder, treachery, insolence, untrustworthiness, ruthlessness, intrafamilial strife, and impiety were seen by Jews and gentiles of the first century, as by us, as difficult and dangerous places to live. The gentiles' present situation may therefore be the result of sin, but it is also a state of punishment and marked by suffering, and while they need forgiveness of their wrongdoings, they just as urgently—like Israel, many times in the past as well as the present—need release from their sufferings. Paul underlines this point again in Romans 5, when he affirms that gentiles and Jews alike are wrongdoers because sin came into the world through Adam and death through sin (5:12). All Adam's descendants, with or without the law, are both wrongdoers by inheritance—even if they did not "sin in the likeness of Adam"—and suffer death because of Adam.

If Jews think they are in a position to condemn gentiles (2:1), however, they are mistaken. They are judged by their own standard and found wanting (2:3). They are stubborn (2:5) and disobedient (2:8). They (or at least some of them) claim to know the will of God and understand what is important (2:18; cf. 2:20), but in practice they constantly break the law (2:21–25) or fail to observe it in a proper spirit (2:29).[90] Those who have constituted themselves "a guide to the blind, a light to those who are in darkness" (2:19), and teachers of the foolish and simple (2:20), have, Paul implies, led others astray too. We may note that these types of sin are not necessarily equal. Those who think they know what is important may be sincere but mistaken, like Paul himself before his call, while those who are led astray by blind guides are presumably sinful by association rather than intention. Well-intentioned but misguided zeal continues to be a risk for Christ-confessors, as Paul makes clear at Rom 14:13 when he tells the Romans not to "put a stumbling-block or hindrance in the way of a brother or sister" who, for instance, thinks differently from themselves about food laws.

At 3:3 Paul describes the failing of "Jews" collectively before as well as after the Christ event as *apistia*, lack of trust or faithfulness toward God, and by implication

---

90. *Bdelussomai* (Rom 2:22), usually refers to idolatry (cf. Isa 2:8, 20 LXX; Dan 11:31 LXX; Wis 14:11; Rev 21:8), but here probably refers to something less extreme.

CHAPTER 1

perhaps a surfeit of trust in themselves, though he does not speak of them individually, since he says, "what if some were unfaithful?" He returns to this idea in Romans 9–11, where he says that some of the branches of Israel have been "broken off because of their *apistia* (τῇ ἀπιστίᾳ ἐξεκλάσθησαν, 11:20)." Paul makes explicit here what is only implied in chapter 2, that Israel collectively is less willfully sinful than misguided. She has genuine "zeal for God" (10:2) and does "strive for the law of righteousness" (9:31), but has sought to establish her own righteousness rather than recognize that righteousness has always comes from God by *pistis* (9:32) and now comes through Christ and trust in Christ (10:4, 8–11; cf. 10:14, 17).[91] In addition, when Paul speaks of some branches of Israel as having been broken off, he hints that *apistia* brings not only alienation but also suffering. A branch that has been torn off its tree is dead wood. For the people of Israel, whether they have been actively *apistos* toward God or are simply associated with those who have been, to be alienated from God is the definition of pain and grief, so the situation of Israel now is not only one of wrongdoing but also one of suffering that seeks relief.[92]

God, however, has not rejected God's people (11:2) and uses even their "stumbling" for good (11:11–12). All will eventually receive mercy (11:32). By keeping in play both the idea that Israel has done wrong and the idea that she has been well intentioned but misguided, Paul captures something of what must have been the complex mindset of many Christ-confessing Jews, for whom the "failure" of other Jews to confess Christ must have been understandable on some level, even as they believed it was wrong.

The idea that preferring one's own judgment and self-trust to trust in God may constitute either wrongdoing or misguidedness, and may also be a cause of suffering, appears in other letters too. At 1 Cor 1:18–23, Paul proclaims that God will destroy the wisdom of those who think they are wise (1:19, cf. 1:18) and reveal it for the foolishness it is (1:20).[93] It is trust in God and Christ, not human wisdom, that saves (1:21).[94] "Jews demand signs and Greeks desire wisdom, but we proclaim Christ crucified, a stumbling-block to Jews and foolishness to gentiles" (1:22–23).

---

91. *Apistia* here is collective, but since Paul assumes that people can choose whether or not to trust, he probably sees individuals as having responsibility too.

92. We may also wonder why Jews have failed in trust. Does Paul's attack on those who trust their own judgment about the law hint at some loss of confidence in God at a time of political upheavals and increasing oppression?

93. Paul cannot be using *mōria* here in the sense of something wicked but in the sense that the message of the cross is paradoxical, which makes it more possible that he does not use *mōros* in the sense of willfully wicked foolishness in Romans.

94. The focus here is on both God and Christ as the power and wisdom of God (1 Cor 1:24), so trust in both may be implied.

74

Wrongdoing and Suffering, Trust and Mistrust

Here, as in Romans 11, Paul's imagery hints at more than his immediate point. When some people stumble over the stumbling-block of the cross, their stumble suggests not only their wrongdoing but also the height of the bar of trust to be cleared and the pain of stumbling over it.

Paul (except when talking about himself) does not make a major theme of the idea that *apistia* might be an honest mistake or not a person's own fault, not least because he evidently wants community members to take responsibility for what they think and do and continue to trust in God and Christ. But we can already see indications that he recognizes, within a group that is collectively capable of wrong, different kinds and degrees of wrongdoing and responsibility. This recognition resonates with our own experience that wrongdoing comes in many forms and degrees, and also that all kinds of wrongdoing can damage trust. Sometimes, foolishness, inherited bad behaviors, misplaced trust, and misplaced good intentions can be as damaging to relationships of trust as willful wrongdoing.

For Paul, as we have noted, God's people are still God's people and always will be (cf. Rom 11:1), and Jews and gentiles have arrived at their present condition by different routes. Even so, they have much in common. Instead of recognizing the *pistis* of God and answering it with their own, both groups, collectively if not necessarily individually, have preferred to rely on their own wisdom (1:22) or knowledge (2:20) and to judge for themselves whom or how they should worship.[95] As a result they (or some of them) have failed in trust in various damaging ways. Because of their collective wrongdoing, they are collectively suffering, and both their wrongdoing and suffering need to be addressed.

We saw above that reminding ourselves of the acutely difficult political and social situation in which the scribes and Pharisees of Israel found themselves, in both Jesus's and the evangelists' day, allows us to hear what Matthew's Jesus, for instance, calls the religious authorities' failures of justice, mercy, and trust as, at least in part, responses to Israel's suffering. We can hear similar tensions underlying Paul's letters. When, for example, in 1 Cor 1:22 Paul says that "the Jews demand signs," he suggests that they want to trust in God, but by asking God to send what they can trust themselves to recognize as a sign, rather than simply trusting God to reveal to them what God chooses at the time God chooses (1:21), they fail to recognize Christ and the proclamation of Christ crucified (cf. 1:23) as trustworthy. But in a political context in which all the subjects of the Roman Empire were always at risk of harsher exploitation, the retraction of what freedoms and privileges they

---

95. To put it another way, they have practiced inappropriate self-trust, relying on their ability to assess who is God and how to worship God, rather than trusting God to communicate what God requires.

75

CHAPTER 1

had, or brutal suppression, and in which there were, in some quarters, aspirations to resistance, hopes for salvation, or rumors of rebellion, many must have been looking for signs of divine activity. It must have been a matter of urgent concern and much anxiety whether a sign had really been seen, or what constituted a trustworthy sign, or how to interpret alleged signs. Inevitably, individuals and groups must have felt they had to exercise and trust their judgment in seeking and identifying signs. In such an environment, both sign seeking and, as Paul sees it, the misunderstanding of signs, are themselves powerful signs of people's suffering.

Similarly, as we saw above, when the Galatians trust other apostles and allow themselves to be persuaded to keep the law, Paul implies that they have been stupid if not culpable. We can go further and acknowledge what Paul does not: how risky it was for the Galatians to put their trust in the new proclamation about Jesus Christ in the first place, and how worrying it must have been when different apostles of Christ passed through Galatia with different teachings. The Galatians' desertion of Paul's teaching, as he sees it, may be caused by understandable doubt and anxiety in an uncertain situation. Nor should we assume that Paul's early audiences would not have thought of this. They knew from daily experience that in a complicated and conflicted world it was difficult to know where, among humans or gods, to put one's trust. We referred at the beginning of this chapter to "bad moral luck," the idea that a person may sometimes find herself in a situation in which it is impossible to make a morally good decision. If the situations of the Corinthians and Galatians were not impossible, they were certainly insecure and potentially stressful, and under that kind of pressure it is easy to make what to those like Paul, who possess an extremely strong sense of religious direction, look like bad decisions.[96]

The Power of Evil

Throughout this chapter we have focused on forms of human wrongdoing and the interrelation of wrongdoing and suffering, but since we have finished with Romans, and Romans will be our starting point in chapter 3, we should say a little more about a topic of long-standing concern to interpreters, particularly in relation to this letter. Is Paul's thinking dominated by the idea that human beings

96. We do not know how the Galatians received Paul's letter, but the existence of (at least) two Corinthian letters suggests that some communities were capable of taking Paul's advice under their own advisement and not necessarily accepting his judgment of their behavior.

Wrongdoing and Suffering, Trust and Mistrust

are guilty of disobedience to God and stand in need, above all, of forgiveness, or by the idea that sin is a diabolical metaphysical power under which human beings languish until they are released by God's action through Christ?[97] We cannot do justice to the complexity of this debate here, but we can make some observations that are relevant to our theme of the relationship between sin and suffering.

We have noted that the Hebrew Bible and Second Temple writings preserve several strands of tradition about sin and evil. Most (though not all) are dominated by the assumption of human moral responsibility, but the Dead Sea Scrolls introduce the possibility that human beings are corrupted and led astray by metaphysical powers hostile to God.[98] Martinus de Boer has shown that broadly the same categories influence Paul, particularly in Romans.[99] Both Jews and gentiles are capable of doing wrong for which they are morally responsible—though, as we have seen, not every member of each group may be personally responsible, and some wrongdoings are consequences of others or even punishments for others. Paul can also speak of sin as a power by which people can be led astray (e.g., Rom 7:8, 11), "under" the power of which they can be trapped (e.g., Rom 3:9; cf. 6:12), to which they can be enslaved (e.g., Rom 6:6, 17; 7:14), and which leads to death (e.g., Rom 5:12; 7:11; 8:10). (This points not only to the power of sin over people, but also to their suffering when they are "under" it.[100]) Paul can also speak of Satan or Beliar, the evil power that opposes God (Rom 16:20; cf. 1 Cor 5:5; 2 Cor 6:15) and seeks to lead human beings astray, thwart their good purposes, and destroy them (1 Cor 7:5; 2 Cor 2:11; 11:14; 12:7; 1 Thess 2:18). Those who succumb to Satan or sin count as wrongdoers, but they are less than willfully disobedient toward

97. The issues are discussed by Simon Gathercole, "'Sins' in Paul," *New Testament Studies* 64 (2018): 143–61, with a survey of recent scholarship. Gathercole argues, surely rightly, that though both themes are present in Paul, we should not underestimate the importance for him of forgiveness of sins. Nor, though, should we neglect the different shades of sin in play, or the possibility that people are also released from suffering by the Christ event.

98. Pp. 38–39.

99. Martinus C. de Boer, "Paul and Jewish Apocalyptic Eschatology," in *Apocalyptic and the New Testament: Essays in Honor of J. Louis Martyn* (ed. Joel Marcus and Martin L. Soards; Sheffield: JSOT Press, 1989), 169–90.

100. On being released from the power of sin, see Rom 6:7; cf. 3:9; 5:21; 6:6, 9, with Beverly Roberts Gaventa, "The Cosmic Power of Sin in Paul's Letter to the Romans: Toward a Widescreen Edition," *Int* 58 (2004): 229–40, though I am not convinced that we need to see sin as a metaphysical power. Taking sin not as a metaphysical power but nevertheless as a force that people can experience as personal and that can enslave people in devastatingly destructive ways is Matthew Croasmun, *The Emergence of Sin: The Cosmic Tyrant in Romans* (New York: Oxford University Press, 2017).

CHAPTER 1

God. In 1 Cor 7:5, for example, Paul refers to the danger of succumbing to Satan through lack of self-control rather than ill will.[101] Similarly, those who are under sin may be less than willful wrongdoers. If, for instance, as at Rom 7:7–8, one is a well-intentioned, law-abiding Jew who would not have known the meaning of covetousness if the law had not forbidden it and "produced in me every kind of covetousness," one is surely something less than willfully disobedient to God.

This leads to a further observation about both Satan and sin. Paul's Satan occasionally seems to be God's tester or executioner, following two early strands of tradition (1 Cor 5:5; 2 Cor 12:7).[102] Occasionally Paul refers to the idea of cosmic war between God and Christ and other powers, who we assume include Satan, though he is only once mentioned by name (Rom 16:20; cf. 1 Cor 15:24–28; possibly Rom 8:38–39).[103] More often Satan (by whatever name) appears in the undisputed Pauline letters as a force that can be resisted by community members who are "guileless in what is evil" (Rom 16:19), behave appropriately to their spouses (1 Cor 7:5), do not "yoke" themselves with *apistoi* (2 Cor 6:15), and generally remain on their guard against wrongdoing (2 Cor 2:11; 11:13–14; cf. Rom 12:9; 1 Cor 5:13; 1 Thess 5:22).[104] Strikingly, in the passages in which Paul writes in most detail of the situation of people before they are liberated by Christ and Christ-confession, he does not invoke Satan but instead human beings' own attitudes and practices and God's response (e.g., Rom 1:18–2:11; 3:10–18; 7:7–20; Gal 1:13–16). Satan here is less a terrifying cosmic power than a personification of the kind of mindsets and behaviors that Paul wants community members to avoid. In this, Paul's representation of Satan is notably different from his representation of God or of the exalted Christ, who, even as Paul can say that "The Lord is the Spirit" (2 Cor 3:17) and that "Christ lives in me" (Gal 2:20), is also always a heavenly person with whom Paul has a relationship.[105]

101. One can also be thwarted by Satan without counting as a wrongdoer: Paul does not regard himself as sinful for being prevented by Satan from visiting the Thessalonians at 1 Thess 2:18.

102. On the history of the Satan and the relationship between evil and devil, see especially Ryan E. Stokes, *The Satan: How God's Executioner Became the Enemy* (Grand Rapids: Eerdmans, 2019), and Ida Fröhlich and Erkki Koskenniemi, eds., *Evil and the Devil* (London: T&T Clark, 2013).

103. Gal 1:4 probably refers to the this-worldly evils of the present time, in contrast with the time to come, which is in line with usage in Jewish apocalyptic, as noted by H. D. Betz, *Galatians: A Commentary on Paul's Letter to the Churches in Galatia* (Philadelphia: Fortress, 1979), 41–42.

104. On *apistoi* as "outsiders" by definition rather than a group with significant features of their own, see Tobias Wieczorek, *Die Nichtgläubigen—Hoi Apistoi: Über die Funktion abgrenzende Sprache bei Paulus* (Göttingen: Vandenhoeck & Ruprecht, 2021).

105. Teresa Morgan, *Being "in Christ" in the Letters of Paul: Saved through Christ and in His Hands* (Tübingen: Mohr Siebeck, 2020), 162–74.

Wrongdoing and Suffering, Trust and Mistrust

Similarly, Paul's references to sin as a power speak to the real power that the state of sinfulness has over people's sense of themselves and their circumstances, their ability to hope or envision a different future, their ability to put their trust in the right places, and their ability to change. It highlights the suffering of those who are "under" sin as well as their wrongdoing. But this picture, especially in Romans 5–8, remains—as it was usually taken to be before the "apocalyptic turn" in Pauline studies—less than a picture of an independent cosmic power. Sin enters the world through human disobedience (Rom 5:12). Even after Adam sin, though in the world, is not "reckoned" when there is no law (5:13; cf. 7:8): it exists in principle but cannot generate a sphere of operation for itself. Paul, moreover, can speak not only of sin as enslaving human beings and reigning over them but also of death doing the same (5:14, 17). Our desires, meanwhile, can rule us (7:15–20) and the mind that is "set on the flesh" can be hostile to God (8:7; cf. 8:12–13). Alternatively, we can be slaves to obedience and righteousness (6:6, 16, 19) and ruled by grace (5:21). To make his account of righteousing by Christ and the new and transformed life to which it leads as vivid and compelling as possible, in Romans 5–8 Paul personifies a wide range of good and bad attitudes, actions, and states that human beings experience as acting on us even as we experience and enact them, but there is no indication that he regards all these as metaphysical powers, and while sin is a central actor in this drama, it does not need to be seen as an independent metaphysical entity any more than the rest.[106] We saw in the introduction (in the context of trust and mistrust, but it applies to other attitudes and practices too) that psychologists and sociologists now recognize the power of our mindset over our lives and relationships, social configurations, hopes, and ability to change. Paul did not have access to Pierre Bourdieu's concept of *habitus* (though it has been pointed out that the idea goes back, in some form, at least to Aristotle), but he would have appreciated its understanding that people both shape themselves and their environment and are shaped by their environment, often to the point that they cannot easily change a damaging and hated situation or set of attitudes and behaviors.[107] Paul had no

---

106. The debate is well discussed notably in the essays in Beverly Roberts Gaventa, ed., *Apocalyptic Paul: Cosmos and Anthropos in Romans 5–8* (Waco: Baylor University Press, 2013). But one does not have to disagree with Martinus C. de Boer, for instance, in "Paul's Mythologizing Program in Romans 5–8," in *Apocalyptic Paul*, 1–20 that Paul often writes mythologically, not to think that he is doing so with reference to sin in these chapters. Arguing that Paul accepts that a cosmic battle between God, Christ, and hostile powers is ongoing until the end time, but that he is less interested in it than in the human plane and the situation, including the mental, emotional, and moral condition, of community members, see Morgan, *Being "in Christ"*, 165–68.

107. For the use of Bourdieusian *habitus* to emphasize the centrality of relationality to trust, and relational trust as key both to interpreting experience and to seeing potential in the future,

CHAPTER 1

reason to foster a dispute with those in his day who thought in terms of a personal metaphysical power hostile to God, and he uses the idea protreptically to urge his communities to tackle their wrongdoings and fragilities in faith like people going into battle or beating off a hostile power. But in the passages where he reflects on it most extensively, the power of sin over humanity is less the power of a metaphysical enemy of God than the terrible power we have to imprison ourselves and each other in depths of despair and self-destruction. In the next chapter we will see how, in contemporary situations of conflict and conflict resolution, trauma and abuse and their survival, and the social (re)integration of ex-offenders and those at risk of offending, the offer of trust and response of trust can become the first steps on a pathway to reconciliation and renewal. In chapter 3, we will explore how the restoration of trust between God and humanity through Christ makes possible our release from the prisons we construct for ourselves and those we construct for one another.[108]

---

see Morten Frederiksen, "Relational Trust: Outline of a Bourdieusian Theory of Interpersonal Trust," *J. Trust Res.* 4 (2014): 167–92.

108. The fact that people can be depicted as responsible for their wrongdoings raises the question whether Jews or gentiles, absent Christ, could have returned to their right relationship with God. For Paul (and all New Testament writers) the question is counterfactual and so irrelevant, but it arises, in a slightly different form, in the context of recent Two Ways models of Paul's soteriology, which have argued that, for Paul, only gentiles need to put their trust in Christ to be saved; for Jews it is enough to keep the covenant and the temple cult. Apart from the questions that this model raises—if Paul thinks that confessing Christ is for gentiles, why does he confess Christ himself? Why is there no sign that he thinks it odd that other Jews confess Christ? If at-one-ment with God is not through Christ for Jews, what were Paul and the other apostles preaching to Jews?—I am persuaded by the exegetical arguments, for instance, of Richard Bauckham and Bruce Longenecker against this view. See R. J. Bauckham, "The Parting of the Ways: What Really Happened and Why?" *Studia Theologica* 47 (1993): 135; Bruce Longenecker, "On Israel's God and God's Israel: Assessing Supersessionism in Paul," *Journal of Theological Studies* 58 (2007): 26–44. In some passages, Paul is so clear that both Jews and gentiles have sinned, that Jesus is the anointed one of Israel (including Paul himself, e.g., Gal 2:20) as well as the savior of the gentiles, and both Jews and gentiles who become Christ-confessors trust in Christ, that a Paul promoting two ways to righteousness would be at odds with himself and surely with most, if not all, other early communities. On Paul, Israel, and the gentiles see also the balanced assessments of Michael Bachmann, "Paul, Israel, and the Gentiles: Hermeneutical and Exegetical Notes," in *Crosscurrents in Pauline Exegesis and the Study of Jewish-Christian Relations* (ed. Reimund Bieringer and Didier Pollefeyt; London: Bloomsbury, 2012), 72–105 and Michael Bird, "Salvation in Paul's Judaism," 15–40 in the same volume. Gabriele Boccaccini, *Paul's Three Paths to Salvation* (Grand Rapids: Eerdmans, 2020) offers an intriguing alternative, and I appreciate his recognition that New Testament writings do not depict all human beings as sinful, but, from the perspective of this chapter, he underestimates the extent to which those who are not willfully sinful may suffer from the consequences of sin, and the extent to which even those who are not sinful, or not individually, may need saving from suffering.

80

Wrongdoing and Suffering, Trust and Mistrust

Conclusion

This chapter has argued that, for New Testament writers, human beings can fall out of trust with God and put trust in the wrong places through either wrongdoing or suffering. Both wrongdoing and suffering, moreover, are complex and everywhere interlinked. People can trust wrongly because it is their nature; because they choose to do so either willfully or through forgetfulness, foolishness, or negligence; because they allow themselves to be led astray; because they fail to foresee the potential consequences of their actions with the best of intentions; or because they do wrong in reaction to an experience of suffering or betrayal. They can suffer from the consequences of their own wrongdoing or that of others, whether they are innocent or complicit themselves.

This taxonomy pre-echoes a point made especially by liberation theologians that, in most societies, some people are more victims than perpetrators of evil, more sinned against than sinning, and less responsible than others for the nature of their society as a whole. Some may not have done wrong at all and need liberating from the consequences of others' wrongdoing but not their own. At the same time, New Testament writings see people as caught up in situations, relationships, and societies in which wrongdoing is endemic, even if they do not do wrong themselves. This reminds us that in any society, almost no one, if anyone at all, is wholly without agency and therefore wholly without responsibility for the nature of that society. Societies are highly complex networks in which everyone impinges to some degree, however limited, on others, so it is not irrational to envisage everyone as implicated, in some way, in the nature of the society as a whole.

The Christ event, for these writers, changes what is possible for all people, but there is no suggestion in New Testament writings that what God has done through Christ does not seek or need a human response. Human beings are called to put their trust in God and Christ and remain faithful until the end time. New Testament writings (with the possible exception of the few passages that speak in terms of preelection) therefore assume that the damage that wrongdoing and suffering have done to the divine-human relationship do not make it impossible for human beings to trust, given the right circumstances. Like modern theorists of trust, they recognize that trust is so fundamental to all relationships, and to our ability to function in the world, that we must, and do, trust and relearn how to trust, even when our trust has been badly damaged and scarred. When damaged people come to trust, however, they need to be able to trust where trust will be vindicated. For New Testament writers, this means trusting in the "living and true God," in Jesus Christ, and in those to whom God entrusts the gospel and other work for creation. These writings recognize, implicitly if not explicitly, that trusting in the

CHAPTER 1

right places is not straightforward. God may approach humanity through Christ with therapeutic trust, but human beings must recognize and respond to Christ. Even when a person has put their trust in the right place, remaining trusting and faithful through time is not easy. People fail in trust constantly, out of fear, doubt, and lack of understanding, but until the end time the way is always open for them to return to trust.

The diverse traditions inherited by Christians about saviors, Jewish or gentile, recognize that both wrongdoing and suffering damage divine-human relationships. Different images and accounts of saviors, divine or human, envisage the savior figure as saving people from their sins, individual or collective, the painful consequences of their sins, or the suffering caused by others. The complexity of messianic traditions in Judaism, in particular, is well recognized, but the co-existence and interconnectedness of the themes of salvation from wrongdoing and suffering in the New Testament has not influenced theories of atonement as strongly as it could and, arguably, should have. Theories of atonement, moreover, have yet to reflect on the close association of the themes of sin and suffering with the failure of trust in New Testament writings and the equally close link between salvation and the restoration of trust.

The sketches I have offered here of wrongdoing, suffering, and the many ways in which trust can struggle or fail, resonate with our own experience. The *apistia* of Jews and gentiles is the misplaced trust of the gambler who trusts her system to make her fortune, or the mistrust of the patient who refuses a life-saving treatment from his doctor because he is afraid of what it might contain. It reminds us of the person who, longing to belong, puts his trust in a community that turns out to exploit its members and later struggles to extricate himself from it. It is the failure of most people today when we neglect to trust environmentalists who point to the evidence of global warming sufficiently to reduce our individual carbon footprint. The consequences of failures of trust of all kinds are far-reaching. They put us in toxic relationships. They make it more difficult for us to see and respond to those who are trustworthy.[109] They make us behave in ways that hurt ourselves and others. They undermine our trust in ourselves and our sense of self-worth.

Potentially most damaging of all, where we put our trust profoundly affects our sense of reality. When we trust people, we tend to trust their values and (at least

109. No New Testament writer, apart from the possible final redactor of John, suggests that sinful human beings are incapable of responding to God's action through Christ with *pistis*. See the nuanced discussions in John M. G. Barclay and Simon Gathercole, eds., *Divine and Human Agency in Paul and His Cultural Environment* (New York: T&T Clark 2007), with the introduction by Barclay, 1–8.

Wrongdoing and Suffering, Trust and Mistrust

some aspects of) their worldview. We entrust ourselves and (at least some aspects of) our worldview to them. The linguistic link in English between what "matters" and physical "matter" captures that what matters to us is material to us; it is real to us. The people (and ideas and things) we trust matter to us: they are material in our world; they shape its reality. In toxic trust relationships, the assurance, for instance, of an abusive husband that his wife will never find anyone else to love her may seem more real—more trustworthy—to her than the possibility of making a new life for herself. To someone who distrusts the government, the media, or big business, a world of conspiracy theories shared in internet chat rooms may seem more real than what most people regard as reality.

The damaging relationships and worlds we enter by trusting the wrong people, or trusting ourselves misguidedly, or by not feeling able to trust ourselves or others, can be very difficult to leave, even if part of us wants to. We often talk about people who do leave such environments as having "gotten out," as if a set of relationships and a worldview were a physical box or a prison. Alternatively we speak of them as "survivors," as if they lived through a disaster in which others have been injured or died. For Paul and other early Christian writers, the world of *apistia* is a world that shapes us and our lives for nothing but death and destruction (cf. 2 Cor 6:14–15). We have to get right out of it: to die to it and live in a different reality.[110] God, they affirm, makes this possible through Christ, and the means by which it becomes possible is trust.

In chapter 3 we will explore how those who have done wrong may be made right with God in different ways, making different kinds and degrees of change. For someone whose life involves doing active harm to others, such as a slave owner or a domestic abuser, what may be needed is repudiation of that way of life and the determination to think and act differently in the future. For a well-intentioned but misguided zealot, as Paul describes himself as being, what may be needed is for that person to understand that her zeal has been misdirected and a resolution to redirect it. The person who has done little harm in their everyday life, but little good either, may need to recognize that God asks more of humanity than this and resolve to do more. Wrongdoing comes in many forms and so, therefore,

---

110. In passages that are not about atonement, Paul can offer a more pragmatic and arguably more charitable or optimistic approach to those without trust, e.g., 1 Cor 7:12–15, where *apistoi* who are family members of the faithful may be "made holy" by their association with community members and should remain part of their Christian families. In 1 Cor 14:22–24, Paul urges the Corinthians not to speak in tongues, because speaking what appears to be gibberish is liable to put off any *apistos* who comes to a meeting of the church; instead they should concentrate on prophecy, which is more likely to convince noncommunity members that "God is really among you" (14:25).

83

CHAPTER 1

must at-one-ment. But we cannot imagine that God's ingenuity in finding ways to restore our relationship with God is less than humanity's ingenuity in finding ways to damage it. And, as we will see in the next chapter, the restoration of trust is a powerful means of righting relationships damaged by every kind of suffering and wrongdoing.[111]

111. Whether people must respond as individuals or can respond as groups, Paul does not specify; we can assume that most people, baptized as adults, responded as individuals, but we cannot rule out that if households were baptized together (e.g., 1 Cor 1:16), some members did not make an individual profession, or did so under orders.

CHAPTER 2

Trust after Trauma, Conflict, and Offending

Chapter 1 argued that wrongdoing and suffering are deeply entwined in biblical testimony and our own everyday experience. All of us have had the experience of doing wrong in various ways and of being implicated in the wrongdoing of others, and all of us have also had the experience of suffering from the wrongdoing of others and our own. Chapter 3 outlines a model of atonement, rooted in Paul but drawing on other New Testament writings, that seeks to show how, through Christ, God may be understood as offering human beings release from both wrongdoing and suffering through the restoration of trust. Some readers may see the restoration of trust as a weaker means of at-one-ment than some more traditional mechanisms, but this does not do justice to the power of trust to transform relationships and communities. This chapter explores modern examples of the role of trust in the at-one-ment of individuals and societies after political conflict, personal trauma, and lawbreaking, studied by psychologists and sociologists. In these fields, the necessity of restoring trust where it has been broken, and the power of doing so, is widely recognized and often movingly described.

The Role of Trust in Conflict Resolution

"Conflict resolution" in scholarly literature can refer to a process of peacemaking which, in principle, ends a political or military or paramilitary conflict, or a longer process of reconciliation that may begin before peace treaties are made and usually continues long afterward. Whether a study focuses on one or the other depends on whether it is primarily concerned with the activities of governments and leaderships or society more widely. Leaderships and governments negotiate

85

CHAPTER 2

and sign treaties, but the work of reconciliation throughout a society takes longer and involves many more people.

Research on conflict and on how individuals, groups, and societies seek restoration after conflict is a vast field, encompassing work in history, political theory, sociology, and psychology. In theology, the importance of trust in maintaining or restoring relationships is so far little studied, but elsewhere the importance of trust for the good working of individuals, groups, and societies, the extent to which trust is degraded and lost in times of conflict, and the vital importance of (re-)creating trust after conflict, have all been extensively researched.[1]

Some of the earliest studies of the role of trust in conflict resolution saw trust as a "dependent variable," which could be established once peace and justice had been restored. More recently, trust has been seen as integral to processes of peacemaking from their beginnings. A 2020 study by Andrés Casas-Casas of trust and reconciliation in Colombia during the peace process of 2012–2016 is typical, arguing that trust is one of the bases on which peace and justice build, both during peace processes and afterward.[2] "Trust in ex-combatants and in government increases the likelihood of [participants'] having positive attitudes toward future reconciliation and willingness to support not only the peace process but reconciliation activities after war."[3] Writing about Rwanda, Immaculée Mukashema and

1. Angelika Rettberg and Juan E. Ugarriza, "Reconciliation: A Comprehensive Framework for Empirical Analysis," *Security Dialogue* 47 (2016): 517–40 offers an overview of trust in their framework for analyzing post-conflict reconciliation processes. Immaculée Mukashema and Etienne Mullet, "Attribution of Guilt to Offspring of Perpetrators of the Genocide: Rwandan People's Perspectives," *Conflict Resolution Quarterly* 33 (2015): 75–98 argues that although a majority of Rwandans consulted do not think that sin is hereditary, a minority takes the view that it can descend (so far) to the second and third generation, invoking biblical precedent.

2. Andrés Casas-Casas, Nathalie Mendez, and Juan Frederico Pino, "Trust and Prospective Reconciliation: Evidence from a Protracted Armed Conflict," *Journal of Peacebuilding and Development* 15 (2020): 298–315. Cf. Miles Hewstone et al., "Stepping Stones to Reconciliation in Northern Ireland: Intergroup Contact, Forgiveness, and Trust," in *The Social Psychology of Intergroup Reconciliation* (ed. Arie Nadler, Thomas Malloy, and Jeffrey D. Fisher; Oxford: Oxford University Press, 2008), 199–225; Reuben M. Baron, "Reconciliation, Trust, and Cooperation: Using Bottom-Up and Top-Down Strategies to Achieve Peace in the Israeli-Palestinian Conflict," in Nadler, Malloy, and Fisher, *Intergroup Reconciliation*, 275–98; Luca Andrighetto, Samer Halabi, and Arie Nadler, "Fostering Trust and Forgiveness through the Acknowledgment of Others' Past Victimization," *Journal of Social and Political Psychology* 5 (2017): 651–64. Anika Oettler and Angelika Rettberg, "Varieties of Reconciliation in Violent Contexts: Lessons from Colombia," *Peacebuilding* 7 (2019): 329–52 make the point that the lessons societies have learned about reconciliation and the restoration of trust at the end of conflicts are applicable much more widely to societies that suffer endemic, everyday conflict without falling into war.

3. Casas-Casas, Mendez, and Pino, "Trust and Prospective Reconciliation," 298.

Trust after Trauma, Conflict, and Offending

Etienne Mullet argue that "after a period of political violence, a country must . . . rebuild its material infrastructure: roads, schools, hospitals, factories. It must also rebuild its psychological infrastructure; that is, it must rebuild trust and cooperation between people."[4] Article 2 of the Belfast (Good Friday) Agreement of 1998 between the Republic of Ireland and the United Kingdom, which formally ended the "troubles" of the previous thirty years, states, "We must never forget those who have died or been injured, and their families. But we can best honour them through a fresh start, in which we firmly dedicate ourselves to the achievement of reconciliation, tolerance, and mutual trust." James Meernik and Jose R. Guerrero, writing about the Bosnian War of 1992–1995, warn of the risks of not cultivating trust: "Mistrust, a loss of a sense of control of their lives, a negative self-identity, and a lack of positive connections with other groups create psychological barriers for reconciliation amongst formerly warring parties."[5]

In political and military conflicts, some participants do much more harm than others, while others mainly suffer, but many both suffer and do harm. The roots of conflicts, moreover, are often deep and complex, going back generations. The 1994 genocide of ethnic minority Tutsis by majority Hutus in Rwanda is a well-known example. Rwanda was colonized and ruled by Belgium from 1897 to 1918, during which time Tutsis were favored by the authorities and held most local powers. In 1959, a revolution by Hutus forced hundreds of thousands of Tutsis to flee the country, and ethnic violence followed against the small number of Tutsis remaining. In 1990 the Rwandese Patriotic Front, consisting mainly of Tutsis, invaded Rwanda from Uganda. A power-sharing agreement was signed in 1993 but collapsed when a plane carrying the Hutu president, Juvénal Habyarimana, together with the Hutu president of Burundi, Cyprien Ntaryamira, was shot down in April 1994 and both were killed. The genocide began days later in the resulting

4. Immaculée Mukashema and Etienne Mullet, "Unconditional Forgiveness, Reconciliation Sentiment, and Mental Health among Victims of Genocide in Rwanda," *Social Indicators Research* 113 (2013): 121–22. The restoration of trust between individuals and groups works in similar ways, but some studies argue that restoration of trust between groups is harder, because groups have internal resources and sources of support, so they often take longer to recognize their need to reconcile and trust others. On this see also Christopher P. Reinders Folmer et al., "Repairing Trust between Individuals and Groups: The Effectiveness of Apologies in Interpersonal and Intergroup Conflicts," *International Review of Social Psychology* 34 (2021): 1–15. At the time of writing, Rwanda's peace settlement has held for nearly thirty years, and during that time the country has moved significantly up the Australian Institute for Economics and Peace's widely cited Global Peace Index.

5. J. Meernik and J. R. Guerrero, "Can International Criminal Justice Advance Ethnic Reconciliation? The ICTY and Ethnic Relations in Bosnia-Hercegovina," *Journal of Southeast European and Black Sea Studies* 14 (2014): 395.

CHAPTER 2

power vacuum. In three months, at least half a million Tutsis were murdered by Hutu militias, many of them neighbors and former friends. Though Tutsis were the victims of the genocide, both Tutsis and Hutus were both victims and perpetrators in the longer conflict. The genocide has severely affected the mental health of members of both groups, including their capacity to trust: "Emotional harms in the Rwandese society are still far from being repaired. A complex emotional climate prevails involving at one and the same time feelings of anger, resentment, shame, sadness, and distrust."[6] The rebuilding of trust is recognized as indispensable to the ongoing restoration of Rwandese society and for the mental health of Rwandans.[7]

A study by Timothy James Bowyer exposes the degradation of trust suffered by rural peoples of the Andes as a result of decades of violence (political, paramilitary, and drug-related) in Bolivia, Colombia, Ecuador, Peru, and Venezuela.[8] In a chapter entitled "Losing Trust in the World," he investigates the "psychic pain and confusion" that comes from violence, showing how

> the threat of death and destruction made the need for prolonged vigilance as inevitable as much as the feelings of fear, mistrust and isolation . . . Intense surprise, humiliation, helplessness and loss of control intensify the need for protective attachments as much as they cause people to lose trust in themselves, in other people, and in their community as the following testimony demonstrates:
>
> "One night they let my husband go and at about midnight he came back to the house. The military had told him: 'leave with all of your family. If you don't leave, I'll kill them all.' At that point we grabbed our children and went into the hills, with the soldiers watching us. When we got into the hills, they started firing bullets, saying that they would kill us, and that it would've been better for him if he had stayed behind. So, then we hid in a cave.'"[9]

6. P. Kanyangara et al., "Collective Rituals, Emotional Climate and Intergroup Perception: Participation in 'Gacaca' Tribunals and Assimilation of the Rwandan Genocide," *Journal of Social Issues* 63 (2007): 388.

7. Immaculée Mukashema and Etienne Mullet, "Current Mental Health and Reconciliation Sentiment of Victims of the Genocide against Tutsi in Rwanda," *International Journal of Social Psychology* 25 (2014): 33.

8. Timothy James Bowyer, *Beyond Suffering and Reparation: The Aftermath of Political Violence in the Peruvian Andes* (New York: Springer, 2018).

9. Bowyer, *Beyond Suffering*, 65, 68. The testimony is from an interviewee from Wamani (Victoria).

Trust after Trauma, Conflict, and Offending

"In every testimony," Bowyer observes, "the abuse of basic trust is overwhelming."[10] He emphasizes how difficult it is for those who have suffered for so long and in so many ways to regain trust. They do not trust governments, local authorities, NGOs who promise more than they deliver, their neighbors, or even themselves. "For survivors that have witnessed the disintegration of trust, respect, self-esteem, security, and supportive relationships, an appreciation of the current situation and of the individual's own place in the wider context including spiritual needs . . . is a formidable challenge."[11] Even so, those who have suffered have a powerful incentive to work to recover trust, and it is extraordinary how often, over time, they do.[12]

These examples testify not only to the importance of trust but to what is lost when trust is lost, and what is at stake when people seek to (re)establish trust, including a sense of identity, self-esteem, emotional equilibrium, and connectedness with the wider world as well as the ability not always to be hypervigilant, to feel secure, to make relationships, to hope, to act positively and cooperate, and to make a difference for the future. A 2021 study led by Mariska Kappmeier observes, "the fundamental difference between intergroup conflict and intergroup peace is trust."[13] These examples also indicate that the restoration of trust—even if trust, at the beginning, is limited and provisional—is one of the first steps that needs to be taken in a process of reconciliation.

Kappmeier argues that the creation and restoration of trust between groups tends to be even more difficult than that between individuals, because groups tend to be even more competitive, and members of a group feel a less urgent need for cooperation with outsiders than do vulnerable individuals. Drawing on her own earlier work, she proposes that one group that trusts another must be able to see the other as competent (able to deliver on promises), secure or reliable, and compassionate; as having integrity and as being compatible with the needs and desires of the trusting group. All these factors in combination enable the

10. Bowyer, *Beyond Suffering*, 118.

11. Bowyer, *Beyond Suffering*, 133.

12. S. J. Lepore and T. A. Revenson, "Resilience and Post-Traumatic Growth Recovery, Resistance, and Reconfiguration," in *Handbook of Post-Traumatic Growth: Research and Practice* (ed. Lawrence G. Calhoun, Richard G. Tedeschi, and Marianne Amir; New York: Taylor & Francis, 2009), 27; R. Lev-Wiesel and M. Amir, "Growing Out of Ashes: Posttraumatic Growth among Holocaust Child Survivors. Is It Possible?" in Calhoun, Tedeschi, and Amir, *Handbook of Post-Traumatic Growth*, 257.

13. Mariska Kappmeier, Bushra Guenoun, and Kathyrn H. Fahey, "Conceptualizing Trust between Groups: An Empirical Validation of the Five-Dimensional Intergroup Trust Model," *Peace Confl.* 29 (2021): 90, citing a number of earlier studies on the failure of trust as a source and engine of conflict.

CHAPTER 2

first group to feel secure in trusting the second.[14] In the introduction, we saw that New Testament writers address similar concerns in writing about trust between God and humanity, emphasizing the long-term trustworthiness and faithfulness of God, God's and Christ's love for humanity, and the existential importance for human beings of the salvation God offers them.

Other studies emphasize that while being convinced of the reliability, competence, integrity, justice, and so on of an opposing group is an ideal situation in which to make peace, it is rarely the actual situation toward the end of a conflict. In practice, groups that seek peace usually need to take a risk, trusting that the other side will be trustworthy in the absence of proof. A group led by Diego Esparza analyzing the 2016 Colombian peace accord argues that those who were able to take part in negotiations over the agreement had, for whatever reason, a disposition to trust, while only those who were willing to risk trusting the government at that time were likely to accept it.[15] Those who could take at least a first step of trust could also hope, and on that basis proceed. In the introduction, similarly, we noted the aspect of risk-taking on both sides in the new relationship with God that human beings are being offered. Esparza detected a willingness to trust among those negotiating in 2012–2016 but very varied levels of trust in the wider population, which meant that, at the time, it was not at all clear whether the agreement would hold.[16]

A 2022 study by Anastasia Filippidou and Thomas O'Brien argued that the nature of the trust that was holding the Colombia peace accord in place was

---

14. Kappmeier, Guenoun, and Fahey, "Conceptualizing Trust between Groups," 90, 95; cf. M. Kappmeier, "Trusting the Enemy—Towards a Comprehensive Understanding of Trust in Intergroup Conflict," *Peace and Conflict* 22 (2016): 134–44. Kappmeier and others tested these factors in two studies of race and gender relations in America using measures with between twenty and fifty items. The study additionally identified predictability (which is similar to reliability), willingness, and ability to collaborate (which are close to competence and compatibility) as factors in trust creation. Cf. the similar argument made by Alejandro Chavez-Segura, "Can Truth Reconcile a Nation? Truth and Reconciliation Commissions in Argentina and Chile: Lessons for Mexico," *Latin American Policy* 6 (2015): 226–39. Matthew J. Hornsey and Michael J. A. Wohl, "We Are Sorry: Intergroup Apologies and Their Tenuous Link with Intergroup Forgiveness," *European Review of Social Psychology* 24 (2013): 1–31, argue that groups are less likely than individuals to respond to apologies and petitions for forgiveness.

15. Diego Esparza, Valerie Martinez, Regina Branton, Kimi King, and James Meernik, "Violence, Trust, and Public Support for the Colombian Peace Agreement," *Social Science Quarterly* 101 (2020): 1236–54, especially 1242–44. They note the wealth of recent research on dispute settlement, which emphasizes that the trust of those to whom a settlement will apply is key in securing buy-in to it (1242–43).

16. As of early 2024, it still does.

90

complex. Parties to the agreement had been able to develop and maintain what they called "thin" trust—just enough to enable them to work together—while all sides worked to foster "thick" trust with their own supporters, which helped the accord to hold in the wider population.[17] "Thin" trust may look less than ideal, but that does not necessarily make it inadequate in practice.[18] In *The Theology of Trust* I argued, along similar lines, that in New Testament writings, the trust of everyone who encounters Jesus is fragile and imperfect, cut with fear or doubt, and liable to fail. Nowhere in New Testament writings, however, is it suggested that those who sincerely trust and keep trying to trust, however they fail, are excluded from eternal life of the kingdom of God. Even imperfect trust may be adequate for the restoration of societies or for participation in the kingdom of God.[19]

We have seen that for psychologists like Doris Brothers, part of trust is self-trust: the ability to trust one's own judgments and to see oneself as worthy of trust by others.[20] Nurit Shnabel and Johannes Ullrich, also from a psychological perspective, argue that those who participate in processes of reconciliation, whether individuals or groups, need to be able to frame a positive identity for themselves. As part of this they need to be able to esteem themselves, not least by being able to trust their perceptions of others, and to experience that others see and hear them in a way that they can trust.[21]

---

17. Anastasia Filippidou and Thomas O'Brien, "Trust and Distrust in the Resolution of Protracted Social Conflicts: The Case of Colombia," *Behavioral Sciences of Terrorism and Political Aggression* 14 (2022): 1–21. In a similar vein, Janine Natalya Clark, "Reflections on Trust and Reconciliation: A Case Study of a Central Bosnian Village," *International Journal of Human Rights* 16 (2012): 239–56 argues that societies can function, in the aftermath of conflict, with minimal levels of trust or thin trust.

18. It can also support better mental health in contexts where the failure of trust damages mental health and the re-creation of trust and improving mental health support each other. See Mukashema and Mullet, "Unconditional Forgiveness," 27–28.

19. See especially Morgan, *Theology of Trust*, 258–63.

20. Above, pp. 19–20.

21. Nurit Shnabel and Johannes Ullrich, "Putting Emotional Regulation in Context: The (Missing) Role of Power Relations, Intergroup Trust, and Groups' Need for Positive Identities in Reconciliation Processes," *Psychological Inquiry* 27 (2016): 124–32. This, they argue, is one of the ways in which, more broadly, emotions play a key role in processes of reconciliation, taking trust as having an emotional as well as cognitive and active aspect. Individuals and groups may not all find it equally possible to trust in themselves or others. Writing about the Colombian peace process in 2019, James Meernik observes that women are much less likely to trust in the process than men, perhaps because they have suffered more, because they have more socioeconomic challenges to navigate, or because they have less access than men to power and office and hence agency in the process. See James Meernik, "Violence and Reconciliation in Colombia: The Personal and the Contextual," *Journal of Politics in Latin America* 11 (2019): 340.

CHAPTER 2

One of the most important factors enabling trust, however thin, provisional, or imperfect, is access: the ability of individuals or groups to be in contact, to meet face-to-face, and to get to know one another. The development of trust is more possible when we can see and hear the other and judge their facial expressions, tone of voice, body language, and even their smell, and when we can see how they relate to other members of their own group and to outsiders. We need to see and hear how people respond to talk about the past and the future and to be able to judge how they feel about having damaged others or having been damaged. We need to be able to scrutinize them to see whether they are sincere in talking about future change. It is not that other means of communication cannot seek to foster trust, but nothing matches the depth and subtlety of what we experience and detect in the physical presence of others.

A group of senior officers of the US Army reported discovering this during their involvement with the "draw down" of American forces in Iraq in 2011.[22] The 2nd Brigade Combat Team, 10th Mountain Division, met regional religious, political, tribal, security, and nongovernmental leaders to discuss practical ways in which the army could support a transition to peaceful democracy in Iraq. They found, unexpectedly, that the idea of "reconciliation" did not appeal to their interlocutors, but that they had more success when they began to speak of the establishment of trust, hope, and unity.[23] In order for trust to be developed, they found, government at every level needed to connect with local people, so that people felt they knew their leaders and that their leaders had their interests at heart. The officers were, at the time of reporting, optimistic about the capacity of the US Army to act as conciliator in this process and bring sections of society together to foster trust and trustworthiness. (A dozen years later, when the Iraq War, including the draw down at its end, is widely regarded as a catastrophic failure that led to the collapse of Iraq as a state and incalculable damage to Iraqi society, this account also underlines that rebuilding trust in human contexts is a complex and uncertain process.)

These army officers were seeking to act as mediators. In reconciliation processes, mediators are individuals (less often, groups) who are known and recognized as trustworthy by both parties.[24] They seek to present each side to the other and to increase each side's understanding of the other and their sympathy for the

22. Nathan Miniami, David Miller, Michael Davey, and Anthony Sawalhah, "Beyond Reconciliation: Developing Faith, Hope, Trust, and Unity in Iraq," *Military Review* 91 (2011): 52–59.

23. Miniami et al., "Beyond Reconciliation," 55–56.

24. Jennifer E. Beer et al., *The Mediator's Handbook* (4th rev. ed.; Gabriola: New Society, 2012); Daniel Bowling and David Hoffman, "Bringing Peace into the Room: The Personal Qualities of the Mediator and Their Impact on the Mediation," in *Bringing Peace into the Room: How the*

Trust after Trauma, Conflict, and Offending

other's experiences and needs. They typically do not make a deal themselves but help those who have been in conflict to come to an agreement with each other, and we return to their role below.[25]

Laura Stovel's study of postwar Sierra Leone in the early 2000s explores at length the role of trust in the restoration process.[26] Stovel notes that the people she spoke with, who self-identified as Christians, "were quick to say they forgave excombatants for war crimes and would let them return and they defined 'forgiveness' and 'reconciliation' as being willing to forgo revenge. I wanted a deeper sense of how they felt, how they dealt with anger and pain and built trust again."[27] She explores what many studies recognize in passing, without making it their focus: the importance of local and face-to-face encounters in the restoration of trust.[28] It may be important to trust governments and militaries—their ability to keep law and order and willingness to hold free and fair elections—but the dense, complex, multilayered relationships of social trust, which most strongly hold communities together, are (re)developed above all on the local level between neighbors and through one-to-one, small group-to-group, face-to-face encounters.

Stovel argues that trust is a good measure of what she calls "deep reconciliation: reconciliation that goes beyond compromises or physically bring people in

---

Personal Qualities of the Mediator Impact the Process of Conflict Resolution (ed. Daniel Bowling and David Hoffman; San Francisco: Jossey-Bass, 2003), 13–47.

25. There are also mixed findings on the role of third parties in trust processes. A study led by Ying Yu is typical in finding, in a business context, that third parties play a key role in trust repair processes. See Ying Yu, Yan Yang, and Fengjie Jing, "The Role of the Third Party in Trust Repair Process," *Journal of Business Research* 78 (2017): 233–41. In two more targeted studies, Nurit Shnabel, Arie Nadler, and John F. Dovido found that third-party mediators were effective in restoring the trust of conflicted parties by working separately with each party to develop their sense of agency and the other party's moral image in their eyes; see Nurit Shnabel, Arie Nadler, and John F. Dovido, "Beyond Need Satisfaction: Empowering and Accepting Messages from Third Parties Ineffectively Restore Trust and Consequent Reconciliation," *European Journal of Social Psychology* 44 (2014): 126–40. This process enabled each party to come to the process of restoring trust and reconciliation with greater success. Third parties were less effective, however, in restoring trust directly. This makes an interesting parallel with the model of atonement through the restoration of trust in the next chapter, which argues that the relationships between Christ and God and Christ and the faithful, which are conceptually separable though part of the same process, enable human beings to return to trust in God rather than that Christ's death in itself restored trust.

26. Laura Stovel, *Long Road Home: Building Reconciliation and Trust in Post-War Sierra Leone* (Cambridge: Intersentia, 2010).

27. Stovel, *Long Road Home*, 2.

28. The importance of face-to-face interaction, spatial presence, and physical contact in the restoration of trust after violence is well explored by M. Anne Brown, "The Body in the Emergence of Trust," *Ethnopolitics* 19 (2020): 209–27.

CHAPTER 2

conflict together. It is reconciliation that is felt. . . . Long-term national reconciliation in Sierra Leone involves three areas of trust building [two of which take
place on the local level]: creating trust between citizens and the state; building
trust and promoting healing within communities; and reconciling factions or divided segments within the population."[29] As Stovel reports: "When I asked Sierra
Leoneans how they learn to trust excombatants, the answer was almost always,
'We watch them.' These statements are typical":

> (A certain excombatant) has done a lot of harm to the people. It will not be very
> easy for them to trust him again . . . If maybe he had come here, stayed here
> for some time then they watch him, see how he behaves to them, (they might)
> have some trust. But staying far off and just coming like that, it will take them
> some time to have confidence in him. They will still have some fear. Because
> you need to trust somebody (interview, teacher, 'Togo,' May 6, 2003).

> Well, we are watching them. Some of them are still aggressive. They can't
> change totally. They change gradually. So as time goes on they build trust. So
> we are watching them . . . I treat them as they treat themselves (group interview,
> retired civil servant, Port Loko, March 29, 2003).

> When you (an excombatant) are talking, from the tone of your voice and every
> other thing we'll be able to know whether you are saying the truth (village elder,
> 'Togo,' March 29, 2003).

These villagers can be seen as exercising thin trust (though Stovel does not use
this term) by letting ex-combatants return home. Then, day by day, they watched
them to see whether their behavior justified further trust. Stovel argues that "Sierra
Leoneans have largely achieved the peaceful coexistence that many call reconciliation. A look beneath the surface, however, reveals substantial social distrust
and wounds and rifts that will be difficult to mend."[30] To mend that rift more fully
and for the longer term requires more homecomings and the gradual restoration
of thicker trust.

The recognition that people have the best chance of developing trust when
they are able to take the first step of a face-to-face encounter and build on it is
replicated in reports from conflicts around the world. It is also profoundly incarnational. Of all the attitudes and actions that Christians envisage God as extending

29. Stovel, *Long Road Home*, 224.
30. Stovel, *Long Road Home*, 235–36.

Trust after Trauma, Conflict, and Offending

toward humanity and as asking of humanity, trust is perhaps the one that most depends on the incarnation—on God's sending God's Son to be in the world, making face-to-face relationships, inviting and eliciting trust by his words, actions, and example in life, death, and resurrection.[31] By the same token, the centrality of trust-faith between God and humanity in Christian conviction helps to explain why not only teaching collections but biographies or histories of Jesus's presence and activities on earth developed in early churches. For those who did not encounter Jesus in his early life, or have not encountered the exalted Christ, stories about Jesus on earth were and are a means—arguably the strongest means—by which people encounter Jesus, participating in spirit in the narrative of his life, death, and resurrection together with the experiences and later lives and work of his disciples.

In some countries, churches have acted as mediators after conflict. The 1994 genocide in Rwanda caught up in its maelstrom not only Rwandans but also the Roman Catholic Church, the largest Christian organization in the country. In 1994, around two-thirds of Rwandans, of all ethnic backgrounds, were Catholics. Tens of thousands of Tutsis were killed in the grounds of Catholic parishes, schools, and medical centers.[32] A "significant minority" of Catholic priests, religious, and lay catechists "actively collaborated" in the killings, and the Catholic hierarchy did not make any public statement during the early weeks of the genocide.[33] The failure of the church to do anything to lessen ethnic tensions or prevent the conflict was much discussed in its aftermath. The reputation and moral standing of the church both within and beyond Rwanda were badly damaged.

The Catholic Church has also, however, been extensively involved in initiatives of reconciliation through teaching, shared liturgy, and the creation of jus-

---

31. The theme of Jesus's rejection by many of those who encountered him, and how Mark and John in particular treat this theologically, is beyond the scope of this study, but in broad terms we, from the perspective of this study, might relate it to the theme of "therapeutic trust" that we have already encountered. God chooses to send an atypical messiah into the world, trusting that at least some human beings will recognize and respond to him. Perhaps, at this point, God seeks a closer, more human-to-human-like relationship of trust with humanity than could be established by a revelation of divine power or glory, whether because humanity is being invited into a closer relationship with God than ever before, or because humanity will be entrusted with God's work in the world more than ever before, or both. Such a relationship might need to be established through a Son of God who is also human, recognizably trustworthy and trusting in human terms, and the significance of the offered relationship for God might be worth the risk of sending a messiah whom many did not recognize.

32. The story is outlined and the scholarly literature discussed by J. J. Carney, "A Generation after Genocide: Catholic Reconciliation in Rwanda," *TS* 76 (2015): 785–12.

33. Carney, "After Genocide," 786.

CHAPTER 2

tice and peace commissions. J. J. Carney observes that although little theology has been written out of the experience of Rwanda's situation, the church's work for reconciliation can be seen as inspired by liberation theology. One theologian whose work has been shaped not least by the Rwandan massacre is the Ugandan-American Emmanuel Katongole. Katongole calls for a "new theological imagination" shaped by practices of lament, forgiveness, and pilgrimage. He uses the image of the "ambassador of reconciliation," drawn from 2 Cor 5:18–20, to speak of God's reconciliation with the world through Christ and Christ's call to his followers to embrace a ministry of reconciliation throughout the world.[34] Reconciliation, Katongole argues,

> is God's gift of 'new creation' to the world (2 Cor 5:17) and an invitation to enter and experience the world of new creation, which God has made possible through God's reconciling love. For as Paul says, 'If anyone is in Christ, the new creation has come: The old has gone, the new is here! All this is from God, who reconciled us to himself through Christ' (2 Cor 5:17–18). In the context of Africa's turbulent political history, the invitation offers not simply concrete alternatives in the wake of violence, but a basis for a new society founded on God's nonviolent and reconciling love.[35]

Katongole's emphasis is on the reconciling power of love rather than trust, but 2 Corinthians 5 also speaks of the trust of the faithful in Christ (5:8), and the next chapter will argue that Paul's reconciliation language is very close (conceptually and sometimes in the text) to his language of trust.

Another African priest and theologian, Desmond Tutu, also spoke of the theology of reconciliation as a way forward for Africa. The title of one of his books also highlights the importance of physical proximity, including for mediators in reconciliation processes: *Walk with Us and Listen: Political Reconciliation in Africa.*[36] These words come from a comment by Tenda Nkomo, a survivor of the Matabeleland massacre of around 20,000 Ndebele by the Zimbabwean army in 1983–1984: "Don't tell us what to do. Walk with us and listen . . . You will never

---

34. See especially Emmanuel Katongole with Jonathan Wilson-Hartgrove, *Mirror to the Church: Resurrecting Faith after Genocide in Rwanda* (Grand Rapids: Zondervan, 2008); Emmanuel Katongole and Chris P. Rice, *Ambassadors of Reconciliation* (Downers Grove: InterVarsity, 2008). Katongole develops this theology further in his *The Sacrifice of Africa: A Political Theology for Africa* (Grand Rapids: Eerdmans, 2011).

35. Emmanuel Katongole, "The Gospel as Politics in Africa," *TS* 77 (2016): 712.

36. Charles Villa-Vicencio and Desmond Tutu, *Walk with Us and Listen: Political Reconciliation in Africa* (Washington, DC: Georgetown University Press, 2009).

96

Trust after Trauma, Conflict, and Offending

fully understand the journey of our suffering. We suffer alone and we must heal our own wounds. But we need your presence, so stay with us." Nkomo's words are echoed by Pascal Bataringaya, president of the Presbyterian Church of Rwanda, who commented in an interview in 2016, "The churches have something special. They walk with the people, with the perpetrators, with the victims. People feel they are not alone." The Presbyterian Church walked with the people after the genocide by developing multiple local peacemaking groups and initiatives, with the explicit aim of (re-)creating trust.[37] The idea that part of the work of a reconciler is to walk both with those who have suffered and with those who have done wrong echoes the language of Paul in Romans 6, to which we will return in the next chapter, where we are with Christ and Christ is with us as we undergo our necessary death to the power of sin and suffering and journey toward new life.

This sample of studies of the role of trust in the ending of conflicts and the restoration of societies and individual relationships after conflict shows how widely trust is now recognized as integral to every stage of the process. The kind of trust that is willing to take a risk on another person and a process enables peace processes to begin. Trust can keep a process going and develop it. It may start out thin and inadequate, and even periodically fail, but inadequate trust can be enough in its early stages. (Conversely, where not enough sustained effort is found possible, trust can fail, and peace processes fail with it.) Mediators can play a key role in fostering trust, and it works best when the parties can encounter each other directly and, above all, face-to-face. Mediation and face-to-face encounters both foster one of the most important aspects of trust: it encourages individuals and groups to recognize that, whoever was deemed to have "started" the conflict, all sides will have suffered and all sides done harm. In the rest of this chapter we will see similar themes in play in the (re-)creation of trust after trauma and after lawbreaking. In the next chapter, we will see them in play in the crucifixion.

Peace processes that focus on reconciliation and are strongly future oriented—including, for instance, those inspired by South Africa's Truth and Reconciliation Commission, and processes of "restorative justice" that sometimes run in parallel to states' criminal justice systems—are sometimes criticized for not paying enough attention to justice, that is, for not holding wrongdoers to account or exacting appropriate penalties.[38] If wrong has been done, it is argued, someone

37. Christine Schliesser, "From 'a Theology of Genocide' to a 'Theology of Reconciliation'? On the Role of Christian Churches in the Nexus of Religion and Genocide in Rwanda," *Religions* 9 (2018): art. 34, 9–10.

38. See, e.g., discussions in Monika Nalepa, "Lustration as a Trust-Building Mechanism? Transitional Justice in Poland," in *After Oppression: Transitional Justice in Latin America and Eastern Europe* (ed. Vesselin Popovski and Mónica Serrano; Tokyo: United Nations University

CHAPTER 2

must pay for it, and the cost to them must be real and, many would say, painful in order for social and moral order to be restored. Models of atonement that focus on reconciliation have attracted the same criticism. It is clear, moreover, that the justice or righteousness of God, God's condemnation of humanity for its sins, and the threat of judgment at the end time are central concerns of almost all early Christian writings.

The findings of the last chapter and this section so far, however, suggest that there are advantages in putting justice in a wider framework of the restoration of trust. For one thing, wrongdoing is very varied in nature, and though every wrongdoing may need to be addressed, not every kind is equally appropriately addressed by punishment. For another, many, probably most, if not all wrongdoers are also sufferers, and often wrongdoing is instigated in part by suffering, which can also alienate people from one another and from God. If we believe that a just and righteous God seeks the at-one-ment of humanity, and perhaps wider creation, with Godself, then there are attractions in envisaging God as initiating the restoration of trust as a framework within which other relationships, including relationships based on justice, can develop.[39] After conflict and division, a step of trust often needs to be taken before anything else can be done, and it is where trust has been initiated that other relationships become imaginable.[40]

TRUST AFTER TRAUMA

"To experience trauma," writes Lisa M. Cataldo, "is to experience the shattering of the world. In the face of trauma, what has been taken for granted becomes ques-

---

Press, 2012), 333–62; Yutaka Osakabe, "Restoring Restorative Justice: Beyond the Theology of Reconciliation and Forgiveness," *International Journal of Public Theology* 10 (2016): 247–71; Demaine J. Solomons, "Re-Examining a Theology of Reconciliation: What We Learn from the *Kairos* Document and Its Pedagogical Implications," *HvTSt* 76 (2020): art. a5843, https://doi.org/10.4102/hts.v.76i1.5843.

39. In an argument that has points of contact with this, Willard Swartley, *The Covenant of Peace: The Missing Peace in New Testament Theology and Ethics* (Grand Rapids: Eerdmans, 2006) argues that the peace that God offers to humanity is key to reconciliation and the restoration of humanity's relationship with God.

40. It may surprise some that this section has little to say about South Africa's Truth and Reconciliation Commission (TRC), which inspired many similar reconciliation processes around the world. The TRC worked with one (traditional, Christian) model of reconciliation in which reconciliation needs to be preceded by recognition of fault, repentance, and forgiveness, and literature on it has had (perhaps surprisingly) little to say about trust. This chapter focuses on studies of processes in which trust has been seen as central to at-one-ment.

Trust after Trauma, Conflict, and Offending

tionable. One's basic sense of safety, trust in others, and trust in one's own sense of self can be deeply damaged or destroyed . . . For the trauma survivor, there is no 'certainty that God listens to our cry' . . . trauma at any point in life can shatter religious faith—the whole system of trust in a safe world and a good God."[41]

Less has been written about the restoration of trust after trauma or lawbreaking than on trust in conflict resolution, but all three share many of the same themes. One of the most important is how suffering and wrongdoing are entwined in the experience of both perpetrators and victims. In trauma studies and studies of lawbreaking, it is particularly tempting, and often easy, to polarize victims who, we feel, deserve justice and support, and perpetrators, whom we may want to see punished. Research in both sociology and psychology, however, shows that many, probably most perpetrators have been or are also victims, while some victims are also perpetrators. Wrongdoing, moreover, once again comes in many forms: sometimes malevolent, but more often driven by need, bad judgment, misplaced trust, a sense of being trapped by circumstances, or vulnerability to exploitation. Trauma studies tend to focus on physical or violent trauma, but trauma is not necessarily physical or obviously violent. Betrayal, for instance, is a prevalent and profoundly damaging form of trauma and can take many forms. One of its well-known consequences is the loss of "the ability to make healthy decisions about whom to trust," which might include trusting too little, too much, or ill-advisedly.[42]

Victims of trauma notoriously lose trust both in other people and in themselves. At the extreme, as James Bowyer says, "the tortured victim loses trust in the world forever."[43] The international organization Help for Adult Victims of Child Abuse (HAVOCA), established in 2001 by and for abuse survivors, describes its mission as providing "support, friendship and advice for any adult whose life has been affected by childhood abuse . . . HAVOCA believes that every single child abuse victim has the ability to survive and lead a more fulfilling life."[44] HAVOCA

41. Lisa M. Cataldo, "I Know That My Redeemer Lives: Relational Perspectives on Trauma, Dissociation, and Faith," *Pastoral Psychology* 62 (2013): 791–92.

42. Robyn L. Gobyn and Jennifer J. Freyd, "The Impact of Betrayal Trauma on the Tendency to Trust," *Psychol. Trauma* 6 (2014): 505; Melissa G. Platt and Jennifer J. Freyd, "Betray My Trust, Shame on Me: Shame, Dissociation, Fear, and Betrayal Trauma," *Psychol. Trauma* 7 (2015): 398–404.

43. Bowyer, *Beyond Suffering*, 78–79. Antonio Gómez Ramos, drawing on the work of Jean Améry, makes the same point that trust can be fatally damaged by trauma in "Resentment and the Limits of a Politics of Memory," in *Just Memories: Remembrance and Restoration in the Aftermath of Political Violence* (ed. Camila de Gamboa Tapias and Bert van Roermund; Cambridge: Intersentia, 2020), 69–87.

44. Help for Adult Victims of Child Abuse, 2014, https://www.havoca.org.

CHAPTER 2

recognizes how difficult it is for those who are being or have been abused to trust. One contributor describes it like this:

> If I had a pound for every time somebody emailed HAVOCA and said they had trust issues, I'd be a rich man. It is the one characteristic that raises its ugly head on a regular basis—trusting oneself and trusting others . . . Lack of trusting yourself can manifest itself in a lack of trusting others and ultimately a lack of trust in your relationships . . . Learning to trust yourself and others is a big step—it takes time and practice.[45]

Alexis Donkin, a survivor and guest contributor to the website, writes,

> Trust is hard for someone who has suffered abuse. Typically the abusive person is someone close—a family member, lover, or friend. This heightens feelings of betrayal. How could a person do this? How could they hurt me? If this person could do this, then *anyone could.*
>
> And that is the problem. *Anyone can hurt you.* However, the opposite is also true—*anyone can love you.* If you don't trust people, if you don't let them in, they can't hurt you. And of course, if they can't hurt you, they also can't love you because they will never get close enough to know you. In order to experience love, to experience healing, it is necessary to trust. And that requires making yourself vulnerable.
>
> I found this to be the most difficult obstacle to healing after abuse.[46]

Donkin points not only to the damage caused by the loss of trust but also to why it is so important to regain trust if possible. Those who cannot trust struggle to feel whole, to make functional everyday relationships, or to let themselves love or be loved.

Another contributor observes that those who experience or have experienced abuse experience more kinds of suffering than we might expect: suffering from present and past abuse and from the different effects of each, which harm the victim in different ways.[47] The same contribution emphasizes that the way forward for someone who has experienced abuse is not necessarily through direct

---

45. https://www.havoca.org/survivors/trust/trust-others/. The second page goes on to emphasize that changing one's mindset is an essential first step, but only the first step.

46. Alexis Donkin, "Trust," *HAVOCA Blog*, June 13, 2015, https://www.havoca.org/trust/. See further pp. 151–52.

47. Maya Logo, "The Truth about Forgiveness—Revised," *HAVOCA Blog*, December 21, 2022, https://www.havoca.org/the-truth-about-forgiveness-revised/.

Trust after Trauma, Conflict, and Offending

forgiveness of the perpetrator, a theme to which we will return in chapter 5. Aside from the question whether a survivor of abuse is able to forgive, they may more urgently need support from third parties in building self-respect, self-trust, and affirming relationships that give a positive structure and dynamic to their lives. Such relationships have the potential to be stronger, wider-ranging, and more empowering than the damage the survivor has received from abuse. For such relationships to develop, however, survivors need to be able—and often must learn to be able—to trust where trust is merited.

Victims of trauma can be individuals or groups, and trauma can be addressed both individually and in groups. A study of therapy offered to a group of veterans suffering from PTSD emphasizes the importance of interpersonal trust for recovery from the trauma of battle.[48] The veterans were offered therapy in a group, and many found this helpful: the journey toward recovery was easier in company with and with the support of others who knew what they had been through. Chapter 5 will return to this theme, reflecting on the value of communities as places in which trust may be recovered. This study also found that those who had longer-term therapy aimed at rebuilding their self-confidence and ability to make and maintain relationships did better than those who had short-term cognitive therapy. Trust can be a long process, and it took time for the veterans to process what they had experienced and to build the relationships, not least relationships of trust, which helped them toward recovery.

This group had the support of a therapist. Jon G. Allen in *Trusting in Psychotherapy* explores the role of trust in relationships between patients and psychotherapists from the point of view of therapists, who respond to many different kinds of psychological need, including the needs of survivors of abuse.[49] He ob-

---

48. Wright Williams et al., "Group Psychotherapy's Impact on Trust in Veterans with PTSD: A Pilot Study," *Bulletin of the Meninger Clinic* 78 (2014): 335–48. Fanny Guglielmucci et al., "Helping Traumatized People Survive: A Psychoanalytic Intervention in a Contaminated Site," *Front. Psychol.* 5 (2014): art. 1419 argue that trauma to a whole community (in this case perpetrated by its main employer), resulting in shared loss of basic trust and sense of identity, is best addressed by group therapy. Ervin Staub et al., "Healing, Reconciliation, Forgiving and the Prevention of Violence after Genocide or Mass Killing: An Intervention and Its Experimental Evaluation in Rwanda," *Journal of Social and Clinical Psychology* 24 (2005): 297–340 describes an initiative in which psychologists worked with traumatized groups with the additional aim of promoting reconciliation with those who had harmed them.

49. See also Katherine Rachlin, "Trust in Uncertainty: The Therapeutic Structure of Possibility, Turning Points, and the Future of Psychotherapy with Transgender, Nonbinary, and Gender-diverse Individuals," *Studies in Gender and Sexuality* 23 (2022): 93–101, who emphasizes that in this process, neither therapist nor patient can be sure of the outcome; the trust between them also involves trust in the process. The importance of sensitivity and trustworthiness in those who

CHAPTER 2

serves that it is crucial not only that the patient, as a starting point, trusts the goal and process of the therapy, but that therapist and patient trust each other, and that the therapist is recognized as (and is) trustworthy:

> When trust comes transiently into our therapeutic purview, we focus on the patient's problems with it. But trusting makes no sense unless the trusted person is trustworthy, and trustworthiness is almost entirely neglected in the psychotherapy literature. Perhaps our starting point should be: What makes a therapist trustworthy? Moreover, I think psychotherapy goes best when trust is reciprocal, that is, when the patient and therapist are trusting of each other and trustworthy to each other—as it should be in any close relationship.[50]

Therapists also act as a type of mediator, helping patients to describe their experiences, to name what has happened to them and sometimes also what they have done, to understand how their experiences have changed them, and ideally to find routes to healing. In the case of trauma or abuse, therapists are normally not mediating between both parties, and the focus is not on the restoration of trust between victim and abuser. But to an abused person, as we saw above, every person and situation can become a proxy for the abuser and the situation of abuse, so the therapist must try to help the victim (re)learn trust in other people and situations that can be trusted, to help them to live and thrive more normally.

The therapist can also be seen as traveling alongside the patient on their journey toward healing, and knowing that the therapist is with them may be as powerful for the patient as any other aspect of therapy. Lisa Cataldo reports the case of a woman who was on the brink of "one of the most challenging realizations in the mind of the trauma survivor: that history cannot be undone. She said in the voice of her child-self, 'I want you to fix it!' I want you to go back and make it so that it never happened!' And the analyst replied, with genuine feeling, 'I would if I could!' The patient credits this as the turning-point in her healing process."[51] The therapist was traveling imaginatively with the patient, recognizing her pain and her need and wishing she could intervene to prevent it, and experiencing that, in itself, changed the patient's outlook. Jon G. Allen notes that research indicates that the relationship between a therapist and patient influences the outcome of

---

support survivors of abuse is underlined by Karin Örmon, Marie Torstensson-Levander, Charlotta Sunnqvist, and Christel Bahtsevani, "The Duality of Suffering and Trust: Abused Women's Experiences of General Psychiatric Care—An Interview Study," *Journal of Clinical Nursing* 23 (2013): 2303–12.

50. Allen, *Trusting in Psychotherapy*, xxv.
51. Cataldo, "My Redeemer Lives," 803.

Trust after Trauma, Conflict, and Offending

therapy significantly more than the therapist's particular method.[52] The trust-worthy therapist mediates between the survivor and the place of new life that the survivor hopes to reach, showing the survivor a route and traveling it with them. Chapter 3, as already noted, will explore the idea that Christ travels with the suffering and with wrongdoers on their journey to at-one-ment with God, and that the relationship of trust with Christ that makes this journey possible is also the starting point from which people (re)learn trust in one another in this world.

Mediators are not always available after trauma, especially in societies devastated by war. Sometimes, however, victims' own trauma motivates them to work as mediators for the renewal of others' trust. Even before the 1994 genocide, some Rwandans were working at grassroots level for ethnic reconciliation. In 1985, Anne-Marie Mukankuranga, a Tutsi, was attacked with her family by Hutus. In the early 1990s this experience inspired her to found the *Umusamaritani z'impuhwe* ("Merciful Samaritan Association," popularly known as the Good Samaritans) to seek to reconcile Hutus and Tutsis. The Good Samaritans recognized that all sides in Rwanda's ethnic conflict were both wrongdoers and victims of trauma. They fed and helped refugees of all ethnicities and organized community meetings to discuss ethnic tensions. After the genocide—despite strenuous objections by family and friends who were afraid of what might happen to her—Mukankuranga moved into the prisons, newly filled with Hutu militiamen, seeking dialogue and reconciliation with them. Her work bore fruit, many Hutus describing themselves as having conversion experiences that changed their view of themselves and their Tutsi neighbors. Gradually Mukankuranga brought some prison officials and other people to join her ministry. The Good Samaritans continue to help families of both Tutsis and Hutus, especially widows and orphans, with food, shelter, and "sharing" sessions. Mukankuranga is convinced that "God's love has no boundaries."[53] The organization has grown significantly, and although its language is dominantly that of forgiveness and love, its activities can also be seen as acts of trust.[54] As J. J.

---

52. Allen, *Trusting in Psychotherapy*, xxvii.

53. Carney, "After Genocide," 796.

54. Donald E. Millar, *Becoming Human Again* (Oakland: University of California Press, 2020), especially 138–44 describes another similar, Christian Rwandan initiative, Solace Ministries, which also offers support and meetings in which survivors may share stories. He also notes that trust is one of the major casualties of war, leading to loneliness, loss of religious faith, and loss of moral compass (114, 147). Agnieszka Katarzynska, "The Idea of Dialogue, Trust and Reconciliation in the Pilgrimage of Trust on Earth," *Journal for Perspectives of Economic, Political, and Social Integration* 22 (2016): 225–43 describes an initiative by the Taizé community, started in 1962, to bring together young people from Eastern and Western Europe in mass regional meetings that sought to grow trust and reconciliation.

CHAPTER 2

Carney says of Mukankuranga, moreover, her own suffering "has . . . given her a fundamental trust in God that enables her to courageously encounter the inevitable skepticism, adversity, and piecemeal nature of postgenocide reconciliation in Rwanda."[55] For Mukankuranga, reconciliation is always triangular: it involves God as well as the human parties, and it is her trust in God that strengthens her in the process of human at-one-ment.

Survivors of trauma who are able to exercise trust, however risky, in however apparently challenging an environment, can create decisive change not only for their own lives but in the world around them. A study by the psychologist and peace studies researcher Laura K. Taylor argues that willingness to trust has enabled survivors who were primarily or wholly victims in Colombia's civil war to take agency in their communities and engage in successful community building:[56]

> Feeling a lack of safety in the community may motivate those who experience community antisocial behavior to establish bonds with other victims. In the face of both political and community violence, individuals may be motivated to act prosocially and help others through community engagement (Taylor et al., 2014). These results challenge depictions of those exposed to violence as helpless victims; instead, the findings converge with other studies that recognize the agency and constructive ways individuals respond to political violence and community conflict (see Barber, 2009; McCouch, 2009). Of course, this does not suggest that individuals need to be exposed to violence in order to engage in civic life, but rather calls attention to resilience in the face of multiple forms of risk.
>
> Continuing the focus on resilience factors, the findings also suggest the social trust was an important resource to promote civic participation. Deeper trust in friends and neighbors was related to taking on a greater role in civil society. Controlling for experiences related to the conflict and public safety, social trust was related to participation in voluntary organizations (Delhey & Newton, 2003). This finding is consistent with the conceptualization of the

---

55. Carney, "After Genocide," 797. Alongside legal and individual initiatives to restore Rwandan society after 1994, multiple governmental as well as church initiatives have been developed aimed at restoring trust among Rwandans. Hannah Grayson, "A Place for Individuals: Positive Growth in Rwanda," *Eastern African Literary and Cultural Studies* 3 (2017): 115 describes an education program introduced in 2013: "'Ndi Umunyarwanda', which means, 'I am Rwandan', is an overarching program designed to build a national identity based on trust and dignity."

56. Laura K. Taylor, "Impact of Political Violence, Social Trust, and Depression on Civic Participation in Colombia," *Peace Confl.* 22 (2016): 145–52. She defines trust as the enacting positive expectations of others' intentions, motivations, and behaviors (146).

Trust after Trauma, Conflict, and Offending

model, which proposed that social trust was necessary for an individual to decide to take part in community life.[57]

In this case, trust encouraged survivors of trauma to invest in other survivors, and that investment helped to rebuild communities. Taylor also notes, however, that those who suffer from depression as a result of trauma find it harder to trust and harder to participate in civic life.

The literally vital importance of trust for survivors of trauma is underlined in the article by Matthew Ratcliffe, Mark Ruddell, and Benedict Smith to which we referred in the introduction.[58] They show how survivors of torture and other forms of trauma can suffer a catastrophic loss of trust, which makes it almost impossible for sufferers to look forward or have any hope for the future. When early Christian preachers and writers called people to trust in God and Christ for the righting of their relationship with God and ultimate salvation, they also articulated the life-or-death power of trust to engender existential hope in a way that resonates as powerfully today as it did in the first century.[59]

TRUST AND THE REHABILITATION OF EX-OFFENDERS

We have repeatedly emphasized the complex relationship between wrongdoing and suffering, and this relationship is nowhere clearer, or arguably more intractable, than in the case of those who break the law and are convicted and imprisoned. Those who find themselves in prison, are often (perhaps typically) themselves victims of often complex and long-term trauma. Studies in the psychology of prisoners show that such trauma damages trust, which in turn has a damaging effect on interpersonal relationships both outside and within prison.[60] Even if one is not a victim of trauma, prison is a harsh environment in which trust is a constant risk.

---

57. Taylor, "Impact of Political Violence," 149–50.

58. Ratcliffe, Ruddell, and Smith, "Foreshortened Future." Bridget Klest, Andreea Tamaian, and Emily Boughner, "A Model Exploring the Relationship between Betrayal Trauma and Trust," *Psychol. Trauma* 11 (2019): 656–62 argues that the loss of trust after trauma often leads to mistrust of medical services, which has an adverse effect on victims' physical health.

59. Morgan, *Roman Faith*, 55–74, 117–20 explores the fragility of trust in Mediterranean society during the first centuries BCE and CE.

60. Jennifer C. Kao et al., "Associations between Past Trauma, Current Social Support, and Loneliness in Incarcerated Populations," *Health and Justice* 2 (2014): art. 7, 2, with a discussion of past research.

CHAPTER 2

When prisoners find trust difficult, however, they can become prey to loneliness, self-blame, and depression. Depression can lead to hopelessness, and hopelessness to self-destructive thoughts and behavior.[61] It can become harder and harder for a person suffering in this way to access any support offered to them in prison or outside it following their release, creating a negative spiral in well-being that makes them more likely to be both victims and perpetrators of crime in the future.

A research group led by Jennifer Kao recommended, based on a survey of existing literature and their own work, that prison authorities work with prisoners to help them to develop appropriate "incremental trust."[62] (Re)learning trust, they argued, was crucial if prisoners were to survive prison and make any kind of new life on their release. It might be very hard for prisoners to take the risk of trusting in any part of a world or a judicial system that, in many cases, seemed to have been (and may actually have been) stacked against them from childhood. But if they could be helped to discern what trustworthy relationships were available to them, to take a first step of giving trust where it seemed most likely to get a positive response, and to make some stronger and more supportive relationships, then there was hope for their future. This approach, Kao's group argued, had the potential to alleviate loneliness, depression, and self-harm and to foster well-being, resilience, and good functioning in society.[63]

However well prepared they are, on being released from prison ex-offenders notoriously struggle to find work. Trust is regarded as a key concept in the theory of employment relations in general, and never more so than when there is some reason why one partner might not be regarded as trustworthy.[64] Oluwasegun Obatusin and Debbie Ritter-Williams investigated why some employers in Baltimore, Maryland were reluctant to employ ex-offenders and found that a prime factor was their perceived untrustworthiness.[65] "According to participants, the issue of trust was complex as the decision to employ an ex-offender could turn out to be a great experience or a significant risk. According to Participant 1, an ex-offender could not be trusted: 'he is somebody who cannot be trusted and has a tendency

---

61. Kao et al., "Associations between Past Trauma," 2.

62. Kao et al., "Associations between Past Trauma," 9.

63. Kao et al., "Associations between Past Trauma," 9–10.

64. Jeroen de Jong, René Schalk and Marcel Croon, "The Role of Trust in Secure and Insecure Employment Situations: A Multiple-Group Analysis," *Economic and Industrial Democracy* 30 (2009): 510.

65. Oluwasegun Obatusin and Debbie Ritter-Williams, "A Phenomenological Study of Employer Perspectives on Hiring Ex-Offenders," *Cogent Social Sciences* 5 (2019): art. 1571730. Employers' worries about customers' perceptions of ex-offenders were another factor in their reluctance to employ them.

Trust after Trauma, Conflict, and Offending

to violate established laws or procedures.' Participant 3 added that the perception of trust could be temporary or permanent depending on the ex-offender."[66]

According to this study, however, when employers did give ex-offenders an opportunity, they found that employees typically responded with trustworthiness, were much less likely to reoffend, and also readjusted better to "civilian" life. Employers who were willing to accept the risks involved were those who were willing to look beyond the "cage" created by the label "ex-offender," with its implications that a person was irredeemably "evil and untrustworthy," and see the person as talented, skillful, and as having potential to do well.[67] The shocking image of the cage in this account recalls chapter 1, where we discussed how being sinful can be experienced and represented as a place where one is trapped, and out of which one has to break to enter a new life.

Obatusin and Ritter-Williams also found that some employers took more than a superficial interest in the ex-offender's background. What had brought them to offend in the first place? Greed or need? Willful disdain for the law or being in the wrong place at the wrong time?[68] They listened to the potential employee's story and sought to understand the mixture of suffering and wrongdoing in their past. By taking time to attend to the ex-offender as a person and listen to them with some degree of sympathy, these employers began to create new conditions for trust. Some also sought to mitigate risk by seeking references from family members and community leaders. These, they hoped, would indicate that an ex-offender was surrounded by a support system that would help them not to reoffend and hold them accountable if they did.[69] The range of experiences Obatusin and Ritter-Williams described led them to argue that employers would be justified in giving more opportunities to ex-offenders: not stereotyping them as irredeemably evil but helping them to rebuild their lives, and offering "a supportive context to rebuild trust."[70] The creation of trust can be a foundation on which new relationships and new lives are built.

In some Western countries, governmental and nonprofit organizations act as mediators between ex-offenders and wider society, offering support and mentoring and helping ex-offenders to make new lives and not reoffend. In the 1980s and 1990s, six Christian denominations in Cleveland, Ohio, jointly administered a program called Community Re-Entry (CR), which sought to enable ex-offenders

---

66. Obatusin and Ritter-Williams, "Employer Perspectives," 6.
67. Obatusin and Ritter-Williams, "Employer Perspectives," 8.
68. Obatusin and Ritter-Williams, "Employer Perspectives," 9.
69. Obatusin and Ritter-Williams, "Employer Perspectives," 6.
70. Obatusin and Ritter-Williams, "Employer Perspectives," 9.

CHAPTER 2

to reenter and remain part of mainstream society. Part of the program was "Care Team," which was formed of a group of ex-convicts trained to assist vulnerable elderly residents in a local housing authority. Although the CR Program had invested trust and training in Care Team members, and team members had affirmed their intention to be trustworthy, the vulnerable residents initially found it hard to trust them—especially, for instance, with money for buying groceries and other necessities. Gradually, however, the residents were reassured by what they saw as the trustworthiness of the program's administrators and began to take a risk on the ex-offenders. The Care Team members proved highly trustworthy, and deeper trust relationships began to develop. On one landmark day, a Care Team member came into the CR office with three hundred dollars in cash that a resident had entrusted to him to deposit in her bank. There were tears in his eyes. He said, "No one has trusted me like this since I was 13 years old."[71]

The Christian groups that administered this program were committed to the possibility that ex-offenders could, by trusting in and being trusted therapeutically by an organization whose own trustworthiness was rooted in its trust in God and Christ, become trusting and trustworthy in turn and be rehabilitated. They acted as I will suggest Christ acts in his death, and as communities such as churches can act now to enable, by their trust and trustworthiness toward both parties, trust to develop between them. Between about 1980 and when the Community Re-Entry program was described in the 2000 article by Richard E. Sering, more than one thousand offenders took part in the program every year, and at least 93 percent annually stayed out of prison. Trust, together with practical help and the opportunity to practice a new way of life, changed thousands of lives. Not the least striking aspect of this, and similar stories of rehabilitation, is that ex-offenders were invited not only to trust the Community Re-Entry program and let themselves be helped but also to become trustworthy and help others.

A study by Ruth Armstrong examines the nature of the trust involved in mentoring prisoners and ex-prisoners among self-identified Christian volunteers in programs in the United Kingdom.[72] Armstrong observes that most theorists of trust assume that it needs to be well founded: it is foolish, even dangerous to trust someone unless you are reasonably sure they are trustworthy. The Christian volunteers she studied, however, took a different view. For a start, they saw

71. Richard E. Sering, "Reclamation through Trust: A Program for Ex-Offenders," *Christian Century*, December 6, 2000, https://www.christiancentury.org/article/reclamation-through-trust.

72. Ruth Armstrong, "Trusting the Untrustworthy: The Theology, Practice and Implications of Faith-Based Volunteers' Work with Ex-Prisoners," *Studies in Christian Ethics* 27 (2014): 299–317. Hereafter, page references from this work will be given in parentheses in the text.

108

Trust after Trauma, Conflict, and Offending

their activity first and foremost as service to God and an expression of their trust in a trustworthy God. Second, they extended trustworthiness and trust to their "protégés" not in response to their perceived trustworthiness but in the hope of creating trust and trustworthiness.

In one case study, mentor Brian worked with prisoner Big G, a repeat offender. They met several times before Big G was released and continued to meet almost daily after his release. Brian helped Big G to get a job, showing him how to write job applications, drove him to job interviews and then to and from work, secured him a bank loan, and employed Big G himself. After less than three months, however, Big G was reconvicted and imprisoned. Brian reported:

> You've got to build up a closeness and a trust, a level of trust, you know, like Big G when he fell off the wagon there, he called me ... he called me on a borrowed cell phone from under a bridge ... but he knew, I mean he had the trust that I was a person he could call and that I would be there, and that I would come and get him, you know.

On the face of it, despite his sense that he had built a relationship of trust with Big G, Brian's mentoring was a costly failure, but Armstrong argues otherwise. The volunteers in this program held an unarticulated but well-formed theology of trust. As noted above, they understood their mentoring as a gift based on their faith (304–5). It was not, however, a gift from "us" to "them" across a social or moral divide; the mentors recognized the shared humanity and human predicament of everyone involved. "Volunteers' services were delivered in an ambience of subversive altruism. Rather than aiming to assist the state through an interest in prisoners characterized by difference and therefore 'appropriate distance', the language and practice of the volunteers was of transformation through grace—the bestowal of gratuitous trust and acceptance. Volunteering was not about helping 'them', but about being 'us'." The mentors based their activity on a sense of human identity with the offenders and offered them a relationship involving trust that they recognized the offenders needed and which, if their positions were reversed, they would want to be offered themselves. They understood that they would often be disappointed and were fully prepared to take that risk. Armstrong argues that, given the potential benefit to society as a whole, the volunteers' actions were not only an act of grace but were practically "less risky ... [and] more intelligent" than the alternative (309). And often the "gift of trust" did indeed generate "a trustworthy response" (299).

The prisoners, who also identified as being part of a religious tradition (in one case Muslim and in the others Christian), for their part accepted the volunteers'

CHAPTER 2

outreach to them because they saw its motivation as one of "service to God and love of mankind" (306). The trust of the volunteers was not "charity" and did not arise from a sense of superiority or pity. It was seen as assuring the prisoners that they were valuable people, precious to God and to the volunteer. As one female prisoner said, "I remember I told one female [volunteer] in one of them classes when I first got there, I said 'Miss, I don't know you, I don't trust you, I don't wanna talk to you.' And that woman did not give up on me, and you know, she's a good woman, she didn't just give up on me" (307). The prisoner came round and did come to talk to and trust the volunteer.

We can see this as another example of incarnational trust. The mentors offered the prisoners a relationship based on their understanding of their fully shared humanity and offered to be with, and travel with, the prisoners on their long and often rocky road toward a new life. The prisoners were (or came to be) willing to trust them based on their understanding of the mentors' commitment to God, their own willingness to trust in God, and the fact that the mentors offered to be with them and travel with them.

Armstrong concludes that mentoring schemes of this kind have many successes, alongside their failures, because they recognize that people are more than the sum of their failures and offenses, that trust can be elicited by being offered even to the apparently untrustworthy, and that "potential can be realized by being recognized . . . perceptions of possibility can shape what is possible . . . in a dynamic trust relationship, being trusted is an inherent part of being, or becoming, trustworthy" (308–9). She concludes by reporting that when Big G went back to prison, Brian continued to visit him. Brian collected Big G on the day he got out again, helped him to get another job, and several years later, at the time of writing, Big G had not reoffended.

Life-changing trust can take place directly between two parties. Christina Landman and Tanya Pieterse studied how prisoners serving long sentences in South Africa sought to give meaning to their suffering in jail by recognizing God or Christ as suffering alongside them and growing in trust in God in consequence.[73] In this process, God is envisaged as a friend, "the one you can trust and confide in, who is always there for support," who stays with you as you do your time. "Maybe I wasn't trusting God outside," said Prisoner 11 in an interview, "now I do trust God. I do trust God for being in control of my whole life and I know he has got a purpose for everything that happens in my life."[74] Alternatively, as in the Cleveland Community Re-Entry program, trust can be mediated through a third

---

73. Christina Landman and Tanya Pieterse, "(Re)constructing God to Find Meaning in Suffering: Men Serving Long-Term Sentences in Zonderwater," *HvTSt* 75 (2019): art. 5520.

74. Landman and Pieterse, "(Re)constructing God," 5–6.

Trust after Trauma, Conflict, and Offending

party. In a recent report into government-administered Youth Offending Teams (YOTs), which are part of HMI Probation services in the United Kingdom, one young offender attests to the role of his parents in mediating trust between the Youth Offending Team and himself:

> If your YOT worker gets on well with your parents . . . then you, you form a bond, it's like that trust circle in'it? It opens up a bit more because you think well yeah, my parents trust them maybe I can trust them that little bit more. And if, if they get on well and they're chatting and that then it's like it's a good thing because then it makes you feel better about yourself.[75]

This young offender not only recognizes the role of his parents in mediating between himself and the YOT but also puts his finger on a key aspect of trust. At a time when many young people feel worst about themselves and their prospects, mired in the grip of past errors and present difficulties, "it makes you feel better about yourself." The feeling this young man got from seeing trust in action and including him helped to change his view of his situation and so, in itself, changed how it was possible for him to see himself being and acting in the future.

Another group of recent studies has shown the effectiveness of inviting ex-offenders to share their experience of crime, punishment, and rehabilitation with other offenders or groups who, because they have grown up in difficult circumstances, are deemed at higher than average risk of offending.[76] Meeting people with whom they can identify, who have offended, whose lives and values have subsequently changed, and who encourage and support them in taking a different path, can change the course of offenders' or potential offenders' lives. As Sean Creaney observes, change is brought about less by tools or programs than by "the existence of a trusting, empathetic and consistent relationship which provides sources of hope."[77] We might be reminded of what Paul and other New Testament writers

---

75. Cath Larkins and John Wainwright, *'Just Put Me on the Right Track': Young People's Perspectives on What Helps Them Stop Offending* (Preston: University of Central Lancashire Press, 2013), 15.

76. E.g., M. Barry, "The Mentor/Monitor Debate in Criminal Justice: What Works for Offenders," *British Journal of Social Work* 30 (2000): 575–95; I. Boyce, G. Hunder, and M. Hough, *St. Giles Trust Peer Advice Project: An Evaluation* (London: St. Giles Trust, 2009); Gillian Buck, "The Core Conditions of Peer Mentoring," *Criminology and Criminal Justice* 18 (2017): 190–206; Gillian Buck, "'I Wanted To Feel the Way They Did': Mimesis as a Situational Dynamic of Peer Mentoring by Ex-Offenders," *Deviant Behavior* 38 (2017): 1027–41.

77. Sean Creaney, "Children's Voices—Are We Listening? Progressing Peer Mentoring in the Youth Justice System," *Child Care in Practice* 26 (2020): 22.

CHAPTER 2

never forget: that the death and resurrection of Christ makes possible the release of wrongdoers not only through encounter with Christ himself but also through the example and testimony of those who have encountered him and been changed.

We saw in the introduction and above that the ability to trust oneself is a significant part of trust and the ability to trust and be trusted by others. Self-trust is well recognized as one of the aspects of trust that is damaged by trauma and abuse. More unexpectedly, perhaps, it is also damaged by offending:

> Research has demonstrated that for an offender a transgression results in the elevation of the psychological need for belonging . . . Specifically, offenders experience a threat of exclusion; of being marginalized, stigmatized, and socially tainted because of their own wrongdoing. Social exclusion or marginalization of an offender is one way a community deals with a violation of group norms and values . . . Whether exclusion is used because the offenders' behavior indicates to the group that they are an untrustworthy group member, or as a form of punishment, or as a way of communicating the group's condemnation of the behavior, the exclusion (or possibility of exclusion) threatens the offenders' fundamental need to belong . . . Thus, a transgression results in offenders having an elevated need for belonging and acceptance by others . . . However, this need for acceptance includes the need to reestablish that one is a good and appropriate group member, that one understands group moral values, and is able to conform to them . . . This is expressed by the offenders needing others to understand their side of the story, empathize with their experience, and recognize that they are agreeable people.[78]

One of the ways in which offenders seek to establish that they are "agreeable people" is by affirming and demonstrating their trustworthiness. Part of this process is the (re)establishment of self-trust, which the authors define in this context as "confidence that [one] can and will act more appropriately in the future," or, to put it another way, trust in one's own ability to be trustworthy.[79] The (re)development of self-trust may come about through therapy or by the offender working with themselves or with the help of a third party, who might be friends, family members, or fellow members of a community such as a religious community.[80]

78. Lydia Woodyatt and Michael Wenzel, "A Needs-Based Perspective on Self-Forgiveness: Addressing Threat to Moral Identity as a Means of Encouraging Interpersonal and Intrapersonal Restoration," *Journal of Experimental Social Psychology* 50 (2014): 126.

79. Woodyatt and Wenzel, "Needs-Based Perspective," 128.

80. Many studies of conflict resolution and rehabilitation take the view that for reconciliation or rehabilitation to occur, wrongdoers must come to recognize their wrongdoing, feel

Trust after Trauma, Conflict, and Offending

CONCLUSION

The examples in this chapter, drawn from three different fields of the social sciences and psychology, share some striking findings and conclusions. They agree that trust is essential where individuals or groups hope to mend broken relationships, whether after war, trauma, or offending. Trust is central to every stage of the process of reconciliation and restoration, however long it takes. An act of trust can initiate a relationship. It affirms that the truster has something to offer and that the truster thinks the trustee also has something to offer, which affirms the value of the trustee and can encourage and empower them to respond. Particular situations often shape our perceptions so that we identify one group or individual as having done wrong and another as having suffered, but the reality is usually more complicated. Suffering and wrongdoing are everywhere intertwined; many people have both suffered and done wrong, and wrongdoing comes in many kinds and degrees. The restoration of trust, however, can be initiated from any side in a complex situation and address all kinds of damage done and suffered.[81]

Trust is a very practical attitude and act: it says that the problems of wrongdoing and suffering that pervade the world can be addressed by people acting together. It underpins many other kinds of relationship, making them more likely to hold. The development of trust can involve many setbacks, but even when trust is fragile, imperfect, and prone to fail, thin or imperfect trust can be good enough to enable relationships to begin and develop. As it begins to work, ideally, trust gradually deepens, enabling cooperation and mutual support and expanding the worldview of everyone involved. It allows participants to look to the future and prepare for it. That future may be quite specific, involving a particular goal, or it may be very open-ended.

Studies of trust in social sciences tend to focus on trust as an act, while psychology tends to focus on it as an attitude. We saw in the introduction that in the ancient world, including in early Christian writings, it can be either or both, and

---

empathy for the victim and shame for their behavior, and acknowledge and repent of it. There are, though, circumstances in which this is not practically or psychologically possible. There are also circumstances in which someone who has suffered cannot practically wait for an offender to feel shame or repent before moving on with their own lives (however that is understood). We return to this theme below, pp. 212–18.

81. We have focused here on sincere and often successful efforts to restore trust, but we should also note that trust can be elicited with empty words and promises, and people sometimes trust wrongly. See, e.g., Schniter, Sheremeta, and Sznycer, "Building and Rebuilding Trust"; Christopher P. Reinders Folmer et al., "We Can't Go On Together with Suspicious Minds: Forecasting Errors in Evaluating the Appreciation of Denials," *J. Trust Res.* 10 (2020): 4–22.

CHAPTER 2

it is usually taken to be ideally both.[82] In practice, the same is true in the cases we have described, and the relationship is often reciprocal: sometimes taking an attitude of trust enables one to act with trust, and sometimes taking a step of trust enables the attitude to follow. The fact that the attitude and act of trust do not always go together, however, underlines how risky trust can be. Sometimes to establish or foster trust, one person or group needs to act when they are not sure they can trust or respond to an action without being sure of its motives.

Some of the case studies in this chapter focused on two parties, but often a mediator was involved. In many different situations, mediators can help to foster trust by representing different parties to one another, by helping them to understand each other better, and by being with and traveling with those who need to grow in trust. Modern theories of mediation argue that mediation can not only change participants' relationships to one another but can change their sense of identity, their sense of where they belong, and the "truth" they inhabit.[83] The practice of mediation, meanwhile, combines care, the creation of new structures and life goals that participants may inhabit, and the creation of new (secular) belief or faith.[84] This describes well the kind of change human beings need to be freed from the prison that our suffering and wrongdoing often create around us and live at one with God and Christ, which we began to explore in the last chapter and will trace further in the next.

Among the studies of trust we have described are several in which participants or mediators self-identify as Christian. Christians may root their own capacity for trust or trustworthiness in the trustworthiness and trust of God and Jesus Christ. Their response to that fundamental trust is sometimes found to make them more willing than usual to take a risk on other people. Sometimes they do so explicitly in imitation of Christ, who took a risk on those he called to follow him and be reconciled with God. It is tempting to speculate that some of the initiatives to establish or foster trust we have seen that are not explicitly inspired by Chris-

---

82. See further Morgan, *Roman Faith*, 224–34, 444–72.

83. Arie Nadler and Nurit Shnabel, "Instrumental and Socioemotional Paths to Intergroup Reconciliation and the Needs-Based Model of Socioemotional Reconciliation," in *The Social Psychology of Intergroup Reconciliation* (ed. Arie Nadler, Thomas E. Malloy, and Jeffrey D. Fisher; Oxford: Oxford University Press, 2008), 37–56; Ida Helene Asmussen, "Mediation in Light of Modern Identity," in *Nordic Mediation Research* (ed. Anna Nylund, Kaijus Ervasti, and Lin Adrian; Cham: Springer, 2018), 133–43.

84. Neil H. Katz, "Enhancing Mediator Artistry: Multiple Frames, Spirit, and Reflection in Action," in *The Blackwell Handbook of Mediation: Bridging Theory, Research, and Practice* (ed. Margared S. Hermman; Oxford: Blackwell, 2006), 374–83, especially 374–76.

Trust after Trauma, Conflict, and Offending

tianity may be influenced by it, especially since the majority of studies in conflict resolution to date focus on parts of the world (Africa, South America, Europe) that have a strong Christian heritage or are strongly Christian now. Against this, there is little discussion of trust in Christian theology, so peace or reconciliation initiatives have little formal Christian work on trust from which they can draw. Then again, there is a good deal of popular interest in trust among Christians, so it is not impossible that much of the interest in trust in the spheres we have been looking at owes something, even if subconsciously, to a strain of popular and untheorized but implicitly theological Christian thinking.[85]

We have seen that, in these studies, trust is profoundly incarnational. Even where it is very difficult to establish trust, it is easier when—with or without the offices of a mediator—people can inhabit the same space, see each other, listen to each other, speak, and know that they are heard. As we saw Laura Stovel put it earlier, the kind of trust that is created by face-to-face encounter is the measure of "deep reconciliation . . . reconciliation that is felt."[86] The mediators who featured in the stories above did not die in the process of mediation, but that does not make them as different from Jesus Christ as we might assume. For many, especially those working in the aftermath of conflict, mediation was and is an extremely risky process. In undertaking it, they put themselves in daily danger of being attacked or killed. Many, moreover, undertake this work because they have been attacked in the past, tortured, threatened with death, and have seen members of their families and friends killed (some have also perpetrated these crimes). They have been face to face with death, and their survival to work for peace is its own kind of resurrection. Survivors of trauma or abuse have often been all but destroyed by what they have suffered physically, psychologically, and emotionally. Those who go on to work with other victims know every step on that road of suffering. Those who have been convicted and incarcerated, meanwhile, know what it is to have been despised and rejected by their society, condemned, excised from everyday life, and entombed. If, on leaving prison, they learn to (re)make trusting relationships and work with other vulnerable people to help them not to offend, they, too, have risen to a new life. The experience of suffering and wrongdoing alike marks all these groups as indelibly as the imprints of nails or a spear. They never

---

85. There is a wealth of popular books about trusting God on the market in many languages: e.g., Tomas Trigo, *En los brazos del Padre: Confianza en Dios* (Casablanca: Editorial, 2013); Jerry Bridges, *Trusting God* (Colorado Springs: NavPress, 2016); J. Martin, *Trust God's Plan: Finding Faith in Difficult Times* (Niles: Forever Young, 2020); Eugen Drewermann, *Vertrauen kann man nur auf Gott* (Oberursal: Publik-Forum, 2020).

86. Above, pp. 93–94.

115

CHAPTER 2

lose it, but it also allows them to walk alongside others who have done wrong and suffered, extend trust and trustworthiness to them, and show them a way to new life. In the next chapter I will argue that the incarnate Christ, who is fully human among sinful and suffering humanity, also mediates between humanity and God, offering trust and trustworthiness to both, and accompanying humanity on its journey out of suffering and wrongdoing into new life.

CHAPTER 3

The Trust and Trustworthiness of Jesus Christ

In chapter 1 I noted the many images of at-one-ment that are scattered through-out New Testament writings, some of which appear only once and others a handful of times. Only one, the idea of Jesus's death as sacrifice, is developed by a writer at some length, in the Letter to the Hebrews. In contrast, *pistis* language appears several hundred times across the New Testament corpus, in connection with revelation, salvation, healing, righteousness, people's response to Jesus and preaching about him, and discipleship. This in itself should be enough to make us wonder about the nature of the connection between *pistis* and at-one-ment, but *pistis* language also appears in a number of passages that proclaim specifically the significance of Jesus's death and resurrection. It is therefore perhaps surprising that early churches in posttestamental writings do not seem to have canvassed a trust-based model of atonement.

Several explanations are possible. One is that, faced with criticism from both Jews and gentiles for the novelty and implausibility of their teaching and keen to emphasize Christianity's continuity with the Jewish scriptures and tradition, early Christians emphasized and elaborated images of divine-human at-one-ment that appear in the Jewish scriptures, several of which were already associated with messianic hope. Another is that from the second century onward *pistis* was used increasingly of Christians' attitude and practice toward God ("faith") and for the teaching handed down through the generations ("the faith"), so explicit ref-erences to the trust or faithfulness of God and Christ receded somewhat into the background. Yet another is that, consciously or subconsciously, later generations of Christians took for granted that the faithfulness of God reaches out through grace to humanity, which enabled them to respond with "faith" in turn, but saw this as the framework within which mechanisms of atonement took place rather than as a model in its own right.

CHAPTER 3

As we have seen, however, modern research demonstrates the central importance of trust in at-one-ment after conflict, alienation, wrongdoing, and suffering, and this points us back to the New Testament's language of *pistis* in relation to Christ's death. This chapter draws on Paul, with support from other writers, to argue that *pistis*, in its trust/trustworthiness/faithfulness/entrustedness meanings, is not only the leitmotif of every part of the Christian narrative of God's at-one-ment with humanity but also describes how at-one-ment takes place specifically through the death of Jesus Christ. This chapter therefore takes up the implicit challenge of the introduction, which noted that although almost all Christians through time have recognized the death (and sometimes also the resurrection) of Jesus as decisive for humanity's at-one-ment with God, they have given and continue to give themselves great freedom in exploring how it is decisive. Following chapter 1, this chapter will try to show how trust and its close relatives work to restore both wrongdoers and the suffering, together with all those who fall into both categories. In the process we will build on the examples in chapter 2, which showed how mediators who are trustworthy and trusted can help to restore relationships after offending, conflict, and trauma.

I will argue that the trust between God and Christ and between Christ and humanity makes possible the restoration of trust between God and humanity, creating a relationship that is also a framework within which other changes can take place, including repentance and forgiveness, reconciliation between human beings, and (re)new(ed) life and hope.[1] Some of the more traditional images of atonement also have a place within this process. The texts I examine offer not one but a cluster of reasons why Christ dies, which speak both to the nature of Jesus Christ himself and humanity's varied needs of him. I will also try to show that though the resurrection is not a necessary sequel to the crucifixion, it is, like the Christ event as a whole, a grace that makes possible a restoration of trust that otherwise might not have been possible for Jesus's followers. I will explore how a "trust" model of at-one-ment might work for one who suffers and for a wrongdoer who has also suffered and argue that Jesus Christ dies not only—perhaps not even mainly—because he has to, but because *we* have to die to the power of our wrongdoing and suffering, and God, through Christ, wills that that death should culminate in eternal life.

I begin by developing a trust-based model of atonement out of Paul's Letter to the Romans supported by passages from Galatians and Philippians. Romans not

---

1. Corneliu Constantineanu, "Pauline Scholarship on Reconciliation" argues for the link between reconciliation language, peace, and new creation in Deutero-Isaiah as background for Paul.

118

The Trust and Trustworthiness of Jesus Christ

only offers an account of how Christ saves by restoring righteousing, life-giving trust between God and humanity but, as we have seen, also has more to say about wrongdoing and *apistia*, and their relationship with suffering, than any other letter.[2] Romans 3:21–26, Gal 2:15–21, and Phil 3:7–11, with some related passages, share the vision that, through God's grace (Rom 3:24; Gal 2:21; cf. Phil 1:2), Jesus Christ acts for humanity (in a way variously described at Rom 3:24–25; Gal 2:20; cf. Phil 2:7–11), human beings respond with trust (Rom 3:22; Gal 2:16; Phil 3:9), and this relationship, which brings new life to humanity in right relationship with God (Rom 3:24, 26; Gal 2:16, 20; Phil 3:9; cf. Phil 3:11), also involves, in some sense, dying or being crucified with Christ or being conformed to his death (Gal 2:19; Phil 3:10; cf. Rom 6:3–11).

PISTIS, AT-ONE-MENT, AND THE MEDIATION OF JESUS CHRIST

At Rom 5:10 Paul affirms that "we were reconciled to God [κατηλλάγημεν τῷ θεῷ] through the death of his Son." This reconciliation—which is identified with being made right with God (5:1, 9), having peace with God (5:1), standing in grace (5:2), and living in hope of salvation and glory (5:2, 9)—comes about through *pistis* (5:1). A few verses earlier (5:1) Paul has referred to the trust human beings put in "him who raised Jesus our Lord from the dead" (4:24), so *pistis* at 5:1 is probably human trust in God. But at 3:21–26 Paul has already placed *pistis*, together with *dikaiosynē* and *charis*, in a more complex configuration to affirm what God has done through Christ.[3]

As we saw in chapter 1, Paul claims that Jews and gentiles alike are under sin and suffering (e.g., Rom 1:18; 3:9–10; cf. 2:1), and at 3:3 specifies that some Jews have been *apistos*.[4] Both Jews and gentiles therefore stand in need of the righting of their relationship with God (cf. 3:22–23).[5] God, however, remains *pistos* explicitly

---

2. In *The Theology of Trust*, I argued that a saving relationship of trust with God and Christ can be initiated when people encounter Jesus Christ in any part of his earthly life, death, resurrection, or risen or exalted life. The relationship between the saving or life-giving power of trust in Jesus in his earthly life, in particular, and the necessity of his death is somewhat different in different New Testament writings, but Paul has no doubt that Jesus's death and resurrection are central to human righteousing and the restoration of divine-human *pistis*.

3. This passage, with Gal 2:15–21 and Phil 3:7–11, is discussed at greater length in Morgan, *Roman Faith*, 267–74, 288–94, 302–4.

4. Above, pp. 73–76.

5. Cf. p. 75.

CHAPTER 3

toward Israel (3:3) and implicitly toward everyone.[6] God's righteousness is revealed in the gospel "from *pistis* to *pistis*," which suggests that *pistis* belongs first to God and then to human beings.[7] Paul also confirms that when the people of Israel are in their right relationship with God they have *pistis*. In Rom 1:5 he says that he has been sent to bring about the "obedience of *pistis*" among the gentiles too.[8] At Rom 1:12, moreover, as elsewhere, Paul describes Christ-confessors as having *pistis*. At 3:21–26 he sketches Christ's role in the process by which human beings return to their right relationship with God, making use of some phrases that he probably inherited but also using *pistis* language.

Paul proclaims that the gracious righteousness of God has been revealed "apart from the law" (3:21, cf. 3:24) διὰ πίστεως Ἰησοῦ Χριστοῦ (3:22) for all who trust— which could refer to trust in God, Christ, or both[9]—through the death of Christ. Much debate about the meaning of the phrase διὰ πίστεως Ἰησοῦ Χριστοῦ, here and at Gal 2:16 and Phil 3:9, has focused on whether it refers to the faithfulness of Christ to God, or the trust or "faith" that human beings put in Christ. I have argued rather that Paul uses the phrase to describe the faithfulness and trustworthiness of Jesus Christ both to God, as God's Son, and toward humanity, as its savior, which invites humanity's trust in him.[10] This exploits the fact that *pistis* is an "action nominal," a noun that characterizes the two ends of a relationship as complementary, together with the fact that Paul understands Christ, in general, as being in relationship both with God and with human beings and as being the mediator between them as central to the new relationship between God and humanity.[11]

6. Above, p. 75.

7. P. 71.

8. Here I take *pistis* with most commentators as a subjective genitive. C. R. Cranfield, *A Critical and Exegetical Commentary on the Epistle to the Romans* (2 vols.; 6th ed.; Edinburgh: T&T Clark, 1975), 1:66–67 discusses several possible alternatives.

9. Most commentators take this as referring to trust in Christ, but since gentiles must come to trust in God, too, it probably refers to both.

10. Morgan, *Roman Faith*, 31, 53, 263 n. 7, 273.

11. The most recent significant contribution to this debate is Kevin Grasso, "A Linguistic Analysis of *Pistis Christou*: The Case for the Third View," *JSNT* 43 (2020): 108–44. Grasso argues that *pistis Christou* cannot bear an objective meaning and is more likely to mean "Christ-faith," referring to "a system or set of beliefs" (109) than to bear the subjective meaning. I agree that in Greek in general *pistis* with an objective genitive is, at least, rare (not least because most writers prefer the verb to the noun), and that trust/belief in Christ is not all that is at issue in these passages. But I doubt that the objective genitive is "not an option" for the phrase *pistis Christou* (130). *Elpis* "hope," for instance, can operate grammatically similarly to *pistis*, and we find it in New Testament writings and elsewhere with both subjective and objective genitives (e.g., Acts 28:20; Phil 1:20 [subjective]; Acts 16:19; Rom 5:2; Gal 5:5; Eph 1:18; 4:4; 1 Thess 5:8 [objective]) as well as with a preposition of the object of hope (e.g., Acts 24:15; 1 John 3:3). Nor does

120

The Trust and Trustworthiness of Jesus Christ

Having affirmed the *pistis* of God (3:3), Paul now affirms that God's righteousness is manifest in the renewed possibility for human beings of returning to their right relationship with God (3:21). Whatever has happened διὰ πίστεως Ἰησοῦ Χριστοῦ is God's initiative, and it is clear that human beings must actively trust in order to respond and be made right with God (3:22, 26), but what is Christ's role?

God, Paul says at verse 25, "put forward" Christ to die, but Paul also takes for granted, here and everywhere, that Christ's obedience to God is voluntary: the obedience of a son who shares his father's intentions and acts on his behalf.[12] A growing number of commentators have argued that Christ's willingness to die for humanity, here and elsewhere, is an expression of his faithfulness toward a God who is trustworthy (cf. Rom 1:16; 3:3; 1 Cor 1:9; 2 Cor 1:18; 1 Thess 5:24) and his trust in God's new initiative for humanity.[13] We can add to this that the affirmation of

---

the absence of the article in instances of *pistis Christou* mean that it cannot be subjective, since Koine Greek often leaves out the article where older or more literary Greek would not. Grasso is right that *pistis* often refers to the content of Christian teaching in second-century writers and later, but then *hē pistis* is used by itself (this is one of several ways in which Christians gradually extend the meaning of *pistis* language). Paul would only need to specify that the content of his teaching was *pistis Christou* if *pistis* were already used to refer to a body of teaching. The phrase could mean "what is entrusted about Christ," but the idea of something being entrusted to people, where it is used in the New Testament, looks derivative of the trust people put in Christ, so it would be surprising to find it of what righteouses in Rom 3, Gal 3, or Phil 3. Alternatively, the phrase could mean "the argument about Christ" in a rhetorical sense, but that seems implausible in context. My main concern with the "third view," however, is that it suggests that it is (believing or trusting in) the content of preaching or teaching that righteouses and saves. This surely does not do justice to Paul, who seems to make clear throughout his writings that putting one's trust in Christ as Lord and Savior and living under obedience to Christ as to God righteouses and saves—that is, it is a personal relationship with the person of Christ, which is implied but is much more than acceptance of a body of teaching. My interpretation, here and elsewhere, follows none of the three ways Grasso discusses but proposes that people come to put their trust in Christ through the faithfulness and trustworthiness—for short, the relationship of trust—between God and Christ and between Christ and humanity, which enables Christ to mediate between them. Grasso recognizes this and does not dispute it, but says that this is not "how language ordinarily works, and it takes a very special context for that to be plausible" (137 n. 52). Morgan, *Roman Faith*, 95–104, however, shows that *pistis* language is used in this way when it is used of mediators in diplomatic or legal relations; in addition, Paul's talking about how Christ righteouses and saves surely is a "very special context," and we have abundant later evidence that this context leads Christians to develop *pistis* language in multiple directions.

12. Cf. Rom 5:6–7; Gal 2:20; Phil 2:6–7. For Christ's willingness to suffer and die see also, e.g., Matt 20:26–28 // Mark 10:43–45; Matt 26:39 // Mark 14:36 // Luke 22:42; John 12:26–27 with Brown, *John I–XII*, 475–77. In Heb 3:6 Christ's faithfulness to God is that of a son of the house whose loyalty is both taken for granted and enacted.

13. See especially chapter 4 of Richard Hays, *The Faith of Jesus Christ: The Narrative Substruc-*

CHAPTER 3

3:22 that Christ's *pistis* is "for all who trust" points to Christ as trustworthy toward human beings. If we assume that at 3:22 and 26 πίστις Ἰησοῦ Χριστοῦ refers either to the trust of those who put their trust in Christ rather than any attitude or action by Christ himself or to the content of preaching about Christ, then Christ plays no active role in at-one-ment here: he is God's tool and preaching about him is the object of human trust. It fits better with Paul's view of Christ elsewhere (not to mention that of other writers) to see Christ as playing an active role here, in relation to both God and humanity, and the grammar of the phrase πίστις Ἰησοῦ Χριστοῦ allows us to do so. The righteousness of God, says Paul (3:21–26), has been revealed through Christ's trust and faithfulness toward God as trustworthy and toward humanity as capable of responding to him with trust for all who trust (in God or Christ but, for Paul, undoubtedly both). God put Jesus Christ forward as a supplicatory offering—probably a term inherited by Paul[14]—to reveal God's righteousness so that the person who puts their trust in Christ may be righteoused. The relationship of trust between God and Christ allows Jesus to let himself be put forward, and the trust both God and Christ—implicitly but necessarily[15]—put in humanity to respond is justified when human beings do put their trust in Christ and are righteoused.[16]

This double bond of trust, between God and Christ and Christ and humanity, is what makes possible humanity's return to right standing with God through Christ. Christ, who, in a world in which all have sinned (Rom 3:23), is uniquely without

---

ture of Galatians 3:1–4:11 (2nd ed.; Grand Rapids: Eerdmans, 2002); on the history of the debate see, e.g., Matthew C. Easter, "The *Pistis Christou* Debate: Main Arguments and Responses in Summary," *CBR* 9 (2010): 33–47; Chris Kugler, "*Pistis Christou*: The Current State of Play and Key Arguments," *CBR* 14 (2016): 244–55.

14. P. 2 n. 4; p. 47. The phrase *dia pisteōs* at 3:25 may not be original.

15. Victor Paul Furnish, *Jesus according to Paul* (Cambridge: Cambridge University Press, 1993), 109–10, 113–17 notes that when Paul refers to Christ as giving himself up or being given up, the verb *paradidonai* can bear the meaning "entrust" as well as "hand over," and may have that resonance, e.g., at Rom 8:32.

16. Cf. Rom 5:6–7. God also entrusts Paul and the Jews with his plans for humanity, e.g., Rom 3:2; 1 Thess 2:4. As a willing collaborator Christ does more than just obey, but in speaking of the crucifixion Paul emphasizes the humanity of Christ (e.g., 1 Cor 15:3–4, 21) and his self-emptying and subordination (Phil 2:7–8) as well as distinguishes Christ's "gracious gift" from God's own grace (Rom 5:15). God and Christ cannot compel humanity to respond, and it is hard to see how a human response would be valid or valuable to God if it were compelled. Trust, however, cannot be compelled. Hays, *Faith of Jesus Christ*, 170 argues that Romans is strongly theocentric and Paul never says explicitly that people put their trust in Christ, but since Paul affirms clearly elsewhere that people trust in Christ, there seems no strong reason to deny that trust in Christ is implicit in Romans. There is no reason to think that trust in Christ diminishes Paul's sense of the importance of trust in God.

The Trust and Trustworthiness of Jesus Christ

wrongdoing (2 Cor 5:21), is also uniquely trusting toward God and worthy of divine trust.[17] By the same token he is uniquely trustworthy toward human beings and worthy of their trust.[18] The trust between God and Christ enables Christ to be faithful even to death and offers a vehicle for divine grace. The trust between Christ and human beings enables human beings to trust Christ, who acts for them, and for Christ to trust them to respond to him and through him to God's grace. Through this double bond of trust and trustworthiness, trust is restored between humanity and God. To this we can add one more element that we have mentioned before: that God trusts humanity to be able to respond, immediately or eventually, to the revelation of God's righteousness and trustworthiness through Jesus Christ, even though Jesus is not any of the kinds of messiah that God's people might have expected.

Galatians 2:15–20 and Philippians 3:7–11 outline the same understanding of the working of trust between God, Christ, and humanity in Christ's death, though, being written in different circumstances, they do not parallel Romans exactly. In Phil 3:9–11, Paul says that any right standing he has with God comes "through *pistis Christou*, the righteousness from God based on *pistis*. I want to know Christ and the power of his resurrection and the sharing of his sufferings by becoming like him in his death, if somehow I may attain resurrection from the dead." Though the role of *pistis* is not spelled out here, it is clear that right relationship with God comes from God through Christ and that its basis is *pistis*. As in Romans 3, if we understand Christ as taking an active role in this process, we should read *pistis Christou*, as in Rom 3:22, as the trust between Christ and God that makes God's action through Christ possible, and the trust Christ puts in human beings to put their trust in him, along with the trust Paul has (implicitly but undoubtedly) put in Christ.[19]

In Gal 2:15–20, Paul refers several times to *pistis* in an argument that is primarily about the law of Moses.

> [15] We ourselves are Jews by birth and not gentile sinners, [16] yet we know that a person is justified not by the works of the law but through the *pistis* of Jesus Christ [διὰ πίστεως Ἰησοῦ Χριστοῦ]. And we have come to believe in Christ Jesus, so that we might be justified by the *pistis* of Christ [ἵνα δικαιωθῶμεν ἐκ

17. Taking Rom 5:21 with Thrall, "Salvation Proclaimed," 229–30 as meaning that Christ was made like sinful humanity though sinless himself.

18. This does not explain in itself how atonement comes about, just the configuration of relationships that makes it possible.

19. Paul's trust may be implied by the phrase "depending on trust" in verse 9. He has already described the Philippians as actively trusting in Christ (1:29; cf. 1:25).

CHAPTER 3

πίστεως Χριστοῦ] and not by doing the works of the law, because no one will be justified by the works of the law. [17] But if, in our effort to be justified in Christ, we ourselves have been found to be sinners, is Christ then a servant of sin? Certainly not! [18] But if I build up again the very things that I once tore down, then I demonstrate that I am a transgressor. [19] For through the law I died to the law, so that I might live to God. I have been crucified with Christ, [20] and it is no longer I who live, but it is Christ who lives in me. And the life I now live in the flesh I live in [the] *pistis* of the Son of God [ἐν πίστει ζῶ τῇ τοῦ υἱοῦ τοῦ θεοῦ], who loved me and gave himself for me. I do not nullify the grace of God, for if righteousness comes through the law, then Christ died for nothing.[20]

Leaving aside most of the notorious complexities of this passage, it is clear that Christ loves Paul, has given himself up for him, and has died to enable Paul to come to his right relationship with God (2:20–21). Paul has already made another, very similar statement: Christ "gave himself for our wrongdoings to set us free from the present evil age, according to the will of our God" (1:4). These expressions, like those of Rom 3:21–26, show Christ oriented simultaneously toward God and humanity. He does God's will, so he can be called trusting and faithful toward God, and he also loves and acts for human beings.[21] God's care for human beings is linked elsewhere in the Jewish scriptures and in New Testament writings with his being *pistos* in the sense of "trustworthy" toward them and, similarly, Christ is seen as worthy of trust by Paul because of his self-giving love. Christ can therefore be understood as *pistos* toward both God and human beings. Finally, human beings can trust Christ to enable them to come into right standing with God. Here, as in Romans and Philippians, Christ forms the center of the nexus of divine-human *pistis*: faithful, trustworthy, and trusted by both sides.

Understanding *pistis* in these passages as doubly reciprocal resolves a long-standing impasse in interpretation. It also fits with Paul's understanding of the role of Christ in his language of reconciliation and elsewhere. Indeed, to read Christ as both trusting and trustworthy toward both God and humanity is an obvious way to read his *pistis* when he is acting as mediator or conciliator.[22] Throughout the

20. Translation is a modified version of the NRSV.

21. On the relationship between *pistis Christou* and Jesus's faithfulness and obedience in the gospels see P. Bolt, "The Faith of Jesus Christ in the Synoptic Gospels," in *The Faith of Jesus Christ: Exegetical, Biblical, and Theological Studies* (ed. Michael F. Bird and Preston M. Sprinkle; Milton Keynes: Paternoster, 2009), 209–22; W. Salier, "The Obedient Son: The 'Faithfulness' of Christ in the Fourth Gospel," in Bird and Sprinkle, *Faith of Jesus* Christ, 223–38.

22. See P.-D. Dognin, "La foi du Christ dans la théologie de Saint Paul," *Revue des sciences*

The Trust and Trustworthiness of Jesus Christ

ancient world, one of the key qualities of conciliators, mediators, ambassadors, and anyone in public or private life who sought to reconcile others or enable new relationships was their ability and willingness to trust and be trusted by all parties. Being trusting, trustworthy, and trusted by those who have not yet trusted each other or whose trust is broken is essential to bringing people together. We can go further and observe that although Paul uses explicit reconciliation language only rarely, *pistis* language, as he uses it in these passages, is itself language of reconciliation and adds weight to the "reconciliation" theme in the letters.

Though it is beyond our scope here, it is worth noting that some of Paul's followers make use of his image of Christ as reconciler and combine it with language of mediation that Paul himself does not use.[23] They also use *pistis* language in conjunction with reconciliation language, suggesting that they understand *pistis* and reconciliation as closely related, and in places may point to the kind of double bond of trust that we have seen in the undisputed letters (2 Tim 1:8, 10; cf. 3:10–16). The author of Hebrews also sees Jesus Christ as *pistos* in his death and as mediating between God and humanity (e.g., 2:17–18). To give just one example, at the beginning of chapter 3 Jesus is described as "the apostle and high priest of our confession," who was *pistos* to the one who appointed him, just as Moses was "in all his house" (3:1–2). By the time of the author of Hebrews Moses was sometimes portrayed as angelic or divine, especially in his role as mediator between God and the people of Israel.[24] The author then says that Moses was "*pistos* in all his house as a servant" (cf. Num 12:7), but that Christ was "faithful over God's house as a son" (3:5–6).[25] The *pistis* of Christ here seems to be greater than that of other mediators

---

philosophiques et théologiques 89 (2005): 713–28; cf. Anthony Bash, *Ambassadors for Christ: An Exploration of Ambassadorial Language in the New Testament* (Tübingen: Mohr Siebeck, 1997). On the *pistis/fides* of mediators, conciliators, and ambassadors in the wider Roman Empire see Morgan, *Roman Faith*, 99–104, 114–16. Alan Segal's discussion of the Son of Man in the Parables of Enoch also offers parallels; see *Two Powers in Heaven: Early Rabbinic Reports about Christianity and Gnosticism* (Leiden: Brill, 1977), 202–3.

23. Discussed in Morgan, *Theology of Trust*, 159–62. Paul does not call Christ "reconciler" in so many words (e.g., in 2 Cor 5:18–19 it is God who reconciles), but Rom 5:10 affirms that humanity is reconciled to God through the death of God's Son, and 2 Cor 5:19 states that God was reconciling the world to himself "in Christ," so it is no stretch to see Christ as acting as reconciler in the sense that he is the mediator of God's initiative of reconciliation.

24. Cf. Ezekiel the Tragedian, *Exagoge* frags. 6–7 (*apud* Eusebius, *Preparation for the Gospel* 9.29.4–6), Philo, *Life of Moses* 1.158; Testament of Moses 1.14; 4Q374; 4Q377 (though here the writer may have had Moses's humanity mainly in mind).

25. Alan C. Mitchell, *Hebrews* (Collegeville: Liturgical, 2007), 81 argues that Jesus is not only faithful to God here but worthy of God's trust. The omission may be only for reasons of stylistic

CHAPTER 3

between God and humanity but similar to it. Christ is faithful to and trusted by God as well as faithful to and trusted by his people.

It is worth noting that although I have argued for an interpretation of Christ as trusting and trustworthy toward both God and humanity based on a number of Pauline and other passages, the idea of Christ's double trust and trustworthiness does not depend only on these readings. The assumption that a mediating figure will be trusting and trustworthy toward both parties is so widespread in the ancient world, and the idea that a relationship of *pistis* between God and his messiah and between the messiah and his people will in each case be two way is so logical that even if no New Testament passage referred to it explicitly, we could still reasonably infer it. This interpretation, however, does raise further questions. Why do the participants in this double bond trust one another? For trust between God, Christ, and humanity to be (re)established, did Christ have to die? If so, why? How does this model show how Christ's death makes possible the release of humanity from both wrongdoing and suffering? And is the (re)establishment of divine-human trust a means to an end, or is it also an end in itself, an intrinsic part of that relationship?

WHY DO GOD, CHRIST, AND HUMANITY TRUST EACH OTHER?

Paul has at least two and possibly three ways of conceptualizing the trust between God and Jesus Christ. It is the strongest possible form of the trust that exists between God and any human being who is faithful to God. If Paul has heard that Jesus was anointed with the spirit at the beginning of his earthly ministry, then from that moment the trust between Jesus and God was part of their common purpose for humanity's at-one-ment with God.[26] When Paul refers to Jesus Christ as preexisting, he presumably takes for granted that trust between Christ and

---

balance. In Heb 3:2 the author calls Jesus *pistos* but omits the word from his quotation about Moses; this time he leaves *pistos* in his quotation about Moses but omits it from his description of Christ.

26. See, e.g., James D. G. Dunn, *Baptism in the Holy Spirit: A Re-Examination of the New Testament Teaching on the Gift of the Spirit in Relation to Pentecostalism Today* (London: SCM, 1975), 318–26; Dunn, *The Christ and the Spirit: Collected Essays of James D. G. Dunn* (2 vols.; Grand Rapids: Eerdmans, 1998), 1:126–53; though Gordon D. Fee, *God's Empowering Presence: The Holy Spirit in the Letters of Paul* (Peabody: Hendrickson, 1994), 831–34 argues against this. John R. Coulson, *The Righteous Judgment of God: Aspects of Judgment in Paul's Letters* (Eugene: Wipf & Stock, 2017), 81–82 argues that Paul calling Jesus "Christ" indicates that he thinks that Jesus was anointed by the spirit as Messiah and Son of God in his lifetime, despite what may be the partially inherited formulation of Rom 1:4.

The Trust and Trustworthiness of Jesus Christ

God has been part of their relationship from before creation.[27] In Jesus Christ's risen or exalted life, the trust between God and Christ is the trust of the Father and Son who live and work together eternally. In Christ's earthly and exalted life alike, God must trust Christ to do God's work for at-one-ment in the world, and both God and Christ must trust humanity to respond to Christ. Both must trust humanity because when one person seeks to connect with another in hope of restoring any relationship, there are only two ways to do it. You can trust them to respond to you—with all the overtones of risk-taking and hope which that implies, which we can also see in New Testament writings[28]—or you can try to force them to respond, and nowhere in New Testament writings or later Christian tradition is God or Christ imagined as forcing a new relationship or new covenant on humanity.

I have argued at length elsewhere that the whole of Jesus's earthly life and ministry and his risen and ascended life as well as his death offer reasons for people to trust him.[29] In his earthly life, Jesus proclaims the coming of God's kingdom together with God's judgment and mercy and teaches people how to respond. He sees and meets their needs for healing and liberation, hope and direction. In his exalted life he continues to oversee and support communities of his followers.

Human beings trust Jesus not only because of what he teaches and what he does for them, however, but also because of his relationship with God. By his unbreakable relationship of trust with God throughout his earthly life and work, in his death, and in his risen or exalted life, Jesus shows a world that has fallen out of trust with God all it means to live in trust. When some people respond to his earthly mission by attacking, betraying, and eventually crucifying him, he refuses to be drawn into the vicious circle of failed trust, where loss of trust leads to suffering and harm, and suffering all too often leads to harming others and further suffering. In this, Jesus is a model of trust and trustworthiness, but he is more than a model. His actions break the cycle of failed trust, disrupting what people have come to understand as the way relationships work and creating a kind of "firebreak" to the spread of evil and pain (cf. 1 Pet 2:23). By showing humanity that the cycle can be broken, he changes people's sense of what is possible, and thereby what is possible for them.[30] He replaces ingrained human patterns of thought and behavior with the basis for new relationships, divine and human. We

27. Since all three are possible readings of Paul, we do not need to choose between them for our purposes.

28. Morgan, *Theology of Trust*, 68–72.

29. Morgan, *Theology of Trust*.

30. See further below, pp. 136–43, 144–49.

CHAPTER 3

can also see this action in terms of two traditional images of atonement. Jesus, by his trust and trustworthiness, acts as a kind of sacrifice or supplicatory offering, allowing himself to be crucified to break the cycle of suffering and wrongdoing at its most brutal moment, and he combats evil by living and dying in such a way as not to be overcome by it, offering humanity a relationship in which humanity, too, will not be overcome.

Jesus's actions as model and firebreak point to the relationship between trust and grace in this model of at-one-ment. Divine grace offers human beings therapeutic trust, which changes how it is possible for human beings, struggling in suffering and wrongdoing as they are, to respond to God.[31] The trust of Jesus Christ to both God and humanity mediates God's grace, bringing it into the world in a form in which humanity can encounter and recognize it. The cross marks the extremity of human wrongdoing and suffering, and so reveals God's grace and trust, in every sense, in extremis, inviting humanity to respond as humanly possible and be restored to its right relationship with God.

Jesus's action in accepting his death in trust is a revelation of who he is and why he is trustworthy. His suffering does not change his relationship with humanity or with God. It demonstrates that his charisma and power, his preaching and trustworthiness, were not predicated on his personal safety or success. Nothing about him, what he has revealed about God, his call to others, or what humanity can hope for from God changes because of his death.[32] His death also demonstrates the lengths to which he is prepared to go as mediator. By accepting his treatment at the hands of those who have not put their trust in him, not evading them or cutting off relations with them, he shows that there is nothing they can do that puts human beings beyond God's trust or God's confidence in their ability to respond to God. As a human being, Jesus demonstrates this commitment to those he has come to save. As a human being, he cannot know what will emerge from his death, but he enacts his confidence that God will bring good out of it. As God's Son, he enacts his confidence that God will let God's Son act for humanity, whatever it takes. As much as anything the cross is God's revelation to humanity of itself: of how precious it is, even in the depths of its wrongdoing; of what confidence God has in it, such that no human behavior will make God or Christ abandon it; and of what is possible for humanity in response to it.

31. I therefore read Eph 2:4–8, for example, as referring to the grace that is extended by God through the *pistis* of Christ and makes possible humanity's response of *pistis*, and Phil 2:13 to the power of therapeutic trust to change those who experience it. Human beings might, in principle, have been able to put their trust in God, e.g., simply by recognizing God in creation (cf. Rom 1:19–20) but in practice, it seems, they cannot.

32. On Jesus's prayer in Gethsemane see p. 69; Morgan, *Theology of Trust*, 261–63.

128

The Trust and Trustworthiness of Jesus Christ

Just as Jesus's action in accepting betrayal and death makes him a model and more than a model, we can also see it as making him a martyr and more than a martyr. The "cause" for which he dies is humanity itself, and his death proclaims to humanity that even in the depths of its wrongdoing and evil it is loved and trusted by God and God's Son, and there is a path to at-one-ment with God. Humanity can betray God's commitment to it, but it cannot put itself outside God's commitment to it. In the introduction and chapter 2 we saw how the making of relationships of trust changes people's sense of themselves as well as of themselves in relationship and therefore changes how it is possible for them to live in the world and even the reality in which they live. By revealing God's and his own unbreakable trust in humanity on the cross, Jesus Christ embraces humanity in a relationship that has the power to change human beings' sense of themselves, how it is possible for them to live, and the reality in which they live.

Christian understandings of Jesus's death are shaped at every point by the experience of the resurrection and the conviction of Christ's exaltation and future coming. In the past century, however, there has been much more exploration of what we can say about the cross from the perspective of people who are, spiritually or emotionally, still living between the disaster of the crucifixion and the vindication of the resurrection.[33] In recent generations, human beings have suffered abuse, torture, and destruction on such an unprecedented scale that many people (not only Christians) have lost confidence and conviction of God. Even committed Christians sometimes feel closer to the disciples on Easter Saturday than on Easter Sunday. We are so conscious of the evil that pervades our world that we may doubt whether, through Christ, the decisive battle between God and the powers of evil really has been won.

Even before the resurrection, however, Jesus on the cross shows that humanity in trust with God is not trapped or corrupted, damaged or destroyed by evil. As we have seen, he breaks the cycle of wrongdoing and suffering, offering trust in place of harm and offering no foothold for evil. He shows humanity that it is so dear to God that nothing can end its relationship with God, and that at any moment when it begins to respond to God's therapeutic trust, it will begin to emerge from the world of wrongdoing into a new reality. He makes out of the human horror of

---

33. Explored by Ian G. Wallis, *Holy Saturday Faith: Rediscovering the Legacy of Jesus* (London: SPCK, 2000). The incarnational focus of this proposal has points of contact with Timothy Hegedus's analysis of the theology of Douglas John Hall in "Douglas John Hall's Contextual Theology," 26, which shows the force of Hall's insistence that "the basic orientation of the theology of the cross is incarnational, 'the identification of God with humankind in the totality of the human condition.'" Hegedus here is quoting from Douglas John Hall, "Rethinking Christ," in *Antisemitism and the Foundations of Christianity* (ed. Alan T. Davies; New York: Paulist, 1979), 181.

CHAPTER 3

the cross a place and a space in which God is present, offering to humanity trust and a new way of being in relationship with God. For humanity to meet God at the cross it will need to take a step of trust into that space, but the space and the power to take the step have been given to it. Both were created by Jesus's ministry in Galilee, too, but the crucifixion is a different kind of revelation and invitation. In the midst of a chaotic political, religious, and social situation, in a moment of extreme injustice and cruelty, Jesus's trust shows, as Paul puts it, that "neither death, nor life, nor angels, nor rulers, nor things present, nor things to come, nor powers, nor height, nor depth, nor anything else in all creation will be able to separate us from the love of God in Christ Jesus" (Rom 8:38–39).

If contemporary Christians sometimes feel that we are still stuck between the cross and the resurrection experiences and struggle to step into the space created by the cross with confidence in our at-one-ment with God, we can take some comfort from Jesus's disciples. The passion narratives suggest that Jesus's arrest and crucifixion at best damaged, if not destroyed, their trust; there is certainly no sign that it confirmed or strengthened it (though Matt 27:54 and Mark 15:39 affirm that it brought others to recognition of Jesus as Son of God for the first time). It was not until Jesus's followers experienced his resurrection that their trust was confirmed. For later generations that did not share the resurrection experiences, the call to trust became the climax of the preaching of the crucifixion and resurrection together. This suggests that even if the work of Christ is fully revealed, and God's and Christ's side of it is accomplished at the crucifixion, the resurrection experiences act as an extra revelation: an added grace that helps people to respond. Paul's (and other writers') linking of *pistis* language with the idea of reconciliation underlines the importance of humanity's response. An ambassador, for instance, cannot simply be authorized by one people to make peace with another and consider that by that token peace has been achieved; any movement to reconciliation can only be fulfilled when all parties opt into it.

THE GRACE OF REVELATION IN THE RESURRECTION AND LATER

Since we have noted that the trust of Jesus's followers, shattered by his arrest, is remembered as not being restored until their resurrection experiences, while to later generations Jesus's death and resurrection were preached together, it is worth saying a little more about the role of ongoing revelation, after the crucifixion, in the restoration of trust.

In Paul's account at 1 Cor 15:3–5 of the preaching that he received and handed on, four events are listed: Christ died, was buried, was raised, and appeared to

The Trust and Trustworthiness of Jesus Christ

Cephas and others. Whatever is achieved on the cross, the resurrection experience (among which Paul includes his own experiences of Christ) is integral to the story. For Paul, moreover, it is not only the death and resurrection of Christ that reveal what God has done: so does preaching of them and even the presence of the preacher. At Rom 1:16–18 the gospel is the power of God for salvation, "for in it the righteousness of God is revealed." In 2 Cor 2:14, God "through us spreads in every place the fragrance that comes from knowing him," and later Paul tells the Corinthians that he is "always carrying about in the body the death of Jesus, so that the life of Jesus may also be made visible in our body" (4:10; cf. 4:11).[34] In Gal 4:9 Paul reminds the Galatians that they came to know God through God's Son (4:4) and through Paul himself, who appeared to them like an angel or like Christ himself (4:14).

Revelation also continues through the work of the holy spirit. In 1 Cor 2:4 Paul reminds the Corinthians, "My speech and my proclamation were . . . with a demonstration of the spirit and of power" (cf. 1 Thess 1:5). The spirit reveals (cf. 2:7) what human eyes and ears cannot (cf. 2:9) and illuminates what the faithful have been given by God (cf. 2:12). Later in the letter, the spirit enables people to recognize Jesus as Lord (12:3).

The process of revelation continues until the end time.[35] The "day of wrath," Paul says (Rom 2:5), will also be a day of revelation, and the sufferings of the present time are nothing to the glory that will be revealed in the eschatological future (Rom 8:18). In 1 Cor 1:7 Paul reminds the Corinthians that they are waiting for the final "revealing of our Lord Jesus Christ" at "the end" (1:8), and in 4:5 that when the Lord comes, he "will bring to light the things now hidden in darkness and will disclose the purposes of the heart."[36] Every stage of the revelation of God and Christ can generate a response of trust, and since trust needs to be maintained and even strengthened through the present time, it is appropriate that revelation also continues until the "day of the Lord." The divine-human trust relationship made possible through the Christ event will not be realized, beyond failure, development, or extension to new participants until the *parousia*.

A similar theme is detectable in stories of the aftermath of the crucifixion in the gospels. When Jesus is betrayed and arrested, most of the disciples disappear,

34. In 2 Cor 4:6 God's revelation of Christ continues through Paul's preaching; cf. Gen 1:3. In 2 Cor 3:18 putting one's trust in Christ leads to gazing with unveiled face on Christ's glory. Paul claims that his preaching makes the gospel clear (2 Cor 11:6), while in Phil 1:12–13 even his imprisonment advances it.

35. Cf. pp. 71, 79 n. 106, 178, 202.

36. In 1 Cor 3:13 everyone's work will also be revealed on that day in an echo of the end-time parables and the responsibility of a good steward for that with which God has entrusted him or her; cf. p. 208.

CHAPTER 3

and though Peter (with one other, according to John 18:15) follows Jesus to the high priest's impromptu court, he denies knowing him.[37] It seems that the disciples' trust in Jesus, and perhaps also their trust in themselves to be faithful to him, has been overwhelmed by fear. Luke and John temper this picture somewhat. According to Luke (23:49) Jesus's followers, including the women, stand at a distance from the cross and witness the crucifixion. John goes further, depicting Jesus's mother, her sister, Mary the wife of Clopas, and Mary Magdalene, together with "the disciple whom Jesus loved," all standing by the cross until Jesus's death (19:25–26). We can see these actions as expressing faithfulness toward Jesus to the end, but whether this faithfulness would still affirm Jesus as the Messiah, the Son of God, or the one with the words of eternal life, the writers do not say.

In all four gospels Jesus tells the disciples that he will be raised or that he will see them again (e.g., Mark 8:31; 9:31; 10:34 and Synoptic parallels; John 16:16). Even so, after his death all his followers act as though they expect this to be the end of his story. Mark and Luke describe the women as going to the tomb to anoint a dead body. Matthew and John suggest that Mary Magdalene, alone or with another Mary, went to visit the grave, presumably to grieve.

In Mark's Gospel the women are told not to be afraid and that Jesus has been raised (16:6) but, for reasons that remain mysterious despite intensive debate, are said to run away in fear and tell no one what they have seen (16:8). In Matthew's Gospel, the women respond to the revelation of the empty tomb with both fear and joy (28:8), and their joy is vindicated when they meet Jesus himself on the road (28:9–10). Luke describes how the fearful women, reminded by the men they meet at the tomb that Jesus prophesied his resurrection, do remember his words and return to report to the disciples what they have seen and heard (24:1–11). The men, however, think they are talking nonsense and do not *pisteuein* them.[38]

Later the same day, two disciples walking to Emmaus meet a stranger and tell him about the empty tomb (Luke 24:13–35). The stranger says, "how foolish you are and how slow of heart to *pisteuein* all that the prophets have declared" (24:25). *Pisteuein* is usually translated "believe," which is appropriate since the object is the words of the prophets. At the same time, only those who put their trust in Jesus and followed him would be likely to believe that certain prophecies applied to him, and the disciples confirm that they hoped that Jesus would be Israel's

37. On the fragility of the disciples' trust see Morgan, *Theology of Trust*, 258–63.

38. Since the women are the object of the verb, Luke leaves open whether the men did not believe what they said or did not trust them as reliable witnesses. Peter responds (Luke 24:12) by going to look at the tomb himself, which suggests less that he thinks the women were not telling the truth than that they were untrustworthy. At this point, the disciples' trust seems to be at least suspended.

132

The Trust and Trustworthiness of Jesus Christ

redeemer (24:21). The stranger's reproach points to the fragility or failure of the disciples' belief and trust alike, and his exposition of the scriptures addresses both. At the end of the story the stranger is revealed to be Jesus, and the disciples immediately return to Jerusalem to report their experience to the other disciples, who have their own experience to share (24:33–34). As they do so, Jesus appears and, despite what they have already experienced or heard (and, in redaction-critical terms, presumably because this was originally a separate pericope), the disciples are terrified, thinking that Jesus is a spirit (24:37). Jesus asks them why they are frightened and doubtful, and he shows them his hands and feet, but they are still *apistountes* for joy (24:38–41). It is only later at the point of Jesus's ascension that the disciples seem finally to accept what has been revealed to them and bow to the ascended Jesus as Lord (24:52).

All these stories emphasize Jesus's followers' confusion and fear, and in several their fear and lack of understanding are implicitly or explicitly criticized. They should, it seems, have grasped what happened in the crucifixion, but they are granted encounters with messengers and Jesus himself to help restore their understanding and trust. In John's Gospel, trust begins to be restored sooner after the resurrection than in the other gospels, when the disciple whom Jesus loved enters the tomb, sees the grave cloths, and, John says, *pisteuein* though the disciples did not yet know the scripture that Jesus must rise from the dead (John 20:8–9). Even so, the weeping of Mary Magdalene before she encounters Jesus (20:11–14), and the joy of the disciples as a group when Jesus appears to them (20:19–20), suggests that their belief or trust was not secure. When Jesus appears to most of the disciples, moreover, Thomas is not with them and does not believe that they have seen him.[39] When Jesus appears to Thomas (20:26–29), he shows him the wounds of crucifixion and challenges him to stop doubting and trust in him.[40] Thomas does in triumphal terms: "My Lord and my God!" But Jesus says, "Have

39. In John 20:25, where Thomas says that he will not *pisteuein* unless he sees the evidence of Jesus's hands and side, it is clearly belief that is at issue.

40. The climax of his invitation to Thomas is often, understandably in light of John 20:25, translated "do not doubt, but believe" (καὶ μὴ γίνου ἄπιστος ἀλλὰ πιστός; 20:27). But this would involve an extremely rare meaning of *pistos* and probably an unparalleled meaning of *apistos*. Some classical authors (e.g., Theognis, *Elegiacs* 283; Aeschylus, *Prometheus Bound* 917) use *pistos* with the possible meaning of "believing," but the word more likely means "relying on" in such examples, which are all early and poetic. LSJ wrongly cites 1 Cor 6:6 as a semantic outlier, meaning "unbelieving." In itself, we should expect this phrase in John 20:27 to mean, "Become not untrusting [or "faithless"] but trusting [or "faithful"]." This interpretation fits well with the strongly relational meaning of *pisteuein* throughout the Gospel of John and with the following two verses.

CHAPTER 3

you trusted because you have seen me? Blessed are those who have not seen and yet have trusted" (20:29).[41]

Jesus's words here may be intentionally multivalent. They are usually taken as a blessing on later Christians, who trust without the benefit of the resurrection experiences. They may also obliquely comment that, after the revelation of God and God's glory that is Jesus's earthly life (cf. John 5:19–26; 8:18–19, 29; 9:3; 11:4) and the revelation of the cross (cf. 3:14; 8:28; 12:28; 17:1), the disciples should not have needed the further revelation of the resurrection appearances. Jesus's appearances, however, are an added expression of God's love, which sent God's Son into the world to save it (cf. 3:16–17). In addition, in John 20:22 Jesus gives the disciples the spirit, which will continue to reveal what God wants humanity to understand about "sin and righteousness and judgment" (cf. 16:8), to guide the disciples into truth (16:13), and to glorify Jesus (16:14). Luke also highlights the ongoing revelation to the disciples and those to whom they preach through the spirit, making the risen Jesus promise the disciples that they will receive the spirit (Acts 1:5), and then describes how they receive it at Pentecost (2:1–40). Matthew's Jesus confers his authority on the disciples (Matt 28:18–19) and promises that he will remain with them until the end of the age (28:20). Revelation continues to enlighten the disciples whose trust has never been perfect and future generations who will need help in coming to trust and remaining faithful until the end time.

DID JESUS HAVE TO DIE?

Our second and third questions on page 126 were whether, to establish a new relationship of trust between God, Christ, and humanity, Jesus had to die, and, if so, why. We have already explored one response: that the cross opens up a space of trust in which humanity can meet God even in the extreme of human political, social, and religious chaos as well as cruelty, injustice, and suffering. That Jesus creates this space on the cross shows that nothing can destroy the person who is in trust with God, and that God's commitment to humanity is unbreakable. It reveals humanity to itself as infinitely precious to God and capable of responding to God and proclaims that no hostile power, human or superhuman, can separate trusting

41. At John 20:31 both belief and trust may be involved, but this refers to the whole gospel, not just the resurrection experiences. Earlier, Jesus has said, "if you do not believe/trust that I am, you will die in your wrongdoings ... when you lift up the Son of Man, then you will realize [*gnōsesthe*] that I am" (8:24, 28). This suggests that not only knowing but trusting will come of his raising up, which conflates the crucifixion and resurrection. Cf. John 12:32; 3:14; 6:39–40, 44, 54.

134

The Trust and Trustworthiness of Jesus Christ

humanity from God. As the cross holds Jesus, he holds his arms open to humanity and invites it to take a step of trust into that space to meet God. The idea of Christ as mediator in the divine-human relationship, however, raises further questions, not least because it is not normally necessary for mediators or conciliators to die to do their work.[42] It also points to further layers of meaning in Jesus's death.

On one level, the death of Jesus was simply a fact with which his early followers had to deal, and they did so by interpreting it as part of God's plan of salvation. In the ancient Mediterranean and Near Eastern worlds, however, the deaths of great men who were taken up to heaven were treated in very varied ways.[43] Even if their deaths were remembered, and even if they were traumatic, they were not usually seen as central to the significance of the person's earthly or heavenly life: typically, resurrection or (more often) ascension would "trump" death. Early Christian interpretations of Jesus's death as necessary express a distinctive, early, and persistent conviction that the crucifixion was more than a contingent human event. It was always, in some way, part of God's plan.

Christian understandings of Christ's death were distinctive in their early cultural contexts in another respect. In Jewish scripture and tradition and Mediterranean myth and history, it is rare for the earthly and heavenly life of a great figure to be equally significant or storied. Most early Christians, however, seem to have recognized both Jesus's earthly existence and his heavenly existence as vital to their understanding of his identity and to their understanding of his identity in his earthly life and death as fully continuous with his identity in his risen and exalted life (and, for some, also his preexistence). Another response to the questions whether and why Christ needed to die is therefore that he dies because he cannot be other than he is.[44] As the person who has always been trusting and trustworthy toward God and toward humanity and whose work is to restore trust between humanity and God, he could not, for instance, try to evade the arrest that was the consequence of his work on earth. To do so would have been to fail

42. Nor is a death normally needed for divine revelation. We also noted in chapter 2 that mediators of trust on the human plane do not normally die in the process of mediation, though many have been tortured, threatened with death, or incarcerated.

43. Teresa Morgan, "Big Little Innovations: The Death and Resurrection of Jesus Christ," in *Innovation and Appropriation in Early Christianity: Authors, Topics, Texts, Genres* (ed. S. L. Jónsson, S. Luther, and J. P. B. Mortensen; Göttingen: Vandenhoeck & Ruprecht, forthcoming).

44. It is a recurrent idea cross-culturally that a trusting/trustworthy person may be tested by extreme or tragic circumstances. E.g., Abraham went to sacrifice Isaac because he had put his trust in the "unwavering steadfastness" (*anendoiaston bebaiotēta*) of God (Philo, *That God Is Unchangeable* 4). Regulus, as a prisoner/ambassador from Carthage to Rome, was remembered as keeping his word and returning from his embassy to Carthage to die (Livy, *History of Rome* 18; Gaius Sempronius Tuditanus *apud* Aulus Gellius, *Attic Nights* 7.4.1; Horace, *Carmina* 3.5).

135

CHAPTER 3

to trust that God would work even with his suffering and death and to fail to trust humanity to be able to trust even one betrayed and crucified. At the same time, God must trust Christ to remain trusting and trustworthy even through death and must trust humanity to be able to trust even one crucified and the God who allows his crucifixion. Jesus's death therefore reifies to the extreme his relationship with God and with humanity, which even suffering and death cannot change. It reveals his trust and trustworthiness and invites humanity to respond.[45] On this understanding of his death, Christ needs to die not for a discrete purpose—to act as a sacrifice or to defeat the powers of evil—but because he is who he is, and it is only as the person he is that he can reconcile humanity with God.

Did Jesus also have to die to reveal humanity to itself? In the situation in which he found himself, in his last week in Jerusalem, my argument so far suggests that he did. To evade arrest would not only have been to deny the person he was but also to deny what the cross reveals to humanity about itself. The cross proclaims that humanity is not precious to God and reconcilable with God up to a point, but that it is precious unconditionally and reconcilable from any state, and the unconditionality of God's commitment to humanity, expressed by grace, is what enables humanity to take a first step toward new life in a new reality.

In Galatians and Philippians we saw that Paul refers to himself as being crucified with Christ or conformed to his death, and we noted that this language of dying with Christ is also central to Romans 6. This image, I suggest, adds a further dimension to the meaning of Christ's death. For Paul, if Christ's death affirms the continuity of who and what he is, it changes radically what it is possible for human beings to be. It enables them to die, because it is, above all, human beings who have to die: not, in this context, physically, but to the power of wrongdoing and suffering.[46]

Paul has the highest hopes for humanity.[47] He is waiting and working for the time when all the faithful will be with Christ under God's reign (cf. 1 Cor 15:50; Gal 5:21). He envisages them as coheirs with Christ (cf. Gal 4:1–7), victorious (1 Cor 15:57) and glorified (cf. Rom 8:29–30) in God's presence (cf. 2 Cor 4:14) for eternal life (cf. Rom 2:7; 6:23).[48] He awaits the fulfillment of this vision at the

---

45. Roger Haight, *The Future of Christology* (New York: Continuum, 2005), 86–101 argues similarly that, through his death, Jesus can be understood both as involved in the process of salvation and as revealer of it, and that the cross itself does not save, but God saves in spite of it. He too finds this pattern of thinking in Paul.

46. Phil 1:21–23 indicates that as long as Paul is in right standing with God he sees physical death as insignificant; all the more, perhaps, if at the coming of Christ the faithful will be taken up dead or alive (cf. 1 Thess 4:16–17).

47. See further Morgan, *Being "In Christ"*, 199–200.

48. On Paul's *syn-* language see B. McGrath, "*Syn* Words in Saint Paul," *CBQ* 14 (1952): 219–26,

The Trust and Trustworthiness of Jesus Christ

parousia, but following the resurrection he already understands the faithful as a "new creation" (2 Cor 5:17), who are "dead to wrongdoing and living for God under the authority of Christ Jesus" (Rom 6:11).[49] Those who trust in God and in Christ aspire already to live, here and now, enacting the qualities and relationships that distinguish God's kingdom, including grace, truth, mercy, peace, freedom, holiness, and love.

To come into that relationship, however, and become part of the new creation, human beings must leave behind lives dominated by wrongdoing, failures of trust and trustworthiness, and the suffering that is created by toxic relationships. As we often say of those who are suffering from addiction or abuse, they need to "get out," rejecting a path of life that leads to destruction and becoming survivors in a different world. They must take a step of trust into a new reality, in which they can make new and renewed relationships and learn to hope. Paul has no doubt that life governed by wrongdoing and *apistia* has no future but death and destruction (e.g., 2 Cor 2:15; 4:3; Phil 1:28).[50] The only life that gives life is lived in trust with God and Christ.

To get out of one situation, set of relationships, and view of the world and take a step of trust into new relationships and a new life is itself a kind of death: one that is metaphorical but, in many people's experience, transformatively powerful. In several passages Paul describes this process as dying with Christ, being buried with him, and living a new life with him, using a number of terms compounded with *syn-*, "with," including "suffer with" (*sympaschō*, Rom 8:17), "be crucified with" (*systaurōmai*, Rom 6:6; Gal 2:19), "be buried with" (*synthaptomai*, Rom 6:4), "live with" (*syzaō*, Rom 6:8), and "be conformed to" (*symmorphizomai*) (Phil 3:10) together with "grown together with" (*symphytos*, Rom 6:5) and "in the same shape as" (*symmorphos*, Rom 8:29; Phil 3:21).[51]

In this powerful imagistic language, trusting in response to Christ's crucifixion and resurrection allows human beings to be freed from the power of wrongdoing, suffering, the flesh, and death and to enter new life under the authority of Christ.[52]

---

with Peter Sieber, *Mit Christus Leben: Eine Studie zur paulinischen Auferstehungshoffnung* (Zurich: Theologischer Verlag, 1971) and Douglas A. Campbell, *The Deliverance of God: An Apocalyptic Rereading of Justification in Paul* (Grand Rapids: Eerdmans, 2012), 217–36. Dorothea H. Bertschmann, "Suffering, Sin, and Death in Paul," in *Suffering and the Christian Life* (ed. Karen Kilby and Rachel Davies; London: T&T Clark, 2020), 4–10 argues (against Schweitzer and Tannehill), that dying with Christ is the route to life, not a continuous and lifelong process.

49. My translation.

50. Cf. 1 Cor 1:19, if this refers to physical beings.

51. Paul's followers use further *syn-* language: *synkakopatheō* (2 Tim 1:8; 2:3), *synapothnesko* (2 Tim 2:11), *syzōopoieō* (Eph 2:5; Col 2:13), *synthaptō* (Col 2:12).

52. I have some sympathy here with, though I do not entirely follow, Robert Tannehill, *Dying and Rising with Christ: A Study in Pauline Theology* (Berlin: Töpelmann, 1967), 30, 39–40, who

CHAPTER 3

When, in Gal 2:19–20, Paul says, "I have been crucified with Christ," he is both proclaiming what the crucifixion means to him and asserting his authority as an apostle to affirm that *pistis* leads to justification (cf. Gal 2:16).[53] Paul's own trust led him to be crucified to his old life, and now he lives for God (2:19). Christ lives and works in and through him (2:20), and he cannot "nullify the grace of God" (2:21) by denying that it is *pistis*, rather than works of the law, that makes righteousness possible (cf. 2:16).[54] In Rom 6:5 Paul changes the metaphor and describes the faithful as being "grown together" with Christ through the crucifixion and resurrection: "If then we have grown together with [Christ] by the likeness of his death, so we will be [grown together with him by the likeness] of the resurrection."[55] Those who trust and are baptized do not die and rise physically, but they experience a death to the power of wrongdoing over them (cf. Rom 6:2) and the suffering that wrongdoing brings with it. They "rise" symbolically into a new life (cf. 6:4), and through this death and new life they grow with Christ like plants on the same rootstock.[56] Later in Romans (11:17–24), Paul uses another plant image to describe how the gentiles are "grafted," through trust, like a wild olive shoot onto the "rich root" of the tree that is Israel. This tree has thrived (implicitly, at 11:20) because of its long relationship of trust with God, but, in the present time, some branches have been broken off "because of *apistia*" (11:20). If these shoots of Israel do not return to trust in both God and Christ (cf. 11:23), then they will wither and die.[57] These images, as we saw in chapter 1, express how literally vital it is for Paul that human existence is rooted in God and Christ and grows with them. Being in trust with God and Christ is to be alive, growing, and bearing fruit; any other existence means brokenness and death.[58]

---

sees these passages as representing the death of Christ as an "inclusive event" that frees human beings from the dominion of the old eon and releases them into the power of Christ in the new.

53. Morgan, *Being "in Christ"*, 64–68, 114–15.

54. J. L. Martyn, *Theological Issues in the Letters of Paul* (Edinburgh: T&T Clark, 1997) shows that Paul is summarizing his refutation of the teachers' charge against him here, arguing that they, not he, nullify God's grace, which resides in God's rectifying power and Christ's faithful death, not in the law.

55. Εἰ γὰρ σύμφυτοι γεγόναμεν τῷ ὁμοιώματι τοῦ θανάτου αὐτοῦ, ἀλλὰ καὶ τῆς ἀναστάσεως ἐσόμεθα.

56. In this chapter as a whole, much of which is interested in the life of the faithful as God's "weapons of righteousness" (Rom 6:13), "slaves of righteousness" (6:18), or "slaves of God" (6:22), the faithful, by being *symphytos*, may also be following Christ's example in his earthly life, death, and exalted life. This fits with the language of *homoiōma* that Paul also uses at 6:5, which Morgan, *Being "in Christ"*, 148–55 argues should be taken ethically.

57. Even broken branches can be bound back onto a tree and regrow.

58. Gal 6:8 offers another agricultural analogy: those who sow "for the flesh" reap corrup-

The Trust and Trustworthiness of Jesus Christ

We may still wonder why, to make it possible for human beings to die with him to *apistia*, wrongdoing, and death, Christ should have had to die physically. How do we imagine his death as making a difference? I have suggested that Jesus accepts his betrayal and death because he cannot break trust with God by being other than who and what he is, or do other than affirm to humanity what it is in God's eyes. The continuity of Christ's identity through and after his death is a revelation of the unbreakability of his relationship with God and with humanity, which no human wrongdoing or suffering can destroy, and perhaps only a revelation as powerful as this could persuade human beings to put their trust in God and Christ and let themselves die to the world of *apistia*. This is coherent with what I have already argued as far as it goes, but it does not do full justice to the image of human beings as dying *with* Christ. Paul's *syn-* language expresses metaphorically how real—how material—human beings' death to *apistia* and new life of *pistis* are for them, but it may mean even more than that.

It is notable that the language of dying with Christ is present not only in Paul's lengthy exploration of what God has done through Christ in Romans but also in his much briefer accounts of it in Galatians and Philippians. It is evidently a central part of his thinking about how people respond to Christ and what must follow for their relationship with God to be restored. In Gal 2:19, Paul has "been crucified with Christ," so that he no longer lives in the world as he lived in it before. In Phil 3:10, Paul wants to share Christ's sufferings by becoming like Christ in his death in the hope eventually of being raised from the dead. Dying with Christ is not only an essential step in human beings' at-one-ment with God, but also central to their faithful following of Christ and work for Christ and their hope of eternal life.

On one reading, Paul's *syn-* language tells those who trust that they "died with" Christ, live under Christ's authority, and will "live with" Christ at the resurrection (Rom 6:8, 11; cf. 6:5). From another perspective, *Paul's syn-* language tells the faithful that they died and will live "with Christ." As they go through their death to the world of *apistia* and enter the new life with God that the Christ event has made possible, they do so *with Christ*.[59] It is evidently important to Paul both that the faithful die metaphorically as Christ died and that they do so with Christ, but in these two phrases the emphasis is slightly different. Commentators usually focus

---

tion, which they will then have to consume and which will not fortify their life and might poison them, while those who plant "for the spirit" reap life. Cf. also Paul's agricultural image of community growth in 1 Cor 3:6–7 and the description of the faithful as "rooted" in Christ and established in trust in Col 2:7.

59. C. F. D. Moule, *The Sacrifice of Christ* (London: Hodder & Stoughton, 1956), 40 cites an argument of C. H. Dodd that in Rom 6:3 human beings have died in solidarity with Christ.

CHAPTER 3

on the first perspective, but the second also offers something significant for a *pistis* model of atonement.[60]

Imagine a young child who lives, say, in Vermont. We'll call him Lee. Lee is invited to visit his grandparents on their ranch in California. He loves his grandparents and is longing to visit the ranch, which he has never seen, but between Vermont and California is a complex journey by air. Lee is too young to make this trip alone, so his mother, Katie, takes him. Katie does not urgently need to visit her parents just now: she knows that they are well; they are in touch regularly; and part of her is always with them, in spirit, in the place where she grew up. But she cannot risk that Lee will get lost on the journey, and she knows that if they travel together he will be joyfully confident, trusting her to get him there safely. She arranges to travel with him so that he can travel with her.

Lee trusts his mother because they have a loving relationship and because she has much more experience than he has, especially of air travel. He feels safe when he is with her. Although they travel together, however, in one sense they are not on the same journey. Katie knows the journey and what it will be like; she is fully prepared and not worried about it. For Lee, it is a revelation. He is traveling where he has never been, and everything is new, exciting, and just a little scary. By the time they arrive in California, he will be a slightly different person. He will have traveled, seen new places, taken a step toward growing up, and his life will never be quite the same again.

The Christ who is with those who trust is both the crucified and the exalted Christ. As we will see in chapter 5, Paul sometimes describes the exalted Christ as near the faithful: he guides them and they are in his hands. When Christ is with them, those who trust can travel confidently through their death to the world of wrongdoing and *apistia*, knowing that Christ has taken the journey before and is with them now. They are not on the same journey as Christ because Christ did not need to die to wrongdoing, and his identity and relationship with God were not changed by his physical death.[61] But for those who trust, traveling in company with the person who knows and has shown that leaving one's old life behind leads only to a new and more glorious life helps them to persevere until they reach their longed-for destination.

60. E.g., when one person *syngignōskein*, "agrees with" another in Greek, the *syn* creates the meaning "agreement," but if one person *syngēraskein*, "grows old with" another, he is growing old anyway and the *syn* adds the idea of doing it with another person.

61. Though if Christ was anointed at the beginning of his ministry, he may be thought of as having died then to wrongdoing and death.

The Trust and Trustworthiness of Jesus Christ

The gospels too, in a different way, draw attention to the connection between traveling with Jesus through death and new life. In Mark's Gospel, the women who visit Jesus's tomb on the third day and receive the first revelation of the resurrection are named as Mary Magdalene, Mary the mother of James, and Salome (Mark 16:1).[62] They are also the three named among the women who dare to witness the crucifixion (15:40). Mark, for his own reasons, makes them run away from the tomb in fear and say nothing, but in Matthew's Gospel when Mary Magdalene and "the other Mary" (Matt 28:1) leave the tomb, they meet Jesus and evidently report the meeting to the disciples (28:9–10; cf. 28:16). In John's Gospel, the first person to visit the empty tomb and *pisteuein* (John 20:8) is "the disciple whom Jesus loved," who had stood by the cross with Jesus's mother Mary, Mary Magdalene, and Mary the wife of Clopas, while the first person to whom the resurrection is announced and the risen Jesus appears is Mary Magdalene (20:11–18). The first witnesses to the resurrection, in these narratives, are among the few who went with Jesus throughout his crucifixion.[63]

Jesus is not the only one who rises to new life in these stories. The disciples had left everything to follow him and had high hopes of him. For a time, he was their life. Then, when he was in danger, they gave up on him and ran away. We can see the three days from Jesus's crucifixion as a death for the disciples as much as for Jesus himself: the death of their trust in Jesus as their leader, of everything they had believed in and hoped for, and of their vision not only of Jesus but of themselves. By the same token, the resurrection experiences are not only experiences of Jesus raised from the dead but also experiences of the disciples' own resurrection. From the tomb of failure, despair, and self-loathing they had dug for themselves, they were brought to renewed life, trust, and hope. The resurrection is, symbolically, as much theirs as Christ's and, as for Paul, those who died with Jesus in the failure of their discipleship are raised to new life with him.

To return to the journey to California: in one sense, Katie's experience of past journeys acts as a sign of the journey that Lee will now be able to take. Similarly, the death of Christ acts as a sign of the journey that those who are in a state of wrongdoing and/or suffering can now hope to take.[64] In another sense, a journey that has been made once creates and maps the route for others. In a third

---

62. Joy Ann McDougall, "Rising with Mary: Re-Visioning a Feminist Theology of the Cross and Resurrection," *Theology Today* 69 (2012): 166–76 focuses on the witness of the women at the cross to develop a feminist theology of the cross, though in slightly different terms from here.

63. Luke's version is slightly different because he says that "all [Jesus's] acquaintances," including the women, witnessed the crucifixion from a distance (23:49).

64. Cf. pp. 153–54.

CHAPTER 3

sense, Katie's journey is an example to Lee, but the fact that she travels with him makes her journey more than an example. If Katie had assured Lee that she had taken the journey before and he would be able to do it too, he might have been reassured enough to travel alone, but when they travel together his experience is quite different. Similarly, when those who trust understand themselves as dying with Christ, they are doing more than following a path that has been taken before. They are acknowledging that they travel with the one who knows what it is to have arrived at their hoped-for end and who guides and reassures them at every stage of the journey.[65] They are recognizing that, with Christ, unless they willfully lose themselves on the way, they will undoubtedly come to glory.

In chapter 2 we heard stories of reconcilers who have not physically died but have often come close to dying. Some have been tortured, some have been all but destroyed psychologically or emotionally, and some have been entombed in prison. They, and those with whom they work, often describe what one person can do for another who is struggling to (re)learn trust as "being with" or "walking with." "Walking with" has also become a widely used term in Christian communities that work with survivors of all forms of trauma. As noted earlier, Desmond Tutu entitled one of his books about the peace and reconciliation process in South Africa, *Walk with Us and Listen*.[66] Another Christian organization describes its mission on its website: "To walk with someone . . . means to stand by their side through everything. It is a long-term commitment to be a part of someone's life."[67] A mental health professional who is also a trauma survivor says of working with other trauma survivors, "we must walk with survivors on their path to assure them above all else that they are worthy of help holding the weight and that someday it will not feel so heavy."[68] The experience of those who have been through the trauma of suffering or wrongdoing (or both) says to those who are still in captivity, "There is a way through and out of this into new life. I can guide you, if you trust me, and I will stay with you as you travel." It is partly because they have been where the other is now that such guides are trusted. When one person, in spirit, goes with another who has a difficult and uncertain journey to make, knowing the road even though he or she is no longer traveling it themselves, the journey becomes

---

65. Here Christ's mediation in his death converges with the mediating activity of the exalted Christ; cf. Morgan, *Theology of Trust*, 122–27.

66. P. 96.

67. "What It Means to Walk with Survivors," RAHAB Ministries, May 13, 2022, https://www.rahab-ministries.org/what-it-means-to-walk-with-survivors/.

68. Ali W. Rothrock, "For Those Who Walk with Others on the Path to Healing," *Psychology Today*, August 24, 2022, https://www. https://www.psychologytoday.com/us/blog/after-trauma/202208/those-who-walk-others-the-path-healing.

The Trust and Trustworthiness of Jesus Christ

a different one: less painful and more manageable with a clearer destination in which the traveler can have more confidence.

On the understanding of the crucifixion I have been developing, Jesus's death is a scandal and an act of human evil. It is also an act of divine grace that makes possible what might otherwise have been too big a step for human beings to take, from wrongdoing and suffering into new life. In this act of grace, Christ dies as humanity's representative, leader, and carer. Just as we can imagine Lee's grandparents trusting Katie to bring him safely to California, Katie trusting them to welcome him, Katie trusting Lee to stay close as they travel, and Lee trusting Katie to guide him and keep him safe, so we can envisage the double bond of trust between God and Christ and Christ and humanity making possible the safe delivery of humanity to God.[69]

This discussion has not made much reference to traditional models of atonement other than mediation, but some of the New Testament language on which other models draw, if not the models themselves in their developed forms, is compatible with this "trust" model. By allowing himself to be arrested and executed; by trusting God to use even his death to bring humanity to trust and new life; by showing humanity to itself as infinitely precious in God's eyes and capable of responding to God; by creating a space in which humanity can meet God in trust even in the extreme of human wrongdoing and suffering; by showing humanity the way through death to life and traveling it with them, Christ can be seen as offering himself as a sacrifice "for" humanity on its behalf.[70] His actions can be seen as enabling the "release" or "redemption" of human beings from the powers of evil, wrongdoing, and suffering (e.g., Gal 1:4; 3:13; 4:5; cf. Rom 3:24; 1 Cor 1:30) that hold humanity captive.

I referred above to the work some psychologists have done, showing how important trust is for giving us the sense that we are real in the world around us and that the world is real to us. Whom and what we trust or do not trust shapes our reality: where we can see ourselves and act and make relationships with people who are real to us. Paul understands this instinctively and deeply. He recognizes that when we choose to trust in God and Christ, we opt to be real in the reality of God and Christ and to live, work, and make relationships in that reality.[71] We choose life in an existence that is already partly realized in the present time and

---

69. Cranfield, *Romans*, 296, discussing Rom 6:1–14, notes that Christians die and are raised in several different senses in this passage: at the beginning of the relationship, as "a matter of present obligation," and in the eschatological future.

70. Cf. e.g., John 1:29; Rom 3:25; 1 Cor 5:7; Heb 9:26; with Luke 22:20; 1 Cor 11:25; cf. Matt 26:28 // Mark 14:24.

71. Cf. Martyn, *Theological Issues*, 121; on the realities in which we choose to live see pp. 82–83.

CHAPTER 3

will be fully realized at the *parousia*. In light of this reality, Paul implicitly offers readers a question. Where you put your trust will determine the reality in which you live, for the present and for eternal life. Whom do you trust?[72]

JESUS'S SUFFERING AND DEATH AS EXEMPLARY

The last two sections both mentioned the role of exemplarity in Christ's death.[73] Imitation of Christ plays a significant part in Paul's letters and becomes increasingly important in later writings.[74] For early Christians it is, above all, the suffering of Christ that is exemplary, and the faithful who imitate Christ express trust and faithfulness to God even when it leads to their own suffering.[75] Through imitation they seek to become more like Christ and to take part in God's ongoing work of salvation. The imitability of Christ can also be seen as contributing to humanity's at-one-ment with God. For all these reasons, imitation is worth exploring a little further.

In 1 Thess 1:6–7 Paul reminds the Thessalonians, "You became imitators [*mimētai*] of us and of the Lord, for in spite of persecution you received the word with joy from the Holy Spirit, so that you became an example [*typos*] to all the faithful in Macedonia and Achaia."[76] The Thessalonians seem to have come under some kind of attack for their conversion (cf. 1:8). In 2:14 Paul adds that they have become imitators of the churches of Judea, "for you suffered the same things from your compatriots as they did from the Jews."[77] These passages have been inter-

---

72. Most of us are further familiar with the experience that relationships of trust, for instance, within families or between lovers, lead to the sharing of experience and perspective.

73. Joachim Duyndam, "Hermeneutics of Imitation: A Philosophical Approach to Sainthood and Exemplariness," in *Saints and Role Models in Judaism and Christianity* (ed. Marcel Poorthuis and Joshua Schwarz; Leiden: Brill, 2004), 7–21 discusses exemplarity from a philosophical viewpoint, particularly in relation to sainthood.

74. It has been noted that imitation in Paul deserves more scholarly attention: e.g., Wayne Meeks, *The Moral World of the First Christians* (Philadelphia: Westminster, 1986), 136–43; Richard B. Hays, *First Corinthians* (Louisville: Knox, 1997), 215–24. Note, however, that the language of imitating Christ is not straightforwardly identifiable with practicing virtue, since it centers on trust and obedience to God rather than on the kind of self-regulation with which virtue is associated in the gentile world. For linking moral exemplarism and atonement see recently Oliver Crisp, "Moral Exemplarism and Atonement," *SJT* 73 (2020): 137–49; Craig, *Atonement*, 74 argues that "moral influence" is an inadequate theory of atonement on its own, but it is used here as part of a more complex model.

75. On imitation of the exalted Christ, see Morgan, *Theology of Trust*, 135–36.

76. Translation modified from the NRSV.

77. This clause may be a post-Pauline gloss.

The Trust and Trustworthiness of Jesus Christ

preted as meaning that the Thessalonians should console themselves by reflecting that Christ, Paul, and other churches have suffered too.[78] Paul's words, however, suggest that suffering also expresses the Thessalonians' trust, makes them more like Christ, and even strengthens their *pistis* (cf. 1 Thess 3:10, 13).

In 1 Cor 4:16–17, Paul encourages the Corinthians to imitate him, their father in Christ. A little earlier, he has affirmed his own trustworthiness as a servant of Christ and steward of the mysteries of God (4:1–2) who will be judged by God (4:3–5).[79] As God's servant he has endured all kinds of suffering and humiliation (4:9–13) and "we are fools for the sake of Christ" (4:10), but this foolishness is wiser than the wisdom and pride (cf. 4:6) of the Corinthians. This kind of foolishness, Paul insists, with all that comes with it, is what the Corinthian faithful should be pursuing. He is telling them this not to shame them but to admonish them (4:14–15), and to help them he is sending Timothy to remind them of his "ways in Christ Jesus" (4:17). Paul's "ways" are likely to be more than just his teaching (especially if we want to avoid tautology at 4:17): probably both his teaching and his example as servant of Christ.

This passage is sometimes interpreted as a demand by Paul that the Corinthians acknowledge his authority despite his sufferings and humiliations, but this does less than justice to the link between chapter 4 and chapters 2–3, where Paul characterizes the message of the cross as foolish in the eyes of the world and the wisdom of God as radically different from the wisdom of the world.[80] By being trustworthy servants and stewards of the message of the cross, Paul and Timothy live out the foolishness of the cross and the mysteriousness of God's wisdom in their lives and

---

78. So, e.g., W. Michaelis, "μιμέομαι," *TDNT* 4:666–67. The Thessalonians and others, of course, have not suffered in the same way as Christ suffered. There is no indication, e.g., that they are being executed, and their suffering is not salvific.

79. There may be a link between the mysteries and the idea of imitation; H. D. Betz, *Nachfolge und Nachahmung Jesu Christi im Neuen Testament* (Tübingen: Mohr Siebeck, 1967), 138 argues that the language of mimesis itself comes from the mysteries. Fritz Graf, "Lesser Mysteries—Not Less Mysterious," in *Greek Mysteries: The Archaeology and Ritual of Ancient Greek Secret Cults* (ed. M. Cosmopoulos; London: Routledge, 2003), 256 describes local mysteries of the early Roman Empire as reducing, even eliminating, the distance between initiates and the God they worshiped. If so, we should not take mimesis as mystical in the modern sense, because what made mystery cults mysteries was that their rituals were not open to public view, and only initiates could learn and take part in them, so Paul's point would be that only those who trust can imitate Christ.

80. Raymond F. Collins, *First Corinthians* (Collegeville: Liturgical, 1999), 192–93 notes that 1 Cor 4:8–13 echoes Greek and Jewish lists of tribulations or peristatic catalogues, which measure a person's virtue by the way he overcomes adversity. The reference to Paul's toil may refer to both his apostolic and practical work.

CHAPTER 3

actions, just as they speak of it in their teaching.[81] In their life they die continually to all the aspects of this world that would separate them from God, and as Christ is trusting and trustworthy toward God even in suffering and death, so Paul is trusting and trustworthy toward Christ and Timothy toward Paul (4:17). Through Paul's and Timothy's imitative *pistis*, therefore, the power of God (cf. 1:18) is proclaimed and more people are brought to trust. To understand this, the Corinthians must stop trying to be wise or to judge Paul (cf. 4:5) but rather imitate him and his trust.[82]

At 1 Cor 10:31–11:2, Paul says

> [31] So, whether you eat or drink or whatever you do, do everything for the glory of God. [32] Give no offense to Jews or to Greeks or to the church of God, [33] just as I try to please everyone in everything I do, not seeking my own advantage but that of many, so that they may be saved.
>
> [11:1] Be imitators of me, as I am of Christ [μιμηταί μου γίνεσθε καθὼς κἀγὼ Χριστοῦ]. [2] I commend you because you remember me in everything and maintain the traditions, just as I handed them on to you.

The traditional chapter division connects 11:1 more closely with 11:2 than with the preceding passage, but 11:1 reads at least as well as the climax of the previous few verses, in which Paul has again been telling the Corinthians to do as he does. The following verse can then be read as a summation of the whole passage, in which Paul praises the Corinthians both for remembering him and for following his teachings. On this interpretation, 11:1 means, "Imitate me, as I imitate Christ, in seeking the benefit of the many, so that they may be saved."[83] Paul's preaching and his actions as one who is *pistos* both further the saving work of Christ in the world.[84]

The theme of imitation is implicit in several other passages. Paul introduces the "Christ hymn" in Phil 2:5–11 by encouraging the Philippians to have among

81. Discussed by Anthony C. Thiselton, *The First Epistle to the Corinthians: A Commentary on the Greek Text* (Grand Rapids: Eerdmans, 2000), 365–68.

82. Cf. 1 Cor 15:4 with its possible allusion to Ps 16:8–11 (15:8–11 LXX) where God will not allow his holy one to see corruption (16:10), and 2 Cor 4:13 with its reference to Ps 116:10–15 (115:1–6 LXX) where the psalmist puts his trust in the Lord because the death of his holy ones is precious in the Lord's eyes.

83. On imitating God or Christ see also Eph 5:1–2; 1 Pet 2:21, 23–24; on imitating Paul see also 2 Thess 3:7–9.

84. Paul is probably not explicitly looking forward to his physical death here, nor does he conflate his apostolic activity with Christ's salvific activity, but there is reason to think that, as elsewhere, he sees following Christ as a death to the world; he has just described the celebration of the Lord's Supper as a sharing in the body and blood, that is, the sacrificial death of Christ (1 Cor 10:16–17, cf. 10:18).

The Trust and Trustworthiness of Jesus Christ

themselves the same attitude that was also theirs in Jesus Christ—the "mind" that led Christ to empty himself, take the form of a slave, humble himself, and become obedient to death on a cross. It seems likely that the Philippians are being invited here not only to be humble and obedient but to model their *pistis* on the the self-emptying humility of Christ.[85]

Imitating Christ by acting with humility and accepting the suffering that comes from one's commitment to God therefore is an expression of trust, makes the faithful person more like Christ, and furthers the saving work of Christ in this world. In other passages, Paul mentions other activities that are associated with Jesus during his earthly life. In 1 Cor 12:8–10, for example, the faithful are described, among other things, as healing, doing mighty deeds, prophesying, and discerning spirits. Here and elsewhere, however, activities like these are described as gifts of the spirit rather than explicitly as ways in which the Corinthians follow Christ (though these are obviously connected).[86] When Paul speaks, directly or indirectly, of people following or imitating Christ, he consistently associates them with Christ's suffering and death.[87]

Returning once more to Katie and Lee on their journey to California, we can see how the theme of imitation might also play a part in helping Lee to travel and arrive safely. It is a common sight on public transport to see a young child carefully imitating everything his or her parent does. We can imagine Lee pulling his own small suitcase and carrying his own sizable backpack. He follows Katie closely, spotting the signs as they navigate through security and find their departure gate. In the plane he stows his backpack next to hers and follows her example as she buckles her seatbelt. He is reassured not only by her presence and the fact that she knows her way around but by the fact that he can model his actions on hers at every point.

In time, Lee may himself become a model for his younger brother Jamie to imitate. Similarly, when Paul describes himself as *pistos* and exhorts others to

---

85. Rom 15:1–3 states that the faithful should tolerate the failings of the weak and not please themselves, as Christ did not. In recent years, criticism has been leveled at Paul's language of imitation, or interpretation of it, on the grounds that it encourages those who are already vulnerable to "empty" themselves and allow themselves to be downtrodden or abused. See, e.g., the recent discussion by Jane Heath, "*Imitatio Christi* and Violence to the Self," *J. Disabil. Relig.* 27 (2023): 247–83. I follow Heath, Dustin Ellington, "The Impulse toward the Disadvantaged in the Gospel Preached by Paul," *Scriptura* 115 (2016): 1–13, and others in the view that this is by no means Paul's intention. In the terms of this study, the call to imitation, if anything, empowers the disempowered by recognizing their entrustedness by God with work to do as followers of Christ, without determining how they do it (cf. Morgan, *Theology of Trust*, 312–19), and recognizes their agency in undertaking it.

86. Rom 12:6–8; 1 Cor 12:28–31; 14:1–2; 1 Thess 5:19–20; cf. Eph 4:11.

87. Hebrews also speaks of imitating Christ in suffering and death; e.g., 12:1–3.

CHAPTER 3

imitate him as he imitates Christ, he understands himself as continuing, in his own apostolic work, God's work of salvation through Christ, and so as playing his part in God's ongoing revelation and action in the world, which will enable people to continue to come to trust and live in trust until the *parousia*.[88]

For Paul, his willingness to imitate Christ and accept suffering is an expression of trust in God and Christ, trust in the gospel, and trust in his own entrustedness with the gospel by which he has become part of God's ongoing revelation and work for the world. In his willingness to accept suffering, there may even be a hint (cf. 1 Thess. 1:6) that suffering is the inescapable obverse of life in the spirit. The more overflowing life in the Christian community is with life and spirit, the more liable it is to attract suspicion and hostility from outside; but if life is to be gained, then suffering must be borne.[89] Imitating Christ has yet another implication that would have been familiar in Paul's world. Those who follow and imitate Christ not only hold certain atittudes, such as trust and hope, and practice certain types of action, such as love and generosity, but also follow a path. Following a path based on a (religious or philosophical) commitment is the beginning of what Christians and others call a *hodos*, a "way"; and following a way that has acknowledged leaders and authorities, in company with others who are following it, gives followers

88. It is worth noting that Paul's and others' discourse of imitation of the suffering of Christ does not fit easily within the typology of imitation developed by scholars of exemplarity in the Greek and Roman worlds and adopted by some New Testament scholars. In Greek and Roman moralizing literature, when great men and women are held up as examples to be imitated, their exemplarity normally consists in either a virtue or an action. For example, Horatius Cocles defends Rome from the invading Etruscans in the sixth century BCE by holding the Sublician Bridge with two comrades until it can be destroyed behind them (Polybius, *Histories* 6.55; Livy, *History of Rome* 2.10). Note also Achilles and Ajax, who in different ways exemplify courage, and Odysseus and Nestor, who exemplify wisdom (Plutarch, *Moralia* 243c–d). For recent discussions of the workings of Greek and Roman exemplarity see Rebecca Langlands, *Exemplary Ethics in Ancient Rome* (Cambridge: Cambridge University Press, 2019); Matthew Roller, *Models from the Past in Roman Culture: A World of Exempla* (Cambridge: Cambridge University Press, 2019). Suffering is neither a virtue nor an action, and although Christ-confessors may undergo suffering, Paul never suggests that it is an intrinsically good thing or that they should seek it out. To do justice to Paul's understanding of *imitatio Christi*, we need a third category of imitation, which we might describe as embracing the consequences of a commitment one has made in the trust and hope that, however challenging, they will ultimately be justified.

89. Paul may also see imitating Christ by being willing to accept suffering as marking the difference between God's values and those of this age and revealing the faithful as belonging to God's kingdom; cf. Betz, *Nachfolge*, 186–89. Embracing the consequences of a commitment one has made has something in common with martyrdom, of which Christ's suffering is treated as a model elsewhere but is a broader category.

148

The Trust and Trustworthiness of Jesus Christ

not only a cultic or intellectual identity but also a social one.[90] Paul's call to *pistis*, as he never forgets, therefore invites people into not only a new relationship with God and Christ but also into a new community and way of life.

Last but not least, as we have seen, the suffering and death of Christ, and preaching about it, change human beings' understanding of how it is possible to live for God, and by that token change how they can live for God. We might compare what happened when, in 1954, Roger Bannister became the first athlete to run a mile in less than four minutes or, in 1983, Carl Lewis ran the first sub-ten-second one hundred meters. Within a very short time, a number of other athletes had also done what many people had long thought impossible, and now all elite athletes aim for times quicker than these. By changing everyone's understanding of what is possible for the human body, many athletes have changed what is possible.[91] This analogy, however, does not go far enough for our purposes because it does not factor in the relationship between Christ and his followers or the idea that Christ travels with those who trust him on their necessary death to the things that hold them captive and into new life. Imagine that the first person to run a dramatically new time in a distance race has a close friend, and the first runner runs with her friend as she seeks to break the same barrier, supporting and encouraging her all the way. Anyone who has taken a long hike in company, been befriended within a support program for ex-offenders, or made the long journey of survival from abuse in the company of someone who is further on that same journey knows how much difference it makes to take such a journey alongside someone who knows the way and is convinced that they can make it. The presence of another person who knows the way can make the difference between failure and success, between remaining imprisoned in an old way of life and breaking out into the new.

At-One-Ment for the Suffering and the Wrongdoer

So far, we have recognized that although every aspect of Jesus Christ's earthly life, death, resurrection, and exalted life can be seen as salvific, almost all Christians

90. Noted by Michaelis, "μιμέομαι," 4:668.

91. This phenomenon is also recognized in the slogan "You can't be what you can't see," attributed to the American civil rights activist Marian Wright Edelman and widely referenced in arguments for equal rights and opportunities. It is explored in relation to the idea of Christ as mediator in the African American systematic theology of James H. Evans, *We Have Been Believers: An African-American Systematic Theology* (2nd ed.; Minneapolis: Fortress, 2012), especially 89–113.

CHAPTER 3

have understood his death as central to his work of salvation, so our model of atonement through trust must offer an account of the place of the cross in the restoration of the relationship between God and humanity. We have explored how Paul envisages Jesus Christ as trusting and trustworthy toward both God and humanity in his suffering and death, and how his relationship of trust with both makes possible their reconciliation. We proposed that by his relationship of trust with God, Jesus shows humanity what it means to live in trust. He allowed himself to be taken and crucified because to avoid the consequences of his commitment to God and to human beings would have been to deny the person he was and is, and it is as that person that he is able to at-one God and humanity. By refusing to give up his trust, even in suffering and death, Jesus creates a firebreak in the spread of evil, breaking the cycle of wrongdoing and suffering which alienates people from God. He also shows humanity to itself as inalienably precious to God, incapable of breaking God's commitment to it even in the extreme of wrongdoing, and capable by the grace of therapeutic trust of responding to God.

The cross is a human evil, but God, through Christ, uses it to create a space in the extreme of this world's chaos, suffering, and wrongdoing in which God meets humanity for its at-one-ment. To take part in the restoration of its relationship with God, humanity must respond to God's therapeutic trust and take their own step of trust into that space. Those who take the step must die spiritually to a world ruled by wrongdoing and pain as well as become part of a new creation. To make that possible Jesus dies before them, so that they can die with him and he, in his exalted life, is with them as they travel.

Both for those who have yet to take the step of trust, and for those who have been through death and are trying to live faithfully as "slaves of God" (Rom 6:22), Jesus is an example and more than an example. His trust and trustworthiness, even in death, change what human beings recognize is possible for them, and by that token make it possible as he goes with them. Because, however, the trust of Jesus's disciples is remembered as having been damaged, if not destroyed, by his death—as ours so often is by the power of evil in our own world—the resurrection experiences, and later revelations of many kinds, are added as a grace out of love to strengthen the fragility of our trust. As a model of at-one-ment this is a more complex narrative than some, though all models are narratives of some kind and have several stages. Its elements are mutually compatible, and we have noted that some older images of atonement can be fitted into it. Another fictional scenario may help us to reflect on it further. What follows imagines the situation of someone who has suffered and now perpetrates abuse along with someone who suffers abuse, and it tries to envisage how trust between God and Christ and

150

The Trust and Trustworthiness of Jesus Christ

Christ and human beings might help to release them from their different prisons and bring them to at-one-ment with God.

Flo is a wife, mother of three, and victim of an abusive husband. Her husband, Tom, was himself abused as a child, and as an adult he has not been able to find ways to address his suffering or handle the anger he feels. He vents his feelings on Flo, though not yet on their children.[92] Flo cannot physically stop him, and she does not know how to help him. Under the weight of her suffering and fear for her children, she is slowly sinking into deeper misery and isolation. She has largely lost contact with her own friends and family and has no trust or hope that they can help her. They do not know much about her situation and are confused and resentful of what seems her withdrawal. The more isolated Flo becomes, the more, destructively, she has to rely on her husband, and the harder it becomes to imagine ever getting out of the house.

We saw in chapter 2 how victims of trauma often lose trust both in themselves and in other people. Lack of trust becomes the framework of a person's life, dictating their behavior and relationships. Breaking out of that framework can be frightening, difficult, even impossible, and often can only happen with help. As one victim of trauma expressed it, "In order to experience love, to experience healing, it is necessary to trust. And that requires making yourself vulnerable. I found this to be the most difficult obstacle to healing after abuse."[93]

Even those who have faith in a God of love and justice can find it almost impossible not to retaliate when they are hurt, not to lose faith in the people around them when they are suffering, or to trust when trust has been betrayed in the past. It is all too easy to see how the intertwined suffering and wrongdoing in Flo's home might continue indefinitely, leading to ever more abuse.[94] While rec-

92. Eric Y. Tenkorang, Adobea Y. Owusu, and Gubhinder Kundhi, "Help-Seeking Behavior of Female Victims of Intimate Partner Violence in Ghana: The Role of Trust and Perceived Risk of Injury," *Journal of Family Violence* 33 (2018): 341–53 examines help-seeking behavior in victims of domestic abuse and finds it strongly correlated with existing trust in formal and informal support networks, which, however, themselves tend to be weak in the group studied. Nicole M. Buck et al., "Explaining the Relationship between Insecure Attachment and Partner Abuse: The Role of Personality Characteristics," *Journal of Interpersonal Violence* 27 (2012): 3149–70 finds that male batterers tend to suffer from insecure attachment, including lack of trust.

93. Donkin, "Trust"; cf. p. 100.

94. There are many theological discussions of abuse to which this discussion cannot do justice and discussions of atonement in light of abuse, but see, e.g., Joanne Carlson Brown, "Divine Child Abuse?" *Daughters of Sarah* 18 (1992): 24–28; Margo G. Houts, "Atonement and Abuse: An Alternative View," *Daughters of Sarah* 18 (1992): 29–32; M. H. Schertz, "God's Cross and Women's Questions: A Biblical Perspective on the Atonement," *Mennonite Quarterly Review* 68

CHAPTER 3

ognizing that this is a fictional scenario, and real situations are often even more complex and intractable, can the model of atonement we have been outlining offer something to it?

Neither Flo nor Tom can see a way out of their situation. But if Flo has had any contact with Christianity she may be able to see in God and Christ persons who do not, in any circumstances whatever, accept evil and who act consistently and constantly for love, for healing, and for the flourishing of the world. The vision of God and Christ as just and life-giving testifies that there is a world in which wrongdoing and suffering are not normal or acceptable. Beyond the abuse in which Flo feels trapped, there are a wholly different life and relationships of trust and trustworthiness.

Christ knows how Flo is suffering. Like her, he has been helpless in the face of violence. But he is with her and will never betray her. His absolute refusal to be corrupted by the evil around him, his steadfast trust and faithfulness both to God and to humanity, and the life that God brings out of his death create a space of trust into which he invites Flo to step. He assures her that her suffering is not natural or some kind of punishment and is not inescapable. A new and very different life is possible for her if she dares to follow Christ out of her present situation. There are, moreover, people around her who follow Christ's example of trust and trustworthiness and who can help her on the journey.

None of this, of course, gets Flo and her children physically out of the house into a safe environment. But it has the capacity to change her understanding of her situation, and by that token the situation itself. It assures her that she is not alone. It offers freedom from the power that suffering has over her to make her believe that her life could not be different, or that she does not deserve any better. It tells her that with Christ there is a journey to be undertaken that will lead her to a new life. Knowing this may strengthen her practically as well as spiritually to find a way out of her present situation. It opens up the possibility that her suffering can be transformed into new self-confidence, new power to make new, life-giving relationships, and even the power to inspire and support others who are suffering as she has suffered. Her chances are much better if she also connects with people—a relative or friend, a church or care professional—who can help and support her, and we will return to this in the last chapter.

We have seen that wrongdoing can be a response to suffering, and perhaps the assurance that suffering is not normal or right could reach Tom, too, and he might

---

(1994): 194–208; Katie M. Deaver, "Gentle Strength: Reclaiming Atonement Theory for Survivors of Abuse" (PhD diss., Lutheran School of Theology at Chicago, 2017).

The Trust and Trustworthiness of Jesus Christ

respond. Tom, however, has put his trust in himself and in violence to deaden his suffering. For him, an invitation to trust in God might need to take the form it takes to some groups of *apistoi* in the New Testament, especially the gospels: that of a challenge to recognize that he has put his trust in the wrong place. His choices are doing nothing but damaging his life and those of his family and putting him at risk of being exposed, arrested, and imprisoned. For him, however, just as much as for Flo, God, through Christ, offers a way out of his toxic situation and into a new life. What is more, in showing him this way, God and Christ are not only trustworthy but are ready to trust him, despite everything, with a new and different life and new and life-giving relationships.

Exactly how trust restores people and relationships retains an element of mystery, despite all the investigations of scholars in multiple disciplines. The workings of mediation have something of the same mystery: it is striking how often even handbooks for professional mediators, which describe meticulously what qualifications mediators need and how a mediation process should be prepared and enacted, stop short of describing what happens in the room. In the case of at-one-ment between God and humanity, we might envisage God as like a gardener, who sorts the weeds from the cultivated plants in her garden and adds all the weeds, dead flowers, and worm-eaten fruit to her compost heap. There, mysteriously, they turn back into nutritious soil that the gardener can spread back on the garden next year to grow more flowers and fruit. God takes the worst of human wrongdoing and suffering and "composts" it, turning it back into soil in which new life can grow. Both wrongdoing and suffering can be likened to what the gardener composts because both militate against life and flourishing. Plants do not choose whether to be composted by the gardener, but human beings can entrust themselves, their wrongdoing, and their suffering, through Christ, to the transformational power of God. How God transforms human suffering and evil remains a mystery to human understanding in this life; but it is less the process that human beings need to understand than the result.

For Flo and Tom, God's action through Christ is a sign that this world is not a place in which wrong that is done stays done; where, when people fail, as they constantly do, their failures lead inexorably to suffering and more and more failures; where those who are damaged remain damaged forever and pass their damage on to those around them. Through Christ, this is a world in which suffering and wrongdoing are constantly interrupted by new life, new relationships, and new hope and in which trusting in Christ can transform those who trust. In comparison with models of atonement that understand Christ's death, for instance, as an atoning sacrifice or penal substitution, it may be tempting to think of trust as

153

CHAPTER 3

a rather weak or indirect means of restoring humanity to its right relationship with God. In fact, there is an abundance of evidence to the contrary. As we saw in chapter 2, trust relationships can change people and change the course of their lives in direct and decisive ways.

Our model implies that God is ready to act for humanity at any time, but human beings have to be willing to respond and at least try to trust (granted that few, if any, manage perfect trust in their lifetimes). This raises a further question about those who may struggle to trust because they have suffered or their trust has been betrayed in the past. In describing Flo, I did not suggest that her situation was the result of any wrongdoing on her part (and I did not intend to suggest that she had inherited sinfulness), but we can imagine that, in her suffering, she might well struggle to trust in God. What kind of God allows obstacles to trust, and so to salvation, to stand in the way of those who have suffered?

It is cruel and unjust that Flo's suffering might damage her ability to trust in God. Part of what makes evil evil is the damage it does to the innocent. In the model we have outlined, I have not even suggested that the ability to trust is a gift of the spirit, since I have argued elsewhere that Paul does not think so.[95] But I think the model can respond to this challenge without trivializing it. There is little doubt that both wrongdoing and suffering damage people's ability to trust, but no New Testament writing suggests that the suffering cannot respond to God and Christ with trust.[96] Trust may be difficult, but it is always possible. This conviction, moreover, fits strikingly well with the examples we saw in chapter 2, which overwhelmingly find that trust can be built or rebuilt even among offenders and ex-offenders, victims of crime, the vulnerable, and those who have suffered abuse. The (re)building of trust is often a slow process, but all New Testament writers, more or less explicitly, affirm that God's work of salvation is not yet complete, so there is scope for even a slow process to come to fruition. They also recognize that human trust is fragile and imperfect, but nowhere in New Testament writings are those who want to trust but struggle to do so excluded from among Jesus's followers.

95. For an argument that trust precedes the gift of the spirit see Morgan, *Theology of Trust*, 298–312.

96. In a few passages of John's Gospel some wrongdoers seem not to be elected to *pisteuein*, but in other passages everyone can *pisteuein*, though not all do.

The Trust and Trustworthiness of Jesus Christ

CONCLUSION

This chapter has sought to show how for Paul the trust between God and Jesus Christ, together with the trust which God and Christ seek to establish between Christ and human beings, make possible the restoration of trust between God and humanity. Though Paul develops this model further than other New Testament writers, there are references to the idea of Christ as mediator elsewhere in the gospels and the epistles, while the idea that human beings are called or recalled to salvation through trust in God and Christ is ubiquitous in the New Testament. God's gracious outreach of trust shows humanity, mired and trapped in its wrongdoing and suffering, that to God it is still precious and still worthy of trust, and God invites and enables it to respond. By trusting humanity to respond to Christ, we can also understand God as entrusting it with a share of the power that is needed to bring it back to its right relationship with God.[97] Therapeutic trust, by its nature, empowers the recipient and, by offering therapeutic trust to humanity, God changes what is possible for humanity in return.

God and Jesus Christ trust one another as God and ultimately faithful human being, as Father and Son by the gift of the spirit, and as preexistent Father and Son. Both trust humanity to respond to Jesus in both his incarnate and exalted life. Jesus offers people reasons to trust throughout his life, death, and exalted life, and people respond not only because of what he says and does but because of who he is. Even through death, Jesus's relationship with God is unbreakable. His actions break the human cycle of failed trust, wrongdoing, and suffering. They show humanity to itself as inalienably precious to God, incapable of breaking God's commitment to it, and always capable of responding to God's trust. Out of the human horror of the cross, Jesus creates a space for trust, in which God is present offering trust to humanity and inviting humanity to take a step of trust toward God. We argued that the cross achieves this on its own but that the resurrection and later revelations act as a further grace for the disciples, shattered by Jesus's arrest and death, and for humanity, which still so often feels as if evil and wrongdoing rule our world.

Studies of conflict resolution often propose that trust is more likely to be restored in broken communities when people can meet each other face to face, and also when a mediator can be physically present. By affirming that Jesus Christ is the Son of God and insisting on the continuity of his identity in his earthly life and death and exalted life, New Testament writings affirm the importance of the

---

97. Cf. pp. 207–17.

CHAPTER 3

physical presence of God's Son with humanity, in the incarnation, for bringing people to trust. By implication, and occasionally explicitly (e.g., John 20:21), they also affirm the importance of testimony to Jesus Christ in the words and actions of his followers and their writings as part of the ongoing revelation of God's action through Christ.

Mediators do not normally die (though it is not unknown), but I argued that Jesus had to die because he could not be other than he was, and because to avoid death would have been to affirm humanity as less than it is to God. Beyond that, Jesus dies as a grace, because human beings do have to die to a life dominated by wrongdoing and suffering. We have to "get out" and live as survivors in a new life with new relationships and new hope. So that human beings can go through this death, Christ shows the way; they travel with him in spirit and he goes with them. Jesus's death therefore has an exemplary aspect, but it is much more than just exemplary because by changing humanity's sense of what is possible with God, he changes what is possible for it. He shows the way that humanity must take, and he travels with it so that it can travel with him.

This chapter has reaffirmed what we saw in the introduction and chapter 2: that trust helps to create our reality, the reality in which we can see ourselves, live, and act as real and make relationships with others who are real to us. To choose to trust in God and Christ is to choose to be real in the reality of God and Christ: to be alive in that world that is already partly realized in the present and whose fulfillment is promised at the end time. In a fictional scenario, we considered how the invitation to trust in God and Christ might offer new life to a person who was suffering abuse, and a person who was both a victim and a perpetrator of abuse. Using the image of God as gardener who "composts" wrongdoing and suffering to create new life, I characterized God's action in Christ as a sign that this is not a world in which evil that is done must stay done, creating suffering and more evil as its effects resound through time, place, and relationships. Rather, this is a world in which human wrongdoing and suffering are disrupted by new life and hope, and in which entering a relationship of trust with God and Christ can change those who trust for good. We noted that, in this model, God is always ready to act for humanity and receive humanity back to its right relationship with God, but that God does not force people to trust. People must respond to the revelation of God's and Christ's trustworthiness and the promise of new life by taking the step of trust that has been made possible for them into a space in which reconciliation can occur.

In chapter 1 I noted that several models of the origin of evil coexist in the Hebrew Bible, all of which were inherited by early Christians. In developing the

156

The Trust and Trustworthiness of Jesus Christ

argument that wrongdoing and suffering of many kinds alienate people from God, I have not yet discussed the separate question whether the ultimate cause of wrongdoing is human free will, weakness, original sin, the force of cosmic powers, our own conflicted psychology, or something else. In *Paul and Palestinian Judaism*, E. P. Sanders memorably came to the conclusion that Paul was convinced of what God had done for humanity through Christ, and reasoned back from that "answer" to humanity's plight to its cause—we might add, not always consistently. In a similar spirit, this study focuses more on what trust between God, Christ, and humanity makes possible than on the ultimate cause, if there is a single ultimate cause, of human alienation from God. It is, though, worth noting that the affirmation across New Testament writings that human beings, even under sin and suffering, *can* trust in Jesus Christ and in God implies that trust can act as the route to at-one-ment whether we envisage humanity as trapped in realities governed by hostile metaphysical powers or by our own minds and cultures.

We have also followed Paul in seeing God as always ready to be reconciled to humanity rather than (as witnessed sometimes in the Hebrew Bible) as needing to be reconciled. We have followed research in conflict resolution, the rehabilitation of ex-offenders, and the restoration of survivors of trauma in seeing trust as an essential first step in reconciliation, after which people can begin to face their past or present, articulate it, repent, seek forgiveness, and contemplate offering forgiveness as they need to. Like much of the research in these disciplines, a "trust" model of at-one-ment accepts that facing the past and present, repentance, and seeking and offering forgiveness are all highly demanding forms of mental, emotional, and relational work that can take years and may not be completed within a lifetime. In the last chapter we will return to this and the role that Christian communities may play in the process. For now, we note that in a "trust" model of reconciliation, the first step in trust can precede repentance.

This model also accepts that trust itself often needs time to grow and strengthen from "thin" to "thick." In principle it is possible for people to trust each other fully, unshakably, from the first moment they meet, but even in everyday life it is not the norm, and it is much less likely where people are damaged by suffering and wrongdoing. New Testament writings recognize this too: people sometimes take time to come to trust in God and Christ, and those who have started to trust often waver and fail, but, until the final judgment, the fragility of human trust is not treated as a deal-breaker where human beings continue to seek at-one-ment with God.[98] However carefully the gardener cultivates her flower beds, weeds

---

98. Morgan, *Theology of Trust*, 247–63.

CHAPTER 3

will continue to spring up until the last day. Even right standing with God is only provisional until the end time. The crucifixion, together with the resurrection and ongoing revelations, however, stands as a sign not only of what God has done but of what God through Christ continues to do for humanity. The restoration of trust through the death and resurrection of Christ is not an end point but a beginning: new life, new possibilities, and new hope.

CHAPTER 4

Trust in Creation

So far we have been talking about trust in the at-one-ment of God and human beings. But what about the rest of creation? At a time when we are more conscious than ever of our material and moral inseparability from our environment and the whole cosmos of which we are part, we may wonder whether other parts of that whole can also be estranged from God as a result of the kinds of wrongdoing or suffering we have been exploring. In the fast-growing field of ecotheology, it is well recognized that the rest of creation is the victim of sustained and ongoing human wrongdoing, and non-human creation is increasingly understood not merely as an object of human attentions and often abuse but as a subject in its own right. There is, however, very little discussion so far of whether nonhuman creation can not only suffer but also do wrong, and whether it needs not only to be liberated from the consequences of human wrongdoing but also to be reconciled with God on its own account.[1] This chapter considers whether there is scope to

---

1. E.g., Bron Taylor, ed., *Encyclopedia of Religion and Nature* (2 vols.; London: Continuum, 2005) so far lacks entries on atonement, salvation, or soteriology, while Roger S. Gottlieb, ed., *The Oxford Handbook of Religion and Ecology* (Oxford: Oxford University Press, 2006) includes two brief mentions of salvation but none of soteriology or atonement. We cannot here discuss the large and rich bibliography on ecotheology or theology and evolutionary science in general but must confine ourselves to the question of creation's possible sinfulness and how it might be addressed. Jürgen Moltmann, *The Way of Jesus Christ* (London: SCM, 1990); John Haught, *Deeper than Darwin: The Prospect for Evolution in the Age of Evolution* (Boulder: Westview, 2003); Denis Edwards, "Why Is God Doing This? Suffering, the Universe, and Christian Eschatology," in *Physics and Cosmology: Scientific Perspectives on the Problem of Evil in Nature* (ed. Robert J. Russell, Nancey Murphy, and William Stoeger; Berkeley: CTNS; Vatican City: Vatican Observatory, 2007), 247–66; Willis Jenkins and Ernst M. Conradie, eds., "Ecology and Christian Soteriology," special issue of *Worldviews* 14 (2010); Ted Peters, "Constructing a Theology of Evolution: Building on John Haught," *Zygon* 45 (2010): 921–37; Michael Gorman, *The Death of the Messiah and the Birth*

CHAPTER 4

envisage nonhuman creation as sinful—recognizing, as in earlier chapters, that wrongdoing is often deeply entwined with suffering—and whether, if so, we can envisage nonhuman creation also as restored to its right relationship with God through the trust and trustworthiness of Jesus Christ.

GOD AND CREATION

We can begin with what is least controversial: for Christians, God is the God who creates everything that is. At the beginning of the book of Genesis, God creates the heavens and earth and everything in them. God then goes beyond other creator gods of the ancient Near East and Mediterranean by identifying everything God has created as good. Given the breadth of the Hebrew term for "good" (*ṭôb*) and its Septuagintal translation (*kalos*) we cannot be certain whether God finds creation beautiful, pleasing, harmonious with Godself, morally good, or a combination of them all, but we can be sure that, for Jews and Christians, creation does more than exist: it has a positive status in God's eyes.[2]

---

of the New Covenant: A (Not So) New Model of the Atonement (Eugene: Cascade, 2014); Daniel P. Castillo, "Integral Ecology as a Liberationist Concept," *TS* 77 (2016): 353–76, and, more obliquely, Sallie McFague, *A New Climate for Christology: Kenosis, Climate Change, and Befriending Nature* (Minneapolis: Fortress, 2021) are among those who see the atonement as reconciling all creation to God, though they assume that nonhumans suffer rather than do wrong, and they tend not to be very clear how this kind of reconciliation would work. Critically discussing recent models of "deep incarnation" that focus on the solidarity of God through the cross with all suffering creatures, see Michael E. Lee, "Historical Crucifixion: A Liberationist Response to Deep Incarnation," *TS* 81 (2020): 892–912. Discussions of nonhuman creation's relationship with God tend to assume that these are metaphorical or eschatological, which is well discussed by Mark Harris, "'The Trees of the Field Shall Clap Their Hands' (Isaiah 55:12): What Does It Mean to Say That a Tree Praises God?" in *Knowing Creation: Perspectives from Theology, Philosophy, and Science* (ed. Andrew B. Torrance and Thomas H. McCall; Grand Rapids: Zondervan, 2018), 287–304, but this chapter explores the possibility that seeing atonement as the restoration of trust has more literal potential. Unusual in arguing that atonement might encompass nonhuman creation are David G. Horrell, *The Bible and the Environment: Towards A Critical Biblical Theology* (London: Equinox, 2010), 42–44, who also argues (49–61) that the theme of creation's praise of God in the psalms decenters humanity from creation, and Celia Deane-Drummond, "Shadow Sophia in Christological Perspective: The Evolution of Sin and the Redemption of Nature," *Theology and Science* 6 (2008): 13–32. Deane-Drummond argues that the self-emptying of Christ as divine Wisdom on the cross might meet the wrongdoing of nonhuman as well as human creation, understood, in the language of Sergii Bulgakov, as "shadow sophia." She argues, however, that understanding atonement in this way cannot help nonhuman creation in any literal way (23).

2. The so-called approval formulate that "God saw that . . . was good" appears seven times in

Trust in Creation

Both Genesis's creation stories describe God anthropomorphically for a human audience as acting, resting, speaking, planning, giving creatures autonomy to multiply, and creating humanity in some aspect of God's likeness (Gen 1:26).[3] Once humanity is created, God interacts anthropomorphically with it within the text.[4] But God also rebukes the snake in terms that the snake presumably understands (3:14–15), and later books of the Hebrew Bible envisage God interacting with many other parts of creation in ways they understand. The book of Job, for example, describes how God guides the bear and her cubs (38:39), brings the wild ox to serve God (39:9), commands the eagle (39:27), and makes a covenant with Leviathan (40:25–28). Creation responds according to its kind. Mount Zion celebrates God's judgments (Ps 47:12) and the heavens proclaim God's justice (Ps 50:1–6). Young lions seek their food from God (Ps 104:21) and young ravens cry to God for food and are not disappointed (Ps 147:9). The singer of Psalm 148 calls all creation—animal, vegetative, and inanimate—to praise the Lord, and Ps 150:6 urges, "Let everything that has breath praise the Lord."[5]

In *The Hebrew Bible and Environmental Ethics*, Mari Joerstad investigates biblical accounts of the interaction of the inanimate world particularly with God and humanity. She describes this as "an exercise in taking [the texts' anthropomorphic language] seriously; I don't mean literally—there is plenty of metaphor here—but seriously."[6] Through the lenses of "new animism" and metaphor theory, she argues

---

Gen 1; as Gordon Wenham, *Genesis 1–15*, 18 notes, "goodness" in God's works reflects God's own goodness and God's recognition that God's own goodness is reflected in God's works.

3. On the history of interpretation of the image of God in Genesis, see, e.g., Yair Lorberbaum, *In God's Image: Myth, Theology, and Law in Classical Judaism* (New York: Cambridge University Press, 2015). Karl Barth, *Church Dogmatics* (vol. 3.1, *The Doctrine of Creation, Part I*; trans. G. W. Bromiley; Edinburgh: T&T Clark, 1986), 183–87 argues that humanity's divine image means that God can enter relationships with human beings, speak to them, and make covenants with them; cf. Claus Westermann, *Genesis* (Neukirchen-Vluyn: Neukirchener, 1970), 1–11. Catherine McDowell, *The Image of God in the Garden of Eden* (Philadelphia: Pennsylvania University Press, 2015), 185, 201–2 argues that the idea of being in God's image is also language of sonship, so Adam is characterized here as God's son. These strengthen the reading of God's relationship with humanity in Gen 1–3 as one of care.

4. Elizabeth Burns, "Must Theists Believe in a Personal God?" *Think* 8 (2009): 77–86 notes that this does not commit us to positing a personal God, but that God enables creation to interact with God within its capacities. Gen 3 also assumes that, at this point, snakes and humans can communicate with each other.

5. The earth responds to the presence of God with earthquakes and rain (Ps 68:9); God makes the wind God's messenger (Ps 104:4)

6. Mari Joerstad, *The Hebrew Bible and Environmental Ethics: Humans, Non-Humans, and the Living Landscape* (Cambridge: Cambridge University Press, 2019), 2. Joerstad draws on Jane Bennett, *Vibrant Matter: A Political Ecology of Things* (Durham: Duke University Press, 2010),

CHAPTER 4

that by representing inanimate creation as living and active, as interacting with God, and as acting on humans biblical texts represent humanity as part of a whole, interrelated landscape of creation. Human beings are shaped by this landscape as much as they shape it, and they live appropriately—in a way that is "good"—when they live in harmony with the rest of creation and all creation lives in harmony with God.[7] This kind of existence, Joerstad shows, is represented as bringing joy both to human beings and to the rest of creation, animate and inanimate. Joerstad's concern, in addition to the illumination of a biblical worldview, is the questions that taking this language seriously raises for humanity's understanding of the environment and our relationship with it. She does not, however, explore the possibility that inanimate creation may not only recognize God's presence, praise God, grieve over human or natural suffering, react to human wrongdoing, and become polluted by human wrongdoing and unfit for God's presence, but also that it may transgress, intentionally or unintentionally, on its own account. Jonathan Morgan takes this approach further and argues that in Leviticus 18–27 the land is a "semi-autonomous moral agent," which, for instance, "vomits" out inhabitants who have defiled it (18:25, 28; cf. 20:22), devours lawbreakers (26:38), and deserves to be able to rest and enjoy every seventh agricultural year (25:2, 4–5; 26:34).[8] In this chapter I will go further still and argue that zoology and botany offer a new framework for "new animist" discourse, within which we can express our sense of the complex interactivity of creation not only through metaphor but also through the language of empirical science.

The Hebrew Bible also affirms that God's relationship with creation from the beginning is one of care, evident in God's sense of what is good for creation and God's actions on creation's behalf, and that part of God's care for creation is to give parts of it into the care of one another.[9] In Genesis's first creation story (1:26), human beings are made in God's likeness and given dominion over other earthly

---

which argues for the agency of inanimate creation and human-made "things" and assemblages of things. Though this is a work of political theory not theology, Bennett's approach—"I am looking for a materialism in which matter is figured as a vitality at work both inside and outside of selves, and is a force to be reckoned with without being purposive in any strong sense" (62)—offers a route for theological thinking about inanimate creation.

7. Graham Harvey defines "new animists" as "people who recognize that the world is full of persons, only some of whom are human, and that life is always lived in relationship with others." See Harvey, *Animism: Respecting the Living World* (New York: Columbia University Press, 2006), ix.

8. Jonathan Morgan, "Transgressing, Puking, Covenanting: The Character of the Land in Leviticus," *Theology* 112 (2009): 172–80.

9. Alan J. Hauser, "Genesis 2–3: The Theme of Intimacy and Alienation," in *Art and Meaning: Rhetoric in Biblical Literature* (ed. Alan J. Hauser, David M. Gunn, and David J. A. Clines;

Trust in Creation

beings. What it means to be made in God's likeness has been debated since antiquity, but the story suggests at least that human dominion is not simple power but involves the responsibility to ensure that creation remains, as God made it, good (e.g., 1:4, 25), dazzlingly varied (1:11–25), fruitful (e.g., 1:12, 22, 28), and surrounded by plenty to sustain it (1:29–30). In the second story, the human is given responsibility for cultivating and caring for Eden (2:15, 18). The woman God creates out of the human is given the role of partnering the man as no other animal can (2:18, 20) while the garden has the responsibility of feeding them (2:9) with river branches that water the garden and other parts of the land (2:10–14). If being good can have more than one meaning, part of the goodness of created beings in these stories surely consists in their taking care of each other.

The relationship between God and humanity, and humanity and the rest of creation, in Genesis is soon undermined. The acts of Adam and Eve in eating the apple are the first instance of human rebellion against God, but we sometimes gloss over the fact that, in the story, the first creature to put itself at odds with God is the snake, and in corrupting the humans the snake also subverts God's plans.[10] God is well aware of this and curses the snake first (3:14–19). For the writer of the story, it is not only humanity that is capable of wrongdoing for which it is morally responsible and appropriately punished, and humanity is not even the first part of creation to err.

Despite this, throughout Genesis God continues to care for creation, reordering its relationship with God repeatedly after episodes of wrongdoing and punishment described in the stories of the flood, Sodom and Gomorrah, Esau and Jacob, and beyond. These stories set a pattern not only for God's relationship with humanity but also for God's relationship with creation more widely and for relationships among created beings. When any participant mistreats any other, the symbiosis between them is disturbed, and life becomes more difficult. Human beings and snakes try to harm each other (3:15). The ground yields thorns and thistles instead of good sustenance (3:17–18), shouts in outrage when human blood is spilled on it (4:10), and refuses afterward to grow crops (4:12). When God decides to wipe out humanity with a flood, God decides to wipe out animal (and plant)

London: T&T Clark, 1982), 20–36 discusses the intimacy of this relationship, and the alienation that follows.

10. Assuming, with most modern commentators both Jewish and Christian, that the snake is not Satan in disguise, 3:14 nevertheless makes clear that it does something that calls for divine punishment. Claus Westermann, *Genesis 1–11: A Commentary* (Minneapolis: Augsburg, 1984), 237–38, in the context of arguing that the story of the snake does not, as might appear at first sight, explain the origin of evil, notes that although "the words of the serpent are . . . directed against God . . . this does not become a theme of the narrative."

CHAPTER 4

life too (6:5–7): "Now the earth was corrupt in God's sight and the earth was full of violence . . . And God said to Noah, 'I have determined to make an end of all flesh, for the earth is filled with violence because of them'" (6:11–12). We do not hear that nonhuman beings have done wrong themselves at this point, but they are corrupt by association with humanity (whether because created beings ultimately form one group, or because of their particular relationships with humans) such that it is evidently appropriate for them to share humanity's punishment.

I argued in chapter 1 that God's relationship with Adam and Eve is not only one of care but also one of trust, and that trust is damaged in two stages when the snake induces Eve to doubt God and then Eve and Adam disobey God. Trust as a theme remains implicit in the creation stories, but elsewhere in the scriptures, especially in the psalms and books of wisdom, the connection between God, creation, care, and trust is clear and sometimes explicit. Psalm 32 LXX, for instance, has a strong creation theme: "The word of the Lord is upright, and all his works are trustworthy [or perhaps "performed in good faith"; πάντα τὰ ἔργα αὐτοῦ ἐν πίστει]" (32:4). God loves mercy and justice, and the earth is full of his mercy (32:5). By God's breath and word the heavens and all their hosts were established, and God gathers the waters of the sea and puts them in store (32:5–7). The Lord brought all the inhabitants of the world into being (32:8–9, cf. 32:15). He looks down on them (32:13): "the eyes of the Lord are on those who fear him, those who hope in his mercy to rescue their souls from death and to keep them alive in famine. Our soul waits for the Lord, because he is our helper and protector" (32:18–20). The trustworthiness and care of God for the whole of creation frame the whole of existence, and the capacity of created beings to trust God is made possible by God's care. Psalm 18 LXX links the trustworthy (*pistos*, 18:8) witness of the Lord, which makes infants wise, with God's creation of the world and the whole world's celebration of God's glory. "The heavens tell the glory of God, and the firmament proclaims the work of his hands" (18:1). All created beings are in a relationship of trust with God as creator and grow in wisdom within that trust.[11]

In the New Testament, Adam and Eve are referenced only rarely, but the creation of the world is invoked many times and often in a prominent position at or near the beginnings of books.[12] Given that God's creativity and care are linked

11. W. H. Bellinger Jr., "The Psalms, Covenant, and the Persian Period," in *Covenant in the Persian Period: From Genesis to Chronicles* (ed. Richard J. Bautch and Gary N. Knoppers; Philadelphia: Pennsylvania University Press, 2015), 309–21 shows that some psalms use creation imagery to appeal to God's faithfulness to Israel as an instance of God's faithfulness to creation as a whole.

12. 1 Cor 15:22, 45; Rom 5:14; Luke 3:38. On Genesis motifs in the New Testament in general see Paul Sevier Minear, *Christians and the New Creation: Genesis Motifs in the New Testament*

Trust in Creation

with trust in God in the Hebrew Bible, it would not be surprising to find New Testament writings invoking the trustworthiness of God as creator when they urge people to put their trust in God. More often, in fact, they use creation to make a claim about Christ: that Jesus Christ, who preexisted with God and took part in creation, is trustworthy as God is trustworthy and cares for creation as does Godself.[13]

The writers of John's Gospel and 1 John may both be adapting existing hymns when they begin their texts by proclaiming that Christ was (with) God before creation, or was the firstborn of creation through whom everything else was made (John 1:1–4; 1 John 1:1–2). John's Gospel uses *pisteuein* nearly a hundred times, nearly always to refer to trusting or believing (relationally) in Jesus, and one of its principal themes is that human beings can and must trust in Jesus as they do in Godself.[14] By identifying Jesus with the preexistent Word, both John's Gospel and 1 John insist that Jesus is trustworthy just as the creator God is trustworthy.

Those who put their trust in Jesus in John's Gospel do so because they recognize him as the one with whom (i.e., God) they are already in a relationship from their creation. Some of Jesus's "I am" sayings indicate that this relationship is also one of care. Jesus is the light of the world, without which creation cannot come into being (8:12; cf. 1:9).[15] Jesus is the bread of life that feeds all who come to him (6:35).[16] He is the shepherd who looks after his sheep at the risk of his own life; the protecting door of the sheepfold (10:9, 11), and the vine whose branches depend on it for life and nourishment (15:4–5). By describing Jesus's care for others using images from the natural world, the writer also suggests that created beings care

---

(Louisville: Westminster John Knox, 1994). On God's care for all creation and creation's response in New Testament writings, though not discussing the cross, see Robert Murray, *The Cosmic Covenant* (London: Sheed & Ward, 1992); Richard Bauckham, *Bible and Ecology: Rediscovering the Community of Creation* (London: Darton, Longman & Todd, 2009); Richard Bauckham, *Living with Other Creatures: Green Exegesis and Theology* (Bletchley: Paternoster, 2012); Horrell, *Bible and the Environment.*

13. They also refer to creation to claim that the faithful have been chosen and preelected by God, or to affirm that both Jews and gentiles can and should put their trust in God. The theme of Christ's preexistence also draws on wisdom literature, where trusting in God is also prominent (e.g., Prov 3:3, 5; 16:20; 29:25; Wis 1:2; 3:1; 10:7; cf. Wis 10:5; 12:2; 16:24–25; Sir 2:6, 8, 10, 13; 32:24), so linking Christ with God the creator via the idea of Christ as God's wisdom strengthens the idea that one should trust Christ in the same way as the creator God.

14. Morgan, *Roman Faith*, 397–403.

15. John 8:12 also refers to the nightly lighting of lamps during the feast of tabernacles, which is the setting of this story.

16. Philo, *On the Change of Names* 259–260 and Mekilta Exodus 13.17 speak of manna being assimilated into the bodies of the Israelites eating it.

CHAPTER 4

for one another (light gives life to everything else; the grain and the vine feed others; the shepherd takes care of his sheep). First John 1:1–4 treats some of the same themes. The Word of life has been made visible, so that human beings can see it and testify to it (1:2). Those who see and recognize it (cf. 1:1) are brought into fellowship or unity (*koinōnia*) with the Father and his Son, Jesus Christ (1:3), and are cleansed once for all from all sin (1:7, 9).

Colossians 1:15–20 may draw on another existing hymn to the preexistent Christ: "He is the image of the invisible God, the firstborn of all creation, for in him all things in the heavens and on earth were created, things visible and invisible, whether thrones or dominions or rulers or powers—all things have been created through him and for him" (1:15–16). Here again, to have a relationship of trust and faithfulness with Christ (1:2, 4, 23; cf. 1:7) means to have a relationship that is tantamount to the relationship of human beings with the creator God.[17] It is also to be reconciled and at peace with God and Christ (1:20–21), to be part of the unity of all things (1:17), and to "share in the inheritance of the saints in the light" (1:12).

The Letter to the Hebrews applies the creation passage of Ps 101:26–28 LXX to Christ:

> [10] In the beginning, Lord, you founded the earth, and the heavens are the work of your hands; [11] they will perish, but you remain; they will all wear out like clothing; [12] like a cloak you will roll them up, and like clothing they will be changed. But you are the same, and your years will never end. (Heb 1:10–12)

The writer has already called Christ God's Son and the "imprint" of God's being (1:3) through whom the universe was created (1:2).[18] Now God's "sure [*bebaios*] word" (2:2) has been revealed through Christ (2:3–4) for the salvation (2:3) of those who trust in Christ (2:13).

Paul in Rom 1:18–23 and Luke's Paul in Acts 17:22–31 both appeal to creation theologies, proclaiming that God makes Godself known through creation and therefore that everyone should give glory and thanks to God (Rom 1:21) or should repent and put their trust in God and Christ before Christ returns to judge the world (Acts 17:30–31).[19] In Rom 1:19–20, Paul says that the gentiles should have

17. This could be the case whether *eikōn* refers to Christ as the manifestation of God, as creator and reconciler of the universe, or as acting on and with the world with God; see Morgan, *Theology of Trust*, 87 n. 228.

18. Attridge, *Hebrews*, 50 notes that the writer understands Ps 44:7–8 LXX as addressing the Son of God.

19. C. K. Barrett, *Acts of the Apostles: A Shorter Commentary* (London: T&T Clark, 2002), 269 notes that the idea of God as creator is common to Jews and Greeks, which is broadly

166

Trust in Creation

recognized God and worshiped God because the whole of creation reveals God's power and nature. Luke's Paul tells the Athenians that the God for whom they have been "groping" (Acts 17:27) and have half-recognized (17:23–24) is the creator God of Israel.[20] He emphasizes God's parental relationship and care for creation with two citations from Greek authors: "in him we live and move and have our being" and "we too are his offspring."[21] Paul, meanwhile, tells the Romans that gentiles who reject their relationship with God (1:28) become incapable of other functional relationships: they become insolent, haughty, boastful, wicked, and rebellious toward their (human) parents (1:30; cf. 1:31) as well as destructive toward themselves and each other (1:26–27). For both writers, it is as part of creation that human beings need to be restored to their right relationship with God, and that relationship is one of trust (cf. Acts 17:34; Rom 3:26).

Creation and eschatology are closely linked in these and other passages that celebrate Christ as creator with God.[22] Eschatology is also the focus of the most famous passage about the relationship between creation as a whole and God in Paul's letters in Rom 8:18–25.[23] Paul describes "the whole creation" as "groaning together as it suffers together the pains of labor" (8:22). The imagery of groaning as if in labor recalls passages such as Isa 13:8, Jer 4:31, and Hos 13:13, in which Israel or her enemies groan in knowledge of their own sins and in anticipation of God's punishment.[24] This suggests that creation may be in a state of sin, and this sug-

---

true though Greek myths are more diverse, but also shows how many echoes of scripture are threaded through this speech.

20. Both link the idea that gentiles are under God's judgment with the idea that they have failed to see and understand God for who and what God is (Acts 17:23–24; Rom 1:20–21). See the discussion of Robert Jewett, *Romans: A Commentary* (Minneapolis: Fortress, 2007), 157–59.

21. The first is often thought to be Stoic but is not a known quotation; the second quotes Aratus, *Phenomena* 5.

22. E.g., Eph 1:3–6; cf. Eph 1:1, 13; Titus 1:1–4; 1 Pet 4:7–5:4; Rev 21:1–4 (without trust language). Trust language does not appear in the New Testament's few visions of existence after the *parousia*, but it may be imagined as continuing to be part of the restored divine-human relationship. See Morgan, *Roman Faith*, 473–75.

23. Cf. Gen 3:17–18; Job 31:38–40, where human sin causes the rest of creation to groan. Paul does not say that the rest of creation sins as humanity does, but we can see the rest of creation as implicated in human sin and as sharing its consequences, which could include the reactive creation of more suffering and wrongdoing. Counseling caution for when we are tempted to read Romans 8 as a source for either nonanthropocentric theology or optimism that righteoused humanity can contribute to the liberation of creation, however, is Horrell, *Bible and the Environment*, 74–80.

24. David Horrell, "A New Perspective on Paul? Rereading Paul in a Time of Ecological Crisis," *JSNT* 33 (2010): 19–20 argues, particularly on the basis of this passage and 1 Cor 15, that "Paul's soteriological vision is literally all-encompassing," incorporating creation as well as humanity.

CHAPTER 4

gestion is strengthened when Paul refers in Rom 8:23 to "not only creation but we ourselves," who are distinct in that we have received the spirit but, like the rest of creation, are groaning as we wait for adoption. Those who have put their trust in Christ, been righteoused, and received the spirit await the *parousia* in a different state from the rest of creation. Paul has already said, however, that "creation was subjected to futility, not of its own will, but by the will of the one who subjected it, in hope that the creation itself will be set free from its enslavement to decay and will obtain the freedom of the glory of the children of God" (Rom 8:20–21). This points to creation as being not in a state of willful sin, like the ancient Israelites or Babylonians according to the prophets, but something closer to that of non-Christ-confessing Jews who, as we saw in chapter 1, have not necessarily done wrong intentionally (though some have), and many of whom have been faithful, but who have become sinners "under the law" (cf. Rom 2:12) and need to be redeemed (cf. 8:23).[25] This suggests that we can see creation as possibly being, in some parts, willfully sinful, but in some other parts as suffering from its adherence to laws that no longer pertain after the crucifixion and resurrection.[26] In this new existence, not only the faithful but everything that exists is waiting in hope of salvation.

Most of these New Testament passages occur at or close to the beginnings of books (we could add the vision of a new heaven and earth at the climax of Rev 21:1–5), framing their writers' arguments about what God has done through Christ, and how humanity is called to respond. Creation imagery is only one of several ways in which New Testament writers envision the restored relationship between God, Christ, and humanity, but their prominent location and often powerful hymnic language mean that these passages are particularly memorable. Drawing on a scriptural vision that sees the relationship between God and all creation as one of care and trust, they affirm that human beings can and should trust God and Christ because they are part of creation and, more broadly, that creation as a whole needs to be restored to its right relationship with God through Christ.[27]

25. Pp. 73–75.

26. Gerd Theissen, *Psychological Aspects of Pauline Theology* (Edinburgh: T&T Clark, 1987), 333 points to the "profound correspondence" between humanity and the rest of nature in this passage. He is not proposing the interpretation above but his comment is compatible with it.

27. A number of commentators recently have argued that creation theology underlies much covenant theology in the Hebrew Bible, and the breaking of covenants harms creation as a whole. Some Pauline scholars have argued that this theme underlies Paul's understanding of the relationship between human wrongdoing and the suffering of the rest of creation not only in Romans 8 but elsewhere. They focus on creation as the innocent victim of human sin, but this approach also opens up the possibility that creation as a whole is implicated in the breaking of covenants insofar as humans are part of it; see Morgan, *Theology of Trust*, 89–90. It may sound odd to some readers to speak of nonhuman creation having, losing, or being restored to trust,

Trust in Creation

The Wrongdoing and Suffering of Creation

Few readers will be surprised by the idea that (at least animate) nonhuman beings can suffer, but to many it will be a less familiar and less intuitively plausible claim that nonhuman creation can do wrong or sin. Here, however, recent research in life sciences and philosophy offers food for thought.

The idea that human beings are part of the natural world, not distinct from it, became embedded in the life sciences through the work of eighteenth-century natural historians such as Carl Linnaeus, Gilbert White, and Alexander von Humboldt. I have already mentioned in relation to biblical writings that creation can be said to do wrong insofar as human beings, who are part of creation, do wrong. By the same token, creation can be said to suffer insofar as human beings suffer for their own wrongdoings, and it is also easy to see some parts of the natural world as suffering for the wrongdoings of others. In the twenty-first century, there is no doubt that other parts of creation have suffered for human damage to the environment: their habitats degraded or destroyed, their sources of food polluted or obliterated, and their numbers driven into decline or extinction.

Created beings other than humans have not often been seen as capable of morally culpable wrongdoing, because they have not been seen as moral agents or as responsible for their actions in the way that humans are usually assumed to be. In recent years, however, some biologists and philosophers have argued that an increasingly wide range of other animals can experience and act on what may be called emotions with moral content.[28] The moral philosopher Mark Rowlands has drawn a wealth of this scholarship together in a study that sets the arguments of philosophers from Aristotle to Wittgenstein about the moral capacities of animals alongside recent research in zoology. Rowlands argues that the case made by many philosophers against the moral capacities of animals is conceptually too limited. Typically, it has been assumed that animals cannot be moral agents because they lack the capacity for reflection, which would enable control over their motivations

---

but exercising what we recognize as trust need not require a high level of intelligence or self-consciousness, as some of the examples below show.

28. David DeGrazia, *Taking Animals Seriously: Mental Life and Moral Status* (Cambridge: Cambridge University Press, 1996); Paul Shapiro, "Moral Agency in Other Animals," *Theoretical Medicine and Bioethics* 27 (2006): 357–73; Mark Rowlands, "Animals That Act for Moral Reasons," in *The Oxford Handbook of Animal Ethics* (ed. T. Beauchamp and R. G. Frey; New York: Oxford University Press, 2011), 519–46; Rowlands, *Can Animals Be Moral?* (Oxford: Oxford University Press, 2012), 15–32; Judith Benz-Schwartzburg and Andrew Knight, "Cognitive Relatives and Yet Moral Strangers?" *Journal of Animal Ethics* 1 (2011): 9–36; Simon Fitzpatrick, "Animal Morality: What Is the Debate About?" *Biology and Philosophy* 32 (2017): 1151–83.

CHAPTER 4

and behavior. Rowlands agrees that animals lack this capacity but argues that this is more than is required for a creature to act morally. He argues that animals can act for "moral reasons" that take the form of emotions with moral content. Emotions, in this context, are identified as "intentional states," which may have very varied content, and Rowlands defends the attribution of such states to animals. Animals that can act for moral reasons can be identified as "moral subjects," who may act on moral motivations even without being held responsible for their actions in the sense that a human moral agent, capable of reflection, would be. Rowlands gives a wide range of examples of animals, especially social animals (including many mammals and some reptiles and birds) that have been identified by experimental zoologists as showing what he calls emotions with moral content, such as sympathy, compassion, kindness, tolerance, patience, anger, indignation, malice, and spite as well as "a sense of what is fair and what is not."[29]

> Binti Jua, a gorilla residing at Brookfield Zoo in Illinois, had her fifteen minutes of fame in 1996 when she came to the aid of a three-year-old boy who had climbed onto the wall of the gorilla enclosure and fallen twenty feet onto the concrete floor below. Binti Jua lifted the unconscious boy, gently cradled him in her arms, and growled warnings at other gorillas that tried to get close. Then, while her own infant, Koola, clung to her back, she carried the boy to the zoo staff waiting at an access gate.[30]

> A young female elephant suffers from a withered leg and can put little weight upon it. A young male from another herd charges the crippled female. A large female elephant chases him away and then, revealingly, returns to the young female and gently touches her withered leg with her trunk. Joyce Poole, who described this event, concludes that the adult female was showing empathy.[31]

> On a busy highway in Chile, a dog has been hit by a vehicle and lies unconscious in the middle of the road. Another dog weaves in and out of the traffic, and manages to drag the dog to safety.[32]

---

29. Rowlands, *Can Animals Be Moral?*, 32, 40; see also Susana Monsó, Judith Benz-Schwarzburg, and Annika Bremhorst, "Animal Morality: What It Means and Why It Matters," *Journal of Ethics* 22 (2018): 283–310.

30. Marc Bekoff and Jessica Pierce, *Wild Justice: The Moral Lives of Animals* (Chicago: Chicago University Press, 2009), 1–2.

31. Rowlands, *Can Animals Be Moral?*, 4; cf. Joshua M. Plotnik and Frans B. M. de Waal, "Asian Elephants (Elephas Maximus) Reassure Others in Distress," *PeerJ* 2 (2014): art. e278, https://doi.org/10.7717/peerj.278.

32. Rowlands, *Can Animals Be Moral?*, 6.

Trust in Creation

Most of the emotions with moral content that have been studied are what are broadly known as altruistic emotions, and altruism in the animal kingdom has become a matter of much popular as well as scientific interest and occasionally headline news. An increasingly wide range of animals, including many primates, pigeons, and rats, has been observed as acting altruistically, helping others when it does not help them or even damages their own prospects to do so. In addition, corvids, canines, primates, elephants, voles, and budgerigars are among animals that show signs of empathy by apparently seeking to console others in distress.[33] Primates, canines, and rats are among those that have been observed acting to correct inequalities between members of a group.[34]

The other side of the moral coin, however, for other animals as for humans, is wrongdoing, especially deliberate wrongdoing or malevolence. The idea that nonhuman animals can do wrong has attracted less scholarly attention than altruism and is still largely unknown to the wider public. Its existence is more controversial than the existence of altruism (though human beings, used to our own moral ambiguity, might think that where one is, the other is likely to be too), but a growing number of studies attest to its presence. The pioneer in this field was William D. Hamilton who, in the 1960s, was working on altruism among animals when he realized that he was also encountering an increasing number of cases of what appeared to be its opposite. He called this behavior "spite," which has be-

---

33. E.g., Russell Church, "Emotional Reactions of Rats to the Pain of Others," *Journal of Comparative and Physiological Psychology* 52 (1959): 132–34; James T. Greene, "Altruistic Behavior in the Albino Rat," *Psychonomic Science* 14 (1969): 47–48; Dale J. Langford et al., "Social Modulation of Pain as Evidence for Empathy in Mice," *Science* 312 (2006): 1967–70; Judith Burkart et al., "Other-Regarding Preferences in a Non-Human Primate: Common Marmosets Provision Food Altruistically," *PNAS* 104 (2007): 19762–66; Orlaith N. Fraser, Daniel Stahl, and Filippo Aureli, "Stress Reduction through Consolation in Chimpanzees," *PNAS* 105 (2008): 8557–62; Venkat R. Lakshminarayanan and Laurie R. Santos, "Capuchin Monkeys Are Sensitive to Others' Welfare," *Current Biology* 18 (2008): R999–R1000; Orlaith N. Fraser and Thomas Bugnyar, "Do Ravens Show Consolation? Responses to Distressed Others," *PLoS ONE* 5 (2010): art. e10605; Zanna Clay and Frans B. M. de Waal, "Bonobos Respond to Distress in Others: Consolation across the Age Spectrum," *PLoS ONE* 8 (2013): art. e55206; Yuko Ikkatai, Shigeru Watanabe, and Ei-Ichi Izawa, "Reconciliation and Third-Party Affiliation in Pair-Bond Budgerigars (*Melopsittacus Undulatus*)," *Behaviour* 153 (2016): 1173–93; Martin Schmeltz et al., "Chimpanzees Return Favors at a Personal Cost," *PNAS* 114 (2017): 7462–67.

34. Sarah F. Brosnan and Frans B. M. de Waal, "Monkeys Reject Unequal Pay," *Nature* 435 (2003): 297–99; Sarah F. Brosnan, Hillary C. Schiff, and Frans B. M. de Waal, "Tolerance for Inequity May Increase with Social Closeness in Chimpanzees," *Proc. R. Soc. Lond. B* 272 (2005): 253–58; Sarah F. Brosnan et al., "Mechanisms Underlying Responses to Inequitable Outcomes in Chimpanzees, Pan Troglodytes," *Anim. Behav.* 79 (2010): 1229–37; Friederike Range et al., "The Absence of Reward Induces Inequity Aversion in Dogs," *PNAS* 106 (2008): 340–45; Lina Oberliessen et al., "Inequity Aversion in Rats, *Rattus Norvegicus*," *Anim. Behav.* 115 (2016): 157–66.

CHAPTER 4

come the standard term for negative moral behavior among animals (sometimes known as "Hamiltonian spite").

In a groundbreaking paper, Hamilton observed that "incidents in which an animal attacks another of the same species, drives it from a territory, or even kills and devours it are commonplace."[35] Some of these he identifies as cases of the Darwinian "struggle for existence," where, for instance, a family cannot support two warring dominant males or a territory for more than a limited number of individuals. But sometimes one animal is observed harming another where there is no evident benefit to itself. For example, many male birds sing or display in some way to attract a mate, but male bowerbirds not only build their own bower but destroy those of others, even when there are plenty of females in the area. When a clutch of corn ear worms hatches into caterpillars, the first to hatch eats all its siblings, even though a corn cob is large enough to support several caterpillars. Spite, Hamilton argues, is not common in nature because, for most species most of the time, cooperation and coexistence are better survival strategies. Where it does occur, in his view, it may have distant roots in the struggle for existence, but even if it does, it can persist long after any need for a particular survival strategy has passed.[36] "Spite" is now standardly defined in the life sciences as any kind of social behavior that inflicts harm on another without direct benefit to the actor.[37]

For reasons that are still not well understood, spite seems to be particularly common among social insects, though it has been observed elsewhere, notably among monkeys and microbes. The parasitic wasp *Copidosoma floridanum*, for example, lays its eggs inside a moth egg. Some of the eggs develop into regular larvae while others grow into "soldier larvae," which are sterile. Soldier larvae need regular larvae for the species to reproduce and continue, but despite this they routinely kill regular larvae for no apparent reason.

35. W. D. Hamilton, "Selfish and Spiteful Behavior in an Evolutionary Model," *Nature* 228 (1970): 218.

36. Studies of spite include, e.g., L. Rózsa, "Spite, Xenophobia, and Collaboration between Hosts and Parasites," *Oikos* 91 (2000): 396–400; K. R. Foster, T. Wenseleers, and F. L. W. Ratnieks, "Spite: Hamilton's Unproven Theory," *Annales Zoologici Fennici* 38 (2001): 229–38; L. Lehmann, K. Bargum, and M. Reuter, "An Evolutionary Analysis of the Relationship between Spite and Altruism," *Journal of the European Society for Evolutionary Biology* 19 (2006): 1507–16; W. L. Vickery, J. S. Brown, and J. G. Fitzgerald, "Spite: Altruism's Evil Twin," *Oikos* 102 (2003): 413–16; F. Dionysio, "Selfish and Spiteful Behavior through Parasites and Pathogens," *Evolutionary Ecology Research* 9 (2007): 1199–210; Andy Gardner et al., "Spiteful Soldiers and Sex Ratio Conflict in Polyembryonic Parasitoid Wasps," *American Naturalist* 169 (2007): 519–33; Stuart A. West and Andy Gardner, "Altruism, Spite, and Greenbeards," *Science* 327 (2010): 1341–44.

37. Patrick Forber and Rory Smead, "The Evolution of Fairness through Spite," *Proc. R. Soc. Lond. B* 281 (2014): art. 20132439, abstract.

172

Trust in Creation

While drafting this chapter, I was watching one spring's clutches of ducklings and goslings growing up on the river Thames in Oxfordshire. Anyone who watches ducks and geese cannot help noticing that geese are much the better parents. On my stretch of river, most of the ducks are mallards, which live alongside several species of geese. One never sees goslings accompanied by just one adult: two are the norm, and it is not uncommon to see three. Up to a dozen ducklings, however, are regularly overseen by just one adult or are left apparently to fend for themselves. One afternoon I watched four ducklings—one quite large, two slightly smaller, and one smaller still—swimming together upstream. No adult duck was in sight. The smallest duckling kept dropping behind and having to paddle furiously to catch up with the group. As it paddled, it cheeped loudly and insistently, obviously trying to attract the group's attention and apparently communicating something like, "Wait for me! Don't leave me behind!" The rest of the group ignored it, and no sooner had it caught up and stopped paddling so hard than it would start to drop behind again. I wondered how much longer it would survive. Far more ducklings than goslings die every year, caught by large fish in midstream or by predators on the river bank. Given that ducks and geese belong to the same family (as do the river's mute swans who, like geese, are careful parents), it is hard not to think that ducks would be capable of parenting their young more carefully. Clutches of ducklings tend to be larger than those of goslings and cygnets, and one Darwinian-type theory would be that ducks simply calculate that hatching more offspring and looking after them less well than do other birds serves them adequately as a reproductive strategy. But observation of groups of ducklings suggests that this is not the whole story. The smallest duckling I saw this year evidently had a sense that it belonged to the group (very likely they were siblings). It was clearly distressed by not being able to keep up, and it was trying to persuade the group to notice its distress and respond by letting it catch up and return to relative safety. The group was choosing to ignore it, despite the fact that, one might think, in Darwinian terms, a larger number of ducklings grouped together would be more likely to discourage predators from attacking, and if it did not, it would serve the stronger members of the group to have one obviously weaker member that a predator would be likely to take first. The behavior of the bigger siblings was not only indifferent but apparently actively spiteful, against their own interests, and very unlike that of closely related birds living alongside them. Here, as in the positive examples of animal behavior we saw above, it seems plausible to see moral instincts and moral choices in play. In this case, the moral choice of the group seemed to be causing the unnecessary suffering of one of their number and making its premature death more likely.[38]

38. This is not the norm among other avian families either, cf. Joane L. Edgar et al., "Avian Maternal Response to Chick Distress," *Proc. R. Soc. Lond. B* 278 (2011): 3129-34.

CHAPTER 4

Susana Monsó, Judith Benz-Schwarzburg, and Annika Bremhorst have pointed out that understanding a wide range of animals as moral subjects, as they do, undermines human claims of superiority over the rest of creation and challenges the basis on which human beings exploit other animals.[39] They argue further that nonhuman moral subjects, like human beings, are subject to specific kinds of harm and share certain rights or entitlements with human beings. Human beings need not only to consider the welfare of these animals, ensuring that they are not victims of abuse, but to treat them with respect and consideration as fellow living beings. Other beings, moreover, deserve not only care or protection but also justice and that their quality of life, their mental and moral capacities, and their freedom of action not be thwarted. Nonhuman animals deserve, in other words, to be seen and related to (not just "treated") as human beings would wish to be seen and related to themselves. If, however, the mental and moral capacities many animals share with human beings mean that human beings have a responsibility to interact with them according to certain moral standards, then a door is opened, in principle, to holding other animals according to their capacities to the same or related standards. It becomes possible to contemplate that those that do not act toward others with justice, respect, and consideration can be seen, like human beings, as responsible for any damage they do to one another by their failings and wrongdoings.

The idea that some animals have moral emotions and may be considered as moral subjects began with studies of primates, but it has extended steadily to other animals, including what we normally think of as much less intellectually developed animals, birds, and fish. We do not yet know how much further research may extend to more diverse and simpler organisms, but, at a minimum, to err in the direction of moral integrity human beings must surely extend respect and consideration as widely as possible across the realm of created beings. By the same token, we can see a very wide cross section of creation as subject to moral standards analogous to ours.

If there are grounds to see some animals as capable of spite or wrongdoing, a much larger sector of creation can be seen as suffering the effects of wrongdoing and potentially as reacting negatively to suffering, including with loss of trust. For example, in the modern Western world many people may not feel ready to attribute moral capacity or responsibility to plants. (Though it has been argued that one highly influential ancient Indian legal text, the *Manu Smriti* or "Laws of Manu," composed in Sanskrit between 200 BCE and 200 CE, attributes moral standing to both animals and plants, and a few modern Western philosophers have also explored the moral standing of plants.[40]) But we have adopted in common speech

39. Monsó, Benz-Schwarzburg, and Bremhorst, "Animal Morality."
40. Christopher G. Framarin, "The Moral Standing of Animals and Plants in the *Manusmrti*," *Philosophy East and West* 64 (2014): 192–217.

Trust in Creation

the idea, adapted by botanists from physics and medicine, that plants and fungi can suffer stress, often because of selfish and exploitative activity by other beings. Stress hinders growth, development, and reproduction and causes harmful genetic mutations, cell death, and, in severe cases, the death of the whole organism.[41] Plants and fungi undergoing stress suffer in the sense that they endure damage, even if we do not understand how that suffering is experienced, and they respond not only directly with changes at the level of their biochemistry, cell function, and the function of the whole organism but also indirectly. The signals that certain trees, including willows, poplars, and sugar maples, send each other to warn of an impending insect attack, which enables trees not yet under attack to produce chemicals that will put off the insects, have become a celebrated example of plant communication. They suggest that plants, in some sense, both experience insect attacks as suffering—as dangerous and damaging to them—and act with something like empathy to prevent other trees of the same kind sharing the same fate.[42]

Even inorganic parts of creation respond to stress, and even if we hesitate to attribute suffering to them, we commonly talk about their stress responses as doing harm and causing suffering to other parts of creation. We might compare the woman's response in Genesis 2 to being put under stress by the snake, which causes behavior that is described as damaging humanity for the indefinite future. Farming practices insensitive to local conditions cause soil degradation and erosion. Building on naturally wet ground causes floods. The increase of atmospheric carbon dioxide is causing increasingly destructive high temperatures around the globe, rising sea levels, coastal erosion, high winds, uncontrollable wildfires, and more and deeper droughts. Suffering, in the natural as in the human world, leads to damage which causes further suffering in a destructive cycle.

This suggests that many animals that would not, in the past, have been thought capable of moral subjectivity or moral choices may now be seen as capable of both, and we do not know how much further across the animal or even plant kingdom these findings may be extended in the future. Even parts of creation that we do not currently find easy to imagine as having moral subjectivity, moreover,

---

41. Ilse Kranner et al., "What Is Stress? Concepts, Definitions and Applications in Seed Science," *New Phytologist* 188 (2010): 655–73, reviewing the recent literature; Angela Kallhoff, Marcello di Paola, and Maria Schorgenhumer, eds., *Plant Ethics: Concepts and Applications* (London: Routledge, 2018).

42. The earliest experiments were with trees that signal about insect attacks, but communication between plants is now thought to be much broader than that; see, e.g., Hirokazu Ueda, Yukio Kikuta, and Kazuhiko Matsuda, "Plant Communication: Mediated by Individual or Blended VOCs?" *Plant Signaling & Behavior* 7 (2012): 222–26; Anja K. Meents and Axel Mithöfer, "Plant-Based Communication: Is There a Role for Volatile Damage-Associated Molecular Patterns?" *Frontiers in Plant Science* 11 (2020): 1–13.

CHAPTER 4

can suffer harm and retaliate by doing harm. We will return below to how far we can see nonhuman animals and even plants as exercising, responding to, or failing in trust, but first we turn back to the New Testament and to the theme of trust between God, Christ, and creation there.

Trust in Creation in the New Testament

The gospels describe Jesus's relationship with the rest of the created world in varied terms and with a greater wealth of detail than any other part of the New Testament. Leaving aside the occasions when God or Jesus explicitly intervenes in nature (opening the heavens, changing water into wine, turning a few loaves and fish into a feast, stilling a storm), a star rises to mark Jesus's birth (Matt 2:2), fish rush to be caught by his future followers (Luke 5:6), water supports his weight (Matt 14:25 // Mark 6:48; cf. John 6:19), darkness covers the land during his crucifixion (Matt 27:45 // Mark 15:33 // Luke 23:44), and at his death the earth shakes and rocks are split (Matt 27:51).[43] We take these as symbolic pointers to Jesus's identity, but studies like Joerstad's of the earth's response to God in the Hebrew Bible suggest that they also signal that the earth itself recognizes and responds to the Messiah. Psalm 67:6, Isa 11:6–9 and 41:18–19, and Ezek 34:27 foretell that, at the coming of the messiah or God's salvation, the land will yield an abundance of fruit and crops, predators and prey will live together in harmony, and the earth will be filled with the knowledge of God. In Jesus's earthly lifetime the coming of God's kingdom was not yet complete, but the land's response to Jesus signals that the Messiah had begun his work.

The earth may also trust or fail to trust in God. In Matthew 6 Jesus criticizes those to whom he is preaching as *oligopistoi*, people of little trust in God, because they worry about what they will eat, drink, and wear (Matt 6:30–31 // Luke 12:28–29). He contrasts them with wild lilies, which are spectacularly clothed by God, and birds, which are fed (Matt 6:26, 28 // Luke 12:24, 27). The birds and the lilies, he implies by contrast, are *pistoi*, trusting in God.

Mark's Jesus tells a parable about the collaboration between God and agricultural land:

> 26 The kingdom of God is as if someone would scatter seed on the ground,
> 27 and would sleep and rise night and day, and the seed would sprout and grow,

---

43. In several second-century texts, but in what may be a much earlier tradition, the birth of Jesus causes a range of cosmic disturbances; see Sarah Parkhouse, "The Incarnation as Cosmic Disturbance in the Long Second Century," *EC* 14 (2023): 340–59.

Trust in Creation

he does not know how. [28] The earth produces of itself first the stalk, then the head, then the full grain in the head. [29] But when the grain is ripe, at once he goes in with his sickle, because the harvest has come. (Mark 4:26–29)

Though there is no trust language in this passage, there is trust language in other end-time parables, and here, as in several of those stories, we can see God the farmer as entrusting the seed to the earth, which responds to his trust by growing the grain.[44]

Both these pericopes point to nonhuman creation as trusting in God and responding to being entrusted with something by God. Elsewhere, creation is less collaborative. Matthew and Mark (Matt 21:18–20 // Mark 11:12–14, 20–21) tell a story of Jesus being hungry, passing a fig tree by the roadside, finding it has no fruit, and cursing it so that it withers (immediately in Matthew, later in Mark). The Matthean disciples are amazed at how the tree withered, and Jesus implies that it was by his faith (Matt 21:20–21), but the disciples do not ask why the tree withers, and we are left to infer that it is because it provided nothing to feed the Son of God. The fact that it was punished for not doing so suggests that its failure is meant to be seen as "spiteful," not simply a consequence of the fact that it is spring and not the season for figs.[45] Mark presents the story slightly differently, noting explicitly that it is not fig season (Mark 11:13), but also that Jesus "cursed" (*katarasasthai*) the tree, which again suggests that we are meant to infer that the tree has done something wrong. When Peter points out that the tree had withered, Jesus responds, "Have trust in God" (11:22). He goes on to give the teaching about trust moving mountains (11:23–24), but his initial imperative "trust in God" can be read as referring backward to the tree as well as introducing the next teaching. If it does, then Mark goes beyond Matthew's implication that the tree has done something wrong to indicate that its failure is one of trust. This may suggest that the tree, which sticks to its normal fruiting pattern instead of feeding the Messiah when he comes, is intended as an image for all the law-abiding people in Israel who do not recognize and trust in Jesus when they encounter him. It may further hint that the land of Israel itself should recognize and respond to the Messiah, and that though, in the course of the gospels, it sometimes collaborates with God in revealing Jesus for who he is, it can also fail to do so.[46]

---

44. Morgan, *Theology of Trust*, 291–92.

45. Modern readers are sometimes indignant at what seems Jesus's harsh response to a harmless tree, and perhaps Luke was too, because he converts the story into a parable (Luke 13:6–9) about a nonbearing fig tree that is given four years and plenty of manure to mend its ways before it is threatened with being cut down.

46. Fruiting trees are also an image for human beings, in this case true or false prophets in Matt 7:15–20. "You will know them by their fruits," Jesus tells the disciples (7:20), which may be

CHAPTER 4

The story of the storm at sea, which blows up when Jesus and his disciples are on the way to Gerasa or Gadara (Matt 8:23–27 // Mark 4:35–41 // Luke 8:22–25), finds the wind and the waves of the sea apparently rebelling against Jesus, being censured (*epitimein*) by Jesus for their behavior, and subsiding. *Epitimein* is commonly used of responses to wrongdoing, often in a judicial context, so the winds and waves are depicted not just as inanimate forces under Jesus's control, but as powers that can behave in right and wrong ways. When Jesus and the disciples reach the other side, the gospels offer a different story of creation doing wrong and suffering. The Gerasene or Gadarene demoniac (Matt 8:28–34 // Mark 5:1–20 // Luke 8:26–39) is tormented by a legion of demons or unclean spirits: nonhuman beings whose whole existence consists of rebelling against God. Jesus summons them out of the man, but they beg to be allowed to enter a nearby herd of pigs. For the evangelists, this is no doubt acceptable because pigs are unclean in Mosaic law. The fact that the demons ask to enter the pigs, however, suggests that demons can thrive by tormenting pigs as they can by tormenting human beings, and the response of the pigs seems to confirm it. They are immediately driven to self-destruction, running down a steep bank into the sea where they are drowned. Apparently another animal is capable of suffering under the power of a demon or unclean spirit as a human being is.

In these stories, Jesus represents God to the nonhuman world as he does to human beings. Like human beings, the rest of creation variously puts its trust in him, suffers, rebels, is censured, and is either punished or returns to its right relationship with God.[47] Like human beings, the rest of creation can expect to endure stress and suffering before the end time (e.g., Matt 24:7 // Mark 13:8 // Luke 21:10–11), final judgment, and new life at the fulfillment of the kingdom of God. Occasionally (Rom 8:19–21; Rev 21:23; 22:1–2) the promise of the end time is described as transforming the natural world as much as human life. The scriptural traditions on which New Testament writers draw concerning the active engagement of the whole of creation with God, which Western tradition has lost over centuries of regarding the rest of creation as a tool to be used and an object to be exploited,

---

good (*agathos*) or bad (*poneros*). Elsewhere in Matthew and Luke, both John the Baptist and Jesus use the image of fruit bearing as an image of repentance or virtue: "Bear fruit worthy of repentance . . . every tree that does not bear good fruit is cut down and thrown into the fire" (Matt 3:8, 10; Luke 3:8–9); "Every tree that does not bear good fruit is cut down and thrown into the fire. Thus you will know them by their fruits" (Matt 7:19–20). We assume that a parallel is being drawn between a tree that is axed because it is not useful, and people who are punished for willful sin, but the evangelists may also be pointing to the moral involvement of the land itself in welcoming or not welcoming the Messiah.

47. Healing miracles are not included here because we are not discussing natural suffering and, in addition, I do not want to argue that nonnormative physical states are necessarily to be "cured"; see Morgan, *Theology of Trust*, 250–55.

Trust in Creation

are now coming back into view at a time when the sciences are also increasingly revealing the subjectivity, even the moral subjectivity, of other created beings.

If, however, we find biblical support for the idea that at least some nonhuman beings are subjects capable of wrongdoing as well as suffering, is there scope to understand atonement through Jesus Christ as making possible the righteousing and salvation not only of humanity but of creation more widely?

Before exploring this idea, we should recognize the possibility that at-one-ment through Christ might not be *intended* for nonhuman creation. If God, as tradition affirms, can give more than one revelation to human beings and can communicate with the snake in the snake's terms and the eagle in the eagle's terms, then we should consider the possibility that God makes at-one-ment possible for other beings by means appropriate to them, which human beings may not be able to detect or even conceive of. But given the increasing acknowledgment by scientists and theologians alike that human beings are indivisibly part of the whole of creation, and the Jewish and Christian intuition that God relates to and acts for all creation in (at least some) ways that we do experience and recognize, and given the New Testament's witness that Jesus Christ in his earthly life had a relationship with nonhuman as well as human creation, it is worth exploring whether at-one-ment through trust in the trust and trustworthiness of Jesus Christ is conceivable as a possibility for nonhuman as well as human nature.

CREATION AND ATONEMENT: THE NEW TESTAMENT

As what Col 1:15 calls "the firstborn of all creation," and as one who lived an earthly life, Jesus is part of creation. As such, he is arguably well positioned to mediate between God and nonhuman creation as well as between God and human beings.[48] Most of the images of how Jesus reconciles God and humanity on which we focus when discussing atonement are drawn from the human sphere (ransom, redemption, penal substitution) or could refer to either humans or animals (sacrifice, offering, curse). The best-known exception is the image of the lamb of God, but New Testament writings also offer a scatter of other images of Jesus's death and resurrection that reference creation more widely.[49]

In John's Gospel, Jesus foretells his death using the image of the grain of wheat: "unless a grain of wheat falls into the earth and dies, it remains just a single grain.

---

48. Mediators can but do not need to belong to both the groups between which they mediate, but they do need, at a minimum, to have something in common with each group that can form a basis for trust.

49. Jesus's followers can also follow example, e.g., by acting as salt or light (Matt 5:13–14).

179

CHAPTER 4

But if it dies, it bears much fruit" (12:24). The grain comes from the earth and its chemical elements are the elements of creation as a whole. The image—appropriate to John, for whom the glorification of Jesus is more significant than the suffering of the cross—focuses on neither any violence that might be done to the wheatear in the process of harvesting nor any suffering of the grain, but rather on the collaboration between the grain, the earth of which it is a part, and God who created and oversees the whole, which leads to new and more abundant life.[50]

John also likens Jesus to the natural world in some of his "I am" sayings. Jesus is the grain and water combined as bread (6:34, cf. 6:27), which is fed to others to end the suffering of hunger and give life. He is the light (8:12) that exists to give light to others, making possible all life and reproduction and guiding people to eternal life.[51] He is the vine that nourishes others and enables them to bear their own fruit (15:1–5), and the force of life itself that brings life even out of death and never dies (11:2–6). Again, John uses these images to focus on the life that comes from Jesus's life, of which his death is seen in these passages almost more as an organic part in collaboration with God and God's earth than as the outrage and conflict with hostile forces that it is for the Synoptic evangelists.

At the Last Supper (Matt 26:26 // Mark 14:22 // Luke 22:19; cf. 1 Cor 11:24) Jesus foretells that he will be broken like bread to feed and give life to others. As the bread is consecrated to God by Jesus's blessing, Jesus has been consecrated since his baptism to serve God by serving others, and as consuming the bread signals acceptance of its power to give life, symbolically consuming Jesus's body signals acceptance of Jesus's power to give life through his service. In this image, Jesus's death acts not like a ransom, a punishment for others' sins, or even (as the wine does) a sacrificial offering. The emphasis is on the fact that he offers those who trust him what they most fundamentally need: the staple of life. They, in a common English metaphor, "eat it up"—wholly absorb it—and it changes them from

50. In Mark's parable of the sower, the sower, according to Jesus, sows the word of God (Mark 4:14 // Luke 8:11). We might also hear the seed that is sown as the kingdom of God, which, when sown in fertile ground, bears fruit abundantly. On this reading the seed parallels the mustard seed of Mark 4:30–32 (// Matt 13:31–32 // Luke 13:18–19), which Jesus identifies with the kingdom of God, and of which he says that when it is sown in the ground it grows to become the greatest of all shrubs, giving shade to the birds of the air. Remembering John 12:24, we can also hear the unnamed seed and the mustard seed as Jesus himself, whose death and burial in the earth bring forth abundant new life. The double tradition's parable of the leaven (Matt 13:33 // Luke 13:20–21) is another which is used of the kingdom but could also refer to Jesus himself: the fragment of leaven is buried in three measures of flour, but it makes the whole batch of bread rise.

51. Cf. John 1:9–10, where the "true light" is that through which the world was created and which inheres (1:4) in the life-giving Word. Cf. also 1 John 1:5, where God is light, which, similarly, both draws people to itself and lights their way.

180

Trust in Creation

the inside out. The brokenness of the bread points to the soon-to-be-brokenness of Jesus's body, but the image of bread itself points beyond the crucifixion to every aspect of Jesus's life, death, and work, which has fed and changed, and will continue to feed and change, those who accept it. To be bread is to enable life itself by giving oneself to feeding, sustaining, and changing others.

In 1 Cor 15:20–23 Paul's focus is less on the crucifixion than the resurrection, and he uses the tradition of the firstfruits that are offered to God as an image for the resurrection of Jesus.[52] As the firstfruits consecrate the rest of the harvest, Paul assures the Corinthians that Christ's resurrection will be followed by that of everyone else at the end time. But the firstfruits have also come from the burial of the grain of wheat, the olive pit, or the grape pip in the earth, which has enabled the seeds to grow. Just before these verses Paul references Christ's death for human sins (15:3), but this image points in a different direction. By allowing himself to die, giving himself to the earth to which God consigned Adam—"for you are dust, and to dust you shall return," Gen 3:19; cf. 1 Cor 15:21–22—and being raised from it to new life, Paul's Jesus collaborates with God and the earth to change the relationship of humanity with both. In dying and being raised in this way, moreover, as Paul develops further in Romans 8 and we saw in the previous chapter, Jesus shows the way that the faithful can travel with him, following his lead and allowing themselves to be conformed to his image (Rom 8:29).

These images allow us to envisage Jesus not just as a human being who lives, dies, and acts on behalf of other human beings and calls them to respond, but as a part of creation that lives, dies, and acts on behalf of creation as a whole and calls creation to respond. They offer glimpses of models of atonement that commentators have often overlooked while focusing on images from the human—public, political, and male-dominated—sphere. They point to Jesus, in collaboration with God and God's world, acting to create new and more abundant life, to nourish and change those who encounter him, to show the way to eternal life, and to enable other beings to bear fruit in their turn. In these processes, vitally, the world, in the form of the earth of the farmer's field or the tomb, responds to Jesus's gift of himself and plays its part. The earth is not simply the passive backdrop to the Christ event—not only a respondent to the Christ event—but a partner in it: it is only in this material world, with the collaboration of the world, that Jesus can die to death and be raised to glory.

By acting in these ways, moreover, Jesus acts as a great range of created beings are capable of acting. Animals and plants, as we will see below, can everywhere be

---

52. Cf. Exod 23:16; Neh 10:35. In Rom 16:5 and 1 Cor 16:15 Paul also uses this imagery of the first converts in a region, following Jer 2:3, and in Rom 8:23 firstfruits are the gift of the spirit, which is a foretaste of resurrection life.

CHAPTER 4

seen giving life to others, nourishing and changing them, and offering themselves as an example and companion: parents to offspring, siblings to siblings, group members to one another, cohabitants of a particularly locality to each other, and members of different species with no previous connection to one another.[53] By using images of Jesus's death and resurrection from the natural world, New Testament writers identify Jesus not only with humanity but also with creation much more widely, and what he does as something that not only a human being could do but that many plants and animals are capable of doing as well. They point to Jesus not just as the human but as the universal being in whose life-giving life God is made known.

Like humanity, much or perhaps all of creation is capable of wrongdoing, suffering and inflicting suffering. Much or all of creation is also capable of change and renewal. Much or all of creation is capable, even if not self-consciously, of self-giving: the seed to the next generation of wheat, the yeast to the dough, the altruistic gorilla or dog from the stories earlier in this chapter to the human child or the wounded fellow dog, the worn-out body to the ecosystem that is capable of breaking it down and re-forming it into other bodies. Just as Jesus's death as a human being is envisaged as liberating others from the power of both wrongdoing and suffering, so his death as part of creation has the capacity to bring new life out of the damaging and damaged past.

Even if we envisage Jesus as part of creation acting for creation as Jesus, as human being, acts for humanity, however, previous chapters have argued that what Jesus accomplishes by his death and resurrection is the possibility of the restoration of trust between God and humanity, and for this to happen I have argued that human beings must respond to God's and Christ's trust, and what God has done through Christ, with their own trust. Can we, analogously, imagine a way in which creation might be understood as capable of responding to the death and resurrection of Christ? Can we envisage calling a restored relationship between creation and God a relationship of trust?

CREATION AND ATONEMENT: THE NONHUMAN WORLD

The introduction to this book offered a definition of trust that was intended to be uncontroversial to most of those who have worked on it. Trust can be an attitude, an action, or both. It involves putting something (which could be an object, an

---

53. Biologists distinguish between "true altruism," which does not expect a return, and "reciprocal altruism," which does, in some form, at some point.

Trust in Creation

action, or a person) in someone else's hands with the belief, hope, assumption, or wager that the other can and will respond positively. I could, for instance, trust you to buy a carton of milk on the way home from work, or trust you with my spare house key or with my life. Trust involves the making or invoking of some kind of relationship (which can be more or less profound, wide-ranging, or life-influencing). It very often involves cooperation for an end, and it is also an end in itself, making everyday life, for most people, more positive, more life-enhancing, and more hopeful.

Biologists do not often talk about trust in the animal kingdom, perhaps because it is hard to know what other animals are thinking, except insofar as actions and reactions are guides to thought processes. A large body of research, however, does explore group cooperation, conflict resolution, and social learning, along with altruism, in various parts of the animal kingdom, especially among primates, some other highly social mammals, corvids, a few other birds, and some fish. Some researchers have pointed out that many of these behaviors, if they were observed among human beings, would be identified as examples of trust, so even when it is hard to speculate what an animal is thinking, we can entertain the possibility that he or she is acting with what we recognize as trust. (We need not be too worried that we generally cannot know in any detail what an animal is thinking, given that we attribute trust, for instance, to infants and prelinguistic young children whose thought processes are similarly difficult to access.)

Many kinds of animals live in organized groups, which interact with other groups of the same species or those of other species, and many studies explore how such groups work to maintain themselves and hold their own in complex ecosystems.[54] Animals cooperate to find, secure, and share food; to keep warm, create shelters or food stores, and warn each other of predators; to defend themselves; to raise young; and sometimes in grooming, comforting each other, and conflict solving. All these, in a human context, would be readily understood as involving trust in the ability and willingness of individuals to help others even when it involves time, effort, or risk to themselves.

When Robert Trivers developed the concept of "reciprocal altruism" in an influential 1971 article, many of the examples he gave could also be seen as involving trust.[55] For example, in different parts of the world, small "cleaner fish" clean the teeth or scales of larger fish and other forms of marine life. The larger animal

54. E.g. Jean-François Gariépy et al., "Social Learning in Humans and Other Animals," *Frontiers in Neuroscience* 8 (2014): 1–13.

55. Robert Trivers, "The Evolution of Reciprocal Altruism," *Quarterly Review of Biology* 46 (1971): 35–57.

CHAPTER 4

not only allows the cleaner fish to do its work, feeding itself in the process, but sometimes signals to the cleaner when it is leaving the area or chases off threats to the cleaner fish's safety. It does not seem outlandish to suggest that, whatever the thought processes involved, the cleaner acts with trust that the larger animal will not harm it, while the larger animal trusts that the work the cleaner does is worth more to it than simply eating the small fish.

Reciprocity in nature is not always direct but can also be generalized, such that one beneficiary "pays forward" what she or he has received to benefit another. Throughout the plant and animal kingdoms, for example, mature plants and animals respond to their parents' care for them by caring for their offspring. Generalized reciprocity has been detected across a wide range of life forms, from bacteria to primates, and can also be seen as involving trust or perhaps a combination of trust and hope.[56] A much cited study of Norway rats led by Claudia Rutte tested the conditions under which female rats would pull on a stick attached to a tray of food in order to provide food for other rats. It found that, at the beginning of the experiment, the rats typically worked to provide food not only for close relatives but also for strangers. If they were then given some experience of other rats helping them, they became even more likely to help others, but even those that were not helped often continued to help others. Experience, and perhaps also intuition, told these rats that what we might call trustworthiness to others, combined with trust in others, was worthwhile.[57]

When trust and cooperation between individuals and groups break down, some species have been observed enacting a range of practices of conflict resolution. A series of studies of pigtailed macaque monkeys in captivity showed that a small number of individuals within the group had a specific role "policing"

56. R. Axelrod and W. D. Hamilton, "The Evolution of Cooperation," *Science* 211 (1981): 1390–96; Daniel J. Rankin and Michael Taborsky, "Assortment and the Evolution of Generalized Reciprocity," *Evolution* 63 (2009): 1913–22; Gerrit Sander van Doorn and Michael Taborsky, "The Evolution of Generalized Reciprocity on Social Interaction Networks," *Evolution* 66 (2011): 651–64; Zoltán Barta et al., "Cooperation among Non-Relatives Evolves by State-Dependent Generalized Reciprocity," *Proc. R. Soc. Lond. B* 278 (2011): 843–48; Natassja Gfrerer and Michal Taborsky, "Working Dogs Cooperate among Each Other by Generalised Reciprocity," *Biology Letters* 14 (2018): 1–6.

57. Claudia Rutte and Michael Taborsky, "Generalized Reciprocity in Rats," *PLoS Biology* 5 (2007): 1421–25 describe this behavior as generous and altruistic (1422). They implicitly assume that the basis of this altruism was ultimately self-interest, but their findings are also compatible with, for instance, the rats' valuing the flourishing of the group as a whole. Manon K. Schweinfurth et al., "Male Norway Rats Cooperate according to Direct but Not Generalized Reciprocity Rules," *Anim. Behav.* 152 (2019): 93–101 differentiates between levels of altruism in female and male Norway rats.

184

Trust in Creation

conflicts among group members.[58] The "policers" were dominant males (though not necessarily the most high-status males in a group), who had what observers characterized as the respect of both parties in the conflict. Sometimes policers intervened impartially to stop a fight, treating both combatants the same, and sometimes they intervened to protect the weaker party. They did not typically have to stop the conflict by force: it was normally enough to assert their dominance and remind those in conflict that they were taking a risk if they made trouble. What the policer was communicating to the stronger party in the conflict, or to both parties if both were equally strong, looks in part like trustworthiness or reliability: trust me to make you stop if I have to.[59] In cases where there was a weaker party in the conflict, moreover, it may have taken trust for the weaker party to stop resisting, because stopping would put it at risk unless the policer could be trusted to protect it. In groups of primates with dominant males, these males did not simply tyrannize over the other members of the group, but also led and protected them, so a display of power was not only a display of power but also a reminder of the care dominant males gave to other group members. Displays of power may also communicate to group members in conflict that they should remember the benefits of group membership, and trust the dominant male when he asserts that the group works best with minimal conflict.

It is not only dominant males that can reconcile group members in conflict. Among macaques and vervet monkeys, relatives of the victim of an attack have been observed approaching and grooming the attacker, apparently as a way of making peace on behalf of the victim.[60] In this scenario, we can envisage that both the victim and his or her relatives need to trust the aggressor to accept their approach for the sake of peace and trust that they will not put themselves in more danger by doing so. Female primates have also been observed acting as conciliators toward males in conflict. In this pattern, the female typically approaches

58. Jessica C. Flack, Frans B. M. de Waal, and David C. Krakauer, "Social Structure, Robustness, and Policing Cost in a Cognitively Sophisticated Society," *American Naturalist* 165 (2005): E126–E139; Jessica C. Flack et al., "Policing Stabilizes Construction of Social Niches in Primates," *Nature* 439 (2006): 426–29. Cf. Brianne A. Beisner et al., "Social Power, Conflict Policing, and Role of Subordination Signals in Rhesus Macaque Society," *American Journal of Physical Anthropology* 160 (2016): 102–12.

59. On the difference between trust and reliance in general, see p. 13.

60. Frans B. M. de Waal, "Primates: A Natural Heritage of Conflict Resolution," *Science* 289 (2000): 589; cf. Annemieke K. A. Cools, Alain J.-M. van Hout, and Mark H. J. Nelissen, "Canine Reconciliation and Third-Party-Initiated Postconflict Affiliation: Do Peacemaking Social Mechanisms in Dogs Rival Those of Higher Primates?" *Ethology* 114 (2008): 53–63; Amanda M. Seed, Nicola S. Clayton, and Nathan J. Emery, "Postconflict Third-Party Affiliation in Rooks, Corvus Frugilegus," *Current Biology* 17 (2007): 152–58.

CHAPTER 4

and grooms one male and then the other, implying, researchers infer, that her peaceful relationship with both of them is grounds for their making peace with each other.[61]

Yet another form of conflict resolution by third-party intervention has been identified among chimpanzees. In a typical scenario, one group member attacks another and several other group members come to the aid of the attacked, screaming and chasing off the aggressor. After the conflict has died down, a tense silence is broken by the whole group breaking out in hoots, in the midst of which the original aggressor and victim embrace and kiss, restoring harmony in the group.[62] Studies like these emphasize that for most social animals most of the time, it is worth finding ways to resolve the inevitable tensions and conflicts that arise within groups, and that mediation is one way of doing so. The behaviors of the mediating individuals or groups suggest that although they are not always the most powerful group members, they can be trusted to restore a viable peace in which is worthwhile for both conflicted parties to invest. Nor are these various strategies for conflict resolution confined to primates: studies have found similar behaviors among ravens.[63]

Mediating behaviors like these are risky because the mediator cannot usually be sure that neither of the other parties will turn on them, and they can be seen as performing trustworthiness and enacting trust toward others. Their trust may sometimes be therapeutic: by enacting trust they aim to create it and the goods it brings. Social behavior also involves social learning, in which individuals learn from each other rather than by direct experience of their environment, and social learning is extensively studied in many species in its own right.[64] By living alongside and observing others, individuals learn what to eat, where to find water and shelter, what to fear, and how to solve problems. Social learning explains, for

61. Frans B. M. de Waal and Angeline van Roosmalen, "Reconciliation and Consolation among Chimpanzees," *Behavioral Ecology and Sociobiology* 5 (1979): 55–66; Claudia Rudolf von Rohr et al., "Impartial Third-Party Interventions in Captive Chimpanzees: A Reflection of Community Concern," *PLoS ONE* 7 (2012): 1–9.

62. De Waal, "Primates"; cf. Giada Cordoni, Elizabetta Palagi, and Silvana Borgognini, "Reconciliation and Consolation in Captive Western Gorillas," *International Journal of Primatology* 27 (2006): 1365–82.

63. Orlaith N. Fraser and Thomas Bugnyar, "Ravens Reconcile after Aggressive Conflicts with Valuable Partners," *PLoS ONE* 6 (2011): art. e18118.

64. Ruud van den Bos, Jolle W. Jolles, and Judith R. Homberg, "Social Modulation of Decision-Making: A Cross-Species Review," *Frontiers in Human Neuroscience* 7 (2013): 1–16 set human and animal studies side by side; see also Gariépy et al., "Social Learning"; Lucy M. Aplin et al., "Experimentally Induced Innovations Lead to Persistent Culture via Conformity in Wild Birds," *Nature* 518 (2015): 538–41.

Trust in Creation

instance, why two groups of chimpanzees living fairly close together with the same range of foods available can develop a preference for different fruits. Group members appear to trust one another when they prefer imitating the eating habits of another group member to experimenting for themselves.[65] Often, moreover, members of a group trust and imitate some individuals within the group but not others, suggesting that some members, for some reason, are considered more trustworthy (in their level of knowledge, perhaps, or judgment) than others.[66] There is also some evidence that in groups in which social learning is particularly important for survival, individuals are more likely to act in conformity with the majority.[67] Conformity can not only be an act of trust but can also signal that you trust other group members and that they can trust you to identify with the group, and so strengthens the group by affirming members' trust in each other. This type of action leads to some of the most dramatic forms of group behavior observable in nature, from the movements of shoals of fish to avoid predators to the migration of large flocks of birds and crowd behavior among human beings.

Early studies of learning across the animal kingdom, especially in primates, corvids, and some species of fish, assumed that while one individual may learn from another by observation and imitation, animals other than humans do not teach. In recent years, this model has increasingly been challenged. Many animals are now seen as using very varied tactics of social manipulation, including active teaching.[68] Wild chimpanzee mothers, for example, have been observed teaching their offspring to crack nuts by leaving tools, such as a stone hammer and anvil, around near the nuts (nonmothers have not been seen to do this), by showing their offspring how to use the hammer and anvil, and by intervening to correct them so that they place the nut in the best position and use the hammer most effectively.[69] Killer whales appear to teach young members of a pod how to strand their prey.[70] Many species of animal gaze fixedly at something significant, such as a source of food, to indicate its whereabouts to others. Great apes, octopuses, and

---

65. A. Whiten et al., "Imitative Learning of Artificial Fruit Processing in Children (*Homo Sapiens*) and Chimpanzees (*Pan Troglodytes*)," *J. Comp. Psychol.* 110 (1996): 3–14.

66. K. N. Laland, "Social Learning Strategies," *Learning Behavior* 32 (2004): 4–14.

67. Laland, "Social Learning."

68. Alex Thornton and Nicola J. Raihani, "The Evolution of Teaching," *Anim. Behav.* 75 (2008): 1823–36; Richard W. Byrne and Lucy A. Bates, "Primate Social Cognition: Uniquely Primate, Uniquely Social, or Just Unique?" *Neuron* 65 (2010): 815–30.

69. Christopher Boesch, "Teaching among Wild Chimpanzees," *Anim. Behav.* 41 (1991): 530–32.

70. C. Guinet and J. Bouvier, "Development of Intentional Stranding Hunting Techniques in Killer Whale (*Orcinus Orca*) Calves at Crozet Archipelago," *Canadian Journal of Zoology* 73 (1995): 27–33.

CHAPTER 4

several species of fish are among those who have been shown to use referential gestures to inform or instruct others hunting with them.[71]

We do not know how far across the animal kingdom cooperation, group learning, conflict resolution, and altruism extend, but the trend over the last few decades has been to find them ever more widely. They can even be seen periodically in species that spend much of their lives solitarily or that live in groups with little social complexity, such as cattle and sheep, especially when young are being raised. Such behaviors are increasingly recognized as having counterparts in the plant kingdom too.[72] We have already noted that some plants after being attacked by predators such as insects release chemicals into the air that are detected by neighboring plants, which can then strengthen their chemical defenses before they are attacked. In places of dense vegetation, networks of mycorrhizal fungi between plants enable them to share water and sugars. Some established plants donate to young plants to strengthen them. Some dying plants donate phosphorous and nitrogen that they will soon no longer need to healthy neighbors. Not only do plants of the same species do this but also plants of different species.[73] A celebrated series of studies led by Suzanne Simard, Brenda Twieg, and Leanne Philip found that in the forests of British Columbia carbon was exchanged seasonally between paper birch trees and Douglas fir seedlings, despite the fact that they could be seen as competing for the same resources. The birches "fed" the seedlings while they were heavily shaded during the summer, and the firs reciprocated while

71. D. A. Leavens and W. D. Hopkins, "The Whole-Hand Point: The Structure and Function of Pointing from a Comparative Perspective," *J. Comp. Psychol.* 113 (1999): 417–25; M. Tomasello and J. Call, "Intentional Communication in Nonhuman Primates," in *The Gestural Communication of Apes and Monkeys* (ed. J. Call and M. Tomasello; Mahwah: Erlbaum Associates, 2007), 1–15; Alexander L. Vail, Andrea Manica, and Redouan Bshary, "Referential Gestures in Fish Collaborative Hunting," *Nature Communications* 4 (2013): 1–7.

72. In the tradition of classical Darwinism, one might think that these activities are the result of the preferential survival of some species and strains over others as a result of what turn out to be advantageous behaviors. This, though, cannot be the case in the animal examples above, where adaptations for survival and flourishing happen much more quickly, and this casts doubt on the assumption that this must be true in the plant kingdom too. It is now more common to take adaptation to involve an element of strategy, however understood, in the adaptive actions of plants too.

73. Steven D. Johnson and Florian P. Schiestl, *Floral Mimicry* (Oxford: Oxford University Press, 2016), 1–15 describe the history of research and define and outline the range of plant mimicry. See also K. J. Beiler et al., "Architecture of the Wood-Wide Web: Rhizopogon Spp. Genets Link Multiple Douglas-Fir Cohorts," *New Phytologist* 185 (2009): 543–53; Y. Y. Song et al., "Defoliation of Interior Douglas-Fir Elicits Carbon Transfer and Stress Signalling to Ponderosa Pine Neighbors through Ectomycorrhizal Networks," *Scientific Reports* 5 (2015): art. 8495.

Trust in Creation

the birches were leafless during the winter.[74] Flowers, meanwhile, can apparently, in some sense, observe the appearance of other plants or animals and mimic them in order to put off predators or attract pollinators. They imitate food sources of other plants, potential mates, or oviposition sites in order to induce pollinators to visit multiple plants of the same species. They design their flowers, in color and pattern, to attract pollinators and point them to where to seek nectar.[75] They give off scents that aim to attract pollinators or potential prey. A description of one dramatic example is given by H. Bänzinger:

> An encounter in a steamy rain forest with a flowering *Rhizanthes zippelii* makes an intruder wonder. The look of the flowers is more akin to a tentacled animal—a starfish or a medusa—than to a member of the plant kingdom. But at the same time the reddish globe with crater, embedded in a tangle of rufous hairs, reminds one of the blood-shot orifices of a furry mammal. This perplexing aspect is part of an intricate set of lures: visual, tactile, olfactory, and gustatory . . . Behind this disconcerting look hide potent insect-manipulating powers to entice, appease and deceive a disparate cohort of nectar thieves, opportunists, female-chasing males and predators, as well as dupes which lay hundreds of ill-fated eggs on the flowers.[76]

There are signs that plants also act to resolve conflicts in their interactions with animals. Many plants, for example, entice ants onto their foliage: the plants offer the ants food and nesting places, while the ants spread their seeds and defend them from other insects that are predators.[77] The presence of ants, however,

---

74. Suzanne Simard et al., "Net Transfer of Carbon between Ectomycorrhial Tree Species in the Field," *Nature* 388 (1997): 579–82; Brenda D. Tweig, Daniel M. Dural, and Suzanne W. Simard, "Ectomycorrhizal Fungal Succession in Mixed Temperate Forests," *New Phytologist* 176 (2007): 437–47; Leanne J. Philip and Suzanne W. Simard, "Minimum Pulses of Stable and Radioactive Carbon Isotopes to Detect Belowground Carbon Transfer Between Plants," *Plant and Soil* 308 (2008): 23–35; Suzanne Simard, "Mycorrhizal Networks Facilitate Tree Communication, Learning, and Memory, in *Memory and Learning in Plants* (ed. F. Baluska, Monica Gagliano, and Günther Witzany; Cham: Springer, 2018), 191–213.

75. Some of these patterns are visible to the human eye, others only to insects; see W. R. Thompson et al., "Flavonols: Pigments Responsible for Ultraviolet Absorption in Nectar Guide of Flower," *Science* 177 (1972): 528–30.

76. H. Bänzinger, "Ecological, Morphological and Taxonomic Studies on Thailand's Fifth Species of Rafflesiaceae: *Rhizanthes zippelii* (Blume) Spach," *Natural History Bulletin of the Siam Society* 43 (1995): 337.

77. Matthew P. Nelsen, Richard H. Ree, and Corrie S. Moreau, "Ant-Plant Interactions Evolved through Increasing Interdependence," *PNAS* 115 (2018): 12253–58.

CHAPTER 4

can discourage the plant's normal insect pollinators, such as bees and butterflies, from visiting its flowers. Fleur Nicklen and Diane Wagner have shown how *Acacia constricta* gives off a scent that repels ants without affecting its pollinators, so that ants avoid newly opened flowers or contact with their pollen, leaving the flowers free to be visited by pollinators.[78] The study of conflict resolution in the plant kingdom is in its early stages but, by analogy with work on the animal kingdom, we may guess that future research will show that, like other forms of social life and communication among plants, it is more complex than we realized. I have not discovered any research into the possibility that plants teach one another, but since plants are increasingly recognized as communicating with one another, helping one another, and warning one another of dangers, it is not impossible that they will be found to be doing something analogous to teaching in the animal kingdom.

How far creatures other than humans have self-consciousness is much debated, but we do not need to assume that animals or plants are highly self-conscious (if at all) in order to recognize that they cooperate, learn from each other, act altruistically, and actively resolve their conflicts. Nor do we need to assume that they need to be self-conscious to hypothesize that they exercise trust. Trust, as we have noted, can, as far as we can tell, predate self-consciousness in infants, and adult humans regularly trust others without consciously weighing the pros and cons of doing so. It may sound oddly anthropomorphic to describe animals or plants as exercising trust when they act cooperatively or altruistically, learn from one another, or seek to resolve conflicts, but given that trust can occur without self-consciousness even in adult humans, and often is only observable as an action, there is no strong reason to think that by attributing trust to animals or plants we are, in fact, inappropriately anthropomorphizing.

Some of the examples we have given so far have been of activities within communities of the same nonhuman species or between different nonhuman species. We can add to these our everyday experience that some animals are able and willing to cooperate with human beings and become part of social groups that may consist of human beings and other beings of different species to minimize and even resolve conflicts within such groups as well as to learn from human beings. Human beings around the world commonly create and sustain social groups that include a wide range of animals (and also plants). In some of these relationships, the role of trust is clear. A farmer who works a sheepdog must first train and then trust the dog not to attack the sheep, while the dog trusts the farmer to provide it with food and companionship that are worth more than easily accessible sheep

78. E. Fleur Nicklen and Diane Wagner, "Conflict Resolution in an Ant-Plant Interaction: *Acacia Constricta* Traits Reduce Ant Costs to Reproduction," *Oecologia* 148 (2006): 81–87.

Trust in Creation

meat. Whether trust between human beings and plants will one day be identifiable, we do not know, but given the trajectory of recent research it presumably cannot be ruled out.[79]

The significance of the existence of cooperation, social learning, conflict resolution, and altruism among animals and even plants, between as well as within species, begins to suggest an answer to the question we posed earlier in the chapter, whether we can envisage a way in which creation may be understood as capable of responding to the death and resurrection of Christ within a trust-based model of atonement, and whether we can envisage calling a restored relationship between creation as a whole and God a relationship of trust. That animals and perhaps plants are capable of behaviors that, in human beings, we would readily understand as involving trust, suggests that trust is possible for animals and perhaps also plants, and that it is possible between as well as within species. We can therefore envisage that it is possible, in principle, that not only human beings but also the rest of the created world might be released from the power of wrongdoing and suffering through trust.

But can we envisage other animals or plants coming to trust by encountering, in any sense, the trustworthiness of God through the death of Jesus Christ at a particular moment in history? We have seen indications that some nonhuman animals can generalize from the experience that practical help is a good thing to the idea that giving help and, in the process, being trustworthy and trusting others are worthwhile even when they have no immediate benefits. We can infer that some creatures can interpret the significance of a negative experience as not being what it appears to be. We have seen that human and nonhuman beings alike can relate to others, including with altruism and trust, across species boundaries. But if nonhuman beings can remember a distant shared past and relate it to their present, if they can experience spiritual encounters, if they can make meaning at the level of complexity that even the most minimal grasp of a concept like atonement through the cross might seem to require, we do not yet know it.

Even if other forms of life are much more like us in some of their behaviors than we used to believe, in the current state of research it is hard not to think that, in many respects, human beings are still very different from other species.[80] But our model of atonement has a response to this built into it. However great the gulf

---

79. Rachel Nussbaum Wichert and Martha Nussbaum, "Can There Be Friendship between Human Beings and Wild Animals?" *Journal of Human Development and Capabilities* 22 (2021): 87–107 argue that this type of relationship can exist.

80. Brian Boyd, "The Evolution of Stories: From Mimesis to Language, From Fact to Fiction," *WIREs Cognitive Science* 9 (2018): 1–16 discusses the uniqueness of human beings as story makers and interpreters of experience through fiction and history.

CHAPTER 4

between human beings and other animals, not to mention other parts of creation, Christians have long accepted that the gulf between creation and God is even greater. It is axiomatic that no created being can understand the nature or purposes of God. The story of the Christ event, however, affirms Christians' conviction that God sent God's Son into the world as a human being to live as human beings lived in a specific place and time and to communicate and make relationships as human beings do. If God is beyond the grasp of human understanding, Jesus Christ is not, and human beings can put their trust in Christ as God's representative, trust Christ to act as their representative, and so hope to be reconciled with God.

But if God understands the gulf between Godself and creation and acts in Christ to bridge the gap, enabling human beings to come to salvation by putting their trust in Christ, then the question in relation to the rest of the created world is not how could it put its trust in the Christ event, as remembered and interpreted by human beings, or even in the exalted Christ as encountered by Christians today, but rather, what would it take for nonhuman beings to come to trust in the power that creates, sustains, and holds together all life in one great network of creation?

One possibility, as we have already mentioned, is that other life forms may have received or will receive in the future other revelations and routes to atonement in terms they recognize. Another possibility is that the evidence of recent research that cooperation, social learning, conflict resolution, and altruism are possible among many species, and also across species, offers a model for the restoration of trust as we are called to it through the Christ event. In the next chapter I will suggest that as God entrusts Christ with bringing those who encounter him to trust, so both God and Christ entrust Christ's followers with a wide range of work on behalf of God for the good of the world, and that work includes care for and stewardship of creation.[81] On that basis we might argue that as Jesus Christ represents God, God's trust and care for humanity, and God's hope for humanity's return to trust and right standing with God to other human beings, so other human beings are tasked with representing God's hope for the world to other beings.

If so, then human beings would need to find ways of being trustworthy to other beings and fostering trust in them, which might look different from the means by which they themselves learn about God's actions through Christ. Christianity, however—drawing not least on prophetic images of ages governed by rulers sent by God, such as Isa 11:1–9—has a long tradition of stories of relationships of trust and friendship between human beings and animals, which offer a vision of the world of created beings living in harmony with one another and with God. We might remember, among many others, Abba Anthony and his pig; Jerome and his lion; Giles and his deer; Columba and his packhorse; Cuthbert, who befriended

81. Cf. also Morgan, *Theology of Trust*, 282–98.

Trust in Creation

birds and sea creatures; Philip Neri the vegetarian; and, most famously, Francis, who preached to animals and reputedly mediated between the people of Agobio and a wolf. (In addition, anyone who has owned a pet has probably had the experience of needing to return to at-one-ment with a nonhuman being after some kind of suffering or wrongdoing.) Stories like these speak to a Christian intuition that the restoration of trust between God and humanity, which we believe has been made possible through Christ, should and, through creative human action, can extend to other created beings in their relationships with human beings and potentially also in their relations with each other.

Theologians have not explored what it might take for human beings or Christians in general to communicate the possibility of life-transforming trust to other beings. The most obvious starting point is surely that Christians must show themselves as consistently, benevolently, and caringly trustworthy toward other beings. Other beings must find themselves able to trust humanity, as many have not been able to do for hundreds of generations. The idea of restoring trust between humanity and the rest of creation is obviously so vast that we may be tempted to abandon it and fall back on the idea that God offers at-one-ment to other parts of creation through their own revelations. (This would not mean human beings' abandoning any care for creation, which we should practice on the separate grounds that what is created by God is not to be abused by humanity.) But if Christians understand themselves as called to imitate Christ, not least in seeking to bring others to at-one-ment with God, and also recognize that we are in continuity and community not only with all human beings but with all creation, then I do not think we can lightly abandon the idea that we should seek to foster trust wherever we can in creation (defined as widely as possible for this purpose). It is hard to imagine that the content of such trust for any nonhuman being involved would be recognizable as specifically Christian, but it would not be less real or less Christian from the human point of view, or potentially less transformative for that, any more than the trust of a small child or an adult with limited mental capacity is less real or transformative because they do not know about or grasp the significance of the Christ event. No one, axiomatically, fully understands God, and people vary enormously in their capacity to comprehend religious teachings, but it seems that everyone can trust, and by that token everyone can be saved. If that is true of human beings, then not only theology but biology and ecology allow the possibility that it is true of all beings.

Conclusion

This chapter has explored whether we can envisage not only human beings but also nonhuman creation as potentially estranged from God by wrongdoing, suf-

CHAPTER 4

fering, and the loss of trust, and as reconcilable with God, directly or indirectly, through the trust and trustworthiness of Jesus Christ and trust in God and Christ. We have acknowledged that it may seem counterintuitive to propose that nonhuman beings could have any concept of what Christian atonement means, but we saw that there are reasons, on many fronts, to think that this proposition is not as strange as it may at first sound.

It is now beyond doubt that human beings are inextricably part of creation as a whole and, moreover, that we have far more in common with other animals, plants, and other life forms than we believed until recently (at least in the Near East and the Western world). Conversely, nonhuman beings are increasingly recognized across multiple fields of research as more like human beings than we assumed, not least in that many are now seen to have moral emotions, to be moral subjects, and to make moral choices, which suggests that they can not only suffer but can also do wrong. At the same time, biologists increasingly argue that a wide range of animals and plants can act in ways (with cooperation, reciprocal altruism, group learning, conflict resolution, and mediation) that we would recognize as involving the practice of trust and trustworthiness.

From a theological perspective, the God of Jewish and Christian tradition has always been understood as the God of the whole of creation who creates, cares for, trusts, and is trustworthy to creation, and who relates to all parts of creation in ways they can understand. The Hebrew Bible affirms that every part of creation is created good but is also capable of action and change for better or worse. Multiple New Testament writings recognize Jesus Christ, with God, as creator, carer, truster, and trustworthy. Jesus, moreover, in his earthly ministry has a rich relationship with the natural world. People, animals, plants, and even the elements can trust in him, as in God, or fail to trust and be held responsible. God and Christ entrust the kingdom of God, the preaching of the kingdom, and Jesus himself to the world as the farmer entrusts seed to the earth. Jesus mediates between God and creation not only as a human but also as a created being. A strand of New Testament imagery portrays Jesus as many nonhuman forms of creation (including light, a seed, a vine, and the ingredients of bread), which act with generosity, self-giving, care, and empathy, doing what others need of them for their good, and enabling them to bear fruit.

It may be that other beings have their own revelations and routes to trust, which human beings cannot see or understand (or, perhaps, have simply not been looking for). But if Christians understand themselves as not only entrusted with the Christ event and responding to it with trust but also as entrusted by God and Christ with imitating Christ and enacting various kinds of work in the world, we must take seriously the possibility that we are tasked with seeking to restore

Trust in Creation

trust between other created beings and God as well as between other beings and ourselves. In this, we do not need to assume that other beings share our level of self-consciousness or intellectual sophistication, given that we recognize, for instance, that pre-self-conscious infants and adults with less than normative intellectual capacity can exercise and respond to trust. It is also salutary to bear in mind that, prima facie, the gulf of understanding between humanity and God is even greater than between humanity and any other created being. We must, though, acknowledge that in seeking to establish trust with other parts of creation, Christians in the contemporary world start from a shamefully low base. To be seen as trustworthy by the rest of creation, we have hard work to do in relearning to care for other beings, to act generously and altruistically toward them, and to do what they need of us rather than almost always what we want for ourselves.

One final possibility is worth raising. We are used to thinking of Jesus Christ as a human being mediating between God and humanity, but some of the imagery we have looked at in this chapter points in a different direction. We have suggested that, in the incarnation, Jesus is a created being as well as specifically a human being.[82] At a time of crisis in humanity's relationship with the natural world, perhaps we should be looking to practices of trust and trustworthiness in the animal and plant worlds as much as in the human world to call us back to a better relationship with God the Creator. In this generation it is perhaps Christ the grain of wheat, the gentle gorilla, the brave elephant, the mediating macaque, the exemplary lily, and the self-giving fir tree that have the most to teach us about our right relationship with God. Seeking inspiration for our own relationship with God in these exemplary creatures might restore us to some of the respect and humility in the face of the rest of creation that we need to end our own wrongdoing and the suffering we are causing to our fellow creatures.

---

82. To images from the plant kingdom, we can add the image of the lamb, with which Jesus is described by John 1:29; 1 Cor 5:7; and Rev 6:16; 7:14; 12:11; 13:8; 14:4; 17:14; 21:27; 22:3.

CHAPTER 5

As We Forgive

Most of this study, with the exception of chapter 2, has explored at-one-ment between God and humanity or God and creation. Tradition and experience however, both tell us that at-one-ment is equally important in human beings' relationships with one another as well as those with other beings.

Christian discussions of at-one-ment in human relations traditionally focus on the need for repentance when we have willfully done wrong, and for forgiveness of those who willfully do us wrong. They draw, above all, on the two biblical versions of the Lord's Prayer (Matt 6:7–15; Luke 11:1–4; cf. Mark 11:25), in which the faithful ask God to forgive the sins they have committed, or "debts" they have incurred, to God and affirm that they are willing to forgive other people. Discussions of the Lord's Prayer usually read debts as referring to deliberate wrongdoing, but chapter 1 argued that wrongdoing, in biblical writings and everyday experience, can be collective or inherited, foolish, unintended, or even unlucky and is often a consequence of actual or perceived suffering.[1] We can therefore hear the Lord's Prayer as referring to at-one-ment after all kinds of wrongdoing, and nothing in the text or context of the prayer in the gospels precludes such a reading.

In the at-one-ment of humanity with God, however, this study has focused not on the role of repentance and forgiveness but on trust and the central role of Christ as mediator in the restoration of trust. This is not, of course, to suggest that repentance and forgiveness are not involved or not important, but at various

---

1. As in Matt 6:12 and Luke 11:4, "debts" is a conventional way of referring to wrongdoings against God because sin puts one in debt to God. See Davies and Allison, *Matthew*, 1:611; Hans Dieter Betz, *The Sermon on the Mount* (Minneapolis: Fortress, 1995), 399–404, though the prayer does not limit debts to those incurred deliberately. Anthony Bash, *Forgiveness and Christian Ethics* (Cambridge: Cambridge University Press, 2009), 6–8 points out that wrongdoing comes in many kinds and degrees, but that forgiveness addresses them all.

As We Forgive

points we have indicated that repentance and forgiveness may be part of a reconciliation process made possible by the establishment of trust—even if that trust is, at least initially, thin and fragile. One of the themes of this chapter is that the same is true of repentance and forgiveness between human beings: they can take place as part of a process that is made possible by the establishment or reestablishment of trust. In chapter 2 we encountered a number of studies of conflict resolution, recovery after trauma, and the social rehabilitation of ex-offenders, which showed potential participants in a process as taking an initial step of trust in order to create a space within which change might become possible. Trust in these contexts may begin as provisional and precarious, but if it finds a response it has the potential to develop and strengthen, supporting relationships in which it is possible for participants to face their suffering and wrongdoing, repent, seek and offer forgiveness, and be reconciled, and in which people can come to look and move forward together. In chapter 3 I argued that we can see a similar pattern in Paul's account of the role of *pistis* in the Christ event. God the Father takes a step of trust toward humanity by entrusting the gospel to Jesus Christ, and God and Christ invite humanity to respond with trust even before they repent, their sins are forgiven, their righteousness is restored, or new life is given to them.[2] At the crisis of the event, the cross reveals the space into which God invites human beings to step, insisting that nothing will destroy God's and Christ's trust in them, and reveals human beings to themselves as so precious to God that God will not abandon them. It calls humanity to respond with a step of trust into the space in which change becomes possible, and in which, with Christ, it can begin the journey out of suffering and wrongdoing into new life.

Christian repentance and forgiveness between human beings are always understood, in line with the Lord's Prayer, in light of our relationship with God. Christians forgive out of their experience of being forgiven by God or in hope of forgiveness, normally both.[3] In everyday situations of repentance and forgiveness,

---

2. Though Jesus's initial preaching, according to Mark (1:15) and Matthew (4:17), calls people to repent, the only story of a disciple who recognizes his sinfulness before following Jesus is Luke's story of the call of Peter (5:8, where, at the point Simon says "I am a sinful man" he is asking Jesus to leave him, and Jesus has to reassure him before he follows Jesus). Those who come to Jesus for healing do not express repentance for sins first, but they are sometimes praised for their faith before they (or those for whom they are petitioning) are healed. At Matt 9:2 // Mark 2:5 // Luke 5:20 Jesus forgives the sins of the paralytic, but first he praises the trust of those who brought him. Even at Luke 7:36–50 it is the love and trust of the woman that Jesus says have led to the forgiveness of her sins (7:47, 50), not the repentance that is implied by her tears (7:38).

3. On human forgiveness in the Lord's Prayer see recently Robert Morgan, "Human Forgiveness in the Lord's Prayer," *ExpTim* 134 (2023): 164–72. On the complexity of traditions about

CHAPTER 5

however, whether hoped for or enacted, repentance and forgiveness are often envisaged, in practice, in bilateral terms, as something that is the responsibility of each party to do and is in their power to do.[4] It is well recognized that this can be an extremely demanding model. It requires people who have done wrong to face their wrongdoing honestly, admit it, and ask forgiveness: all separately, let alone cumulatively, difficult things to do. It can be seen as challenging people who have suffered serious, perhaps life-changing physical, material, mental, or emotional harm, or harm to those close to them, to receive the wrongdoer(s) back into relationship at whatever risk to themselves or others.[5] Even more demandingly, this model is often seen as analogous, in aspiration, to God's forgiveness of humanity. To admit one's wrongdoings to God, however, is different from admitting them to one's neighbor, and the God who is able and willing to forgive humanity is, by definition, a different order of being from humanity. God may be understood as grieved or angered by human wrongdoing, but God is not envisaged as capable of being damaged by wrongdoing in any way that fundamentally alters or destroys God. The human condition is different, inasmuch as wrongdoing can destroy a human life or badly damage it.

Another theme of this chapter is that rather than seeing repentance and forgiveness as bilateral, under God, we should see them as mediated by Jesus Christ and so, under God, as trilateral or triangular at every point.[6] Christ is

---

Christian forgiveness, and importantly placing it in its cosmological context, see especially James K. Voiss, *Rethinking Christian Forgiveness: Theological, Philosophical, and Psychological Perspectives* (Collegeville: Liturgical, 2015). On whether Christians are called to universal, unconditional forgiveness, see, e.g., Heidi Chamberlin Giannini, "Grounds for Forgiveness: A Christian Argument for Universal, Unconditional Forgiveness," *Journal of Religious Ethics* 45 (2017): 58–82 (for Giannini forgiveness is rooted in hope rather than trust). On Christians as more likely to take this view than non-Christians, and clergy more likely than lay Christians, see Ann Macaskill, "Defining Forgiveness: Christian Clergy and General Population Perspectives," *Journal of Personality* 73 (2005): 1237–65. Arguing that the Christian idea of forgiveness is highly culturally specific and does not coexist easily with other attitudes toward wrongdoing, see Rey Chow, "'I Insist on the Christian Dimension': Forgiveness . . . and the Outside of the Human," *Differences: A Journal of Feminist Cultural Studies* 20 (2009): 225–49.

4. The sacrament of penance and absolution, going back to at least the second century, is differently configured: the church, through a bishop or priest, communicating God's forgiveness to the penitent. Though the church plays a mediating role in this, in one sense of the term, this is not comparable with Christ who mediates in his own right as Son of God, so the focus of this chapter is different from that of the sacrament.

5. It is often assumed that the attitude and act of forgiveness go together, though in principle they can be separated. What is said here about the relationship between forgiveness and trust, however, holds whether we are talking about the attitude or action or both.

6. This is always implicit in Christian thinking but not explicit or explicated as often as

198

As We Forgive

the mediator between God the Father and humanity in the Christ event and continues to be present in and to oversee all Christian life. Christ also shares the human experience that wrongdoing can be catastrophically destructive for created beings, and that at-one-ment is proportionately risky and demanding even for those who are faithful to God. If at-one-ment between human beings is in any way analogous to at-one-ment between humanity and God, then it is appropriate, even essential, to understand it as made possible by the involvement of Jesus Christ.

One major debate in writing about human forgiveness is whether or not it *requires* repentance or at least the recognition of wrongdoing, and many people worry that forgiving people who have not repented amounts to offering them a "get out of jail free card."[7] The idea that at-one-ment begins with the extension of trust and first steps in trust may help us to see this question in a slightly different light. Where there has not been repentance, and forgiveness is offered without immediate hope of repentance or reconciliation, we can see the act as taking place within a framework of trust in God and Christ. Those who see themselves as living in trust with God and Christ, and (as we will see below) as entrusted with Christ's work of at-one-ment in the world, may extend therapeutic trust toward another and forgiveness as a particular expression of that trust, knowing that the one to whom it is offered may not (or not yet) be able to respond but trusting that the initiation of the relationship may create a starting point for change. In this, forgiveness is by no means a "get out of jail free card" but is rather an expression of the offering of a space for relationship, which is possible for forgivers because of their trust relationship with God and Christ and their acceptance of their entrustedness.

This chapter outlines a model in which at-one-ment between human beings (and potentially other beings, but we will focus on humans here) is mediated by Jesus Christ, the *pistis* of Christ, and *pistis* toward Christ, which is extended by the faithful as trust toward other human beings. Understanding human-to-human at-one-ment as based on the creation or restoration of trust, made possible by our trust relationship with Jesus Christ and with God the Father, has some promising features. It highlights that human beings are never alone in seeking reconciliation with one another but always act within the divine-human relationship of trust, in

---

we might expect, though see, e.g. Susan Eastman, "The Lord's Prayer," in *Prayer: Christian and Muslim Perspectives,* eds. David Marshall and Lucinda Mosher (Washington DC: Georgetown University Press, 2013), 79–90: 81–82.

7. On some of the "careless" ways in which Christians sometimes characterize forgiveness see Diane Leclerc and Brent Peterson, *The Back Side of the Cross: An Atonement Theology for the Abused and Abandoned* (Eugene: Cascade, 2022), 172–81.

CHAPTER 5

company with Christ and with Christ's example before them.[8] It allows us to see at-one-ment as a process—often a lengthy process—in which repentance and forgiveness may become possible within a framework of growing trust.[9] And it reminds us that humanity is part of creation as a whole and that our relationship of trust with God and Christ as part of creation is also a resource for our relationships with each other.

CHRIST AND THE RESTORATION OF TRUST BETWEEN HUMAN BEINGS

We have already been reminded that in the incarnation God takes a primary step of therapeutic trust in order to restore humanity's damaged relationship with God. God takes this step not by direct revelation but through the person of Jesus Christ on the human plane. In the gospels, much of Jesus's teaching in his earthly life concerns the importance of living in harmony with one's neighbors and, where needed, being reconciled with them. Among much else we can point to Jesus's articulation of the love commandment (Matt 22:37–39 // Mark 12:30–31 // Luke 10:27; cf. John 13:34–35), his sharpening of traditional teachings against anger, adultery, divorce, retaliation, and hatred of enemies (Matt 5:17–48 // Luke 6:27–28, 32–36; 12:57–59; 16:18), and his guidelines for community problem solving (18:15–20). Paul (on whom I drew largely in developing a trust-based model of atonement) takes a high view of the degree of love, peace, mutual tolerance, and so on that should be possible in his communities under the authority of God and Christ (e.g., Rom 14:13–15:6; 2 Cor 6:16–18; Gal 6:1–10; Phil 4:4–9; 1 Thess 5:14–15) and through the power of the spirit (1 Cor 12:4–6; 12:31–14:1; Gal 5:16–26; cf. 1 Cor 6:19). "Owe no one anything except to love one another" he tells the Romans (Rom 13:8).[10] The faithful are not to fall out over their different beliefs or practices (e.g., Rom 14:1–23; 1 Cor 1:10; Phil 4:2) but must work to build up the community as a whole (Rom 15:2; 1 Cor 8:1; 1 Thess 5:11).

Those who put their trust in Christ to restore their relationship with God have a reason a fortiori to trust Christ when he is remembered as teaching them to

8. Cf. pp. 137–50.

9. Some investigations of forgiveness show how even affirmations of unreserved forgiveness in the wake of wrongdoing can mask a more complicated reality, in which forgiveness is a long-term process that may never be complete; see, e.g., Donald B. Kraybill, Steven M. Nolt, and David L. Weaver-Zercher, *Amish Grace: How Forgiveness Transcended Tragedy* (San Francisco: Wiley, 2007), 79–80, 113–21.

10. My translation. Followed by, e.g., Eph 4:1–7; 4:25–5:5; Col 3:5–17. Cf. also Jas 4:1–12; 1 Pet 1:22; 1 John 2:3–11; 3:11–18.

200

As We Forgive

live harmoniously in trust with one another and how to restore their relationships when they fail. But the importance for Christian communities of living in trust, love, peace, and the rest is not only that they are commanded to do so or that it works better for communities in general to live that way. They must also cooperate because their relationship with Christ and with the spirit is such that they cannot be and do other than what God determines as right and be in that relationship. "Nobody speaking by the spirit of God," Paul says, "says 'Jesus be accursed'" (1 Cor 12:3). Nobody who sincerely confesses Christ and has received the spirit can be in conflict with other community members without being in breach of their relationship with Christ. Paul uses the vivid metaphorical language of incorporation: "Your bodies are members of Christ" (1 Cor 6:15); they "are" Christ's body, with many coordinating parts that depend on one another for the life of all (1 Cor 12:12–27).[11] This organic connection with Christ is the converse of Christ's connection with humanity when he allows himself to suffer in humanity's place: "For Christ did not please himself, but, as it is written, 'The insults of those who have insulted you have fallen on me'" (Rom 15:3). As Matthew's Jesus expresses the same theme in an end-time parable, "whatever [good or bad] you did for one of the least of these brothers of mine, you did for me" (Matt 25:40). The relationship of Christians with one another is, by its nature, triangular. It exists and persists as the relationship it is with reference to Christ, and a relationship between Christians can only be a Christian relationship if Christ is also in it. By the same token, at-one-ment between human beings can only be Christian at-one-ment if it is tripartite and Christ is in it.

A community that aspires to live in trust with Christ and with itself needs to recognize the different needs of participants. Those who are in danger of doing wrong need to be seen and understood, to be both challenged and helped to behave differently. Those who suffer from the behavior of others need to know that a community of the faithful will always be working to keep them from further harm. Given that most people both suffer and do wrong, community members need to share responsibility for holding themselves and one another to account, taking different roles at different times for the good of the community as a whole.

In chapter 3 I argued that Jesus trusted God, trusted humanity to respond to him, and sought to bring people to trust in God through him. I did not accept that his suffering and death were instrumental goods but argued that Jesus accepted them because he could not be who he was and abandon his trust in God or hu-

---

11. I take this to be an expression of the relationship of the faithful with Christ rather than of their participation in Christ; see Morgan, *Being "in Christ"*, 127–36. But the point about the triangular nature of Christians' relationship with one another holds on either interpretation.

CHAPTER 5

manity. By not abandoning God or humanity, even in the extreme of suffering, Jesus acted as a firebreak to evil, breaking the cycles of wrongdoing and retaliation and wrongdoing and suffering that alienate people from God. In the resurrection experiences, his followers recognized his trust as vindicated and God as bringing new life and hope even out of the worst that humanity can do. Jesus's trust therefore revealed the triumph of trust even over death for those who kept faith, renewed their trust, or came afterward to trust in him.

To wrongdoers, Jesus's trust, its vindication, and the response of his followers testify that trust in God and Christ makes possible a new life that is more empowered, more joyful (cf. Matt 5:12; Luke 10:20; John 16:24; Rom 15:13; Gal 5:22), and has more potential than anything they can engineer for themselves. To the suffering, Jesus's death testifies that there is no extreme of suffering that Jesus has not experienced and understood. It is from the cross that Jesus asks the suffering to take the risk of trust in him and in God that leads to new life. To all who belong to both groups, the cross offers a way to life that heals and rectifies both their suffering and their wrongdoing.

Since we live human lives on the human plane, trusting in God and Christ has as many implications for everyday life as it does for eternal life. The faithful person has to get up every morning, eat with their family, go to work, spend time with their friends and neighbors, and encounter those whom they have caused to suffer or who have caused them to suffer in the past, or whom they might harm or be harmed by in the future. Until the end time, trust in God and Christ is worked out in all the places and communities in which the faithful live, and life is rarely easy or unconflicted. When we have suffered, moreover, we may not feel sure of our ability to reach at-one-ment with the wrongdoer and may not feel optimistic about the wrongdoer's future behavior. The example of God's and Christ's trust in us, however, challenges us to take the risk of trusting as we are trusted, and the promise of Christ's ongoing presence with us reminds us that we never do it alone. The relationships of trust we have, both divine and human, act as mediators between ourselves and potential future failures of trust, giving us resources to take the risk of trust again.

Chapter 3 also argued that Jesus dies as a grace, so that human beings do not go through their own death to wrongdoing and suffering alone but in spirit with him. A number of passages also emphasize that the risen and exalted Christ continues to be with the faithful on the way, individually and corporately. Matthew's Jesus assures his followers that "where two or three are gathered in my name, I am among them" (18:20) and that "I am with you always, to the end of the age" (28:20).[12] For Paul, "The Lord is near" (Phil 4:5), perhaps in space as well as time,

12. Davies and Allison, *Matthew*, 2:690 note the parallel between 18:20 and 28:20, observing

As We Forgive

listening to those who call on him (1 Cor 1:2), and is active in laying the foundations of communities (1 Cor 3:11) and welcoming new members into churches (Rom 15:7).[13] If trust, as we have seen in earlier chapters, can take time to evolve and is often less an end point than the beginning of a new and open-ended relationship, Christ is envisaged as with the faithful throughout their lives, and their relationship with him is envisaged as informing and shaping all their relationships with other people.

We recognized in the course of this argument that Jesus is an example of trust, though not only as an example, and that part of the importance of examples is that they change our understanding of what is possible and liberate us to envisage and enact new ways of thinking, living, and relating to one another. By holding the example of Christ before them throughout their lives of faith, Christians do not allow themselves to forget that there are ways of living and interacting which, from within our prisons of suffering and wrongdoing, we cannot see but which, through the life, death, and resurrection of Jesus and our response to him, we can see, and which, under his oversight and in his company, we can risk practicing. New Testament writings do not shy away from acknowledging that practicing trust in Christ is not easy; most emphasize that it may involve suffering and persecution by those who do not share that trust. But they are convinced that the transformation of human existence made possible by trust is greater than the suffering it involves. They remind us, moreover, that even Jesus and his first followers wavered in trust at moments of extreme pressure—but that, as their relationship with God and with one another survived those moments, so can ours.[14]

Chapter 4 emphasized the continuity of humanity with the rest of creation and that humanity's relationship with God and Christ, including our relationship of trust, is from the beginning part of the relationship of creation as a whole to its creator and co-creator. Paul (2 Cor 5:17; cf. Rom 8:18) draws on prophetic tradition to affirm that putting one's trust in Christ and being liberated from suffering and wrongdoing amounts to being re-created, probably both in the sense that the trusting individual is re-created, and that the individual becomes part of a new

---

that the idea of the presence of Christ borrows from the *shekinah*, the glory of God that is present with the Jewish faithful, e.g., when studying Torah.

13. The nearness of Christ is usually seen as temporal, but, e.g., Markus Bockmuehl, *A Commentary on the Epistle to the Philippians* (London: A&C Black, 1997), 245–46 suggests that it is both; cf. Markus Bockmuehl, "The Personal Presence of Jesus in the Writings of Paul," *SJT* 70 (2017): 39–60. Paul describes himself as in the presence of Christ or "before the face of Christ" at 2 Cor 2:10; 8:21, while being fallen from grace is described as being "separated from Christ" in Gal 5:4; cf. Rom 8:39; 9:3.

14. Pp. 66–71.

CHAPTER 5

community that looks forward to a new kind of existence.[15] Creation is vast and complex, and at any one time though there are much wrongdoing and suffering, there is also much harmony. For the faithful, putting their trust in God and Christ brings the constant reminder that the whole of creation exists in a relationship of trust with God and, though that relationship may be broken in many places, in many places it is strong. We can go further and argue that our continued existence suggests that at any moment the fabric of creation, in all its multitudinous relationships and forms of trust, is stronger and more whole than otherwise. Every day we trust our fellow created beings (taking that phrase, as in chapter 4, in the widest sense) and they trust us, and, in every imaginable way and many ways that are beyond our current imagining, our trust works and supports us. We trust gravity that holds us to the earth and the plants and animals that produce what we eat and drink and give us shelter. We trust the everyday trustworthiness of human beings, including ourselves, who have developed to live in communities and cooperate for their mutual benefit in the ancient forms of our family and friendship groups and the highly complex forms of contemporary society. Our experience of being part of creation is everywhere an experience of trust and, for most of us, this experience is much more extensive than our experience of failing or being failed in trust. Its very ubiquity means that we tend not to see and appreciate the power of trust in every aspect of our lives; it is always easier to see the relatively few times and places where it fails than everywhere where it is strong.

This experience is a powerful resource when trust wavers or fails. We can imagine the trustworthiness of creation as like the health of a body, while the failure of trust we occasionally experience in a relationship or situation is like a wound or an illness in one part of that body. Just as the body draws on its resources of health elsewhere to heal the illness or mend the wound, so drawing on the trustworthiness of God's and Christ's creation as a whole gives us strength to work to mend a failure of trust in one part of our life. God, and Christ as co-creator, give us an experience of trust and trustworthiness and resources of trust as parts of creation that strengthen us beyond our individual resources to trust and seek to restore trust with those who have damaged us or part of our existence.

My own sense of the power of all the trust relationships in the world around me to fortify my trust and heal those places in my experience where trust has failed gained strength from a conversation I had many years ago with a member of my congregation, whom we can call Sandra. Sandra had grown up in an unhappy family, where relationships between those who might have been expected to love and trust one another were warped by bullying and controlling behavior.

15. E.g., Isa 65:17–25; 66:22–23; cf. Isa 41:18–20; Hos 2:18–19; 2 Pet 3:7–13; Rev 21:1–4.

As We Forgive

She was ashamed of her home life and did not dare to share it with her friends at school, so she was not able to form strong alternative bonds of trust outside the home. She grew up and left home, thinking that she did not and could not trust anyone, and with little experience of being trusted by others. After leaving college, however, she got her first job in a large organization, and here she was fortunate. She had a well-defined role in a sizable office, where her coworkers were competent and civil. She found that she could do her job; she could be, and was, trustworthy, and her coworkers trusted her and appreciated her trustworthiness. At the same time, she realized that she could trust her coworkers to do their part, and gradually she came to trust them. The workers in this office also, in a friendly spirit, shared a certain amount of information about their personal lives, and Sandra too began to risk sharing a little personal information. She remembered vividly where she was the day she realized that she was part of something she had never dared to hope for: a network of trusting relationships. She was standing at the office printer, staring idly at a large Swiss cheese plant that stood beside somebody's desk. This plant, so fragile in its not-very-large pot, so dependent on the goodwill of its owner (or, when its owner was on holiday, her workmates) to feed and water it, but growing so strongly, spreading its glossy leaves so confidently, seemed to epitomize the trust that made the workplace flourish. That cheese plant, Sandra said enthusiastically, was a revelation. Over the years that followed, she used the revelation of the power and fertility of trust in her workplace as a template on which to build other trusting relationships. Many years later, she used the experience to re-form a relationship with her surviving parent, putting down the roots, at least, of trust with him, even though in their lifetime trust never came to full fruition.

Perhaps no New Testament passage expresses the call to human beings to be reconciled with one another more powerfully than Matthew 5:43–47:

> [43] You have heard that it was said, "You shall love your neighbor and hate your enemy." [44] But I say to you: Love your enemies and pray for those who persecute you, [45] so that you may be children of your Father in heaven, for he makes his sun rise on the evil and on the good and sends rain on the righteous and on the unrighteous. [46] For if you love those who love you, what reward do you have? Do not even the tax collectors do the same? [47] And if you greet only your brothers and sisters, what more are you doing than others? Do not even the gentiles do the same?

In this passage Jesus invokes God's benevolence toward the whole of creation as the basis of human beings' relationships with one another. It is also worth observ-

205

CHAPTER 5

ing his choice of examples of love and good community. As we have already noted, for Jews, gentiles and tax collectors are paradigmatic outsiders, but in Matthew's Gospel they are also among those whom Jesus calls, who come to him for help and whose faith he praises. Jesus therefore both tells his followers to mend their fences with enemies and noncommunity members and points to the fact that, as the one who comes to interpret and fulfill God's law (5:17; cf. 5:48; 7:21), he sets an example by doing so. We tend to focus on the affective aspect of love in passages like this, but love is also a practical activity, and even if its practical and affective aspects ideally go together, they can be practiced separately. Jesus may therefore hope that his followers will come to feel love toward neighbors and enemies alike, but we can also hear him recommending love as a practical action.[16]

This passage talks in terms of love rather than trust, invoking Lev 19:18, but the language of trust could be substituted for it with very much the same effect. Jesus calls his followers to recognize that all human beings are equally part of creation, that he comes to call them all and to interpret and fulfill God's law for them, and that he sets them an example by loving, trusting, and offering at-one-ment to good and evil alike. If those listening aspire to follow him, then they must, and can, follow his example. Ideally, they will feel, think, and act equally with love and trust toward their neighbors, but if they struggle to feel as loving or trusting as they might hope, practical action is a good starting point. At the end of the gospel, moreover, Jesus assures them that, as they follow this demanding path, "I am with you always, to the end of the age" (Matt 28:20).

We noted above that existing trust relationships, both divine and human, can mediate between ourselves and future failures of trust, giving us resources to risk trusting again.[17] We can see Christ as mediating between ourselves and our past experience in other ways. As an example of vindicated trust in humanity as well as in God, he changes our sense of what trust makes possible. By traveling with us on our necessary death to wrongdoing and *apistia*, he changes what we are able to hope for. When we forgive others—even when we often know or suspect our trust will not, or not immediately, make them trustworthy—we allow Christ to persuade us to give a chance, as he does, to people like ourselves, who are not already trustworthy but who, in Christ's eyes, are worth taking a risk on. Our relationship with Christ creates a firebreak in our own personal cycle of wrongdoing and suffering as well as in those cycles in communities and societies.

16. On the distinctiveness of Matthew's ethics in general, see recently M. Konradt, *Ethik im Neuen Testament* (Göttingen: Vandenhoeck & Ruprecht, 2022), 260–322, and on this passage 275–78.

17. Pp. 202, 204.

206

As We Forgive

Jesus Christ, then, can be envisaged as mediating in the process of human-to-human forgiveness, at-one-ment, and the restoration of trust in a number of ways. We take the risk of forgiveness because we trust in Jesus, who risked trusting us and asks us to do the same for each other. We take it because we seek to imitate Jesus, who changes our understanding of what is possible for human beings in their relationship with God. We take it because Jesus goes with us on our journey of trust in each other, as in God and himself. We take it because our experience of living as part of Christ's creation helps us to recognize the abundant resources of trust, often unnoticed, that we already have and that we can use to heal the local wounds and damage in our relationships.

This may sound almost as demanding as the bilateral forgiveness we began with. But it also highlights how many resources, and how much support, the faithful have when they seek at-one-ment on the human plane. It also fits a significant aspect of our everyday experience. It is easier to forgive a slight, a wrong, or even a significant harm when we feel rich and fortunate in other relationships and resources. It is when we feel poor, unsupported, and vulnerable that we feel each other's wrongdoings most acutely and they do the most damage. When we recognize how rich we are, in our relationship with God and Christ and with God's creation, we have resources to enable us to risk at-one-ment with each other.[18]

ENTRUSTED: THE FAITHFUL AS MEDIATORS

This study has focused on the attitude and act of trust, but it has also touched from time to time on the idea of entrustedness, including the idea that Christians may be entrusted with work to do on behalf of God and Christ.[19] It is worth saying a little more about entrustedness, because it plays a role where human beings act, in imitation of Christ, as mediators for at-one-ment in everyday life.

The language of entrustedness is most common in the Pauline corpus, where it is usually applied to Paul's entrustedness as an apostle. When Paul describes himself as entrusted (e.g., Gal 2:7–9; 1 Thess 2:4), using *pisteuein* in the passive, he is always entrusted by God or Christ with something specific, above all with preaching the gospel. He sees himself as accountable to God for the way in which

18. A similar point is made by Robert J. Schreiter, *Reconciliation: Mission and Ministry in a Changing Social Order* (Boston: Boston Theological Institute, 1992), 42–43, 59, with reference to humanity's relationship with God rather than Christ.

19. They may also be entrusted with an entity, especially a body of teaching; e.g., 1 Tim 1:15; 3:1; 4:9; 2 Tim 2:11; Titus 3:8; cf. Rom 3:2. The affirmation that these sayings or *logia* are trustworthy suggests that, as the *logia* of God are entrusted to Israel, so these *logia* are entrusted to the faithful.

CHAPTER 5

he fulfills this trust, and he fulfills it with God's help.[20] In Gal 2:9 Paul describes his entrustedness as a grace or gift, echoing Rom 1:5, where he says that through Christ "we have received the grace of apostleship, to bring about the obedience of *pistis* among all the gentiles."[21]

Paul is entrusted not only with the gospel but also, in some passages, more broadly with a "stewardship" (*oikonomia*, e.g., 1 Cor 9:17) as God's slave.[22] Earlier in 1 Cor 4:1–2 Paul has already described himself as a servant of Christ and steward of the "mysteries of God" and affirmed that "it is required of stewards that they be found trustworthy [*pistos*]." Being trustworthy is the correlate of being entrusted with something, so here "trust" language is beginning to define not only the relationship between God, Christ, and the faithful but also relationships of responsibility and authority within the Christian community.

Paul's stewardship takes various forms. He founds and builds up communities (e.g., 1 Cor 3:5–9) and continues to oversee them when he is not with them, writing letters and sending coworkers to "remind you of my ways in Christ Jesus" (1 Cor 4:17; cf. 1 Thess 3:1–8). He encourages community members to imitate his actions as he imitates Christ (1 Cor 11:1) by enduring the suffering that faithfulness sometimes brings. This suggests that he understands himself as entrusted not only with specific tasks but also with a degree of discretion in how he shapes and supports the communities of the faithful. He never forgets, though, that he is answerable to God for all he does. As he says to the Corinthians, he hopes that his influence among them may be greatly enlarged "in accordance with our schedule," or, literally, "according to our rule [that is, God's rule for Paul]" (2 Cor 10:15).[23]

---

20. We can assume that Paul envisages God and Christ working together in entrusting Paul and others, as they do in giving grace and peace; e.g., Rom 1:7; 1 Cor 1:3; 2 Cor 1:2; Gal 1:3; Phil 1:2; 1 Thess 1:1 (grace and peace); Rom 5:2, 15; cf. 1 Cor 8:9 (grace); Rom 5:1 (peace); Rom 3:22–24; 2 Cor 5:21; cf. Rom 5:1; Gal 2:17, 21; Phil 1:11 (right standing or righteousness); Rom 5:2 (hope). Christ also works "in" or "through" Paul in, e.g., 2 Cor 13:2–5; cf. 2 Cor 4:12; Gal 2:20. On Paul as the "reconciled reconciler," see Otfried Hofius, "Erwägungen zur Gestalt und Herkunft des paulinischen Versöhnungsgedankens," *Zeitschrift für Theologie und Kirche* 77 (1980): 186–99. On Paul as mediator, see, e.g., Karl Olav Sandnes, *Paul—One of the Prophets? A Contribution to the Apostle's Self-Understanding* (Tübingen: Mohr Siebeck, 1991), 154–71; John Howard Schütz, *Paul and the Anatomy of Apostolic Authority* (Cambridge: Cambridge University Press, 1975), 204–48.

21. Taking χάριν καὶ ἀποστολήν as meaning that Paul received grace and apostleship simultaneously, as discussed by Jewett, *Romans*, 109–10.

22. He says of this that he cannot refuse it, but there is no hint that he accepts the trust unwillingly (1 Cor 9:17). 1 Cor 9:14 probably refers to Christ, in line with Paul's usage of "the Lord" elsewhere, but the reference to temple services at 9:13 and the echo of 4:1 at 9:17 suggest that Paul may be referring to entrustedness by God too.

23. "In accordance with our schedule," as translated by Margaret E. Thrall, *A Critical and Ex-*

208

As We Forgive

Paul's coworkers can also be entrusted with work for God and Christ. In 1 Cor 4:17, for example, Paul calls Timothy "my beloved and *pistos* son in the Lord." Timothy is not only loyal to Paul but is also evidently worthy of trust, since Paul is sending him to remind the Corinthians of Paul's own "ways in Christ Jesus." As God entrusts Paul with his ministry, so Paul entrusts Timothy with his. Elsewhere I have called the trust that comes from God through Christ to apostles, community leaders, and community members a "cascade" of trust.[24] It is equally a cascade of entrusting and trustworthiness, which not only connects God, Christ, and the faithful in what Ephesians calls "one [relationship of] trust" (4:5) but articulates relationships among Christians in terms of their authority to entrust and the responsibility of being entrusted.[25]

In the Synoptic Gospels, a series of parables of the end time describes "the master" entrusting his slaves with various tasks which they must fulfill faithfully until the master returns. In Matt 24:45–51 and Luke 12:41–48, Jesus's followers must be like "the trustworthy and prudent slave" (ὁ πιστὸς δοῦλος καὶ φρόνιμος) whom his master has set over the household to feed and take care of his fellow slaves (cf. Matt 24:49 // Luke 12:45). *Pistos* here is usually rendered "faithful," and although the good slave no doubt is faithful, he has also been given a specific role and task, so here "trustworthy" in respect to a specific task is a better translation. The description of the slave as trustworthy suggests that he is not simply given his role but is also entrusted with it.[26] If the servant is trustworthy in executing his trust, he will be praised when his master returns, but if he is not, he will be punished. In light of our discussion of human beings as mediators between God and the rest of creation in chapter 4, we can imagine the slave who is set over his master's

---

egetical Commentary on the Second Letter to the Corinthians (Edinburgh: T&T Clark, 1994–2000), 2:635.

24. Morgan, *Roman Faith*, 217–18.

25. Here *pistis* language is used to describe the emerging organization and authority structure of churches, because some people are entrusted with leadership and others are not. In Paul's undisputed letters everyone—whatever they are entrusted with—trusts God and Christ in the same way, but in the Pastoral and Apostolic Letters, community members can be described as practicing *pistis* in different ways according to their status. So, for instance, slaves express their trust in God by obeying their masters and women by obeying their husbands; see Morgan, *Roman Faith*, 316–17, 320–21. The philology of the name *hoi pistoi* for Christians suggests that they are both faithful and trustworthy and, by that token, entrusted, as, e.g., Timothy is *pistos* and entrusted by Paul with representing him.

26. In Luke 12:48 Jesus says that "much will be required of the person to whom much has been given." The related saying at Luke 16:11, "If you are not trustworthy with dishonest wealth, who will entrust [*pisteuein*] you with true wealth?" suggests that being given something, in this context, and being entrusted with something are closely related.

CHAPTER 5

household as stewarding not only his fellow human slaves but also, directly or indirectly, all the other resources of the household: the domestic animals, crops, and other foodstuffs. Stewardship of a household, or a world, may be not only of people but also of all the resources of that world.

The parable of the talents (Matt 25:14–30 // Luke 19:11–27) also explores entrustedness and trustworthiness. A man setting out on a journey leaves three slaves in charge of five talents, two, and one. When he returns, two have doubled their talents and are commended as "good and trustworthy" (Matt 25:20, 22).[27] Since they were *pistos* in small matters, both will be given greater responsibilities (25:21, 23). The slave with one talent, however, was afraid of his master, whom he knows is a hard man (25:24). He thought the least risky prospect was to bury his talent, and now he returns it. The man is angry, calling the slave "wicked and lazy" (25:25–26). He takes back the talent and orders the man to be thrown out (25:30). The master does not call this slave *apistos*, perhaps because, on one level, he has not been unfaithful or untrustworthy—he has not absconded with his talent or thrown it away. But he has not done as the master wanted, so he has not been trustworthy in fulfilling the specific responsibility with which he was entrusted. The faithful, it seems, must be faithful not only in their attitude to the master but also in their actions according to the trust placed in them.

Like other parables of the coming of the Son of Man, this story insists that, when the master returns, those who do not satisfy him will be cast out (cf. Matt 24:50–51; 25:10). The story also hints that the greatest risk in trusting God or Christ may sometimes be the truster's own lack of understanding or weakness, which causes them to fail in trust or trustworthiness despite their good intentions. Though the fate of the slave with one talent fits the point of the parable in its immediate context, however, it is also significant that many modern readers feel sympathy with him. Perhaps he did not know what would be best for him to do with his relatively limited resources. Perhaps he did know but did not trust himself to succeed. Being entrusted with something is demanding, and many of us fail those who trust us in one way or another. As we have seen, in fact, the gospels often recognize and accept this idea. Ideally those who put their trust in God and Christ will not waver or fail, but quite likely they will and, in many stories, if their desire to trust or to be trustworthy persists, the relationship need not be broken.[28]

27. As in the previous parable, "trustworthy" is a better translation of *pistos* than "faithful" because the issue is not simply whether the slaves are, in general, faithful, but whether they have been trustworthy in executing a particular task.

28. Morgan, *Theology of Trust*, 258–63.

As We Forgive

In these passages, it may be God or Christ who entrusts people with work to do. The entrusted also entrust one another with work in a "cascade" of entrusting and hoped-for trustworthiness. In their trustworthiness, the entrusted are role models for others, as Christ is a model for them. Being entrusted is a challenge, and not everyone will fulfill it, and we may have a good deal of sympathy for those who fail, not least because we may well be among them.

The idea of entrustedness and the cascade of entrustedness are especially significant where human beings are called to act as mediators for one another in the process of at-one-ment. At times, when one person or group has wronged another, it may be impossible for forgiveness to take place or for the two to be reconciled. It may not even be desirable for at-one-ment to be sought. Where one person, for instance, has suffered abuse at the hands of another, it may not be psychologically or emotionally possible for the one who has suffered to take part in any attempt to repair the relationship. Even if the abuser expresses remorse, it may be too damaging for the one who has suffered to have anything more to do with them, and in such cases the safety and health of the sufferer must be protected. If a person, or an entire group, that has suffered at the hands of another has died, they cannot take part in a process of reconciliation whether or not they might have been willing to do so, and then it is debated whether any other individual or group has the right to participate in any such process or to seek or accept at-one-ment on their behalf.[29]

Nevertheless, most Christians are committed to the conviction that every wrongdoer and everyone who suffers from wrongdoing can, in principle, come to at-one-ment with God and their neighbors.[30] More than that, they affirm that a God of grace and love wishes atonement for every wrongdoer as for everyone who suffers from wrongdoing. And here people of faith in imitation of Christ, whether as individuals or groups (for instance in churches), may understand themselves as entrusted by God with acting as mediators for one another.[31]

The person who showed me this many years ago was a neighbor whom we can call Martha. Martha came from a family that had been traumatized by domestic violence over three generations. She seemed at first sight to have escaped her

---

29. Explored, e.g., in Simon Wiesenthal, *The Sunflower: On the Possibilities and Limits of Forgiveness* (Paris: Opera Mundi, 1970).

30. The exception being those who believe in double determination.

31. See Emmanuel Katongole and Chris Rice, *Reconciling All Things: A Christian Vision for Justice, Peace and Healing* (Downers Grove: InterVarsity, 2008), 13. Here Katongole draws a connection between 2 Cor 5:18–20, where Christ is the intermediary in reconciliation between God and humanity, and the Christian's graced call to embrace a ministry of reconciliation within the world. He emphasizes that this is not a heroic or utopian aspiration but realistically possible.

CHAPTER 5

family's unhappy past. By the time I knew her she was happily married with a loving husband, her own home, and children who were thriving. But she bore the scars of her family's history. They came out in insecurity, depression, a chronic uncertainty about whom she could trust, and occasionally in harsh verbal attacks on the people closest to her, and she did not know how to heal the pain she continued to feel.

Martha's family also suffered from her suffering, and some of them found it hard to handle. Being less close to her, I found her outbursts less traumatic, and it was also easy for me to see her many wonderful qualities. She was a devoted wife and mother, a superb cook and gardener, a loyal friend, and a caring neighbor. She contributed to her local community in a hundred ways. Despite working hard, she found time to be creative, hospitable, and attentive to the world around her.

Over several years, I began to feel that I played a small but positive role in her life. As a neighbor rather than a family member, less vulnerable because I was less close to her, it was relatively easy for me to like and affirm her, even when she was angry or abrasive. In our relationship I found her entirely trustworthy, and I think she trusted me. Our friendship became, in a small way, a place of at-one-ment. When we were together she could lower her guard a little, relax, and spend time in a space where there were no barriers to trust and affection. I do not know how much difference our friendship ultimately made—we rarely do know—but my sense was that it helped on her journey of at-one-ment with people closer to her and with her traumatic memories. I know that her company and friendship were an education and a delight to me. She taught me that, sometimes, what another person needs from us, and what we can offer, is the strengthening of their sense that they can trust, be trusted, and be trustworthy in one relationship, which may help to strengthen their will and their power to address the wounds of trust betrayed elsewhere.

Martha never came, in this life, to full at-one-ment with those who had hurt her, let alone reconciliation with the wrongdoing and suffering in her past. But she moved toward it, and the change in her made it easier for her children to move further in the same direction. Maybe in another generation, children will be born for whom the family's past traumas leave no legacy, and who do not struggle to trust one another.

In the course of our lives we may meet individuals or groups of whom we find it hard to believe that they are capable of responding to divine trust, but we also recognize that this is not our judgment to make. We may also encounter people whom we recognize that we personally cannot help, or who cannot help us. But if Christians understand themselves as entrusted with work to do on behalf of God and Christ in the present time, then, as a community, we are committed to

As We Forgive

doing everything we can to foster environments in which as many people, and other beings, as possible have the chance to encounter divine trust and grow in trust and trustworthiness toward God and other created beings. Many of us, in addition, have had the experience that a community that offers trust and trustworthiness to us, in times of distress—whether quite ordinary, everyday distress or profound and life-changing distress—can support us through that time and, in small or large ways, change our future.[32]

The Corrymeela Community in Northern Ireland is well known for working to create a space in which people who have been damaged by conflict can come and take first steps in trust. Corrymeela's vision is that Catholic and Protestant Christians together should witness to Christ, who transcends and heals all human divisions, and create a space in which people from all sections of Northern Irish society can meet to "develop new relationships of mutual respect, trust, and co-operation."[33] The community has developed an "experiential" model of community, "which encourages participants to form ideas concerning their own prejudices and life experiences whilst building trusting, open relationships with others in the group" (which includes both perpetrators and victims of violence and those who are both).[34] As one leading participant explains, "it is not enough to 'know' about reconciliation; we need places where people can experience trust and reconciliation and we need people who can 'model' reconciliation (in this they imitate Christ)."[35] A director of the Corrymeela Center in Ballycastle has described the role of trust in the community's life like this:

> It's really difficult when relationships are broken and people don't trust each other. I'm at the stage that if somebody's willing to take a half step towards the other, then that's a good thing, that's good now. I don't expect people to be forgiving each other or for there to be solutions. I see it more in terms of relationships forming and possibilities of friendships emerging and seeing

32. Haddon Willmer, "'Vertical' and 'Horizontal' in Paul's Theology of Reconciliation in the Letter to the Romans," *Transformation* 24 (2007): 151–60 argues persuasively that reconciliation on the human plane in Romans depends on "vertical" reconciliation between God and humanity.

33. John Morrow, quoted in Maria Power, *From Ecumenism to Community Relations: Inter-Church Relationships in Northern Ireland* (Dublin: Irish Academic Press, 2007), 122.

34. Power, *Ecumenism*, 125. Corrymeela was founded in 1965 before the formation of the Truth and Reconciliation Commission in South Africa. It has much in common with TRAC and its relatives in other countries, but it emphasized from the beginning, as TRAC did not, the foundational role of trust in making possible reconciliation, and the community as a place in which first steps in trust can be taken by longstanding adversaries.

35. David Stevens, "Christ's Ambassadors in the Work of Reconciliation," *Corrymeela Magazine,* January 2007, 10.

CHAPTER 5

different perspectives and being more open to hearing stories from the other side, and for me I've been sort of part of that whole story of creating that safe space, where victims and survivors can share their stories in the presence of perpetrators. And there is something very, very sensitive about that and important about that.[36]

Committing ourselves, as individuals and communities, to creating this kind of space of trust for as many people (and other beings) as we can is also one of the ways in which the faithful imitate Christ. One of the effects of gospel stories that focus closely on an interaction between Jesus and someone whom he praises for their *pistis* is the impression they create of a still place and moment in the midst of a great crowd of people and press of action. When the woman with the hemorrhage, for instance, touches the hem of Jesus's garment (Matt 9:20–22 // Mark 5:25–34 // Luke 8:43–48), he immediately knows it, despite the fact that people are pressing in on him from all sides. In Mark's version, he asks who touched him and the woman, trembling with fear, comes forward. Matthew alters this so that as soon as he is touched, Jesus knows it, turns, immediately identifies the woman, and says, "Take heart, daughter; your trust has healed [or saved] you." In that moment, it is as though the rest of the crowd, and their noise and hustle, have ceased to exist. In John's account of Jesus's healing of a man born blind (9:1–41), much of the story involves a series of debates between the man, his parents, Jesus, the disciples, the man's neighbors, and local Pharisees. The impression is of a busy, noisy, and

---

36. Interview with the author, Leah Elizabeth Robinson, "The Influence of Social Context on a Theology of Reconciliation: Case Studies in Northern Ireland" (PhD diss., Edinburgh University, 2011), 203. This aspect of Corrymeela's work is well studied; see, e.g., Stevens, "Christ's Ambassadors." Miroslav Volf, *Exclusion and Embrace* (rev. ed.; Nashville: Abingdon, 2019), 108–10 argues similarly that often we cannot realistically achieve "final reconciliation" in our lifetimes but need to focus on what resources are needed to live together in peace in the absence of such reconciliation. Volf talks of peace rather than trust, but mutatis mutandis the argument here is similar. Linda Radzik, *Making Amends: Atonement in Morality, Law, and Politics* (Oxford: Oxford University Press, 2007) takes an unusual and much discussed approach to wrongdoing and making amends outside religious contexts, which has points of similarity with the argument here. She argues that the aim of atonement is less to repay moral debts than to repair moral relationships, which includes the reestablishment of trust (82); that one party can inspire someone to become trustworthy by their willingness to forgive, which is not far from our concept of "therapeutic trust" (117); and that reconciliation can take place even where the attitude of forgiveness is not possible (117). She does not assume that mediators are needed in these processes, but we have seen how useful they often are in practice. Downing, "Reconciliation," unusual among theological studies of reconciliation, draws on legal theory and practice to argue that for reconciliation to occur, recognition of the need for change and means of change are more important than punishment, reparations, repentance, or forgiveness.

As We Forgive

conflicted scene. But after the man is thrown out of his community, Jesus seeks him out and asks him to put his trust in the Son of Man, and the man responds by trusting and doing obeisance to him (9:35–39). John tells us afterward that there were some Pharisees present then too, but in the moment it is as if Jesus and the man are alone, and all the crowds and conflict around them have disappeared.

Creating a space of trust, in which wrongdoers and those who have suffered may find space and time to develop trust and trustworthiness, does not always mean being very active or interventionist in the process. Often the Quaker saying is apposite: "Attend to what love requires of you, which may not be great busyness."[37] In chapter 2 we heard two survivors of conflicts in sub-Saharan Africa express the same idea in different terms. Tenda Nkomo from Matabeleland says, "Walk with us and listen . . . You will never fully understand the journey of our suffering . . . But we need your presence, so stay with us."[38] Pascal Bataringaya from Rwanda says, "The churches have something special. They walk with the people, with the perpetrators, with the victims. People feel that they are not alone."[39] In chapter 3 we explored how, in the imagery of Romans 6, Christ can be envisaged as traveling with those who put their trust in him, as they go through their necessary "death" to sin. The faithful must go through the process themselves, but they do not go alone.

Entrustedness, as we have seen, is a responsibility, and those who accept and undertake it will be held to account for how they fulfill it. If Christians aspire to see themselves as entrusted with acting as mediators, they must also imitate Jesus in being as trustworthy as humanly possible. The scale of the responsibility of creating a space in which others may come to trust and be trusted means that when people of faith, as individuals, groups, or churches, prove untrustworthy, the betrayal is correspondingly great. The outrage and anger that have been provoked in recent years by the emergence of scandal after scandal of physical and sexual abuse, across churches, are a measure of how profoundly these churches, and many individuals within them, have betrayed the trust of those who trusted them to act as representatives and mediators of the saving trust and trustworthiness of Christ. To claim to be trustworthy, and then to abuse the trust of those who come to you in good faith, is one of the most brutal ways in which one person can damage another. To invoke the trust and trustworthiness of God and Christ, which stand at the heart of the gospel and of Christian tradition, in order to abuse those who trust you is to strike at the heart of the faith: the experience of those

---

37. *Quaker Faith and Practice* (5th ed.; London: Religious Society of Friends, 1995), Advice 28.
38. Villa-Vicencio and Tutu, *Walk with Us*, 1.
39. Schliesser, "Theology of Genocide," 9.

CHAPTER 5

who encountered Jesus in his earthly life, Christian witness, Christian teaching, and Christian community. New Testament writings reserve some of their most blistering criticism for those whom they regard as abusing the care of others with which they have been entrusted: "Woe to you, scribes and Pharisees, hypocrites! For you lock people out of the kingdom of heaven. . . . blind guides!" (Matt 23:13, 24). "If any of you cause one of these little ones who believe in me to sin, it would be better for you if a great millstone were hung around your neck and you were thrown into the sea" (Mark 9:42). "The name of God is blasphemed among the gentiles because of you" (Rom 2:24). At the time of writing, whether some churches will ever recover from their catastrophic failure to be trustworthy and to create a space for the development of trust is highly uncertain.

When individuals and communities do seek, in good faith, to create trustworthy spaces and relationships in which those who have suffered or done wrong may come to trust in God, it is also worth bearing in mind, as we noted in the introduction and have already mentioned in this chapter, that trust and its relatives can be both attitudes and actions, and though attitude and action are usually understood as ideally going together, they do not always do so. It may be reasonable, for instance, for someone to hold an attitude of trust without acting on it at that moment, or for someone to act with "therapeutic" trust even if, at that moment, they are not sure that the attitude of trust would be appropriate.[40] Similarly, in a context in which people of faith are seeking to fulfill what is entrusted to them by God, they may sometimes act to create an environment of trust even when they know their own trust and trustworthiness toward God or other people are not perfect. In the same spirit they may accept that those who come to them seeking trust and trustworthiness may not come to it fully in all its aspects or all at once. Trust is often, if not always, a process, and it can be a long game.

We saw in Jesus's parables of the end time that it is only on the master's return that the faithful will finally be judged; until then, there is time and space to grow in trust. Paul suggests something similar when he tells the Thessalonians and Corinthians to stand firm in their trust or "in the Lord" (1 Cor 16:13; 1 Thess 3:8)

---

40. Gregory D. Paul and Linda L. Putnam, "Moral Foundations of Forgiving in the Workplace," *Western Journal of Communication* 81 (2016): 53–54 discuss the importance of establishing trust as a first step to the restoration of relationships in the workplace, noting that intention and spontaneous feelings here do not always march in step. Angelika Rettberg and Juan E. Ugarriza, "Reconciliation: A Comprehensive Framework for Empirical Analysis," *Security Dialogue* 47 (2016): 517–40 argue that in reconciliation processes it is an effective starting point to focus on day-to-day cooperation and practical trust without probing too deeply into people's attitude or feelings of trust. They also argue that focusing on day-to-day cooperation can be more effective to restoring relationships than focusing on memory, truth, and justice.

As We Forgive

and to grow stronger in their *pistis* (1 Thess 3:2–3), to grow like plants or children (1 Cor 3:6), and to "bear fruit for God" (Rom 7:4). In the interim, working to restore trust when our own trust and trustworthiness are still works in progress, and helping others to feel trust before they can enact it, or enact it before they can feel it, can act as starting points for renewal of life. In Laura Stovel's study of the restoration of trust after conflict in Sierra Leone, we saw how villagers accepted ex-combatants returning home, taking an initial step of trust, but also watched them to see how they changed and built deeper trust gradually as and when they did change.[41] In less traumatic circumstances, many people have had the experience that acting toward another person with trust, even when they did not feel confident in the relationship, allowed the other to feel trusted and to respond by becoming, over time, more trustworthy. The change may be slow and, in this life, it may never be complete, but it may still be significant and, as respondents to Christ's trust in us, Christians are called to take the risk.

Not only time, but place and social complexity are allies in this process. If we cannot trust or be trusted today, something may change so that we find it easier tomorrow. If we cannot trust or be trusted in one environment, we may find another that offers and fosters trust better. If we cannot trust or be trusted by one person or group, we may find trust with another. The created world is highly complex, and the environment that gives life to one type of being may not give life to another; what feeds one creature does not feed another. Christians affirm the complexity and diversity of creation, however, as good in themselves and also for God's purposes. We may hope that all situations and relationships, by grace, eventually lead to at-one-ment, even if they take many routes.

Conclusion

This chapter has argued that at-one-ment between human beings is always a triangular process, involving the human parties and Jesus Christ. In the context of this study, it has explored in particular how Christ is involved in the restoration of trust. Jesus Christ is present where people seek to create or re-create trust as mediator, example, and companion. In his earthly life he taught the importance of living harmoniously with one another, and of reconciliation where relationships are damaged. In his death he revealed and demonstrated the power of trust in reconciliation, showing humanity that his trust could not be broken, showing humanity its own value in God's eyes, acting as a firebreak to evil, and breaking the

---

41. Pp. 93–94.

CHAPTER 5

cycles of wrongdoing and retaliation and wrongdoing and suffering that damage and prevent the repair of damaged relationships.

Christ offers to humanity—both those who have done wrong and those who have suffered—a wholly and transformatively trustworthy relationship with himself and with God. On this basis, he calls humanity to trust and be trustworthy toward God, himself, and other people, and he entrusts us with work of at-one-ment in this world. Entrustedness is a gift, a calling, and a responsibility. Those who accept and undertake it have an obligation to act in and for the world. In this, they are part of the ongoing revelation of God's outreach of trust through Christ in the Christ event, which we discussed in chapter 3. Those who accept the call to entrustedness are also responsible for being as trustworthy as they are humanly able, and they can expect to be held to account at the end time.

Christians take the risk of offering or accepting forgiveness because we trust in Christ; because we seek to imitate Christ; because Christ goes with us on our journey of reconciliation; and because as part of creation we recognize the abundant resources of trust we already have, which we can use to heal the local wounds and damage in ourselves and our relationships. When we are offered the chance of seeking at-one-ment with other people, we can understand Jesus Christ as asking us to give a chance to people like ourselves, who are not yet perfectly trusting, not reliably trustworthy, and not certain to remain faithful, but who are worth taking a risk on. Here, Christ also mediates between us and our own experience, reminding us that what is true of us is true of the rest of creation too; that those who are not perfect are still worth trusting, in hope that they will respond and, through time, respond more fully.

Sometimes what people suffer at each other's hands makes it impossible for the sufferer(s) to be reconciled with the wrongdoer(s). If Christians believe, however, that God reaches out to everyone in trust and everyone has a chance to respond, there is a role for communities to act on behalf of those who have done wrong or suffered, creating a space, through time, in which people other than the sufferer(s) may offer trust and trustworthiness and give the wrongdoer(s) a chance to respond. In offering this, communities, like individuals, recognize that not everyone may be able to respond in their lifetime, and that all our responses are imperfect, but we trust that where there is the possibility of making a start, there is also the possibility of progress. In this process, place, time, and social complexity are our allies, since if trust is not possible in one place, in one social context, or at one time, it may be possible in another.

In chapter 2 we saw examples of the way in which extending and responding to trust, however difficult the circumstance, can be a necessary and vital first step in the restoration of relationships. We have also seen that the call to *pistis*—in its

218

As We Forgive

core meanings of "trust," "trustworthiness," "faithfulness," and "entrustedness"—is at the center of the gospel from before our earliest sources. This suggests that God's outreach of trust through Christ and human beings' response can be seen as the framework within which repentance and forgiveness take place rather than being the precondition of the new relationship. We can already see this model implied particularly in the psalms and postexilic prophecy in the Septuagint, where God is sometimes referred to as *pistos*, and God's call through the prophets to Israel to repent is predicated on an existing relationship of trust and the covenant, which itself reflects a relationship of trust.[42]

Seeing the (re-)creation of trust as the frame within which repentance and forgiveness can take place offers a way around some of the well-recognized difficulties with the idea that relationships between God and humanity or between human beings are not restored until the wrongdoer has repented. One popular Christian understanding of reconciliation demands that those who have done wrong acknowledge it, admit truthfully to it, and sincerely repent before they are forgiven. But what of those who cannot or will not face their wrongdoing or admit to it? Are they simply cast out? What of the situation when both sides, after a conflict, are more conscious of their suffering than their wrongdoing and each demands that the other admit their wrongdoings and repent first? Do we accept a stalemate? Envisaging the first step in at-one-ment as being that those involved take the risk of offering and accepting a degree of trust and the beginnings of a relationship, within which they may become able to talk about wrongdoing and suffering, repentance and forgiveness, offers a potentially more fruitful way forward. As we saw in some of the examples in chapter 2, there is empirical evidence that it works. This model recognizes that trust may begin as something limited and thin, or something that is enacted without necessarily being felt, but finds that once it has begun there is scope for it to develop and deepen.

Seeing trust as the framework within which repentance and forgiveness can take place has advantages over another popular Christian understanding of forgiveness, which is that it should be freely given whether or not the wrongdoer has recognized their wrongdoing, repented or asked for forgiveness.[43] This model is

---

42. On the *pistis* of God in the Septuagint, see Morgan, *Roman Faith*, 196–200.

43. Scholarship on forgiveness is acutely aware of this problem and offers a number of ways of addressing it: see, e.g. the discussion and proposal of John Hare, "Forgiveness, Justification, and Reconciliation," in *The Wisdom of the Christian Faith* (ed. P. Moses and M. McFall; Cambridge: Cambridge University Press, 2012), 77–96; Alan J. Torrance, "Forgiveness and Christian Character: Reconciliation, Exemplarism, and the Shape of Moral Theology," *Studies in Christian Ethics* 30 (2017): 293–13; Bash, *Forgiveness*, 1–22. For most Christians, however, the "popular" model is the dominant one, with all the difficulties it raises. On forgiveness in the cultures

CHAPTER 5

always in danger of looking like a "get out of jail free card," something that it is generally agreed forgiveness should not be. Alternatively, it can amount to the sufferer simply walking away from a person or a relationship and declining to have anything more to do with them. At the time of writing this is also a popular representation of forgiveness in public discourse, which is sometimes articulated as a decision by the sufferer not to give the wrongdoer any more power to make them suffer but to get on with their life.[44] The difficulty with this—apart from the fact that we cannot always, in practice, simply walk away from someone who is in our lives—is evident if we imagine God's walking away from sinful humanity to get on with God's life. This is less forgiveness than the "canceling" of the wrongdoer in the style of contemporary social media, and it is the opposite of what humanity hopes for from God, or how Christians are called to live. However great the wrongdoing and suffering of which we are capable, the idea that wrongdoers might simply be excised from another person's life is the antithesis of at-one-ment. If we understand the (re-)creation of trust as the framework within which repentance and reconciliation take place, however, and also accept that trust sometimes needs to be (re)established by communities acting on behalf of those who cannot enact it themselves, we can envisage a pathway to the restoration of right relationships between human beings, and human beings and God, that does not depend on a specific type of behavior from the wrongdoer, or on the sufferer letting the wrongdoing "out of jail," or on the canceling of the relationship altogether, but that allows change to happen gradually in a place of trust into which God has invited all humanity.

Trust, as we have observed several times, can be a long game. It is not the end of a process but the beginning of an open-ended relationship that has the capacity to take us to places we cannot yet imagine. Fragile and imperfect as it always is, in this life it offers the promise of new and more abundant life, new relationships, new hope, and new possibilities: a new creation.

---

surrounding early Christianity, see David Konstan, *Ancient Forgiveness: Classical, Judaic, and Christian* (Cambridge: Cambridge University Press, 2012).

44. Discussed by Robert Enright, "Is There a Difference between Forgiving and 'Moving On'?" *The Forgiving Life* (blog), *Psychology Today*, September 17, 2018, https://www.psychologytoday.com/us/blog/the-forgiving-life/201809/is-there-difference-between-forgiving-and-moving.

Conclusion

On August 29, 1904, Florence Gertrude Randle, wife of coal miner Arthur Randle, died in Stockingford, a small village in Warwickshire, England, aged forty-two. Her death was not registered until September 17 because of the inquest, which found that she had died of "peritonitis, the result of a kick and injuries from her husband: manslaughter." Thomas Randle was charged with killing his wife and tried. He pleaded not guilty.

A local newspaper covered the case, reporting the testimony of some of the witnesses:

> On the evening of 27th August, about 3.30, the deceased woman was visited by Mrs. Florence Mary Lucas, who remained in the house half an hour talking to her. The deceased was then apparently all right. Between half-past nine and ten the same evening another Mrs. Mary Mary Lucas [*sic*] was called into the house by the deceased's daughter Grace, and she found prisoner in the front room and the deceased in the back kitchen. The deceased woman was in great pain and was vomiting blood into a bowl. With some assistance Mrs. Lucas conveyed the woman to her own cottage some 300 yards away and examined her. She found signs of violence on the lower part of the body and saw bruises which were then in the process of turning black. The unfortunate woman seemed to be in dreadful agony, and Dr. Mason was called and examined her at one o'clock in the morning. The deceased was then helped into her [Mrs. Lucas's] bed.[1]

Florence died two days later at her neighbor's house. In his postmortem report, Dr. Mason found a ruptured large intestine. Florence told her neighbor that her

1. *Leamington Spa Courier*, December 9, 1904, 6.

CONCLUSION

husband had kicked her. On the witness stand, he claimed that she had pulled a chest of drawers over onto herself and that she drank. He was acquitted.

The Randles had eight children, of whom one, Thomas, is remembered in the family as the only eyewitness to the beating that killed his mother. He would have been twelve or thirteen. He grew up to be an abuser himself, who brutalized his own wife, Florence May, until she managed to get away. Of his three children one committed suicide, one was thrown out of the house for some supposed misdemeanor and was lost to the family, and the third was also thrown out when she married a man her father disapproved of. She was my maternal grandmother, also called Florence May.

Nobody remembers what experiences, if any, made Arthur Randle an abuser, but violence reverberated through the family, traumatizing generation after generation and turning successive generations toward other forms of abuse. The story was not all negative. My grandmother was a strong and loving woman who married a kind man from a happy family, and she created great good in her life as well as passing on some of her trauma in the form of verbal and emotional abuse. Her daughters inherited and built on the goodness of both their parents. But four—or perhaps many more—generations later, the suffering and wrongdoing of the past and the passed are still with us.

In the worldwide abomination of human desolation that is much of the past century, these are small stories of small-town lives. There are no gas ovens here, no machetes, no enslavement, no genocide. But human beings do not suffer to scale, and the pain in these lives was, and is, as disfiguring as the pain of much bigger tragedies. We are not, humanly, all we could be. We are not all we can see is possible. We long to break out of the prison of our suffering and wrongdoing and live a different life.

This study has sought to show how suffering and wrongdoing are interwoven everywhere in human experience and biblical witness. Wrongdoing, moreover, takes many forms, from willful transgression to foolishness, collective or inherited sin, and even bad moral luck. In chapter 1 I argued that in the Hebrew Bible messiahs are envisaged as releasing God's people from both suffering and wrongdoing of all kinds, and that the New Testament inherits and reworks these traditions, showing Jesus Christ as addressing—challenging and healing—both wrongdoers and the suffering. In New Testament writings, wrongdoing is sometimes described as *apistia*—loss or failure of trust. The means of human beings' release from suffering and wrongdoing and restoration to their right relationship with God is everywhere called *pistis*—centrally trust, faithfulness, trustworthiness, and entrustedness.

Chapter 2 explored what it means not to have trust, and the difference it makes to be able to trust or have trust restored with the help of various academic disci-

Conclusion

plines that, in recent years, have worked extensively on the role of trust in different spheres of life. In particular it drew on studies of trust in conflict resolution, the restoration of survivors of trauma, and the social rehabilitation of ex-offenders. From all these spheres we heard testimony that when people cannot trust, they lose confidence in themselves and the world around them. They cease to be able to look forward, make plans, or hope for the future. They are liable to become either expressively angry or depressed and withdrawn. They are more likely either to reject relationships entirely or to abuse them. Trust is so important to human life that it can be called our "second nature." Neither societies nor individuals without trust can hold together, and for those who work with victims or perpetrators of conflict, abuse, or offending, nothing is more urgent than the restoration of trust. When individuals or societies can begin to learn or relearn trust—even if they begin with thin, limited, and fragile trust—they begin to be able to make relationships, to look forward and plan, and to (re-)create new societies and new realities in which they can live and thrive. They can begin to be whole, to be, internally and communally, at one.

New Testament writings attest to the vital role of trust and its relatives in bringing the whole of humanity, wrongdoing, and suffering as it is back to at-one-ment with God and so to wholeness and fullness of human life and hope. I have argued elsewhere that every part of the earthly life, suffering and death, resurrection, and exalted life of Jesus Christ helps to make at-one-ment through trust possible, but Jesus's suffering and death on the cross have always stood at the heart of Christians' understanding of how God restores humanity to its right relationship with Godself, so this study focuses on the cross.

Taking Paul as our starting point and drawing on other writings, chapter 3 explored how Jesus Christ is envisaged as trusting and trustworthy toward both God and humanity. This double relationship of trust enables Jesus to mediate between humanity and God and bring humanity back to trust in God. By his relationship of trust with God, Jesus shows humanity all that it means to live in trust. He allows himself to be taken and crucified because to avoid the consequences of his commitment to God and to other people would be to deny the person he is and the work he does. By refusing to break trust, even in suffering and death, Jesus not only reveals himself but acts as a firebreak in the spread of evil, disrupting the cycle of wrongdoing and suffering that alienates people from God. By the same token he reveals humanity to itself, as infinitely and inalienably precious to God. Nothing humanity can do will break God's therapeutic trust in it, stop God through Christ from reaching out to it, or render it incapable of responding to God.

The cross demonstrates the extremity of human evil, but God through Christ uses it to create a space in the chaos of the world, in which God, by grace, offers

CONCLUSION

trust to humanity for its at-one-ment. To meet God there, humanity must respond with its own step of trust, however thin, fragile, or provisional. As the cross holds Jesus, he holds his arms open to the rest of humanity and invites them to take that step of trust. Those who take the step will have to die spiritually to the world ruled by wrongdoing and pain to become part of a new reality—a new creation. To make the journey thinkable and possible, Jesus dies before them, so they can die with him, and he, in his exalted life, is with them as they travel.

For those who have yet to take the step of trust and for those who have been through death and are trying to live faithfully, Jesus is an example, and more than an example. His trust and trustworthiness, even in death, change what human beings understand as possible for them, and therefore what is possible for them. Because, however, the trust of Jesus's disciples is remembered as having been deeply damaged by his death—as ours so often is by the ongoing power of evil in our own world—the resurrection experiences and later revelations of many kinds are added as a grace to strengthen the fragility of our trust.

In the contemporary world, human beings have become sharply and often shamefully aware that we are indivisibly part of creation as a whole, and increasingly we accept that our place in creation is not simply to dominate it and use or abuse it as we choose. Theologians and biblical scholars have increasingly seen the rest of creation as capable of responding to God in many ways and also of suffering. Chapter 4 therefore asked whether other parts of creation could also be envisaged as moral subjects and potentially as doing wrong and needing atonement in their own right, and explored the growing body of research in animal and plant sciences that suggests that this may be the case. If so, I asked whether Jesus Christ could be imagined as living and dying in trust to restore the whole of creation to at-one-ment with God, and we traced various routes by which this might occur. One of these is that human beings, in imitation of Christ, might seek to mediate between Christ and the rest of creation by being more trusting and trustworthy toward the rest of creation and seeking creation's trust in response.

This theme takes us to the last chapter, which considered, first, Jesus Christ's involvement in all human situations of reconciliation and at-one-ment; second, the idea that repentance and forgiveness are made possible within an overarching relationship of trust; and third, human beings' entrustedness, by God and Christ, as individuals and groups with the responsibility of acting on Christ's behalf in the world. We saw some examples of how individuals and groups may mediate between other individuals and groups for their at-one-ment. I acknowledged, however, that being entrusted with this work is a responsibility, in which we are called to a high standard of trustworthiness, and that we can expect to be held to account for the way in which we carry it out. I also acknowledged that the ability

Conclusion

of churches, in particular, to do this work has been seriously damaged by the abuses of trust that have come to light in recent years, and that, in many cases, it will take time, work, and integrity for churches to repair their reputation and become able to do God's work of reconciliation again. If trust is to be restored in any context in this world, those who accept that they are entrusted with the work of at-one-ment must seek to be as trustworthy as Christ himself.

In this model of at-one-ment, the restoration of trust is the indispensable first step to the reconciliation of humanity with God, with itself, and with the rest of creation. To begin to trust is already to begin to seek healing for oneself and one's relationships. Even the beginnings of trust frame a space in which people can meet, communicate, and begin to understand each other and themselves better. Developing trust creates the conditions in which people may come to be able to tell the truth about themselves, to ask for forgiveness for their wrongdoings, and to offer forgiveness for their suffering. We have emphasized at several points that few people come to perfect trust all at once. Where people (or other beings) are damaged by experiences—some lasting years or generations—of suffering and wrongdoing, it may take years or generations for trust to grow and strengthen enough to enable full at-one-ment. In addition, trust may be possible in one environment of trust but not another, and it will not always involve direct contact between a wrongdoer and a sufferer. But God works with the complexity of space and the passage of time as much as with human flesh, blood, mind, and spirit.

This model does not show trust as restoring human beings to at-one-ment either unilaterally without their active involvement or necessarily all at once and once for all. It follows New Testament writings in seeing trust as a response to God's therapeutic outreach of trust through Christ, which receives healing, righteousness, or salvation as the starting point for an existence in trust with God that does not come to full fruition until the end time. In the meantime, the trust of created beings is well recognized by New Testament writings as imperfect: always liable to suffer from fear, doubt, discouragement, or skepticism and prone to waver and fail. New Testament writings, however, never suggest that, before the end time, imperfect trust is a deal-breaker between God and humanity; as long as we are trying to live and progress in trust, we can hope for salvation. In this respect, the "trust" model is somewhat different from other models of atonement, which make more of what is completed at the crucifixion or accomplished by the crucifixion and resurrection. Even models that most strongly affirm the efficacy of Christ's death, however, unless they are doubly predestinarian, accept that human beings must respond by putting their trust or faith in God and Christ. By making humanity's trust in response to God central to our model, I have argued that the

225

CONCLUSION

model both follows biblical witness and coheres with our experience of how trust works between created beings in many other spheres of life.

Trust, as we saw in the introduction, can be "three-place" (trust in someone for something) or "two-place" (part of a relationship that is its own justification). The trust that Christ restores between God and humanity is both. Through it, God seeks to save humanity (and perhaps the whole of creation), and humanity (perhaps the whole of creation) hopes to be saved. In it, humanity, perhaps all creation, lives to the fullest, at one with itself, with other beings, and with God, in a life that is ever more abundant and eternally renewed.

Works Cited

Allen, Jon G. *Trusting in Psychotherapy*. Washington, DC: American Psychiatric Publishing, 2021.

Alston, William P. "Belief, Acceptance, and Religious Faith." Pages 3–27 in *Faith, Freedom, and Rationality*. Edited by J. Jordan and Daniel Howard-Snyder. Lanham: Rowman & Littlefield, 1996.

Andrighetto, Luca, Samer Halabi, and Arie Nadler. "Fostering Trust and Forgiveness through the Acknowledgment of Others' Past Victimization." *Journal of Social and Political Psychology* 5 (2017): 651–64.

Aplin, Lucy M., Damien R. Farine, Julie Morand-Ferron, Andrew Cockburn, Alex Thornton, and Ben C. Sheldon. "Experimentally Induced Innovations Lead to Persistent Culture via Conformity in Wild Birds." *Nature* 518 (2015): 538–41.

Armstrong, Ruth. "Trusting the Untrustworthy: The Theology, Practice and Implications of Faith-Based Volunteers' Work with Ex-Prisoners." *Studies in Christian Ethics* 27 (2014): 299–317.

Asmussen, Ida Helen. "Mediation in Light of Modern Identity." Pages 133–43 in *Nordic Mediation Research*. Edited by Anna Nylund, Kaijus Ervasti, and Lin Adrian. Cham: Springer, 2018.

Attridge, Harold W. *The Epistle to the Hebrews*. Philadelphia: Fortress, 1989.

Audi, Robert. "Belief, Faith, and Acceptance." *Int. J. Philos. Relig.* 63 (2008): 87–102.

———. *Rationality and Religious Commitment*. Oxford: Oxford University Press, 2011.

Axelrod, R., and W. D. Hamilton. "The Evolution of Cooperation." *Science* 211 (1981): 1390–96.

Bachmann, Michael. "Paul, Israel, and the Gentiles: Hermeneutical and Exegetical Notes." Pages 72–105 in *Crosscurrents in Pauline Exegesis and the Study of Jewish-Christian Relations*. Edited by Reimund Bieringer and Didier Pollefeyt. London: Bloomsbury, 2012.

WORKS CITED

Baier, Annette C. "Trust and Antitrust." *Ethics* 96 (1986): 231–60.

Bänzinger, H. "Ecological, Morphological and Taxonomic Studies on Thailand's Fifth Species of Rafflesiaceae: *Rhizanthes zippelii* (Blume) Spach." *Natural History Bulletin of the Siam Society* 43 (1995): 337–65.

Barclay, John M. G. *Paul and the Gift*. Grand Rapids: Eerdmans, 2015.

Barclay, John M. G., and Simon Gathercole, eds. *Divine and Human Agency in Paul and His Cultural Environment*. New York: T&T Clark, 2007.

Baron, Reuben M. "Reconciliation, Trust, and Cooperation: Using Bottom-Up and Top-Down Strategies to Achieve Peace in the Israeli-Palestinian Conflict." Pages 275–98 in *The Social Psychology of Intergroup Reconciliation*. Edited by Arie Nadler, Thomas Malloy, and Jeffrey D. Fisher. Oxford: Oxford University Press, 2008.

Barr, James. *The Concept of Biblical Theology: An Old Testament Perspective*. London: SCM, 1999.

Barrett, C. K. *Acts of the Apostles: A Shorter Commentary*. London: T&T Clark, 2002.

———. *A Commentary on the First Epistle to the Corinthians*. London: A&C Black, 1968.

———. *A Critical and Exegetical Commentary on the Acts of the Apostles* (London: T&T Clark, 1994).

Barry, M. "The Mentor/Monitor Debate in Criminal Justice: What Works for Offenders." *British Journal of Social Work* 30 (2000): 575–95.

Barta, Zoltán, John M. McNamara, Dóra B. Huszár, and Michael Taborsky. "Cooperation among Non-Relatives Evolves by State-Dependent Generalized Reciprocity." *Proc. R. Soc. Lond. B* (2011): 843–48.

Barth, Karl. *Church Dogmatics*. Vol. 3.1, *The Doctrine of Creation, Part I*. Translated by G. M. Bromiley. Edinburgh: T&T Clark, 1986.

Bash, Anthony. *Ambassadors for Christ: An Exploration of Ambassadorial Language in the New Testament*. Tübingen: Mohr Siebeck, 1997.

———. *Forgiveness and Christian Ethics*. Cambridge: Cambridge University Press, 2009.

Bauckham, R. J. *Bible and Ecology: Rediscovering the Community of Creation*. London: Darton, Longman & Todd, 2009.

———. *Living with Other Creatures: Green Exegesis and Theology*. Bletchley: Paternoster, 2012.

———. "The Parting of the Ways: What Really Happened and Why?" *Studia Theologica* 47 (1993): 135–51.

Baxter, Wayne. *Missing Matthew's Political Messiah: A Closer Look at His Birth and Infancy Narratives*. Philadelphia: Pennsylvania University Press, 2017.

Beer, Jennifer E., Caroline C. Packard, Eileen Stief, and Elizabeth Elwood Gates. *The Mediator's Handbook*. 4th rev. ed. Gabriola: New Society, 2012.

Beiler, K. J., Suzanne W. Simard, Sheri A. Maxwell, and Annette M. Kretzer. "Architecture of the Wood-Wide Web: Rhizopogon Spp. Genets Link Multiple Douglas-Fir Cohorts." *New Phytologist* 185 (2009): 543–53.

Beisner, Brianne A., Darcy L. Hannibal, Kelly R. Finn, Hsieh Fushing, and Brenda McCowan. "Social Power, Conflict Policing, and Role of Subordination Signals in Rhesus Macaque Society." *American Journal of Physical Anthropology* 160 (2016): 102–12.

Bekoff, Marc, and Jessica Pierce. *Wild Justice: The Moral Lives of Animals.* Chicago: Chicago University Press, 2009.

Bellinger, W. H., Jr. "The Psalms, Covenant, and the Persian Period." Pages 309–21 in *Covenant in the Persian Period: From Genesis to Chronicles.* Edited by Richard J. Bautch and Gary N. Knoppers. Philadelphia: Pennsylvania University Press, 2015.

Belser, Julia Watts. "Violence, Disability, and the Politics of Healing." *J. Disabil. Relig.* 19 (2015): 177–97.

Belser, Julia Watts, and Melanie S. Morrison. "What No Longer Serves Us: Resisting Anti-Ableism and Anti-Judaism in New Testament Healing Narratives." *Journal of Feminist Studies in Religion* 27 (2011): 153–70.

Bennett, Jane. *Vibrant Matter: A Political Ecology of Things.* Durham: Duke University Press, 2010.

Benz-Schwartzburg, Judith, and Andrew Knight. "Cognitive Relatives and Yet Moral Strangers?" *Journal of Animal Ethics* 1 (2011): 9–36.

Bertschmann, Dorothea H. "Suffering, Sin, and Death in Paul." Pages 3–22 in *Suffering and the Christian Life.* Edited by Karen Kilby and Rachel Davies. London: T&T Clark, 2020.

Betz, Hans Dieter. *Galatians: A Commentary on Paul's Letter to the Churches in Galatia.* Philadelphia: Fortress, 1979.

———. *Nachfolge und Nachahmung Jesu Christi im Neuen Testament.* Tübingen: Mohr Siebeck, 1967.

———. *The Sermon on the Mount.* Minneapolis: Fortress, 1995.

Bird, Michael. "Salvation in Paul's Judaism." Pages 15–40 in *Crosscurrents in Pauline Exegesis and the Study of Jewish-Christian Relations.* Edited by Reimund Bieringer and Didier Pollefeyt. London: Bloomsbury, 2012.

Boccaccini, Gabriele. *Paul's Three Paths to Salvation.* Grand Rapids: Eerdmans, 2020.

Bockmuehl, Markus. *A Commentary on the Epistle to the Philippians.* London: A&C Black, 1997.

———. "The Personal Presence of Jesus in the Writings of Paul." *SJT* 70 (2017): 39–60.

Bockmuehl, Markus, and James Carleton Paget, eds. *Redemption and Resistance: The Messianic Hopes of Jews and Christians in Antiquity.* London: T&T Clark, 2009.

WORKS CITED

Boer, Martinus C. de. "Paul and Jewish Apocalyptic Eschatology." Pages 169–90 in *Apocalyptic and the New Testament: Essays in Honor of J. Louis Martyn*. Edited by Joel Marcus and Martin L. Soards. Sheffield: JSOT Press, 1989.

Boesch, Christopher. "Teaching among Wild Chimpanzees." *Anim. Behav.* 41 (1991): 530–32.

Bolt, P. "The Faith of Jesus Christ in the Synoptic Gospels." Pages 209–22 in *The Faith of Jesus Christ: Exegetical, Biblical, and Theological Studies*. Edited by Michael F. Bird and Preston M. Sprinkle. Milton Keynes: Paternoster, 2009.

Bos, Ruud van den, Jolle W. Jolles, and Judith R. Homberg. "Social Modulation of Decision-Making: A Cross-Species Review." *Frontiers in Human Neuroscience* 7 (2013): 1–16.

Botner, Max. *Jesus Christ as the Son of David in the Gospel of Mark*. Cambridge: Cambridge University Press, 2019.

Bowes, Kimberley, ed. *The Roman Peasant Project 2009–2014: Excavating the Roman Poor*. Philadelphia: University of Pennsylvania Press, 2020.

Bowling, Daniel. "Bringing Peace into the Room: The Personal Qualities of the Mediator and Their Impact on the Mediation." Pages 13–47 in *Bringing Peace into the Room: How the Personal Qualities of the Mediator Impact the Process of Conflict Resolution*. Edited by Daniel Bowling and David Hoffman. San Francisco: Jossey-Bass, 2003.

Bowyer, Timothy James. *Beyond Suffering and Reparation: The Aftermath of Political Violence in the Peruvian Andes*. New York: Springer, 2018.

Boyce, I., G. Hunder, and M. Hough. *St. Giles Trust Peer Advice Project: An Evaluation*. London: St. Giles Trust, 2009.

Boyd, Brian. "The Evolution of Stories: From Mimesis to Language, From Fact to Fiction." *WIREs Cognitive Science* 9 (2018): 1–16.

Breytenbach, Cilliers. "'Christus starb für uns': Zur Tradition und paulinischen Rezeption der sogennanten 'Sterbeformeln'." Pages 95–126 in *Grace, Reconciliation, Concord: The Death of Christ in Graeco-Roman Metaphors*. Leiden: Brill, 2010.

———. "The 'For Us' Phrases in Pauline Soteriology: Considering Their Background and Use." Pages 59–81 in *Grace, Reconciliation, Concord: The Death of Christ in Graeco-Roman Metaphors*. Leiden: Brill, 2010.

———. "Salvation of the Reconciled." Pages 171–86 in *Grace, Reconciliation, Concord: The Death of Christ in Graeco-Roman Metaphors*. Leiden: Brill, 2010.

———. "The Septuagint Version of Isaiah 53 and the Early Christian Formula 'He Was Delivered for Our Trespasses'." Pages 83–94 in *Grace, Reconciliation, Concord: The Death of Christ in Graeco-Roman Metaphors*. Leiden: Brill, 2010.

———. "'Wie geschrieben ist' und das Leiden des Christus: Die theologische Leistung des Markus." Pages 358–73 in *The Gospel according to Mark as Episodic Narrative*. Leiden: Brill, 2020.

Bridges, Jerry. *Trusting God.* Colorado Springs: NavPress, 2016.

Brosnan, Sarah F., and Frans B. M. de Waal. "Monkeys Reject Unequal Pay." *Nature* 435 (2003): 297–99.

Brosnan, Sarah F., Hillary C. Schiff, and Frans B. M. de Waal. "Tolerance for Inequity May Increase with Social Closeness in Chimpanzees." *Proc. R. Soc. Lond. B* 272 (2005): 253–58.

Brosnan, Sarah F., Catherine Talbot, Megan Ahlgen, Susan P. Lambeth, and Steven J. Schapiro. "Mechanisms Underlying Responses to Inequitable Outcomes in Chimpanzees, Pan Troglodytes." *Anim. Behav.* 79 (2010): 1229–37.

Brothers, Doris. *Falling Backwards: An Exploration of Trust and Self-Experience.* New York: Norton, 1995.

Brown, Joanne Carlson. "Divine Child Abuse?" *Daughters of Sarah* 18 (1992): 24–28.

Brown, Joanne Carlson, and Rebecca Parker. "For So God Loved the World?" Pages 1–30 in *Christianity, Patriarchy, and Abuse: A Feminist Critique*. Edited by Joanne Carlson Brown and Carole R. Bohn. New York: Pilgrim: 1989.

Brown, M. Anne. "The Body in the Emergence of Trust." *Ethnopolitics* 19 (2020): 209–27.

Brown, Raymond E. AB 29. *The Gospel according to John I–XII*. New York: Doubleday, 1966.

Buck, Gillian. "The Core Conditions of Peer Mentoring." *Criminology and Criminal Justice* 18 (2017): 190–206.

———. "'I Wanted to Feel the Way They Did': Mimesis as a Situational Dynamic of Peer Mentoring by Ex-Offenders." *Deviant Behavior* 38 (2017): 1027–41.

Buck, Jennifer. "Feminist Philosophical Theology of Atonement." *Feminist Theology* 28 (2020): 239–50.

Buck, Nicole M., Ellie P. E. Leenaars, Paul M. G. Emmelkamp, and Hjalmar J. C. van Marle. "Explaining the Relationship between Insecure Attachment and Partner Abuse: The Role of Personality Characteristics." *Journal of Interpersonal Violence* 27 (2012): 3149–70.

Buford, Thomas O. *Trust, Our Second Nature: Crisis, Reconciliation, and the Personal.* Washington, DC: Lexington, 2009.

Burkart, Judith, Ernst Fehr, Charles Efferson, and Carel P. van Schaik. "Other-Regarding Preferences in a Non-Human Primate: Common Marmosets Provision Food Altruistically." *PNAS* 104 (2007): 19762–66.

Burns, Elizabeth. "Must Theists Believe in a Personal God?" *Think* 8 (2009): 77–86.

Büssing, Arndt, Klaus Baumann, and Janusz Surykiewicz. "Loss of Faith and Decrease in Trust in a Higher Source during Covid-19 in Germany." *Journal of Religion and Health* 61 (2022): 741–66.

WORKS CITED

Byrne, Brendan. "Jesus as Messiah in the Gospel of Luke: Discerning a Pattern of Correction." *CBQ* 65 (2003): 80–95.

Byrne, Richard W., and Lucy A. Bates. "Primate Social Cognition: Uniquely Primate, Uniquely Social, or Just Unique?" *Neuron* 65 (2010): 815–30.

Calloway, Jamall A. "The Purpose of Evil Was to Survive It: Black and Womanist Rejecting the Cross for Salvation." *Feminist Theology* 30 (2021): 67–84.

Campbell, Douglas A. *The Deliverance of God: An Apocalyptic Rereading of Justification in Paul.* Grand Rapids: Eerdmans, 2012.

———. "Reconciliation in Paul: The Gospel of Negation and Transcendence in Galatians 3:28." Pages 39–65 in *The Theology of Reconciliation.* Edited by Colin E. Gunton. London: T&T Clark, 2003.

Cannon, Katie. *Black Womanist Ethics.* Atlanta: Scholars Press, 1988.

Capper, Brian J. "The New Covenant in Southern Palestine at the Arrest of Jesus." Pages 90–116 in *The Dead Sea Scrolls as Background to Postbiblical Judaism and Early Christianity.* Edited by James R. Davila. Leiden: Brill, 2003.

Carney, J. J. "A Generation after Genocide: Catholic Reconciliation in Rwanda." *TS* 76 (2015): 785–812.

Casas-Casas, Andrés, Nathalie Mendez, and Juan Frederico Pino. "Trust and Prospective Reconciliation: Evidence from a Protracted Armed Conflict." *Journal of Peacebuilding and Development* 15 (2020): 298–315.

Castillo, Daniel P. "Integral Ecology as a Liberationist Concept." *TS* 77 (2016): 353–76.

Cataldo, Lisa M. "I Know That My Redeemer Lives: Relational Perspectives on Trauma, Dissociation, and Faith." *Pastoral Psychology* 62 (2013): 791–804.

Chavez-Segura, Alejandro. "Can Truth Reconcile a Nation? Truth and Reconciliation Commissions in Argentina and Chile: Lessons for Mexico." *Latin American Policy* 6 (2015): 226–39.

Chester, Andrew. *Messiah and Exaltation: Jewish Messianic and Visionary Traditions and New Testament Christology.* Tübingen: Mohr Siebeck, 2007.

Chike, Chigor. "Black Christology for the Twenty-First Century." *Black Theology* 8 (2010): 357–78.

Chow, Rey. "'I Insist on the Christian Dimension': Forgiveness . . . and the Outside of the Human." *Differences: A Journal of Feminist Cultural Studies* 20 (2009): 225–49.

Church, Russell. "Emotional Reactions of Rats to the Pain of Others." *Journal of Comparative and Physiological Psychology* 52 (1959): 132–34.

Clark, Janine Natalya. "Reflections on Trust and Reconciliation: A Case Study of a Central Bosnian Village." *International Journal of Human Rights* 16 (2012): 239–56.

Clay, Zanna, and Frans B. M. de Waal. "Bonobos Respond to Distress in Others: Consolation Across the Age Spectrum." *PLoS ONE* 8 (2013): art. e55206.

Collins, John J. "Pre-Christian Jewish Messianism: An Overview." Pages 1–20 in *The*

Messiah in Early Judaism and Christianity. Edited by Magnus Zetterholm. Minneapolis: Fortress, 2007.

Collins, Raymond F. *First Corinthians*. Collegeville: Liturgical, 1999.

Cone, James H. *A Black Theology of Liberation*. Philadelphia: Lippincott, 1970.

———. *The Cross and the Lynching Tree*. Maryknoll: Orbis, 2011.

Constantineanu, Corneliu. "Pauline Scholarship on Reconciliation: A Review of the Related Literature." Pages 245–342 in *The Social Significance of Reconciliation in Paul's Theology: Narrative Readings in Romans*. London: Bloomsbury, 2010.

Cools, Annemieke K. A., Alain J.-M. van Hout, and Mark H. J. Nelissen. "Canine Reconciliation and Third-Party-Initiated Postconflict Affiliation: Do Peacemaking Social Mechanisms in Dogs Rival Those of Higher Primates?" *Ethology* 114 (2008): 53–63.

Cordoni, Giada, Elizabetta Palagi, and Silvana Borgognini. "Reconciliation and Consolation in Captive Western Gorillas." *International Journal of Primatology* 27 (2006): 1365–82.

Coulson, John R. *The Righteous Judgment of God: Aspects of Judgment in Paul's Letters*. Eugene: Wipf & Stock, 2017.

Cousins, Patrick. "Roger Haight's Theology of the Cross." *Heythrop Journal* 58 (2017): 78–90.

Cover, Robin C., and E. P. Sanders. "Sin." Pages 6:31–47 in *Anchor Yale Bible Dictionary*. Edited by David Noel Freeman. 6 vols. New Haven: Yale University Press, 1992.

Craffert, Pieter D. "I 'Witnessed the Raising of the Dead': Resurrection Accounts in a Neuroanthropological Perspective." *Neotestamentica* 45 (2018): 1–28.

Craig, William Lane. *Atonement and the Death of Christ: An Exegetical, Historical, and Philosophical Exploration*. Waco: Baylor University Press, 2020.

Cranfield, C. R. *A Critical and Exegetical Commentary on the Epistle to the Romans*. 2 vols. 6th ed. Edinburgh: T&T Clark, 1975.

Creaney, Sean. "Children's Voices—Are We Listening? Progressing Peer Mentoring in the Youth Justice System." *Child Care in Practice* 26 (2020): 22–37.

Crisp, Oliver. *Approaches to the Atonement: The Reconciling Work of Christ*. Downers Grove: InterVarsity, 2020.

———. "Moral Exemplarism and Atonement." *SJT* 73 (2020): 137–49.

Croasmun, Matthew. *The Emergence of Sin: The Cosmic Tyrant in Romans*. New York: Oxford University Press, 2017.

Davies, W. D., and Dale C. Allison. *A Critical and Exegetical Commentary on the Gospel according to Saint Matthew*. 3 vols. London: Bloomsbury, 1988–1997.

Deane-Drummond, Celia. "Shadow Sophia in Christological Perspective: The Evolution of Sin and the Redemption of Nature." *Theology and Science* 6 (2008): 13–32.

WORKS CITED

Deaver, Katie M. "Gentle Strength: Reclaiming Atonement Theory for Survivors of Abuse." PhD diss., Lutheran School of Theology at Chicago, 2017.

DeGrazia, David. *Taking Animals Seriously: Mental Life and Moral Status.* Cambridge: Cambridge University Press, 1996.

Dionysio, F. "Selfish and Spiteful Behavior through Parasites and Pathogens." *Evolutionary Ecology Research* 9 (2007): 1199–210.

Dognin, P.-D. "La foi du Christ dans la théologie de Saint Paul." *Revue des sciences philosophiques et théologiques* 89 (2005): 713–28.

Domenicucci, Jacopo, and Richard Holton. "Trust as a Two-Place Relation." Pages 149–60 in *The Philosophy of Trust.* Edited by Paul Faulkner and Thomas W. Simpson. Oxford: Oxford University Press, 2017.

Doorn, Gerrit Sander van, and Michael Taborsky. "The Evolution of Generalized Reciprocity on Social Interraction Networks." *Evolution* 66 (2011): 651–64.

Downing, Gerald. "Reconciliation: Politics and Theology." *Modern Believing* 58 (2017): 3–15.

Downs, David J., and Benjamin J. Lappenga. *The Faithfulness of the Exalted Christ: Pistis and the Exalted Lord in the Pauline Letters.* Waco: Baylor University Press, 2019.

Drewermann, Eugen. *Vertrauen kann man nur auf Gott.* Oberursel: Publik-Forum, 2020.

Dunn, James D. G. *Baptism in the Holy Spirit: A Re-Examination of the New Testament Teaching on the Gift of the Spirit in Relation to Pentecostalism Today.* London: SCM, 1975.

———. *The Christ and the Spirit: Collected Essays of James D. G. Dunn.* 2 vols. Grand Rapids: Eerdmans, 1998.

Duyndam, Joachim. "Hermeneutics of Imitation: A Philosophical Approach to Sainthood and Exemplariness." Pages 7–21 in *Saints and Role Models in Judaism and Christianity.* Edited by Marcel Poorthuis and Joshua Schwarz. Leiden: Brill, 2004.

Easter, Matthew C. "The *Pistis Christou* Debate: Main Arguments and Responses in Summary." *CBR* 9 (2010): 33–47.

Eastman, Susan Grove. "The 'Empire of Illusion': Sin, Evil, and Good News in Romans." Pages 153–71 in *Oneself in Another: Participation and Personhood in Pauline Theology.* Eugene: Wipf & Stock, 2023.

———. "The Lord's Prayer." Pages 79–90 in *Prayer: Christian and Muslim Perspectives.* Edited by David Marshall and Lucinda Mosher. Washington, DC: Georgetown University Press, 2013.

Ebeling, Gerhard. *Word and Faith.* London: SCM, 1963.

Eberhart, Christian A. "Atonement." Pages 3–20 in *Atonement: Jewish and Christian Origins.* Edited by Max Botner, Justin Harrison Duff, and Simon Dürr. Grand Rapids: Eerdmans, 2020.

Works Cited

Ebert, Andreas, Meike Kolb, Jörg Heller, Marc-Andreas Edel, Patrik Roser, and Martin Brüne. "Modulation of Interpersonal Trust in Borderline Personality Disorder by Intranasal Oxytocin and Childhood Trauma." *Social Neuroscience* 8 (2013): 305–13.

Edel, May, and Abraham Edel. *Anthropology and Ethics.* Springfield: Thomas, 1959.

Edgar, Joane L., John C. Low, Elizabeth S. Paul, and Christine J. Nichol. "Avian Maternal Response to Chick Distress." *Proc. R. Soc. Lond. B* (2011): 3129–34.

Edwards, Denise. "Why Is God Doing This? Suffering, the Universe, and Christian Eschatology." Pages 247–66 in *Physics and Cosmology: Scientific Perspectives on the Problem of Evil in Nature.* Edited by Robert J. Russell, Nancey Murphy, and William Stoeger. Berkeley: CTNS; Vatican City: Vatican Observatory, 2007.

Eiesland, Nancy L. *The Disabled God: Toward a Liberatory Theology of Disability.* Nashville: Abingdon, 1994.

Ellington, Dustin. "The Impulse toward the Disadvantaged in the Gospel Preached by Paul." *Scriptura* 115 (2016): 1–13.

Enright, Robert. "Is There a Difference between Forgiving and 'Moving On'?" *The Forgiving Life* (blog), *Psychology Today,* September 17, 2018. https://www.psycholo gytoday.com/us/blog/the-forgiving-life/201809/is-there-difference-between -forgiving-and-moving.

Esparza, Diego, Valerie Martinez, Regina Branton, Kimi King, and James Meernik. "Violence, Trust, and Public Support for the Colombian Peace Agreement." *Social Science Quarterly* 101 (2020): 1236–54.

Evans, James H. *We Have Been Believers: An African-American Systematic Theology.* 2nd ed. Minneapolis: Fortress, 2012.

Fee, Gordon D. *God's Empowering Presence: The Holy Spirit in the Letters of Paul.* Peabody: Hendrickson, 1994.

Fiddes, Paul S. *Past Event and Present Salvation.* London: Darton, Longman & Todd, 1989.

Filippidou, Anastasia, and Thomas O'Brien. "Trust and Distrust in the Resolution of Protracted Social Conflicts: The Case of Colombia." *Behavioral Sciences of Terrorism and Political Aggression* 14 (2022): 1–21.

Fitzpatrick, Simon. "Animal Morality: What Is the Debate About?" *Biology and Philosophy* 32 (2017): 1151–83.

Flack, Jessica C., Frans B. M. de Waal, and David C. Krakauer. "Social Structure, Robustness, and Policing Cost in a Cognitively Sophisticated Society." *American Naturalist* 165 (2005): E126–E139.

Flack, Jessica C., Michelle Girvan, Frans B. M. de Waal, and David C. Krakauer. "Policing Stabilizes Construction of Social Niches in Primates." *Nature* 439 (2006): 426–29.

WORKS CITED

Fletcher-Louis, Crispin. "The High Priest in Ben Sira 50." Pages 89–111 in *Atonement: Jewish and Christian Origins*. Edited by Max Botner, Justin Harrison Duff, and Simon Dürr. Grand Rapids: Eerdmans, 2020.

Forber, Patrick, and Rory Smead. "The Evolution of Fairness through Spite." *Proc. R. Soc. Lond. B* 281 (2014): art. 20132439.

Forrest, Ian. *The Trustworthy Men: How Faith and Inequality Made the Medieval Church*. Princeton: Princeton University Press, 2018.

Foster, K. R., T. Wenseleers, and F. L. W. Ratnieks. "Spite: Hamilton's Unproven Theory." *Annales Zoologici Fennici* 38 (2001): 229–38.

Framarin, Christopher G. "The Moral Standing of Animals and Plants in the *Manusmrti*." *Philosophy East and West* 64 (2014): 192–217.

Fraser, Orlaith N., Daniel Stahl, and Filippo Aureli. "Stress Reduction through Consolation in Chimpanzees." *PNAS* 105 (2008): 8557–62.

Fraser, Orlaith N., and Thomas Bugnyar. "Do Ravens Show Consolation? Responses to Distressed Others." *PLoS ONE* 5 (2010): art. e10605.

———. "Ravens Reconcile after Aggressive Conflicts with Valuable Partners." *PLoS ONE* 6 (2011): art. e18118.

Frederiksen, Morten. "Relational Trust: Outline of a Bourdieusian Theory of Interpersonal Trust." *J. Trust Res.* 4 (2014): 167–92.

Fried, Lisbeth. "Cyrus the Messiah? The Historical Background to Isaiah 45:1." *Harvard Theological Review* 95 (2002): 373–93.

Fröhlich Ida, and Erkki Koskenniemi, eds. *Evil and the Devil*. London: T&T Clark, 2013.

Frost-Arnold, Karen. "The Cognitive Attitude of Rational Trust." *Synthese* 191 (2014): 1957–74.

Furnish, Victor Paul. *Jesus according to Paul*. Cambridge: Cambridge University Press, 1993.

Gallagher, Michael Paul. "Truth and Trust: Pierangelo Sequeri's Theology of Faith." *Irish Theological Quarterly* 73 (2008): 3–31.

Gardner, Andy, Ian C. W. Hardy, Peter D. Taylor, and Stuart A. West. "Spiteful Soldiers and Sex Ratio Conflict in Polyembryonic Parasitoid Wasps." *American Naturalist* 169 (2007): 519–33.

Gariépy, Jean-François, Karli M. Watson, Emily Du, Diana L. Xie, Joshua Erb, Dianna Amasino, and Michael L. Platt. "Social Learning in Humans and Other Animals." *Frontiers in Neuroscience* 8 (2014): 1–13.

Gathercole, Simon. "'Sins' in Paul." *New Testament Studies* 64 (2018): 143–61.

Gaventa, Beverly Roberts, ed. *Apocalyptic Paul: Cosmos and Anthropos in Romans 5–8*. Waco: Baylor University Press, 2013.

———. "The Cosmic Power of Sin in Paul's Letter to the Romans: Toward a Widescreen Edition." *Int* 58 (2004): 229–40.

Works Cited

Gfrerer, Natassja, and Michal Taborsky. "Working Dogs Cooperate among Each Other by Generalised Reciprocity." *Biology Letters* 14 (2018): 1–6.

Giannini, Heidi Chamberlin. "Grounds for Forgiveness: A Christian Argument for Universal, Unconditional Forgiveness." *Journal of Religious Ethics* 45 (2017): 58–82.

Gillespie, Nicole. "Trust Dynamics and Repair: An Interview with Roy Lewicki." *J. Trust Res.* 7 (2017): 204–19.

Gilligan, Carol. *In a Different Voice: Psychological Theory and Women's Development.* Cambridge: Harvard University Press, 1982.

Gobyn, Robyn L., and Jennifer J. Freyd. "The Impact of Betrayal Trauma on the Tendency to Trust." *Psychol. Trauma* 6 (2014): 505–11.

Godfrey, Joseph J. *Trust of People, Words and God: A Route for Philosophy of Religion.* South Bend: University of Notre Dame Press, 2012.

Gorman, Michael. *The Death of the Messiah and the Birth of the New Covenant: A (Not So) New Model of the Atonement.* Eugene: Cascade, 2014.

Gottlieb, Roger S., ed. *The Oxford Handbook of Religion and Ecology.* Oxford: Oxford University Press, 2006.

Graf, Fritz. "Lesser Mysteries—Not Less Mysterious." Pages 241–62 in *Greek Mysteries: The Archaeology and Ritual of Ancient Greek Secret Cults.* Edited by M. Cosmopoulos. London: Routledge, 2003.

Granados Rojas, Juan Manuel. *La teologia de la reconciliation en las cartas de san Pablo.* Estella: Verbo Divino, 2016.

Grasso, Kevin. "A Linguistic Analysis of *Pistis Christou*: The Case for the Third View." *JSNT* 43 (2020): 108–44.

Grayson, Hannah. "A Place for Individuals: Positive Growth in Rwanda." *Eastern African Literary and Cultural Studies* 3 (2017): 107–30.

Greene, James T. "Altruistic Behavior in the Albino Rat." *Psychonomic Science* 14 (1969): 47–48.

Guasto, Gianni. "Trauma and the Loss of Basic Trust." *International Forum of Psychoanalysis* 23 (2014): 44–49.

Guglielmucci, Fanny, Isabella G. Franzoi, Chiara P. Barbasio, Francesca V. Borgogno, and Antonella Granieri. "Helping Traumatized People Survive: A Psychoanalytic Intervention in a Contaminated Site." *Front. Psychol.* 5 (2014): art. 1419.

Guinet, C., and J. Bouvier. "Development of Intentional Stranding Hunting Techniques in Killer Whale (*Orcinus Orca*) Calves at Crozet Archipelago." *Canadian Journal of Zoology* 73 (1995): 27–33.

Gunton, Colin E., ed. *The Theology of Reconciliation.* London: T&T Clark, 2003.

Gutiérrez, Gustavo. *A Theology of Liberation.* Maryknoll: Orbis, 1973.

Gutmundsdottir, Arnfridur. *Meeting God on the Cross: Feminist Christologies and the Theology of the Cross.* Oxford: Oxford University Press, 2010.

WORKS CITED

Haight, Roger. *The Future of Christology*. New York: Continuum, 2005.

Hall, Douglas John. "Rethinking Christ." Pages 167–87 in *Antisemitism and the Foundations of Christianity*. Edited by Alan T. Davies, New York: Paulist, 1979.

Hamilton, W. D. "Selfish and Spiteful Behavior in an Evolutionary Model." *Nature* 228 (1970): 218–20.

Hare, John. "Forgiveness, Justification, and Reconciliation." Pages 77–96 in *The Wisdom of the Christian Faith*. Edited by P. Moses and M. McFall. Cambridge: Cambridge University Press, 2012.

Härle, Wilfried, and Reiner Preul. *Glaube*. Marburg: Elwert, 1992.

Harris, Mark. "'The Trees of the Field Shall Clap Their Hands' (Isaiah 55:12): What Does It Mean to Say That a Tree Praises God?" Pages 287–304 in *Knowing Creation: Perspectives from Theology, Philosophy, and Science*. Edited by Andrew B. Torrance and Thomas H. McCall. Grand Rapids: Zondervan, 2018.

Harvey, Graham. *Animism: Respecting the Living World*. New York: Columbia University Press, 2006.

Haught, John. *Deeper than Darwin: The Prospect for Evolution in the Age of Evolution*. Boulder: Westview, 2003.

Hauser, Alan J. "Genesis 2–3: The Theme of Intimacy and Alienation." Pages 20–36 in *Art and Meaning: Rhetoric in Biblical Literature*. Edited by Alan J. Hauser, David M. Gunn, and David J. A. Clines. London: T&T Clark, 1982.

Hawley, Katherine. *Trust: A Very Short Introduction*. Oxford: Oxford University Press, 2012.

Hays, Richard. *The Faith of Jesus Christ: The Narrative Substructure of Galatians 3:1–4:11*. 2nd ed. Grand Rapids: Eerdmans, 2002.

———. *First Corinthians*. Louisville: Knox, 1997.

Heath, Jane. "*Imitatio Christi* and Violence to the Self." *J. Disabil. Relig.* 27 (2023): 247–83.

Hegedus, Timothy. "Douglas John Hall's Contextual Theology of the Cross." *Consensus* 15 (1989): 21–37.

Held, Virginia. *The Ethics of Care*. Oxford: Oxford University Press, 2006.

Hewitt, J. Thomas. *Messiah and Scripture: Paul's "in Christ" Idiom in Its Ancient Jewish Context*. Tübingen: Mohr Siebeck, 2020.

Hewstone, Miles, Jared B. Kenworthy, Ed Cairns, Nicole Tausch, Joane Hughes, Tania Tam, Alberto Voci, Ulrich von Hecker, and Catherine Pinder. "Stepping Stones to Reconciliation in Northern Ireland: Intergroup Contact, Forgiveness, and Trust." Pages 199–225 in *The Social Psychology of Intergroup Reconciliation*. Edited by Arie Nadler, Thomas Malloy, and Jeffrey D. Fisher. Oxford: Oxford University Press, 2008.

Hick, John. *The Metaphor of God Incarnate*. 2nd ed. Louisville: Westminster John Knox, 1993.

Works Cited

Hofius, Otfried. "Erwägungen zur Gestalt und Herkunft des paulinischen Versöhnungsgedankens." *Zeitschrift für Theologie und Kirche* 77 (1980): 186–99.

Holtzen, William Curtis. *The God Who Trusts: A Relational Theology of Divine Faith, Hope, and Love.* Downers Grove: IVP Academic, 2019.

Hook, Joshua N., Daryl R. Van Tongeren, Don E. Davis, Peter C. Hill, M. Elizabeth Lewis Hall, Daniel J. McKaughan, and Daniel Howard-Snyder. "Trust in God: An Evaluative Review of the Research Literature and Research Proposal." *Ment. Health Relig. Cult.* 24 (2021): 745–63.

Horbury, William. *Jewish Messianism and the Cult of Christ.* London: SCM, 1998.

Hornsey, Matthew J., and Michael J. A. Wohl. "We Are Sorry: Intergroup Apologies and Their Tenuous Link with Intergroup Forgiveness." *European Review of Social Psychology* 24 (2013): 1–31.

Horrell, David G. *The Bible and the Environment: Towards A Critical Biblical Theology.* London: Equinox, 2010.

———. "A New Perspective on Paul? Rereading Paul in a Time of Ecological Crisis." *JSNT* 33 (2010): 3–30.

Horsburgh, H. J. N. "The Ethics of Trust." *Philosophical Quarterly* 10 (1960): 343–54.

Houts, Margo G. "Atonement and Abuse: An Alternative View." *Daughters of Sarah* 18 (1992): 29–32.

Hultgren, Arland J. *Christ and His Benefits: Christology and Redemption in the New Testament.* Philadelphia: Fortress, 1987.

Ikkatai, Yuko, Shigeru Watanabe, and Ei-Ichi Izawa. "Reconciliation and Third-Party Affiliation in Pair-Bond Budgerigars (*Melopsittacus Undulatus*)." *Behaviour* 153 (2016): 1173–93.

Jantsch, Torsten. *Jesus, der Retter: Die Soteriologie des lukanischen Doppelwerks.* Tübingen: Mohr Siebeck, 2017.

Jenkins, Willis, and Ernst M. Conradie, eds. "Ecology and Christian Soteriology." Special issue of *Worldviews* 14 (2010).

Jim, T. S. F. *Saviour Gods and Sōtēria in Ancient Greece.* Oxford: Oxford University Press, 2021.

Joerstad, Mari. *The Hebrew Bible and Environmental Ethics: Humans, Non-Humans, and the Living Landscape.* Cambridge: Cambridge University Press, 2019.

Johnson, Elizabeth. *She Who Is: The Mystery of God in Feminist Theological Discourse.* New York: Crossroad, 1992.

Johnson, Steven D., and Florian P. Schiestl. *Floral Mimicry.* Oxford: Oxford University Press, 2016.

Jones, Karen. "But I Was Counting on You!" Pages 90–107 in *The Philosophy of Trust.* Edited by Paul Faulkner and Thomas W. Simpson. Oxford: Oxford University Press, 2017.

WORKS CITED

Jong, Jeroen de, René Schalk, and Marcel Croon. "The Role of Trust in Secure and Insecure Employment Situations: A Multiple-Group Analysis." *Economic and Industrial Democracy* 30 (2009): 510–38.

Kallhoff, Angela, Marcello di Paola, and Maria Schorgenhumer, eds. *Plant Ethics: Concepts and Applications.* London: Routledge, 2018.

Kanyangara, P., B. Rimé, P. Philippot, and V. Yzerbyt. "Collective Rituals, Emotional Climate and Intergroup Perception: Participation in 'Gacaca' Tribunals and Assimilation of the Rwandan Genocide." *Journal of Social Issues* 63 (2007): 387–403.

Kao, Jennifer C., Adam Chuong, Madhavi K. Reddy, Robyn L. Gobin, Caron Zlotnick, and Jennifer E. Johnson. "Associations between Past Trauma, Current Social Support, and Loneliness in Incarcerated Populations." *Health and Justice* 2 (2014): 1–10.

Kappmeier, Mariska, Bushra Guenoun, and Kathyrn H. Fahey. "Conceptualizing Trust between Groups: An Empirical Validation of the Five-Dimensional Intergroup Trust Model." *Peace Confl.* 29 (2021): 90–95.

Käsemann, Ernst. *New Testament Questions of Today.* London: SCM, 1969.

———. "Some Thoughts on the Theme 'The Doctrine of Reconciliation' in the New Testament." Pages 49–64 in *The Future of Our Religious Past: Essays in Honour of Rudolf Bultmann.* Edited by James A. Robinson. London: SCM, 1971.

Katarzynska, Agnieszka. "The Idea of Dialogue, Trust and Reconciliation in the Pilgrimage of Trust on Earth." *Journal for Perspectives of Economic, Political, and Social Integration* 22 (2016): 225–43.

Katongole, Emmanuel. "The Gospel as Politics in Africa." *TS* 77 (2016): 704–20.

———. *The Sacrifice of Africa: A Political Theology for Africa.* Grand Rapids: Eerdmans, 2011.

Katongole, Emmanuel, and Chris P. Rice. *Ambassadors of Reconciliation.* Downers Grove: InterVarsity, 2008.

———. *Reconciling All Things: A Christian Vision for Justice, Peace and Healing.* Downers Grove: InterVarsity, 2008.

Katongole, Emmanuel, with Jonathan Wilson-Hartgrove. *Mirror to the Church: Resurrecting Faith after Genocide in Rwanda.* Grand Rapids: Zondervan, 2008.

Katz, Neil H. "Enhancing Mediator Artistry: Multiple Frames, Spirit, and Reflection in Action." Pages 374–83 in *The Blackwell Handbook of Mediation: Bridging Theory, Research, and Practice.* Edited by Margaret S. Herrman. Oxford: Blackwell, 2006.

Kittay, Eva Feder. *Love's Labors: Essays on Women, Equality, and Dependency.* 2nd ed. Oxford: Abingdon, 2020.

Klest, Bridget, Andreea Tamaian, and Emily Boughner. "A Model Exploring the Relationship between Betrayal Trauma and Trust." *Psychol. Trauma* 11 (2019): 656–62.

Koehn, Daryl. *Rethinking Feminist Ethics: Care, Trust, and Empathy.* London: Routledge, 1998.

Konstan, David. *Ancient Forgiveness: Classical, Judaic, and Christian.* Cambridge: Cambridge University Press, 2012.

Kranner, Ilse, Farida V. Minibayeva, Richard P. Beckett, and Charlotte E. Seal. "What Is Stress? Concepts, Definitions and Applications in Seed Science." *New Phytologist* 188 (2010): 655–73.

Krause, Neil. "Trust in God and Psychological Distress: Exploring Variations by Religious Affiliation." *Ment. Health Relig. Cult.* 18 (2015): 235–45.

Krause, Neil, and R. D. Hayward. "Assessing Whether Trust Offsets the Effects of Financial Strain on Health and Well-Being." *Int. J. Psychol. Relig.* 25 (2015): 307–22.

Kraybill, Donald B., Steven M. Nolt, and David L. Weaver-Zercher. *Amish Grace: How Forgiveness Transcended Tragedy.* San Francisco: Wiley, 2007.

Kugler, Chris. "*Pistis Christou*: The Current State of Play and Key Arguments." *CBR* 14 (2016): 244–55.

Lakshminarayanan, Venkat R., and Laurie R. Santos. "Capuchin Monkeys Are Sensitive to Others' Welfare." *Current Biology* 18 (2008): R999–R1000.

Laland, K. N. "Social Learning Strategies." *Learning Behavior* 32 (2004): 4–14.

Landman, Christina, and Tanya Pieterse. "(Re)constructing God to Find Meaning in Suffering: Men Serving Long-Term Sentences in Zonderwater." *HvTSt* 75 (2019): art. 5520.

Lange, F. de. "The Heidelberg Catechism: Elements for a Theology of Care." *Acta Theologica Supplementum* 20 (2014): 156–73.

Langford, Dale J., Sara E. Crager, Zarrar Shehzad, Shad B. Smith, Susana G. Sotocinal, Jeremy S. Levenstadt, Mona Lisa Chanda, Daniel J. Levitin, and Jeffrey S. Mogil. "Social Modulation of Pain as Evidence for Empathy in Mice." *Science* 312 (2006): 1967–70.

Langlands, Rebecca. *Exemplary Ethics in Ancient Rome.* Cambridge: Cambridge University Press, 2019.

Larkins, Cath, and John Wainwright. *"Just Put Me on the Right Track": Young People's Perspectives on What Helps Them Stop Offending.* Preston: University of Central Lancashire Press, 2013.

Leavens, D. A., and W. D. Hopkins. "The Whole-Hand Point: The Structure and Function of Pointing from a Comparative Perspective." *J. Comp. Psychol.* 113 (1999): 417–25.

Leclerc, Diane, and Brent Peterson. *The Back Side of the Cross: An Atonement Theology for the Abused and Abandoned.* Eugene: Cascade, 2022.

WORKS CITED

Lee, Dorothy A. "Sin, Self-Rejection and Gender: A Feminist Reading of John's Gospel." *Colloquium* 27 (1995): 51–63.

Lee, Michael E. "Historical Crucifixion: A Liberationist Response to Deep Incarnation." *TS* 81 (2020): 892–912.

Lehmann, L., K. Bargum, and M. Reuter. "An Evolutionary Analysis of the Relationship between Spite and Altruism." *Journal of the European Society for Evolutionary Biology* 19 (2006): 1507–16.

Lepore, S. J., and T. A. Revenson. "Resilience and Post-Traumatic Growth Recovery, Resistance, and Reconfiguration." Pages 24–46 in *Handbook of Post-Traumatic Growth: Research and Practice*. Edited by Lawrence G. Calhoun, Richard G. Tedeschi, and Marianne Amir. New York: Taylor & Francis, 2009.

Lev-Wiesel, R., and M. Amir. "Growing Out of Ashes: Posttraumatic Growth among Holocaust Child Survivors. Is It Possible?" Pages 248–63 in *Handbook of Post-Traumatic Growth: Research and Practice*. Edited by Lawrence G. Calhoun, Richard G. Tedeschi, and Marianne Amir. New York: Taylor & Francis, 2009.

Løgstrup, Knud Eijer. *The Ethical Demand*. South Bend: University of Notre Dame Press, 1997.

Longenecker, Bruce. "On Israel's God and God's Israel: Assessing Supersessionism in Paul." *Journal of Theological Studies* 58 (2007): 26–44.

Lorberbaum, Yair. *In God's Image: Myth, Theology, and Law in Classical Judaism*. New York: Cambridge University Press, 2015.

Luz, Ulrich. *A Commentary on Matthew*. 3 vols. Minneapolis: Fortress, 2001–2007.

Macaskill, Ann. "Defining Forgiveness: Christian Clergy and General Population Perspectives." *Journal of Personality* 73 (2005): 1237–65.

Maimela, Simon S. "The Atonement in the Context of Liberation Theology." *International Review of Mission* 75 (1986): 261–69.

Mannering, Helenka. "A Rapprochement between Feminist Ethics of Care and Contemporary Theology." *Religions* 11 (2020): 185–97.

Martin, J. *Trust God's Plan: Finding Faith in Difficult Times*. Niles: Forever Young, 2020.

Martin, Ralph P. *Reconciliation: A Study of Paul's Theology*. Atlanta: Knox, 1981.

Martyn, J. Louis. "The Apocalyptic Gospel in Galatians." *Int* 54 (2000): 246–66.

———. *Theological Issues in the Letters of Paul*. Edinburgh: T&T Clark, 1997.

McCraw, Benjamin. "Faith and Trust." *Int. J. Philos. Relig.* 77 (2015): 141–58.

McDougall, Joy Ann. "Rising with Mary: Re-Visioning a Feminist Theology of the Cross and Resurrection." *Theology Today* 69 (2012): 166–76.

McDowell, Catherine. *The Image of God in the Garden of Eden*. Philadelphia: Pennsylvania University Press, 2015.

McFague, Sallie. *A New Climate for Christology: Kenosis, Climate Change, and Befriending Nature*. Minneapolis: Fortress, 2021.

McGrath, B. "*Syn* Words in Saint Paul." *CBQ* 14 (1952): 219–26.

McIntyre, John. *The Shape of Soteriology.* Edinburgh: T&T Clark, 1992.

McKaughan, Daniel. "Action-Centered Faith, Doubt, and Rationality." *Journal of Philosophical Research* 41 (2016): 71–90.

———. "Cognitive Opacity and the Analysis of Faith: Acts of Faith Interiorized through a Glass Only Darkly." *Religious Studies* 54 (2018): 576–85.

———. "Faith through the Dark of Night: What Perseverance amidst Doubt Can Teach Us about the Nature and Value of Religious Faith." *Faith Philos.* 35 (2018): 195–218.

———. "On the Value of Faith and Faithfulness." *International Journal for Philosophy of Religion* 81 (2017): 7–29.

Meeks, Wayne. *The Moral World of the First Christians.* Philadelphia: Westminster, 1986.

Meents, Anja K., and Axel Mithöfer. "Plant-Based Communication: Is There a Role for Volatile Damage-Associated Molecular Patterns?" *Frontiers in Plant Science* 11 (2020): 1–13.

Meernik, James. "Violence and Reconciliation in Colombia: The Personal and the Contextual." *Journal of Politics in Latin America* 11 (2019): 323–47.

Meernik, James, and J. R. Guerrero. "Can International Criminal Justice Advance Ethnic Reconciliation? The ICTY and Ethnic Relations in Bosnia-Hercegovina." *Journal of Southeast European and Black Sea Studies* 14 (2014): 383–407.

Michaelis, W. "μιμέομαι." *TDNT* 4:666–67.

Millar, Donald E. *Becoming Human Again.* Oakland: University of California Press, 2020.

Minear, Paul Sevier. *Christians and the New Creation: Genesis Motifs in the New Testament.* Louisville: Westminster, John Knox, 1994.

Miniami, Nathan, David Miller, Michael Davey, and Anthony Sawalhah. "Beyond Reconciliation: Developing Faith, Hope, Trust, and Unity in Iraq." *Military Review* 91 (2011): 52–59.

Mitchell, Alan C. *Hebrews.* Collegeville: Liturgical, 2007.

Moltmann, Jürgen. *The Way of Jesus Christ.* London: SCM, 1990.

Monsó, Susana, Judith Benz-Schwarzburg, and Annika Bremorst. "Animal Morality: What It Means and Why It Matters." *Journal of Ethics* 22 (2018): 283–310.

Morgan, Jonathan. "Transgressing, Puking, Covenanting: The Character of the Land in Leviticus." *Theology* 112 (2009): 172–80.

Morgan, Robert. "Human Forgiveness in the Lord's Prayer." *ExpTim* 134 (2023): 164–72.

Morgan, Teresa. *Being "in Christ" in the Letters of Paul: Saved through Christ and in His Hands.* Tübingen: Mohr Siebeck, 2020.

———. "Big Little Innovations: The Death and Resurrection of Jesus Christ." Forthcoming in *Innovation and Appropriation in Early Christianity: Authors, Topics, Texts,*

Genres. Edited by S. L. Jónsson, S. Luther, and J. P. B. Mortensen. Göttingen: Vandenhoeck & Ruprecht.

———. *The New Testament and the Theology of Trust: "This Rich Trust".* Oxford: Oxford University Press, 2022.

———. *Roman Faith and Christian Faith.* Oxford: Oxford University Press, 2015.

———. "To Err Is Human, To Correct Divine: A Recessive Gene in Ancient Mediterranean and Near Eastern Religiosity?" Pages 64–77 in *The New Testament and the Church: Essays in Honour of John Muddiman.* Edited by John Barton and Peter Groves. London: Bloomsbury, 2015.

Moule, C. F. D. *Forgiveness and Reconciliation and Other New Testament Themes.* London: SPCK, 1998.

———. *The Sacrifice of Christ.* London: Hodder & Stoughton, 1956.

Murray, Joyce. "Liberation for Communion in the Soteriology of Gustavo Gutiérrez." *TS* 59 (1998): 51–59.

Murray, Robert. *The Cosmic Covenant.* London: Sheed & Ward, 1992.

Mukashema, Immaculée, and Etienne Mullet. "Attribution of Guilt to Offspring of Perpetrators of the Genocide: Rwandan People's Perspectives." *Conflict Resolution Quarterly* 33 (2015): 75–98.

———. "Current Mental Health and Reconciliation Sentiment of Victims of the Genocide against Tutsi in Rwanda." *International Journal of Social Psychology* 25 (2014): 23–34.

———. "Unconditional Forgiveness, Reconciliation Sentiment, and Mental Health among Victims of Genocide in Rwanda." *Social Indicators Research* 113 (2013): 121–32.

Nadler, Arie, and Nurit Shnabel. "Instrumental and Socioemotional Paths to Intergroup Reconciliation and the Needs-Based Model of Socioemotional Reconciliation." Pages 37–56 in *The Social Psychology of Intergroup Reconciliation.* Edited by Arie Nadler, Thomas E. Malloy, and Jeffrey D. Fisher. Oxford: Oxford University Press, 2008.

Nagel, Thomas. *Mortal Questions.* New York: Cambridge University Press, 1979.

Nalepa, Monika. "Lustration as a Trust-Building Mechanism? Transitional Justice in Poland." Pages 333–62 in *After Oppression: Transitional Justice in Latin America and Eastern Europe.* Edited by Vesselin Popovski and Mónica Serrano. Tokyo: United Nations University Press, 2012.

Nelsen, Matthew P., Richard H. Ree, and Corrie S. Moreau. "Ant-Plant Interactions Evolved through Increasing Interdependence." *PNAS* 115 (2018): 12253–58.

Neusner, Jacob, W. S. Green, and Ernest Frerichs, eds. *Judaisms and Their Messiahs at the Turn of the Christian Era.* Cambridge: Cambridge University Press, 1987.

Works Cited

Newsom, Carol A. "Models of the Moral Self: Hebrew Bible and Second Temple Judaism." *Journal of Biblical Literature* 131 (2012): 5–25.

———. "When the Problem Is Not What You Have Done but Who You Are." Pages 71–88 in *Atonement: Jewish and Christian Origins*. Edited by Max Botner, Justin Harrison Duff, and Simon Dürr. Grand Rapids: Eerdmans, 2020.

Nicklen, E. Fleur, and Diane Wagner. "Conflict Resolution in an Ant-Plant Interaction: *Acacia Constricta* Traits Reduce Ant Costs to Reproduction." *Oecologia* 148 (2006): 81–87.

Novenson, Matthew V. *Christ among the Messiahs: Christ Language in Paul and Messiah Language in Ancient Judaism*. Oxford: Oxford University Press: 2012.

———. *The Grammar of Messianism: An Ancient Jewish Political Idiom and Its Uses*. New York: Oxford University Press, 2017.

Obatusin, Oluwasegun, and Debbie Ritter-Williams. "A Phenomenological Study of Employer Perspectives on Hiring Ex-Offenders." *Cogent Social Sciences* 5 (2019): art. 1571730.

Oberliessen, Lina, Julen Hernandez-Lallement, Sandra Schäble, Marijn van Wingerden, Maayke Seinstra, and Tobias Kalenscher. "Inequity Aversion in Rats, *Rattus Norvegicus*." *Anim. Behav.* 115 (2016): 157–66.

Oettler, Annika, and Angelika Rettberg. "Varieties of Reconciliation in Violent Contexts: Lessons from Colombia." *Peacebuilding* 7 (2019): 329–52.

Oliver, Isaac W. *Luke's Jewish Eschatology: The National Restoration of Israel in Luke-Acts*. Oxford: Oxford University Press, 2021.

O'Neill, Onora. *A Question of Trust: The BBC Reith Lectures 2002*. Cambridge: Cambridge University Press, 2002.

Örmon, Karin, Marin Torstensson-Levander, Charlotta Sunnqvist, and Christel Bahtsevani. "The Duality of Suffering and Trust: Abused Women's Experiences of General Psychiatric Care—An Interview Study." *Journal of Clinical Nursing* 23 (2013): 2303–12.

Osakabe, Yutaka. "Restoring Restorative Justice: Beyond the Theology of Reconciliation and Forgiveness." *International Journal of Public Theology* 10 (2016): 247–71.

Pace, Michael. "Trusting in Order to Inspire Trustworthiness." *Synthese* 198 (2020): 11897–923.

Parkhouse, Sarah. "The Incarnation as Cosmic Disturbance in the Long Second Century." *EC* 14 (2023): 340–59.

Paul, Gregory D., and Linda L. Putnam. "Moral Foundations of Forgiving in the Workplace." *Western Journal of Communication* 81 (2016): 43–63.

Peterman, Gerald W., and Andrew J. Schmutzer. *Between Pain and Grace: A Biblical Theology of Suffering*. Chicago: Moody, 2016.

WORKS CITED

Peters, Ted. "Constructing a Theology of Evolution: Building on John Haught." *Zygon* 45 (2010): 921–37.

Philip, Leanne J., and Suzanne W. Simard. "Minimum Pulses of Stable and Radioactive Carbon Isotopes to Detect Belowground Carbon Transfer Between Plants." *Plant and Soil* 308 (2008): 23–35.

Pirutinsky, Steven, and David Rosmarin. "My God, Why Have You Abandoned Me? Sexual Abuse and Attitudes towards God among Orthodox Jews." *Ment. Health Relig. Cult.* 23 (2020): 579–90.

Platt, Melissa G., and Jennifer J. Freyd. "Betray My Trust, Shame on Me: Shame, Dissociation, Fear, and Betrayal Trauma." *Psychol. Trauma* 7 (2015): 398–404.

Plotnik, Joshua M., and Frans B. M. de Waal. "Asian Elephants (Elephas Maximus) Reassure Others in Distress." *PeerJ* (2014): art. e278, https://doi.org/10.7717/peerj.278.

Poole, Joyce. *Coming of Age with Elephants: A Memoir.* New York: Hyperion, 1996.

Potts, Justine. *Confession in the Greek and Roman World: A History of Religious Transformation.* Oxford: Oxford University Press, forthcoming.

Power, Maria. *From Ecumenism to Community Relations: Inter-Church Relationships in Northern Ireland.* Dublin: Irish Academic Press, 2007.

Putnam, Robert. *Bowling Alone: The Collapse and Revival of American Community.* New York: Simon & Schuster, 2000.

Quaker Faith and Practice. 5th ed. London: Religious Society of Friends, 1995.

Quell, G., J. Bertram, and G. Stählin. "ἁμαρτάνειν κτλ." *TDNT* 1:274–96.

Rachlin, Katherine. "Trust in Uncertainty: The Therapeutic Structure of Possibility, Turning Points, and the Future of Psychotherapy with Transgender, Nonbinary, and Gender-diverse Individuals." *Studies in Gender and Sexuality* 23 (2022): 93–101.

Radzik, Linda. *Making Amends: Atonement in Morality, Law, and Politics.* Oxford: Oxford University Press, 2007.

Räisänen, Heikki. *Beyond New Testament Theology: A Story and a Programme.* 2nd ed. London: SCM, 2000.

Ramos, Antonio Gómez. "Resentment and the Limits of a Politics of Memory." Pages 69–87 in *Just Memories: Remembrance and Restoration in the Aftermath of Political Violence.* Edited by Camila de Gamboa Tapias and Bert van Roermund. Cambridge: Intersentia, 2020.

Range, Friederike, Lisa Horn, Zsófia Viranyi, and Ludwig Huber. "The Absence of Reward Induces Inequity Aversion in Dogs." *PNAS* (2008): 340–45.

Rankin, Daniel J., and Michael Taborsky. "Assortment and the Evolution of Generalized Reciprocity." *Evolution* 63 (2009): 1913–22.

Ratcliffe, Matthew, Mark Ruddell, and Benedict Smith. "What Is a 'Sense of Foreshortened Future'? A Phenomenological Study of Trauma, Trust, and Time." *Front. Psychol.* 5 (2014): art. 1026.

Rego, Aloysius. *Suffering and Salvation: The Salvific Meaning of Suffering in the Later Theology of Edward Schillebeeckx.* Leuven: Peeters, 2006.

Reinders Folmer, Christopher P., David de Cremer, Maarten Wubben, and Marius van Dijke. "We Can't Go On Together with Suspicious Minds: Forecasting Errors in Evaluating the Appreciation of Denials." *J. Trust Res.* 10 (2020): 4–22.

Reinders Folmer, Christopher P., Tim Wildschut, Tessa Haesevoets, Jonas de Keersmae-cker, Jasper van Assche, and Paul A. M. van Lange. "Repairing Trust between Individuals and Groups: The Effectiveness of Apologies in Interpersonal and Intergroup Conflicts." *International Review of Social Psychology* 34 (2021): 1–15.

Rettberg, Angelika, and Juan E. Ugarriza. "Reconciliation: A Comprehensive Framework for Empirical Analysis." *Security Dialogue* 47 (2016): 517–40.

Reynolds, Thomas E. "Theology and Disability: Changing the Conversation." *Disability and Health* 16 (2012): 33–48.

Richard, Lucien. *What Are They Saying about the Theology of Suffering?* New York: Paulist, 1992.

Ricotta, Daniella. *Il Logos, in verità, è amore: Introduzione filosofica alla teologia di Pierangelo Sequeri.* Milan: Ancora, 2007.

Riesner, Rainer. "Back to the Historical Jesus through Paul and His School (The Ransom Logion—Mark 10.45; Matthew 20.38)." *Journal for the Study of the Historical Jesus* 1 (2003): 171–99.

Rizzuto, Ana-María. "Religious Development beyond the Modern Paradigm Discussion: The Psychoanalytic Point of View." *Int. J. Psychol. Relig.* 11 (2001): 201–14.

Robinson, Leah Elizabeth. "The Influence of Social Context on a Theology of Reconciliation: Case Studies in Northern Ireland." PhD diss., University of Edinburgh, 2011.

Roller, Matthew. *Models from the Past in Roman Culture: A World of Exempla.* Cambridge: Cambridge University Press, 2019.

Rosmarin, David H., Kenneth L. Pargament, and Annette Mahoney. "The Role of Religiousness in Anxiety, Depression, and Happiness in a Jewish Community Sample: A Preliminary Investigation." *Ment. Health Relig. Cult.* 12 (2009): 97–113.

Rosmarin, David H., S. Pirutinsky, and Kenneth I. Pargament. "A Brief Measure of Core Religious Beliefs for Use in Psychiatric Settings." *International Journal of Psychiatry in Medicine* 41 (2011): 253–61.

Rothrock, Ali W. "For Those Who Walk with Others on the Path to Healing." *Psychology Today*, August 24, 2022. https://www. https://www.psychologytoday.com/us /blog/after-trauma/202208/those-who-walk-others-the-path-healing.

WORKS CITED

Rowe, Robert D. *God's Kingdom and God's Son*. Leiden: Brill, 2002.

Rowland, Christopher, and Christopher Tuckett, eds. *The Nature of New Testament Theology: Essays in Honour of Robert Morgan*. Oxford: Blackwell, 2006.

Rowlands, Mark. "Animals That Act for Moral Reasons." Pages 519–46 in *The Oxford Handbook of Animal Ethics*. Edited by T. Beauchamp and R. G. Frey. New York: Oxford University Press, 2011.

———. *Can Animals Be Moral?* Oxford: Oxford University Press, 2012.

Rózsa, L. "Spite, Xenophobia, and Collaboration between Hosts and Parasites." *Oikos* 91 (2000): 396–400.

Ruddick, Sara. "An Appreciation of Love's Labour." *Hypatia* 17 (2002): 214–24.

Ruether, Rosemary Radford. "Christology: Can a Male Savior Save Women?" Pages 116–38 in *Sexism and God-Talk: Towards a Feminist Theology*. Boston: Beacon, 1983.

———. *Women and Redemption: A Theological History*. 2nd ed. Minneapolis: Fortress, 2012.

Rutledge, Fleming. *The Crucifixion: Understanding the Death of Christ*. Grand Rapids: Eerdmans, 2017.

Rutte, Claudia, and Michael Taborsky. "Generalized Reciprocity in Rats." *PLoS Biology* 5 (2007): 1421–25.

Ruzer, Serge. *Early Jewish Messianism in the New Testament*. Leiden: Brill, 2020.

Salier, W. "The Obedient Son: The 'Faithfulness' of Christ in the Fourth Gospel." Pages 223–38 in *The Faith of Jesus Christ: Exegetical, Biblical, and Theological Studies*. Edited by Michael F. Bird and Preston M. Sprinkle. Milton Keynes: Paternoster, 2009.

Sandnes, Karl Olav. *Paul—One of the Prophets? A Contribution to the Apostle's Self-Understanding*. Tübingen: Mohr Siebeck, 1991.

Sang, Barry R. "A Nexus of Care: Process Theology and Care Ethics." *Process Studies* 36 (2007): 229–44.

Sawyer, John F. A. *Isaiah through the Centuries*. Hoboken: Wiley-Blackwell, 2018.

Schellenberg, J. L. *Prolegomena to a Philosophy of Religion*. Ithaca: Cornell University Press, 2005.

Schertz, M. H. "God's Cross and Women's Questions: A Biblical Perspective on the Atonement." *Mennonite Quarterly Review* 68 (1994): 194–208.

Schliesser, Christine. "From 'a Theology of Genocide' to a 'Theology of Reconciliation'? On the Role of Christian Churches in the Nexus of Religion and Genocide in Rwanda." *Religions* 9 (2018): art. 34.

Schmeltz, Martin, Sebastian Gruenisen, Alihan Kabalak, Jürgen Jost, and Michael Tomasello. "Chimpanzees Return Favors at a Personal Cost." *PNAS* 114 (2017): 7462–67.

Schniter, Eric, Roman M. Sheremeta, and Daniel Sznycer. "Building and Rebuilding

Trust with Promises and Apologies." *Journal of Economic Behavior and Organization* 94 (2013): 242–56.

Schreiter, Robert J. *Reconciliation: Mission and Ministry in a Changing Social Order.* Boston: Boston Theological Institute, 1992.

Schütz, John Howard. *Paul and the Anatomy of Apostolic Authority.* Cambridge: Cambridge University Press, 1975.

Schweinfurth, Manon K., Jonathan Aeschbacher, Massimiliano Santi, and Michael Taborsky. "Male Norway Rats Cooperate according to Direct but not Generalized Reciprocity Rules." *Anim. Behav.* 152 (2019): 93–101.

Schwöbel, Christoph. "Reconciliation: From Biblical Observations to Dogmatic Reconstruction." Pages 13–38 in *The Theology of Reconciliation.* Edited by Colin E. Gunton. London: T&T Clark, 2003.

Seed, Amanda M., Nicola S. Clayton, and Nathan J. Emery. "Postconflict Third-Party Affiliation in Rooks, Corvus Frugilegus." *Current Biology* 17 (2007): 152–58.

Segal, Alan. *Two Powers in Heaven: Early Rabbinic Reports about Christianity and Gnosticism.* Leiden: Brill, 1977.

Seligman, Adam. "Trust, Experience, and Embodied Knowledge: Lessons from John Dewey on the Dangers of Abstraction." *J. Trust Res.* 11 (2021): 5–21.

Sequeri, Pierangelo. *Il Dio affidabile: Saggio di teologia fondamentale.* Brescia: Queriniana, 1996.

———. *L'idea della fede: Trattato di teologia fondamentale.* Milan: Glossa, 2002.

Sering, Richard E. "Reclamation through Trust: A Program for Ex-Offenders." *Christian Century,* December 6, 2000. https://www.christiancentury.org/article/reclamation-through-trust.

Shapiro, Paul. "Moral Agency in Other Animals." *Theoretical Medicine and Bioethic* 27 (2006): 357–73.

Shnabel, Nurit, Arie Nadler, and John F. Dovido. "Beyond Need Satisfaction: Empowering and Accepting Messages from Third Parties Ineffectively Restore Trust and Consequent Reconciliation." *European Journal of Social Psychology* 44 (2014): 126–40.

Shnabel, Nurit, and Johannes Ullrich. "Putting Emotional Regulation in Context: The (Missing) Role of Power Relations, Intergroup Trust, and Groups' Need for Positive Identities in Reconciliation Processes." *Psychological Inquiry* 27 (2016): 124–32.

Sieber, Peter. *Mit Christus Leben: Eine Studie zur paulinischen Auferstehungshoffnung.* Zurich: Theologischer Verlag, 1971.

Simard, Suzanne. "Mycorrhizal Networks Facilitate Tree Communication, Learning, and Memory." Pages 191–213 in *Memory and Learning in Plants.* Edited by F. Baluska, Monica Gagliano, and Günther Witzany. Cham: Springer, 2018.

WORKS CITED

Simard, Suzanne, David A. Perry, Melanie D. Jones, David D. Myrold, Daniel M. Durall, and Randy Molina. "Net Transfer of Carbon between Ectomycorrhizal Tree Species in the Field." *Nature* 388 (1997): 579–82.

Skinner, John. *A Critical and Exegetical Commentary on Genesis*. 2nd ed. Edinburgh: T&T Clark, 1930.

Slote, Michael. *The Ethics of Care and Empathy*. London: Routledge, 2007.

Sobrino, Jon. *Jesus the Liberator: A Historical-Theological Reading of Jesus of Nazareth*. Maryknoll: Orbis, 1993.

Solomons, Demaine J. "Re-examining a Theology of Reconciliation: What We Learn from the *Kairos* Document and Its Pegagogical Implications." *HvTSt* 76 (2020): art. a5843, https://doi.org/10.4102/hts.v.76i1.5843.

Song, Y. Y., Suzanne W. Simard, Allan Carroll, William W. Mohn, and Ren Sen Zeng. "Defoliation of Interior Douglas-Fir Elicits Carbon Transfer and Stress Signalling to Ponderosa Pine Neighbors through Ectomycorrhizal Networks." *Scientific Reports* 5 (2015): art. 8495.

Stanton, Graham. *Jesus of Nazareth in New Testament Preaching*. Cambridge: Cambridge University Press, 1974.

Staub, Ervin, Laurie Anne Perlman, Alexandra Gubin, and Athanase Hagengimana. "Healing, Reconciliation, Forgiving and the Prevention of Violence after Genocide or Mass Killing: An Intervention and Its Experimental Evaluation in Rwanda." *Journal of Social and Clinical Psychology* 24 (2005): 297–334.

Stendahl, Krister. "Biblical Theology, Contemporary." Pages 1:418–32 in *The Interpreter's Dictionary of the Bible*. Edited by G. A. Buttrick. 4 vols. Nashville: Abingdon, 1962.

Stevens, David. "Christ's Ambassadors in the Work of Reconciliation." *Corrymeela Magazine*, January 2007, 10.

Stokes, Ryan E. *The Satan: How God's Executioner Became the Enemy*. Grand Rapids: Eerdmans, 2019.

Stovel, Laura. *Long Road Home: Building Reconciliation and Trust in Post-War Sierra Leone*. Cambridge: Intersentia, 2010.

Stuhlmacher, Peter. "The Gospel of Reconciliation in Christ: Basic Features and Issues of a Biblical Theology of the New Testament." *Horizons in Biblical Theology* 1 (1979): 161–90.

———. *Reconciliation, Law, and Righteousness: Essays in Biblical Theology*. Philadelphia: Fortress, 1986.

Stump, Eleonore. *Atonement*. Oxford: Oxford University Press, 2018.

Swartley, Willard. *The Covenant of Peace: The Missing Peace in New Testament Theology and Ethics*. Grand Rapids: Eerdmans, 2006.

Swinburne, Richard. *Faith and Reason*. 2nd ed. Oxford: Oxford University Press, 2005.

Works Cited

Tannehill, Robert. *Dying and Rising with Christ: A Study in Pauline Theology.* Berlin: Töpelmann, 1967.

Tanner, Kathryn. *Christ the Key.* Cambridge: Cambridge University Press, 2010.

Taylor, Bron, ed. *Encyclopedia of Religion and Nature.* 2 vols. London: Bloomsbury, 2005.

Taylor, Laura K. "Impact of Political Violence, Social Trust, and Depression on Civic Participation in Colombia." *Peace Confl.* 22 (2016): 145–52.

Tenkorang, Eric Y., Adobea Y. Owusu, and Gubhinder Kundhi. "Help-Seeking Behavior of Female Victims of Intimate Partner Violence in Ghana: The Role of Trust and Perceived Risk of Injury." *Journal of Family Violence* 33 (2018): 341–53.

Theissen, Gerd. *Psychological Aspects of Pauline Theology.* Edinburgh: T&T Clark, 1987.

Thiselton, Anthony C. *The First Epistle to the Corinthians: A Commentary on the Greek Text.* Grand Rapids: Eerdmans, 2000.

Thom, Johan C. "God the Savior in Greco-Roman Popular Philosophy." Pages 86–100 in *Sōtēria: Salvation in Early Christianity and Antiquity. Festschrift in Honour of Cilliers Breytenbach on the Occasion of His 65th Birthday.* Edited by David S. du Toit, Christine Gerber, and Christiane Zimmermann. Leiden: Brill, 2019.

Thompson, Thomas L. "The Messiah Epithet in the Hebrew Bible." *Scandinavian Journal of the Old Testament* 15 (2001): 57–82.

Thompson, W. R., J. Meinwald, D. Aneshansley, and T. Eisner. "Flavonols: Pigments Responsible for Ultraviolet Absorption in Nectar Guide of Flower." *Science* 177 (1972): 528–30.

Thornton, Alex, and Nicola J. Raihani. "The Evolution of Teaching." *Anim. Behav.* 75 (2008): 1823–36.

Thrall, Margaret E. *A Critical and Exegetical Commentary on the Second Letter to the Corinthians.* Edinburgh: T&T Clark, 1994–2000.

———. "Salvation Proclaimed: 2 Corinthians 5.18–21: Reconciliation with God." *ExpTim* 93 (1982): 227–32.

Tillotson, Nicole, Monica Short, Janice Ollerton, Cassandra Hearn, and Bonita Sawatzky. "Faith Matters: From a Disability Lens." *J. Disabil. Relig.* 21 (2017): 319–37.

Toit, Andre B. de. "Forensic Metaphors in Romans and Their Soteriological Significance." *Verbum et Ecclesia* 24 (2003): 53–79.

Toit, David S. du. "Heil und Unheil: Die Soteriologie des Markusevangelium." Pages 186–208 in *Sōtēria: Salvation in Early Christianity and Antiquity. Festschrift in Honour of Cilliers Breytenbach on the Occasion of His 65th Birthday.* Edited by David S. du Toit, Christine Gerber, and Christiane Zimmermann. Leiden: Brill, 2019.

Tomasello, M., and J. Call. "Intentional Communication in Nonhuman Primates." Pages

WORKS CITED

1–15 in *The Gestural Communication of Apes and Monkeys*. Edited by J. Call and M. Tomasello. Mahwah: Erlbaum Associates, 2007.

Torrance, Alan J. "Forgiveness and Christian Character: Reconciliation, Exemplarism, and the Shape of Moral Theology." *Studies in Christian Ethics* 30 (2017): 293–313.

Trible, Phyllis. "Eve and Adam: Genesis 2–3 Reread." Pages 74–83 in *Womanspirit Rising*. Edited by Carol P. Christ and Judith Plaskow. 2nd ed. San Francisco: Harper & Row, 1992.

Trigo, Tomas. *En los brazos del Padre: Confianza en Dios*. Casablanca: Editorial, 2013.

Trivers, Robert. "The Evolution of Reciprocal Altruism." *Quarterly Review of Biology* 46 (1971): 35–57.

Trojan, Jakub S. *From Christ's Death to Jesus' Life: A Critical Reinterpretation of Prevailing Theories of the Cross*. Bern: Lang, 2012.

Tweig, Brenda D., Daniel M. Dural, and Suzanne W. Simard. "Ectomycorrhizal Fungal Succession in Mixed Temperate Forests." *New Phytologist* 176 (2007): 437–47.

Ueda, Hirokazu, Yukio Kikuta, and Kazuhiko Matsuda. "Plant Communication: Mediated by Individual or Blended VOCs?" *Plant Signaling & Behavior* 7 (2012): 222–26.

United Nations. *Istanbul Protocol: Manual on the Effective Investigation and Documentation of Torture and Other Cruel, Inhuman, or Degrading Treatment or Punishment*. Geneva: Office of the United Nations High Commissioner for Human Rights, 1999.

Vail, Alexander L., Andrea Manica, and Redouan Bshary. "Referential Gestures in Fish Collaborative Hunting." *Nature Communications* 4 (2013): 1–7.

Vickery, W. L., J. S. Brown, and J. G. Fitzgerald. "Spite: Altruism's Evil Twin." *Oikos* 102 (2003): 413–16.

Villa-Vicencio, Charles, and Desmond Tutu. *Walk with Us and Listen: Political Reconciliation in Africa*. Washington, DC: Georgetown, 2009.

Villiers, Pieter G. R. de. "Safe in the Family of God: Soteriological Perspectives in 1 Thessalonians." Pages 305–30 in *Salvation in the New Testament: Perspectives on Soteriology*. Edited by J. G. van der Watt. Leiden: Brill, 2005.

Voiss, James K. *Rethinking Christian Forgiveness: Theological, Philosophical, and Psychological Perspectives*. Collegeville, MN: Liturgical Press, 2015.

Volf, Miroslav. *Exclusion and Embrace*. Rev. ed. Nashville: Abingdon, 2019.

Waal, Frans B. M. de. "Primates: A Natural Heritage of Conflict Resolution." *Science* 289 (2000): 586–90.

Waal, Frans B. M. de, and Angeline van Roosmalen. "Reconciliation and Consolation among Chimpanzees." *Behavioral Ecology and Sociobiology* 5 (1979): 55–66.

Wallis, Ian G. *Holy Saturday Faith: Rediscovering the Legacy of Jesus*. London: SPCK, 2000.

Works Cited

Wasserman, Emma. "Paul among the Philosophers: The Case of Sin in Romans 6–8." *JSNT* 30 (2008): 387–415.

Watt, J. G. van der, ed. *Salvation in the New Testament: Perspectives on Soteriology.* Leiden: Brill, 2005.

Weaver, J. Denny. *The Nonviolent Atonement.* Grand Rapids: Eerdmans, 2001.

Weaver, Natalie Kertes. *The Theology of Suffering and Death: An Introduction for Caregivers.* London: Taylor & Francis, 2012.

Wenham, Gordon. *Genesis 1–15.* WBC 1. Waco: Word, 1987.

West, Stuart A., and Andy Gardner. "Altruism, Spite, and Greenbeards." *Science* 327 (2010): 1341–44.

Westermann, Claus. *Genesis.* Neukirchen-Vluyn: Neukirchener Verlag, 1970.

———. *Genesis 1–11: A Commentary.* Minneapolis: Augsburg, 1984.

Whiten, A., D. M. Custance, J. C. Gómez, P. Teixidor, and K. A. Bard. "Imitative Learning of Artificial Fruit Processing in Children (*Homo Sapiens*) and Chimpanzees (*Pan Troglodytes*)." *J. Comp. Psychol.* 110 (1996): 3–14.

Wichert, Rachel Nussbaum, and Martha Nussbaum. "Can There Be Friendship between Human Beings and Wild Animals?" *Journal of Human Development and Capabilities* 22 (2021): 87–107.

Wieczorek, Tobias. *Die Nichtgläubigen—Hoi Apistoi: Über die Funktion abgrenzende Sprache bei Paulus.* Göttingen: Vandenhoeck & Ruprecht, 2021.

Wiesenthal, Simon. *The Sunflower: On the Possibilities and Limits of Forgiveness.* Paris: Opera Mundi, 1970.

Williams, Bernard. *Moral Luck.* Cambridge: Cambridge University Press, 1981.

Williams, Catrin. "'Seeing,' Salvation, and the Use of Scripture in the Gospel of John." Pages 131–54 in *Atonement: Jewish and Christian Origins.* Edited by Max Botner, Justin Harrison Duff, and Simon Dürr. Grand Rapids: Eerdmans, 2020.

Williams, Wright, David P. Graham, Katherine McCurry, April Sanders, Jessica Eiseman, Pearl H. Chiu, and Brooks King-Casas. "Group Psychotherapy's Impact on Trust in Veterans with PTSD: A Pilot Study." *Bulletin of the Meninger Clinic* 78 (2014): 335–48.

Willmer, Haddon. "'Vertical' and 'Horizontal' in Paul's Theology of Reconciliation in the Letter to the Romans." *Transformation* 24 (2007): 151–60.

Wolter, Michael. *Jesus von Nazaret.* Göttingen: Vandenhoeck & Ruprecht, 2019.

Wolterstorff, Nicholas. "The Assurance of Faith." *Faith Philos.* 7 (1990): 396–417.

Woodyatt, Lydia, and Michael Wenzel. "A Needs-Based Perspective on Self-Forgiveness: Addressing Threat to Moral Identity as a Means of Encouraging Interpersonal and Intrapersonal Restoration." *Journal of Experimental Social Psychology* 50 (2014): 125–35.

Yarbro Collins, Adela. *Mark: A Commentary.* Minneapolis: Fortress, 2007.

WORKS CITED

———. "The Metaphorical Use of *Hilastērion* in Romans 3:25." Pages 273–86 in *Sōtēria: Salvation in Early Christianity and Antiquity. Festschrift in Honour of Cilliers Breytenbach on the Occasion of His 65th Birthday.* Edited by David S. du Toit, Christine Gerber, and Christiane Zimmermann. Leiden: Brill, 2019.

Yarbro Collins, Adela, and John J. Collins. *King and Messiah as Son of God: Divine, Human, and Angelic Messianic Figures in Biblical and Related Literature.* Grand Rapids: Eerdmans, 2008.

Yong, Amos. "Many Tongues, Many Formational Practices: Christian Spirituality/Formation across Global Christian Contexts." *Spiritus* 31 (2009): 176–88.

Yu, Ying, Yan Yang, and Fengjie Jing. "The Role of the Third Party in Trust Repair Process." *Journal of Business Research* 78 (2017): 233–41.

Zand, Dale E. "Reflections on Trust and Trust Research: Then and Now." *J. Trust Res.* 6 (2016): 63–73.

Index of Subjects

abuse, cross as addressing, 6n12, 31, 83, 149, 150–54, 156. *See also* trauma, restoration of trust after

Adam, 39–42, 47, 73, 79, 161n3, 163–64, 181

altruism: in animal kingdom, 170–72, 182–84, 188, 190–92; in plant kingdom, 188–91, 194

anti-ableism in exegesis, 57–59

apistia, 21, 29, 63–76, 82–83, 137–40, 206

apistos, 63–64, 67, 74, 83n110, 119, 133n40, 210

atonement: definition, 1–2, 6–7; images of, in New Testament, 2–3, 6–7, 11, 26, 46–50; Jesus as enabling between God and nonhuman creation, 191–93; in liberation theology, 4–6; modern theories/models of, 2–6; "wide" and "narrow," 1n2, 27

at-one-ment, relation to atonement, 1

Beliar. *See* Satan

belief, as a meaning of *pistis*, 7–9, 11, 13n31, 61, 64–65, 67–69, 132–34, 165–66

Cain, 40–41

Christ. *See* Jesus Christ; "with Christ" (*syn*-language, Paul's)

Community Re-entry Program (Cleveland, Ohio), 108–9

conflict resolution: in animal kingdom, 183–87; definition, 85–86; role of churches in, 95–97; role of trust in, 85–86, 89–98

Corrymeela Community (Northern Ireland), 213–14

covenant, 2, 48–49, 80n108, 161, 168n27, 219; new, 47–49, 127

creation: capable of at-one-ment, 179–82; capable of atonement through Christ, 191–93; capable of mediating, 184–87; capable of sin/spite, 32–33, 169–77; capable of suffering, 169–70, 174–76, 178–79; capable of trust, 176–77, 183–87; God's care for, 162–65; Jesus as mediator between God and, 179–82; nonhuman, as having the same rights as human beings, 174; nonhuman, as moral agent, 162–63; relationship with God, 160–68, 203–4; relationship with Jesus Christ, 176–82

cross: as "firebreak," 127–28, 150, 202, 206, 217, 223; necessity of, 134–43; as space where God meets humanity, 30–33, 130, 134–35, 143, 150–52, 155–56, 197–99

devil, 55–57, 62–63, 69. *See also* Satan

dikaiosynē, meaning of, 38n4

disciples: doubt of, 67, 91, 133; fragile trust of, 31, 52–53, 66–69, 129–34, 141, 150, 224

doubt: of disciples, 67, 91, 133; of Eve, 40n11, 164; of Galatians, 76; of Jesus, 31; relationship with trust/faith, 11, 13, 16–18, 23, 41, 71, 82, 164

end time, 50, 53–55, 91, 127, 131, 137, 144, 148, 168, 176; linked with creation, 167–68; parables of, 51, 70–71, 131n36, 201, 209–10, 216

INDEX OF SUBJECTS

entrusted: apostles as, 8, 11, 122, 148; Christ as, 15, 22, 192; Christians as, 11, 29–30, 33, 95n31, 155, 157, 194, 199, 207–17; disempowered as, 147n85; ex-offenders as, 108; Jews as, 122

entrustedness: in parables, 70, 131; relation to mediation and forgiveness, 207–17; relation to *pistis*, 7–8, 10n25, 13, 118, 121n11, 122n15

Eve, 39–41, 163–64

exemplarity: of Jesus's death, 144–49; of Paul, 144–46

ex-offenders, rehabilitation of, 105–13

failure in trust, by churches 33, 95–97, 216

failure to trust, 11, 15, 20–21, 29, 31, 36–37, 63–76, 141; by Adam and Eve, 39–40; by failing to be trustworthy, 64; by nonhuman creation, 177, 194; by over-trusting one's own judgment, 64; cycle broken, 153–55; experience of creation as defense against, 203–4; future, 202, 206; not a deal-breaker, 23, 32, 67–69, 82, 91, 157; as response to suffering, 65–67, 70–71, 210. *See also apistia*

faithfulness: between human beings, 18; of Christ, 69, 120–22, 152; of disciples, 132; of God, 10, 90, 117, 164n11; to God and/or Christ, 24, 45, 51, 55, 69, 72–74, 132, 166, 208; as meaning of *pistis*, 7–9, 118, 218–19, 222

fear: of disciples, 67, 132–33, 141; generated by conflict or abuse, 88, 94, 151; relationship with trust/faith, 11, 12–13, 18, 23, 56, 82, 91, 214, 225

fides, range of meaning, 7–8

forgiveness: divine, 3–4, 30, 32–33, 43, 47–52, 64, 73, 118; human, 86–87, 90–91, 93, 96, 98, 101, 157, 196–220; of self, 112n78

freedom: divine gift to the world, 29; to keep the law, 65, 93; from oppression/suffering, 4–5, 75–76, 114, 124, 138n52, 152, 168; part of life in trust with God, 137, 138n52, 168; from wrongdoing, 2, 114

free will, 17n59, 37–40, 70, 157, 174

Gadarene/Gerasene demoniac, 178

good faith, 7, 164, 215–16

Good Samaritans, the (*Umusamaritani z'impuhwe*, Merciful Samaritan Association; Rwanda), 103

grace: of apostleship, 208; death of Jesus as, 31, 156, 202, 223–24; divine, 15, 62, 79, 117–19, 123–24, 128–30, 138, 143, 150, 211; human, 109–10; necessity of response to, 32; as quality of God's kingdom, 137; resurrection as, 31, 130, 155, 224

healing miracles, relation to trust, 57–59

Help for Adult Victims of Child Abuse (HAVOCA), 99–100

hope: after sin, 79; after trauma, 21, 105, 151; consequence of trusting in God and/or Christ, 2, 5, 9, 31, 128, 148, 156, 206, 220; for creation as a whole, 168; eschatological, 24, 25, 76, 119, 136–37, 139; God's and/or Christ's for humanity, 127, 192, 206, 218; in human sphere, 12, 15–16, 18, 107, 109, 112, 183, 197–99, 202, 211; messianic, 46, 54, 117, 132–33, 141–42, 226; in nonhuman creation, 184; relation to depression, 106; relation to language of trust, 10n25, 12, 120n11; relation to trust, 21, 23, 89, 90, 92, 118, 137, 223

imitation, 32–33, 115, 144–48, 187, 193–94, 207–8, 212–15, 218, 224; by nonhuman creation, 189. *See also* exemplarity

injustice, 5, 37n4, 67, 130, 134

Jephthah, 42

Jesus Christ: death of, as exemplary, 144–49; as restoring trust between God and humanity, 119–30, 149–54, 206–7; suffering of, as exemplary, 144–49; as trustworthy, 31, 75, 122–26, 128, 135–36, 145–46, 153, 165, 218, 223

John the Baptist, 50–51, 53, 55, 178n46

Judas, 67n74, 69–70

justice: of God, 4–6, 19, 55, 72, 97, 151, 161, 164; human, 4–6, 55, 64, 65, 75, 86, 99, 174, 216n40; restorative, 97–98. *See also* righteousness

Katongole, Emmanuel, 96, 211n31

256

Index of Subjects

liberation, by savior figures, 29, 44–46, 54–55, 81–82, 120–27
Lord's Prayer, 196–97
loyalty: aspect of *pistis*, 7–8, 52, 121n12, 209; in friendship, 212

Mary, mother of Jesus, 49, 51, 54
Mary, other, 132–33, 141
mediation: by Christians/churches, 207–17, 224; in human sphere, 28, 30, 33, 92–93, 95–97, 102–4, 108, 111, 114–15; by Jesus, in relation to humanity 22, 27, 32–33, 119–26, 128, 153–55, 179, 196–99, 207, 223; by Jesus, in relation to nonhuman creation, 194–95; in nonhuman creation, 184–86, 194; by relationships of trust, 202, 206; relation to atonement, 2–3, 11
messiah. *See* savior
Moses, 24n82, 44, 47n32, 48, 123, 125

Noah, 42, 164

original sin, 157
ou pisteuein, 63–64

parousia. See end time
Pharisees, 25, 51, 64–66, 75, 214–16
pistis: describing emerging structures of early churches, 209n25; evolution of, in early churches, 9–10; of God in LXX, 219n42; *pistis Christou*, 120n11, 123–25, 128n31, 199; range of meaning, 7–8, 17, 24, 33, 63–64; reconciliation, relation to atonement, 27–28; ubiquity in New Testament, 9, 11, 117
pistos. See faithfulness; trustworthy
preexistent, Christ as, 30, 126, 135, 155, 165–66

reconciliation: between human beings, 197–201; Pauline language, 27–28, 96, 119, 124–25, 130; relation to atonement language, 1n2, 27–28, 150, 156; relation to trust, 92, 93–94, 96, 103–4, 113, 115, 119, 157, 197
repentance: in the New Testament, 49–53, 62, 65n70, 166, 178n46; outside the New Testament, 98n40, 113n80, 118, 157; in relation to forgiveness, 30–33, 118, 157, 196–200

resurrection, 10–11, 22, 31, 58–60, 67, 77, 95–96, 117–19, 129–34, 135–41; in relation to human forgiveness, 202–3, 223–25; in relation to nonhuman creation, 168, 179–82, 191
revelation, as grace, 130–34
righteousness, 9, 117, 134, 208; through Christ, 119, 122–24, 138, 168, 179, 197; of God, 19n67, 38n4, 47n31, 71–72, 79, 98, 120–21, 131; of human beings, 38n4, 42, 49, 55, 61, 63, 65–66, 74, 80n108, 205; as state and/or activity, 38n4, 63n65. *See also* justice
risk: of not trusting, 66, 87; of trust taken by God, and Christ, 10, 18, 28–29, 95n31, 127, 153; of trust taken by human beings toward each other, 23, 90, 97, 104–11, 114–15, 185–86, 198, 205–7, 218–19; of trust taken by human beings toward God and Christ, 18, 22, 76, 199, 202–3, 210, 217. *See also* therapeutic trust

sacrifice, as model of atonement, 2–3, 11, 43, 46–48, 62, 127–28, 143, 153–54
salvation, different models, Jewish and gentile, 46–49
Satan, 52, 62, 77, 78. *See also* devil
savior: different types of, 29, 43–46, 53–55, 82; in gentile culture, 45–46
sin, 3–8, 21, 37; collective or inherited, 37–38, 41n14, 43–44, 49, 57n51, 65n70, 73, 86n1, 167n23; different kinds, 6n13, 35–36, 62n62, 64, 65n70, 73, 77–80; punishment for prior wrongdoing, 73; response to (perceived) suffering, 40, 64–66, 75–76; vocabulary of, 37n4
spite (Hamiltonian), 171–73
stewardship, as entrustedness, 208–10
suffering, 46; of Jesus, as exemplary, 144–49; leads to trust in God, 104; leads to wrongdoing, 29, 36, 40–41, 68, 85, 99, 105–6, 196; many kinds, 25, 37, 43–47, 49–50, 53; natural, 29, 57–58, 162, 178n47; needs restoration of trust, 30, 73–74, 81–82, 98–105, 113–14, 119–30, 149–54, 203–7, 211–12, 219; of nonhuman creation, 32, 35–36, 159, 161–62, 169, 174–75, 178
suffering servant/man of suffering, 42–43

INDEX OF SUBJECTS

syn- language, Paul's. *See* "with Christ" (*syn-* language, Paul's)

therapeutic trust: of God toward humanity, 10, 15, 28, 43, 128n31, 155, 200, 223, 225; as grace, 30, 150; of human beings toward each other, 108, 186, 199, 214n36, 216
time, and development of trust, 217
trauma, restoration of trust after, 98–105, 151–54
trust: between humans and animals, 190–95; double bond of, 122–26, 143; in history, 21–22; incremental, 30, 106; misplaced, 75, 82, 99; one-place, 12n30; in philosophy, 11–15, 36; in philosophy of religion, 15–17; in psychology, 18–19, 36; in psychotherapy, 19–21, 101–3; and sense of reality, 20, 23, 82–83, 144–45, 156, 193; separability of attitude and action, 12, 13, 14, 16, 22–23, 25–30, 114, 210, 214n36, 216; in social sciences, 21–22; theologies of, 10, 17–18, 95–97; "thin," 14, 91–94, 97, 110, 113–14, 157, 197; three-place, 12n30, 226; triangular, trilateral, 33, 104,

198–99, 201; two-place, 14n40, 226. *See also* faithfulness: of Christ; therapeutic trust; trustworthy: Christ as
trustworthy: Christ as, 31, 75, 122–26, 128, 135–36, 145–46, 153, 165, 218, 223; Christian teaching as, 75; followers of Jesus as, 33, 132n38, 192–95, 215–18, 224–25; God as, 10n24, 17, 28, 121, 153, 164; human beings as, 12, 15, 19–22, 30, 70, 82–83, 90, 92–113, 205–12; nonhuman creation as, 187, 191; *pistos*, meaning of, 9n22; and Truth and Reconciliation Commission, South Africa, 97–98
Truth and Reconciliation Commission, 90, 97–98, 213n34
"two ways" model of salvation, 80n108

untrustworthy, people as, 36, 62, 64, 70, 107, 110, 112

"with Christ" (*syn-* language, Paul's), 137–42
wrongdoing. *See* sin

Zechariah, 47n32, 49, 51, 54

Index of Scripture

HEBREW BIBLE

Genesis

1	161n2
1–3	161n3
1:1–2:3	39
1:3	131n34
1:26	161, 162
2	175
2–3	65
2:4–25	39
3	161n4
3–4	72n89
3:14–15	161
3:14–19	163
3:15	163
3:16–19	40n12
3:16–24	39
3:17–18	163, 167n23
3:19	181
4:3–5	40
4:5	40
4:7	41
4:10	163
4:12	163
6:5–6	41
6:5–7	164
6:7	42
6:8–9	42
6:11–12	42, 164
8:21	41

Exodus

20:5–6	41
23:16	181
24:8	49n36
34:6–7	41

Leviticus

3:6–7	48n34
4:2	62n62
4:32–35	48n34
16:21–22	43
18–27	162
18:25	162
18:28	162
19:18	206
20:22	162
25:2	162
25:4–5	162
26:34	162
26:36	162

Numbers

12:17	125
14:18	41
21:8–9	56

Deuteronomy

5:9–10	41
24:16	41n16

Judges

11:29	42
11:29–39	42
11:30–31	42
11:34	42
11:35	42
11:39	42
11:39–40	42

1 Samuel

17:32	43n22

2 Samuel

24:10	39n7

Nehemiah

10:35	181n52

1 Maccabees

1:43	45
2:15	45

Job

16:7	39n7
31:38–40	167n23
38:39	161
39:9	161
39:27	161
40:25–28	161

259

INDEX OF SCRIPTURE

Psalms

15:8–11 LXX	146n82
16:8–11	146n82
18 LXX	164
18:1 LXX	164
18:8 LXX	164
32 LXX	164
32:4 LXX	164
32:5 LXX	164
32:5–7 LXX	164
32:8–9 LXX	164
32:13 LXX	164
32:15 LXX	164
32:18–20 LXX	164
35:1	45
37:10–13	45
44:7–8 LXX	166n18
47:12	161
50:1–6	161
67:6	176
68:9	161n5
93(94):8 LXX	39n7
101:26–28 LXX	166
104:4	161n5
104:21	161
115:1–6 LXX	146n82
116:10	146n82
116:10–15	146n82
147:9	161
148	161
150:6	161

Proverbs

3:3	165n13
3:5	165n13
16:20	165n13
29:25	165n13

Wisdom

1:2	165n13
3:1	165n13
10:5	165n13
10:7	165n13
12:2	165n13
14:11	73n90
16:16–17	56n50
16:24–25	165n13

Ben Sira

2:6	165n13
2:8	165n13
2:10	165n13
2:13	165n13
4:27	39n7
18:18	39n7
19:11	39n7
19:12	39n7
20:13	39n7
20:16	39n7
20:20	39n7
25:2	39n7
32:24	165n13

Isaiah

2:8 LXX	73n90
2:20 LXX	73n90
11:1–9	192
11:6–9	176
13:8	167
32:5–6	39
40:3	50n39
41:18–19	176
41:18–20	204n15
52:1–2	43
52:13	43
53	42, 47n32
53:3	42
53:3–4	43
53:4	43
53:5	43
53:5–6	43
53:6	43
53:7	43, 48n35
53:8	43
53:9	43
53:10–11	43
53:12	43
61:1–2	55
65:6b–7	41n16
65:17–25	204n15
66:22–23	204n15

Jeremiah

2:3	181
4:31	167

| 5:21 LXX | 39n7 |
| 31:31 | 49n36 |

Ezekiel

20:33–38	45
34:27	176
39:2	45

Daniel

11:31 LXX	73n90
12:1–2	45

Hosea

2:18–19	204n15
13:13	167

Habakkuk

2:4	71

Zechariah

9:1–8	45
9:9	45
9:16–17	45
10:2–3	45
10:6	45
10:8–12	45
10:11	45

Malachi

3:1	50n39

NEW TESTAMENT

Matthew

1:21	50
2:2	51n40, 176
3:2	50
3:8	51, 178n46
3:10	178n46
4:1–7	64n69
4:17	50, 197n2
4:24	53n44
5:5–6	55
5:11	55
5:12	202

260

Index of Scripture

5:13–14	179n49	15:21–28	68	25:14–30	210
5:17	206	15:28	69	25:20	210
5:17–48	200	16:19	69n80	25:21	70, 210
5:43–47	205	16:23	52	25:22	210
5:48	206	17:14–18	67	25:23	70, 210
6:7–15	196	17:14–20	52	25:24	210
6:12	51, 196n1	17:14–21	53n44	25:25–26	210
6:22–34	66	17:17	52, 67	25:26	70
6:26	176	17:20	52, 67	25:30	51, 70, 210
6:28	176	18	68	25:40	201
6:30	66	18:6	51, 66, 66n72, 66n73	26:23–25	70
6:30–31	176	18:6–9	64	26:24	69
7:5	51	18:15–20	67	26:26	180
7:7–11	53	18:17	67, 69	26:28	47, 48, 49, 51, 143n70
7:15–20	177n46	18:18	69n80	26:39	69, 121n12
7:19–20	178n46	18:20	202	26:51–54	52
7:21	206	18:34	51	26:52	53n44
7:21–23	51	20:26–28	121n12	27:4	70
8:5–7	69	20:28	46	27:9–10	70
8:10	69	21:18–20	177	27:37	54
8:23–27	178	21:20–21	177	27:45	176
8:26	67	21:23–27	64	27:51	176
8:28–34	53n44, 178	21:32	51	27:54	130
9:2	57, 197n2	21:41	51	28:1	141
9:9	69	22:13	68	28:8	132
9:10	69	22:37–39	200	28:9–10	132, 141
9:11–13	69	23:1–36	64	28:16	141
9:13	51, 64n69	23:2–7	65	28:18–19	134
9:20	58	23:3	64	28:20	134, 202, 206
9:20–22	214	23:3–4	64		
9:32–34	53n44	23:6–12	64	**Mark**	
9:36	53	23:13	64, 216	1:4	50
10:1–36	64	23:13–15	64	1:15	50, 197n2
10:6	53	23:15–16	64	1:23–28	53n44
10:34–36	54	23:23	64, 65	1:24	58n54
11:5	55	23:23–30	64	1:32–34	53n44
11:18–19	64	23:24	216	2:5	57, 197n2
12:22–24	53n44	23:30–36	64	2:17	51
12:24–30	64n68	23:34–35	65	3:11	53n44
13:31	180n50	23:37	64	3:22–27	64n68
13:33	180n50	23:39	65	4:14	180n50
13:42	67	24:4–5	67	4:26–29	176–77
13:50	67	24:7	178	4:30–32	180n50
14:1–2	53	24:45–51	209	4:35–41	178
14:25	176	24:49	209	4:40	67
14:30–31	67	24:50–51	210	5:1–10	53n44
15:1–20	64	25:10	210	5:1–20	178

261

INDEX OF SCRIPTURE

5:7	58n54	**Luke**		9:37–43	52
5:23	58	1:17	51	9:37–43a	53n44
5:25–34	58, 214	1:32–33	51	9:38–42	67
6:14–16	53	1:50–53	49	9:41	52, 67
6:34	53	1:51–55	51	10:12–15	64
6:48	176	1:55	49	10:20	202
7:1–23	64	1:68	47n32	10:27	200
8:31	132	1:68–75	49n37	11:1–4	196
8:33	52	1:71	47n32, 49, 51	11:4	51
9:14–19	53n44	1:72–73	49	11:9–13	53
9:14–29	52	1:73	47n32	11:14–15	53n44
9:16–27	67	1:74	51	11:15	64n68
9:19	52, 67	1:76–78	49n37	11:17–23	64n68
9:24	67	1:77	47n32, 49n37	11:37–44	64
9:29	52	1:77–79	51	11:42	64
9:31	132	2:30	47n32	12:21–44	66
9:42	51, 66n72, 216	2:38	47n32	12:24	176
10:34	132	3:3	50	12:27	176
10:43–45	121n12	3:8	51	12:28	66
10:45	46, 47	3:8–9	178	12:28–29	176
11:12–14	177	3:38	164n12	12:41–48	209
11:13	177	4:1–4	64n69	12:45	209
11:14–15	53n44	4:9–12	64n69	12:46	70n83
11:20–21	177	4:33–37	53n44	12:51–53	54
11:22	177	4:40–41	53n44	12:57–59	200
11:23–24	177	5:6	176	13:6–9	177n45
11:25	196	5:8	197n2	13:18–19	180n50
12:30–31	200	5:20	57, 197n2	13:20–21	180n50
13:4–6	67	5:32	51	13:25–27	51
13:8	178	6:18	53n44	16:11	209n26
14:21	69	6:20–26	55	16:18	200
14:22	180	6:27–28	200	17:2	51
14:24	47, 48, 49, 143n70	6:32–36	200	17:22	66n73
14:36	69, 121n12	6:42	51	18:1–8	55
14:47	52	6:43–44	64n67	18:9	66
15:26	53n44, 54	7:22	55	18:9–14	66
15:33	176	7:36–50	52, 197n2	19:11–27	210
15:39	130	7:38	52	19:17	70
15:40	141	7:40	52	19:22	70
16:1	141	7:48	52	20:16	51
16:6	132	8:11	180n50	21:8–9	67
16:8	132	8:22–25	178	21:10–11	178
16:11	67n75	8:25	67	22:19	180
16:14	67n75	8:26–39	53n44, 178	22:20	47, 48, 143n70
16:16	67n75	8:43–48	58, 214	22:21–22	70
		9:7–9	53	22:22	69

Index of Scripture

22:42	69, 121n12
22:50–51	52
23:38	54
23:44	176
23:49	132, 141n63
24:1–11	132
24:11	67
24:12	132n38
24:13–35	132
24:21	47n32
24:25	132
24:41	67

John

1:1–4	165
1:9	51, 165
1:9–10	180n51
1:9–19	180n51
1:12	51
1:29	47, 48, 50, 55, 143n70, 195n82
3:10–21	56
3:12	63n66, 67
3:14	55, 56, 134n41
3:17	55
3:18	63n66, 64
3:19	55
3:20	56
4:48	63n66, 64
5:14	55
5:19–26	134
5:24	55
5:38	63n66
5:39–40	56
5:47	63n66
6:15	54
6:19	176
6:27	180
6:34	180
6:35	165
6:39–40	134n41
6:44	134n41
6:54	134n41
6:64	63n66
7:19	56

7:22–24	56
8:12	165, 180
8:18–19	134
8:20	56
8:24	55
8:29	134
8:43–44	55
8:44	55
8:45–46	63n66, 64
9:1–41	214
9:2	56n49
9:3	57, 134
9:35–39	215
10:3–4	55
10:4	55
10:9	165
10:11	165
10:14	55
10:20	56
10:25	55
10:25–26	63n66
10:26	64
11:2–6	180
11:4	134
11:21	58
11:48	56
11:50	56
12:4–6	69
12:6	70
12:7	70
12:24	180n50
12:26–27	121n12
12:27	69n81
12:31–32	56n50
12:32	134n41
12:39	63n66, 64
13:2	70
13:18	70
13:27	70
13:34–35	200
14:9	67n76
14:10	63n66
15:1–5	180
15:4–5	165
16:8	134
16:9	63n66, 64

16:13	132
16:14	132
16:16	132
16:24	202
17:12	70
18:10–11	52
18:11	54
18:15	132
18:34	54
18:36	54n47
19:19	54
19:25–26	132
20:8	141
20:8–9	133
20:11–18	141
20:21	156
20:22	134
20:25	63n66, 67, 133n39, 133n40
20:27	133n40
20:31	134n41

Acts

1:5	134
2:1–40	134
2:22–40	65n70
2:38	52
3:11–26	65n70
3:19	52
3:25	49n38
3:26	49n38
5:31	52
7:8	48n38
7:22–31	166
7:35	47n32
7:51–53	65n70
8:1	61n61
8:3	61n61
9:4	61n61, 65n70
10:42	52
16:19	120n11
17:22–31	166
17:23–24	167
17:27	167
17:30–31	166

INDEX OF SCRIPTURE

17:34	167
24:15	120n11
28:20	120n11

Romans

1:4	126n26
1:5	120, 208
1:7	208n20
1:12	120
1:16	71, 121
1:16–18	131
1:17	71
1:18	72, 119
1:18–21	60
1:18–23	166
1:18–2:11	78
1:19	72
1:19–20	72, 128n31, 166
1:20–21	167n20
1:21	72, 166
1:21–22	72
1:22	72, 75
1:23	72
1:24–31	72
1:26–27	73
1:29–31	73
1:32	72
2:1	73, 119
2:3	73
2:5	73, 131
2:7	136
2:8	73
2:12	168
2:18	73
2:19	73
2:20	73, 75
2:21–25	73
2:22	73
2:24	216
2:29	73
3	30, 123
3:2	122, 207n19
3:3	73, 120, 121
3:9	77
3:9–10	119
3:10–18	78
3:21	120, 121
3:21–26	119, 120, 122, 124
3:22	119, 120, 121, 122, 123
3:22–23	119
3:22–24	208n20
3:23	122
3:24	46, 119, 120, 143
3:24–25	119
3:25	47, 121, 143n70
3:26	119, 121, 122, 167
3:30	47n3
4:24	119
5–8	79
5:1	119, 208n20
5:2	119, 208n20
5:6	60n57
5:6–7	121n12, 122n16
5:9	119
5:10	1n2, 125n23
5:10–11	27
5:12	47, 73, 77, 79
5:13	79
5:14	79, 164n12
5:15	122n16, 208n20
5:17	79
5:20	119
5:21	77n100, 79, 123n17
6	97, 136, 215
6–8	39n6
6:1–14	143n69
6:2	138
6:3	139n59
6:3–11	119
6:4	138
6:5	137, 138, 139
6:6	77, 79, 137
6:7	77n100
6:8	137, 138n58, 139
6:11	137, 139
6:12	77
6:13	138n56
6:16	79
6:17	77
6:18	138n56
6:19	79
6:22	138n56, 150
6:23	136
7:4	217
7:7–8	78
7:7–20	78
7:8	77, 79
7:11	77
7:14	77
7:15–20	38n4, 72, 79
8	167n23, 168n27, 181
8:7	79
8:10	77
8:12–13	79
8:17	137
8:18	131, 203
8:18–25	167
8:19–21	178
8:20–21	168
8:22	167
8:23	168, 181n52
8:29	137, 181
8:29–30	136
8:32	122n15
8:33	47n31
8:38–39	78, 130
8:39	203n13
9–11	74
9:3	203n13
9:31	74
9:32	74
10:2	74
10:4	74
10:8–11	74
10:14	74
10:17	74
11	75
11:1	75
11:2	74
11:11–12	74
11:15	1n2, 27
11:17–24	138
11:20	74, 138
11:23	138
11:32	74
12:6–8	86
12:9	78

Index of Scripture

13:8	200
14:1–23	200
14:13	73
14:13–15:6	200
15:1–3	147n85
15:2	200
15:3	201
15:7	203
15:13	202
16:5	181n52
16:19	78
16:20	77, 78

1 Corinthians

1:2	203
1:3	208n20
1:7	131
1:8	131
1:9	121
1:10	200
1:16	84n111
1:18	146
1:18–23	74
1:19	137n50
1:21	75
1:22	75
1:23	75
1:24	74n94
1:27–28	60n57
1:30	46, 47n32, 143
2–3	145
2:4	131
2:7	131
2:9	131
2:12	131
2:14	60n57
3:1–3	60n57
3:5–9	208
3:6	217
3:6–7	139n58
3:11	203
3:13	131n36
4	145
4:1–2	145, 208
4:3–5	145
4:5	131
4:6	145
4:8–13	145n80
4:9–13	145
4:10	145
4:14–15	145
4:16–17	145
4:17	145, 146, 208, 209
4:18	59
5:5	77, 78
5:7	46, 48, 143n70, 195n82
5:8	48
5:13	78
6:6	133n40
6:15	201
6:19	200
7:5	77, 78
7:12–15	83n110
8:1	200
8:9	208n20
9:14	208n22
9:17	208
10:16–17	146n84
10:18	146n84
10:30–11:2	146
11:1	208
11:24	180
11:25	47, 143n70
12:3	131, 201
12:4–6	200
12:8–10	147
12:12–27	201
12:28–31	147n86
12:31–14:1	200
13:3	47n32
14:1–2	147n86
14:22–24	83n110
14:25	83n110
15	167n24
15:3–4	122n16
15:3–5	130
15:4	146n82
15:20–23	181
15:21	122n16
15:21–22	47, 181
15:22	164n12
15:24–28	78
15:45	164n12
15:50	136
15:57	136
16:13	216
16:15	181n52

2 Corinthians

1:2	208n20
1:18	121
2:10	203n13
2:11	77, 78
2:14	131
2:15	137
3:17	78
4:3	137
4:10	121
4:11	121
4:12	208n20
4:13	146n82
4:14	136
5:14	60n57
5:17	96, 136, 203
5:17–18	96
5:18–19	125n23
5:18–20	1n2, 27, 96, 211n31
5:19	1n1, 125n23
5:21	123, 208n20
6:14–15	83
6:15	77, 78
6:16–18	200
8:21	203n13
10:15	208
11:13–14	78
12:7	78
12:20–21	59n56
13:2	59n56
13:2–5	208n20

Galatians

1:3	208n20
1:4	46, 78n103, 124, 143
1:6	60
1:7–9	60
1:13–16	78

INDEX OF SCRIPTURE

1:14	61	1:12–13	131n34	3:13	145
2:7–9	207	1:20	120n11	4:16–17	136n46
2:9	208	1:21–23	136n46	5:8	120n11
2:15–20	123–24	1:28	137	5:10	61n60
2:15–21	119	2:5–11	146	5:11	200
2:16	119, 120, 138	2:6–7	121	5:14–15	200
2:17	208n20	2:7–8	122n16	5:19–20	147n86
2:19	119, 137, 138, 139	2:7–11	112	5:22	78
2:19–20	138	2:13	128n31	5:24	121
2:20	78, 80n108, 119, 138, 208n20	3	121n11	
2:20–21	124	3:4–9	61	**2 Thessalonians**	
2:21	119, 138	3:5–6	61	2:2–12	61n59
3:1	60	3:7–11	119, 120	3:3	61n59
3:3	46	3:9	61, 119	3:7–9	146n83
3:7	60	3:9–11	123	
3:13	47, 143	3:10	119, 137, 139	**1 Timothy**	
4:1–7	136	3:11	119	1:3–7	62
4:4	131	3:21	137	1:12–13	61
4:5	46, 143	4:2	200	1:15	62, 207n19
4:8	60	4:4–9	200	1:20	62
4:9	131	4:5	200	3:1	207n19
4:14	131		3:7	62
5:4	203n13	**Colossians**		4:1–2	62
5:16–26	200	1:15	179	6:5	62
5:21	136	1:15–20	166	6:9	62
5:22	202	2:7	139n58	
6:1–10	200	2:12	137n51	**2 Timothy**	
	2:13	137n51	1:8	125, 137n51
Ephesians		3:5–17	200n10	1:9	62
1:1	167n22		2:3	137n51
1:3–6	167n22	**1 Thessalonians**		2:11	137n51, 207n19
1:13	167n22	1:1	208n20	2:14	62
1:18	120n11	1:5	131	2:16	62
2:4–8	128n31	1:6	60, 148	2:24–26	62
2:5	137n51	1:6–7	144	3:10–16	125
4:1–7	200n10	1:8	144	
4:4	120n11	1:9	60	**Titus**	
4:5	209	1:10	60	1:1–4	167n22
4:11	147n86	2:4	122n16, 207	1:5–9	63n63
4:25–5:5	200n10	2:14	60, 144	1:9	62
5:1–2	146n83	2:18	77, 78n101	1:10–11	63n63
	3:1–8	208	2:14	47n32
Philippians		3:2–3	217	3:3	61
1:2	119, 208n20	3:3	60	3:8	207n19
1:11	208n20	3:8	216	
	3:10	145	

Index of Scripture

Hebrews

1:10–12	166
2:2	62
2:14–15	62
2:17	62
2:17–18	125
3:2	126n25
3:6	121n12
3:8–12	62
4:7–13	62
5:2	62
7:26	62
9:12	47n32
9:13–14	62
9:15	62
9:26	46, 48, 143n70
9:28	62
10:26	62
12:1–3	147n87
13:11–12	62

James

4:1–12	200n10

1 Peter

1:14	63n64
1:18	47n32
1:22	63n64, 200n10
2:9	63n64
2:9–10	63n64
2:21	146n83
2:23	127
2:23–24	146n83
2:24	63n64
3:18	63n64
4:7–5:4	167n22

2 Peter

3:7–13	204n15

1 John

1:1	166
1:1–2	165
1:1–4	166
1:2	166
1:3	166
1:5	180n51

1:7	63n64, 166
1:9	166
2:2	63n64
2:3–11	200n10
3:3	120n11
3:4–10	63n64
3:11–18	200n10

Revelation

1:19	24n82
6:16	195n82
7:14	48, 195n82
7:17	48
21:1–4	167n22, 204n15
21:1–5	168
21:8	73n90
21:23	178
22:1–2	178